the source
combined words edition

the source
combined words edition

the worship collection compiled by
Graham Kendrick

First published in Great Britain in 2001 by
worldwide worship
Buxhall, Stowmarket
Suffolk IP14 3BW
Phone: 01449 737978
Fax: 01449 737834
Email: www@kevinmayhewltd.com

Foreword

Let the word of Christ dwell in you richly as you teach and admonish one another with all wisdom, and as you sing psalms, hymns and spiritual songs with gratitude in your hearts to God. And whatever you do, whether in word or deed, do it all in the name of the Lord Jesus, giving thanks to God the Father through him.

Colossians 3:16-17

It is to encourage the realisation of this kind of worship lifestyle that we have compiled and published **the source**, not least to facilitate the singing of psalms, hymns and spiritual songs, of which you will find here over one thousand of the best.

As an editorial panel we have sought to discharge our responsibilities as faithfully and generously as possible, believing that diversity was vital to the breadth and richness of the material we were considering. The songs in this book restate the teachings of our faith, explore new insights, proclaim hope, protest, express solidarity with the poor, call ourselves and others to repentance and faith; and in all this we celebrate our God and Saviour Jesus Christ, who, in the words of the writer to the Hebrews, 'became the source of eternal salvation for all who obey him'.

the source has, we believe, several claims to uniqueness.

The content of each hymn and song has been carefully assessed and, while we have still included some material that may be described as 'lighter', we believe that the *overall* balance is more substantial than in previous collections. This attention to substance and breadth has also enabled us to produce a book that will appeal to a broad church constituency.

While compiling **the source** we were keenly aware of its prophetic dimension. For the first time we were making choices unencumbered by copyright or any other restrictions: the world was our oyster and we made full use of the freedom offered to us, including songs both new and old which we expect to take their place (or retake in the case of the older songs) among those loved by congregations everywhere. In this sense we have aspired to be like the kind of teacher Jesus affirmed who is 'like a householder who brings both new things and old out of his treasure-store' (Matthew 13:52).

There is also a sense in which we have been like harvesters, reaping and gathering what has been growing in the 'fields' of diverse worshipping communities. The variety of soils has produced a rich variety of styles and indeed emphasis which we hope will excite, intrigue and challenge the user to appreciate and benefit from the many facets of the jewel of worship expression which seeks to reflect the glory of God in the world today.

the source 2 complements the original volume of **the source** with material drawn from all over the English-speaking world, providing worship groups, musicians and leaders with a compilation that is refreshingly international. Not only did we again seek breadth and depth, rich and trustworthy content, but also height: songs which lift us out of ourselves and fill our vision with the attributes of God. Alongside the new we added to the treasury of traditional hymns those not usually found between the same pair of covers, some of which sport new melodies.

We hope that in this diverse and approachable worship collection we have sown some seeds; that is all we can do. It is in the overflow of worship from hearts which are united in a passionate love for Jesus Christ that these seeds must be brought to glorious fruition.

We may exercise a degree of influence as compilers, but the real power is where the rubber hits the road, each time a pastor or worship leader compiles a song list. Use it well!

GRAHAM KENDRICK
Compiler

JONATHAN BUGDEN
RICHARD LEWIS
MATTHEW LOCKWOOD
Compiling Team

1 Dave Bilbrough

Abba, Father, let me be
yours and yours alone.
May my will for ever be
more and more your own.
Never let my heart grow cold,
never let me go.
Abba, Father, let me be
yours and yours alone.

2 Henry Francis Lyte

Abide with me,
fast falls the eventide;
the darkness deepens;
Lord, with me abide:
when other helpers fail,
and comforts flee,
help of the helpless,
O abide with me.

Swift to its close
ebbs out life's little day;
earth's joys grow dim,
its glories pass away;
change and decay
in all around I see;
O thou who changest not,
abide with me.

I need thy presence
every passing hour;
what but thy grace
can foil the tempter's pow'r?
Who like thyself
my guide and stay can be?
Through cloud and sunshine,
Lord, abide with me.

I fear no foe
with thee at hand to bless;
ills have no weight,
and tears no bitterness.

Where is death's sting?
Where, grave, thy victory?
I triumph still,
if thou abide with me.

Hold thou thy cross
before my closing eyes;
shine through the gloom,
and point me to the skies;
heav'n's morning breaks,
and earth's vain shadows flee;
in life, in death,
O Lord, abide with me.

3 Graham Kendrick

Above the clash of creeds,
the many voices
that call on so many names,
into these final days
our God has spoken
by sending his only Son.

There is no other way
by which we must be saved;
his name is Jesus,
the only Saviour;
no other sinless life,
no other sacrifice,
in all creation
no other way.

Before we called he came
to earth from heaven,
our maker became a man;
when no one else could pay,
he bought our freedom,
exchanging his life for ours.

Beneath the cross of Christ
let earth fall silent
in awe of this mystery;
then let this song arise
and fill the nations:
O hear him call, 'Come to me.'

4 Donald Fishel

Alleluia, alleluia,
give thanks to the risen Lord,
alleluia, alleluia,
give praise to his name.

Jesus is Lord of all the earth,
he is the King of creation.

Spread the good news o'er all the earth,
Jesus has died and has risen.

We have been crucified with Christ,
now we shall live for ever.

God has proclaimed the just reward,
life for us all, alleluia!

Come, let us praise the living God,
joyfully sing to our Saviour.

5 Dave Moody

All hail King Jesus!
All hail Emmanuel!
King of kings, Lord of lords,
bright morning star.
And throughout eternity
I'll sing your praises,
and I'll reign with you
throughout eternity.

6 Dave Bilbrough

All hail the Lamb, enthroned on high;
his praise shall be our battle cry;
he reigns victorious, for ever glorious,
his name is Jesus, he is the Lord.

7 Edward Perronet

All hail the pow'r of Jesus' name!
let angels prostrate fall;
bring forth the royal diadem
and crown him, crown him, crown him,
crown him Lord of all.

Crown him, ye martyrs of your God,
who from his altar call;
praise him whose way of pain ye trod,
and crown him, crown him, crown him,
crown him Lord of all.

Ye prophets who our freedom won,
ye searchers great and small,
by whom the work of truth is done,
now crown him, crown him, crown him,
crown him Lord of all.

Ye seed of Israel's chosen race,
ye ransomed of the fall,
hail him who saves you by his grace,
and crown him, crown him, crown him,
crown him Lord of all.

Let every tribe and every tongue
to him their hearts enthral;
lift high the universal song,
and crown him, crown him, crown him,
crown him Lord of all.

O that, with yonder sacred throng,
we at his feet may fall,
join in the everlasting song,
and crown him, crown him, crown him,
crown him Lord of all.

8 Noel and Tricia Richards

All heav'n declares
the glory of the risen Lord.
Who can compare
with the beauty of the Lord?
For ever he will be
the Lamb upon the throne.
I gladly bow the knee
and worship him alone.

I will proclaim
the glory of the risen Lord.
Who once was slain
to reconcile us to God.
For ever you will be
the Lamb upon the throne.
I gladly bow the knee
and worship you alone.

9 Graham Kendrick and Chris Rolinson

All heaven waits with bated breath,
for saints on earth to pray.
Majestic angels ready stand
with swords of fiery blade.
Astounding pow'r awaits a word
from God's resplendent throne.
But God awaits our prayer of faith
that cries, 'Your will be done.'

Awake, O church, arise and pray,
complaining words discard.
The Spirit comes to fill your mouth
with truth, his mighty sword.
Go place your feet on Satan's ground
and there proclaim Christ's name,
in step with heaven's armies march
to conquer and to reign!

Now in our hearts and on our lips
the word of faith is near,
let heaven's will on earth be done,
let heaven flow from here.
Come, blend your prayers with Jesus' own
before the Father's throne,
and as the incense clouds ascend,
God's holy fire rains down.

Soon comes the day when with a shout
King Jesus will appear,
and with him all the church,
from every age, shall fill the air.
The brightness of his coming shall
consume the lawless one,
as with a word the breath of God
tears down his rebel throne.

One body here, by heav'n inspired,
we seek prophetic power;
in Christ agreed, one heart and voice,
to speak this day, this hour,
in every place where chaos rules
and evil forces brood;
let Jesus' voice speak like the roar
of a great multitude.

10 Chris Falson

All honour, all glory, all power to you.
All honour, all glory, all power to you.
Holy Father, we worship you,
precious Jesus, our Saviour,
Holy Spirit, we wait on you,
Holy Spirit, we wait on you,
Holy Spirit, we wait on you for fire, for fire.

11 Graham Kendrick

All I once held dear,
built my life upon,
all this world reveres,
and wars to own,
all I once thought gain
I have counted loss;
spent and worthless now,
compared to this.

Knowing you, Jesus, knowing you,
there is no greater thing.
You're my all, you're the best,
you're my joy, my righteousness,
and I love you, Lord.

Now my heart's desire
is to know you more,
to be found in you
and known as yours.
To possess by faith
what I could not earn,
all-surpassing gift
of righteousness.

Continued overleaf

Oh, to know the pow'r
of your risen life,
and to know you
in your sufferings.
To become like you
in your death, my Lord,
so with you to live
and never die.

Knowing you, Jesus, knowing you,
there is no greater thing.
You're my all, you're the best,
you're my joy, my righteousness,
and I love you, Lord.

12   Terry Butler

All over the world,
all over the world,
your Spirit is moving
all over the world.

Your river is flowing,
your presence has come,
your Spirit is moving
all over the world.
You're touching the nations,
you're bringing us love,
your Spirit is moving
all over the world.
You're touching the nations,
you're bringing us love,
your Spirit is moving
all over the world.

Your banner is lifted,
your praises are sung,
your Spirit is moving
all over the world.
Divisions are falling,
you're making us one,
your Spirit is moving
all over the world.

Divisions are falling,
you're making us one,
your Spirit is moving
all over the world.

13   William Kethe

All people that on earth do dwell,
sing to the Lord with cheerful voice;
him serve with fear, his praise forth tell,
come ye before him and rejoice.

Know that the Lord is God indeed,
without our aid he did us make;
we are his flock, he doth us feed,
and for his sheep he doth us take.

O enter then his gates with praise,
approach with joy his courts unto;
praise, laud and bless his name always,
for it is seemly so to do.

For why? the Lord our God is good:
his mercy is for ever sure;
his truth at all times firmly stood,
and shall from age to age endure.

Praise God from whom all blessings flow,
praise him, all creatures here below,
praise him above, ye heav'nly hosts:
praise Father, Son and Holy Ghost.

14   Cecil Frances Alexander

All things bright and beautiful,
all creatures great and small,
all things wise and wonderful,
the Lord God made them all.

Each little flow'r that opens,
each little bird that sings,
he made their glowing colours,
he made their tiny wings.

The purple-headed mountain,
the river running by,
the sunset and the morning,
that brightens up the sky.

The cold wind in the winter,
the pleasant summer sun,
the ripe fruits in the garden,
he made them every one.

He gave us eyes to see them,
and lips that we may tell
how great is God Almighty,
who has made all things well.

15 J. W. Van De Venter

All to Jesus I surrender,
all to him I freely give;
I will ever love and trust him,
in his presence daily live.

I surrender all, I surrender all,
all to thee, my blessed Saviour,
I surrender all.

All to Jesus I surrender,
humbly at his feet I bow;
worldly pleasures all forsaken,
take me, Jesus, take me now.

All to Jesus I surrender,
make me, Saviour, wholly thine;
let me feel the Holy Spirit,
truly know that thou art mine.

All to Jesus I surrender,
Lord, I give myself to thee;
fill me with thy love and power,
let thy blessing fall on me.

All to Jesus I surrender,
now to feel the sacred flame;
O, the joy of full salvation!
Glory, glory to his name!

16 Austin Martin

Almighty God, we bring you praise
for your Son, the Word of God,
by whose pow'r the world was made,
by whose blood we are redeemed.
Morning star, the Father's glory,
we now worship and adore you.
In our hearts your light has risen;
Jesus, Lord, we worship you.

17 Darlene Zschech

Almighty God, my redeemer,
my hiding-place, my safe refuge,
no other name like Jesus,
no pow'r can stand against you.
My feet are planted on this rock
and I will not be shaken.
My hope, it comes from you alone,
my Lord, and my salvation.

Your praise is always on my lips,
your word is living in my heart
and I will praise you with a new song,
my soul will bless you, Lord.
You fill my life with greater joy,
yes, I delight myself in you
and I will praise you with a new song,
my soul will bless you, Lord.

When I am weak, you make me strong.
When I'm poor, I know I'm rich,
for in the power of your name
all things are possible,
all things are possible,
all things are possible,
all things are possible.

18 John Newton and John Rees

Amazing grace! How sweet the sound
that saved a wretch like me.
I once was lost, but now I'm found;
was blind, but now I see.

Continued overleaf

'Twas grace that taught my heart to fear,
and grace my fears relieved.
How precious did that grace appear
the hour I first believed.

Through many dangers, toils and snares
I have already come.
'Tis grace that brought me safe thus far,
and grace will lead me home.

The Lord has promised good to me,
his word my hope secures;
he will my shield and portion be
as long as life endures.

Yes, when this heart and flesh shall fail,
and mortal life shall cease,
I shall possess within the veil
a life of joy and peace.

When we've been there a thousand years,
bright shining as the sun,
we've no less days to sing God's praise
than when we first begun.

19 Carol Owen

Among the gods
there is none like you, O Lord, O Lord.
There are no deeds
to compare with yours, O Lord.
All the nations you have made will come;
they'll worship before you, O Lord, O Lord.

For you are great
and do marvellous deeds.
Yes, you are great
and do marvellous deeds.
You alone are God, you alone are God.

You are so good
and forgiving, O Lord, O Lord.
You're rich in love
to all who call to you, O Lord.
All the nations you have made will come;
they'll glorify your name, O Lord, O Lord.

Teach me your ways, O Lord,
and I'll walk in your truth.
Give me an undivided heart,
that I may fear your name.

20 Dave Bilbrough

An army of ordinary people,
a kingdom where love is the key,
a city, a light to the nations,
heirs to the promise are we.
A people whose life is in Jesus,
a nation together we stand.
Only through grace are we worthy,
inheritors of the land.

A new day is dawning,
a new age to come,
when the children of promise
shall flow together as one:
a truth long neglected,
but the time has now come,
when the children of promise
shall flow together as one.

A people without recognition,
but with him a destiny sealed,
called to a heavenly vision:
his purpose shall be fulfilled.
Come, let us stand strong together,
abandon ourselves to the King.
His love shall be ours for ever,
this victory song shall we sing.

21 Charles Wesley

And can it be that I should gain
an interest in the Saviour's blood?
Died he for me, who caused his pain?
For me, who him to death pursued?
Amazing love! How can it be that thou,
my God, shouldst die for me?

'Tis mystery all! th'Immortal dies:
who can explore his strange design?
In vain the first-born seraph tries
to sound the depths of love divine!
'Tis mercy all! Let earth adore,
let angel minds inquire no more.

He left his Father's throne above
so free, so infinite his grace;
emptied himself of all but love,
and bled for Adam's helpless race;
'tis mercy all, immense and free;
for, O my God, it found out me.

Long my imprisoned spirit lay
fast bound in sin and nature's night;
thine eye diffused a quickening ray,
I woke, the dungeon flamed with light;
my chains fell off, my heart was free;
I rose, went forth, and followed thee.

No condemnation now I dread;
Jesus, and all in him, is mine!
Alive in him, my living Head,
and clothed in righteousness divine,
bold I approach the eternal throne,
and claim the crown, through Christ my own.

22 Graham Kendrick

And he shall reign for ever,
his throne and crown shall ever endure.
And he shall reign for ever,
and we shall reign with him.

What a vision filled my eyes,
one like a Son of man.
Coming with the clouds of heav'n
he approached an awesome throne.

He was given sovereign power,
glory and authority.
Every nation, tribe and tongue
worshipped him on bended knee.

On the throne for ever,
see the Lamb who once was slain;
wounds of sacrificial love
for ever shall remain.

23 Unknown

A new commandment
I give unto you:
that you love one another
as I have loved you,
that you love one another
as I have loved you.
By this shall all know
that you are my disciples
if you have love for one another.
By this shall all know
that you are my disciples
if you have love for one another.

24 Donn Thomas

Anointing, fall on me,
anointing, fall on me;
let the power of the Holy Ghost
fall on me,
anointing, fall on me.

Touch my hands, my mouth and my heart,
fill my life, Lord, every part;
let the power of the Holy Ghost fall on me,
anointing, fall on me.

25 Peter West, Mary Lou Locke and Mary Kirkbride

Ascribe greatness
to our God, the Rock,
his work is perfect
and all his ways are just.
Ascribe greatness
to our God, the Rock,
his work is perfect
and all his ways are just.

A God of faithfulness
and without injustice,
good and upright is he;
a God of faithfulness
and without injustice,
good and upright is he.

26 Dave Billington

As I come into your presence,
past the gates of praise,
into your sanctuary
till we're standing face to face,
I look upon your countenance,
I see the fullness of your grace,
and I can only bow down and say:

You are awesome in this place,
mighty God.
You are awesome in this place,
Abba, Father.
You are worthy of all praise,
to you our hands we raise.
You are awesome in this place,
mighty God.

27 Martin J. Nystrom

As the deer pants for the water,
so my soul longs after you.
You alone are my heart's desire
and I long to worship you.

You alone are my strength, my shield,
to you alone may my spirit yield.
You alone are my heart's desire
and I long to worship you.

I want you more than gold or silver,
only you can satisfy.
You alone are the real joy-giver
and the apple of my eye.

You're my friend and you are my brother,
even though you are a King.
I love you more than any other,
so much more than anything.

28 Richard Lewis

As the deer pants for the water,
so my soul, it thirsts for you,
for you, O God, for you, O God.
(Repeat)

When can I come before you
and see your face?
My heart and my flesh cry out
for the living God, for the living God.

Deep calls to deep
at the thunder of your waterfalls.
Your heart of love
is calling out to me.
By this I know that I am yours
and you are mine.
Your waves of love are breaking over me.
Your waves of love are breaking over me.
Your waves of love are breaking over me.

29 John Daniels

As we are gathered, Jesus is here;
one with each other, Jesus is here;
joined by the Spirit, washed in the blood,
part of the body, the church of God.
As we are gathered, Jesus is here;
one with each other, Jesus is here.

30 Paul Baloche

Leader	As we lift up your name,
All	as we lift up your name,
Leader	let your fire fall,
All	let your fire fall;
Leader	send your wind and your rain,
All	send your wind and your rain,
Leader	on your wings of love,
All	on your wings of love.
	Pour out from heaven
	your passion and presence,
	bring down your burning desire.

Revival fire, fall, revival fire, fall,
fall on us here in the pow'r of your Spirit,
Father, let revival fire fall;
revival fire, fall, revival fire, fall,
let the flames consume us
with hearts ablaze for Jesus.
Father, let revival fire fall.

Leader	As we lift up your name,
All	as we lift up your name,
Leader	let your kingdom come,
All	let your kingdom come;
Leader	have your way in this place,
All	have your way in this place,
Leader	let your will be done,
All	let your will be done.

Pour out from heaven
your passion and presence,
bring down your burning desire.

31 Dave Bilbrough

As we seek your face,
may we know your heart,
feel your presence, acceptance,
as we seek your face.

Move among us now,
come, reveal your pow'r,
show your presence, acceptance,
move among us now.

At your feet we fall,
sovereign Lord,
we cry 'holy, holy',
at your feet we fall.

32 Derek Bond

At the foot of the cross,
I can hardly take it in,
that the King of all creation
was dying for my sin.
And the pain and agony,
and the thorns that pierced your head,
and the hardness of my sinful heart
that left you there for dead.

And O what mercy I have found,
at the cross of Calvary;
I will never know your loneliness,
all on account of me.

And I will bow my knee before your throne,
'cos your love has set me free;
and I will give my life to you, dear Lord,
and praise your majesty,
and praise your majesty.

33 Caroline Maria Noel

At the name of Jesus
every knee shall bow,
every tongue confess him
King of glory now;
'tis the Father's pleasure
we should call him Lord,
who, from the beginning,
was the mighty Word.

At his voice creation
sprang at once to sight,
all the angel faces,
all the hosts of light,
thrones and dominations,
stars upon their way,
all the heav'nly orders
in their great array.

Humbled for a season,
to receive a name
from the lips of sinners
unto whom he came,
faithfully he bore it,
spotless to the last,
brought it back victorious
when from death he passed.

Bore it up triumphant,
with its human light,
through all ranks of creatures
to the central height,
to the throne of Godhead,
to the Father's breast,
filled it with the glory
of that perfect rest.

Continued overleaf

All creation, name him,
with love as strong as death;
but with awe and wonder,
and with bated breath.
He is God the Saviour,
he is Christ the Lord,
ever to be worshipped,
trusted and adored.

In your hearts enthrone him;
there let him subdue
all that is not holy,
all that is not true;
crown him as your captain
in temptation's hour;
let his will enfold you
in its light and pow'r.

Truly, this Lord Jesus
shall return again,
with his Father's glory,
with his angel train;
for all wreaths of empire
meet upon his brow,
and our hearts confess him
King of glory now.

34   Graham Kendrick

At this time of giving,
gladly now we bring
gifts of goodness and mercy
from a heav'nly King.

Earth could not contain the treasures
heaven holds for you,
perfect joy and lasting pleasures,
love so strong and true.

May his tender love surround you
at this Christmastime;
may you see his smiling face
that in the darkness shines.

But the many gifts he gives
are all poured out from one;
come, receive the greatest gift,
the gift of God's own Son.

Lai, lai, lai . . .

© 1988 Make Way Music

35   David Fellingham

At your feet we fall,
mighty risen Lord,
as we come before your throne
to worship you.
By your Spirit's pow'r
you now draw our hearts,
and we hear your voice
in triumph ringing clear.

I am he that liveth,
that liveth and was dead.
Behold, I am alive for evermore.

There we see you stand,
mighty risen Lord,
clothed in garments pure and holy,
shining bright.
Eyes of flashing fire,
feet like burnished bronze,
and the sound of many waters
is your voice.

Like the shining sun
in its noonday strength,
we now see the glory
of your wondrous face.
Once that face was marred,
but now you're glorified,
and your words like a two-edged sword
have mighty pow'r.

© 1982 Kingsway's Thankyou Music

36 William James Kirkpatrick

Away in a manger,
no crib for a bed,
the little Lord Jesus
laid down his sweet head.
The stars in the bright sky
looked down where he lay,
the little Lord Jesus,
asleep on the hay.

The cattle are lowing,
the baby awakes,
but little Lord Jesus
no crying he makes.
I love thee, Lord Jesus!
Look down from the sky,
and stay by my side
until morning is nigh.

Be near me, Lord Jesus;
I ask thee to stay
close by me for ever,
and love me, I pray.
Bless all the dear children
in thy tender care,
and fit us for heaven,
to live with thee there.

37 Graham Kendrick

Beauty for brokenness,
hope for despair,
Lord, in the suffering,
this is our prayer.
Bread for the children,
justice, joy, peace,
sunrise to sunset
your kingdom increase.

Shelter for fragile lives,
cures for their ills,
work for the craftsmen,
trade for their skills.
Land for the dispossessed,
rights for the weak,
voices to plead the cause
of those who can't speak.

God of the poor,
friend of the weak,
give us compassion, we pray,
melt our cold hearts,
let tears fall like rain.
Come, change our love
from a spark to a flame.

Refuge from cruel wars,
havens from fear,
cities for sanctuary,
freedoms to share.
Peace to the killing fields,
scorched earth to green,
Christ for the bitterness,
his cross for the pain.

Rest for the ravaged earth,
oceans and streams,
plundered and poisoned,
our future, our dreams.
Lord, end our madness,
carelessness, greed;
make us content with
the things that we need.

Lighten our darkness,
breathe on this flame,
until your justice
burns brightly again;
until the nations
learn of your ways,
seek your salvation
and bring you their praise.

38 Morris Chapman

Be bold, be strong,
for the Lord, your God, is with you.
Be bold, be strong,
for the Lord, your God, is with you.
I am not afraid, I am not dismayed,
because I'm walking in faith and victory,
come on and walk in faith and victory,
for the Lord, your God, is with you.

39 Russell Fragar

Because of your love,
everything's changed,
because of your love,
I'll never be the same.
Your love is perfect,
And I'll never be afraid,
because of your love,
everything's changed.
(Repeat)

I have this confidence
that God is on my side.
All of my days are in your hands.
Love so amazing
that it cannot be denied,
that every day I'm in your plan.

© 1995 Russell Fragar/Hillsongs Australia/Kingsway's Thankyou Music

40 Russell Fragar

Before the world began
you were on his mind,
and every tear you cry
is precious in his eyes.
Because of his great love,
he gave his only Son;
everything was done,
so you would come.

Nothing you can do
could make him love you more,
and nothing that you've done
could make him close the door.
Because of his great love,
he gave his only Son;
everything was done
so you would come.

Come to the Father
though your gift is small,
broken hearts, broken lives,
he will take them all.
The power of the Word,
the power of his blood,
everything was done
so you would come.

© 1996 Russell Fragar/Hillsongs Australia/Kingsway's Thankyou Music

41 Dave Bilbrough

Be free in the love of God,
let his Spirit flow within you.
Be free in the love of God,
let it fill your soul.
Be free in the love of God,
celebrate his name with dancing.
Be free in the love of God;
he has made us whole.

For his purpose he has called us,
in his hands he gently holds us.
He will keep us and sustain us
in the Father's love.

God is gracious, he will lead us
through his pow'r at work within us.
Spirit, guide us, and unite us
in the Father's love.

© 1991 Kingsway's Thankyou Music

42 Billy Funk

Be glorified, be glorified.
Be glorified, be glorified.
Be glorified in the heavens,
be glorified in the earth;
be glorified in the temple,
Jesus, Jesus, be thou glorified,
Jesus, Jesus, be thou glorified.

Worship the Lord, worship the Lord.
Worship the Lord, worship the Lord.
Worship the Lord in the heavens,
worship the Lord in the earth;
worship the Lord in the temple,
Jesus, Jesus, be thou glorified,
Jesus, Jesus, be thou glorified.

© 1991 Integrity's Praise! Music/Kingsway's Thankyou Music

43 Geoff Baker

Behold his love.
I stand amazed
and marvel at the God of grace:
that the Alpha and Omega,

the Beginning and the End,
the Creator of the universe
on whom all life depends,
should be clothed in frail humanity
and suffer in my place.
Behold his love
and worship him, the God of grace.

44 Noel Richards and Gerald Coates

Behold the Lord upon his throne;
his face is shining like the sun.
With eyes blazing fire, and feet glowing bronze,
his voice like mighty water roars.
Holy, holy, Lord God Almighty.
Holy, holy, we stand in awe of you.

The first, the last, the living One,
laid down his life for all the world.
Behold, he now lives for evermore,
and holds the keys of death and hell.
Holy, holy, Lord God Almighty.
Holy, holy, we bow before your throne.

So let our praises ever ring
to Jesus Christ, our glorious King.
All heaven and earth resound as we cry:
'Worthy is the Son of God!'
Holy, holy, Lord God Almighty.
Holy, holy, we fall down at your feet.

45 Elizabeth C. Clephane

Beneath the cross of Jesus
I fain would take my stand,
the shadow of a mighty rock
within a weary land;
a home within a wilderness,
a rest upon the way,
from burning heat at noontide and
the burden of the day.

O safe and happy shelter!
O refuge tried and sweet!
O trysting place where heaven's love
and heaven's justice meet!
As to the holy patriarch
that wondrous dream was giv'n,
so seems my Saviour's cross to me
a ladder up to heav'n.

There lies, beneath its shadow,
but on the farther side,
the darkness of an awful grave
that gapes both deep and wide;
and there between us stands the cross,
two arms outstretched to save;
a watchman set to guard the way
from that eternal grave.

Upon that cross of Jesus
mine eye at times can see
the very dying form of One
who suffered there for me;
and from my stricken heart, with tears,
two wonders I confess –
the wonders of redeeming love
and my unworthiness.

I take, O cross, thy shadow
for my abiding place!
I ask no other sunshine than
the sunshine of his face;
content to let the world go by,
to reckon gain as loss –
my sinful self, my only shame,
my glory all – the cross.

46 Graham Kendrick

Be patient, be ready,
look up – the Lord is near.
Be faithful, be fruitful,
until the day that he appears.
Though all things are shaken
and hearts are filled with fear,
keep working, keep praying,
until his kingdom is here.

Continued overleaf

Deep in our hearts there's a cry,
as the Spirit and Bride say:
'Come, Jesus, come, take your white horse
and ride through the heavens. Come!'
(Repeat)

47 David J. Evans

Be still, for the presence of the Lord,
the Holy One is here.
Come, bow before him now,
with reverence and fear.
In him no sin is found,
we stand on holy ground.
Be still, for the presence of the Lord,
the Holy One is here.

Be still, for the glory of the Lord
is shining all around;
he burns with holy fire,
with splendour he is crowned.
How awesome is the sight,
our radiant King of light!
Be still, for the glory of the Lord
is shining all around.

Be still, for the power of the Lord
is moving in this place;
he comes to cleanse and heal,
to minister his grace.
No work too hard for him,
in faith receive from him.
Be still, for the power of the Lord
is moving in this place.

48 Unknown

Be still and know that I am God,
be still and know that I am God,
be still and know that I am God.

I am the Lord that healeth thee . . .

In thee, O Lord, do I put my trust . . .

49 Katharina Von Schlegal trans. Jane L. Borthwick

Be still, my soul:
the Lord is on your side;
bear patiently the cross
of grief and pain;
leave to your God
to order and provide;
in every change
he faithful will remain.
Be still, my soul:
your best, your heav'nly friend,
through thorny ways,
leads to a joyful end.

Be still, my soul:
your God will undertake
to guide the future
as he has the past.
Your hope, your confidence
let nothing shake,
all now mysterious
shall be clear at last.
Be still, my soul:
the tempests still obey
his voice, who ruled them
once on Galilee.

Be still, my soul:
the hour is hastening on
when we shall be
for ever with the Lord,
when disappointment,
grief and fear are gone,
sorrow forgotten,
love's pure joy restored.
Be still, my soul:
when change and tears are past,
all safe and blessèd
we shall meet at last.

50
Irish trans. Mary Byrne and Eleanor Hull

Be thou my vision,
O Lord of my heart,
naught be all else to me,
save that thou art;
thou my best thought
in the day and the night,
waking or sleeping,
thy presence my light.

Be thou my wisdom,
be thou my true word,
I ever with thee
and thou with me, Lord;
thou my great Father
and I thy true heir;
thou in me dwelling,
and I in thy care.

Be thou my breastplate,
my sword for the fight,
be thou my armour
and be thou my might,
thou my soul's shelter,
and thou my high tow'r,
raise thou me heav'nward,
O Pow'r of my pow'r.

Riches I need not,
nor all the world's praise,
thou my inheritance
through all my days;
thou, and thou only,
the first in my heart,
high King of heaven,
my treasure thou art!

High King of heaven,
when battle is done,
grant heaven's joys to me,
O bright heav'n's sun;
Christ of my own heart,
whatever befall,
still be my vision,
O Ruler of all.

51
Bob Gillman

Bind us together, Lord,
bind us together
with cords that cannot be broken.
Bind us together, Lord,
bind us together,
bind us together with love.

There is only one God.
There is only one King.
There is only one Body.
That is why we sing:

Made for the glory of God,
purchased by his precious Son.
Born with the right to be clean,
for Jesus the victory has won.

You are the family of God.
You are the promise divine.
You are God's chosen desire.
You are the glorious new wine.

52
Frances Jane van Alstyne

Blessed assurance, Jesus is mine:
O what a foretaste of glory divine!
Heir of salvation, purchase of God;
born of his Spirit, washed in his blood.

This is my story, this is my song,
praising my Saviour all the day long.
This is my story, this is my song,
praising my Saviour all the day long.

Perfect submission, perfect delight,
visions of rapture burst on my sight;
angels descending, bring from above
echoes of mercy, whispers of love.

Perfect submission, all is at rest,
I in my Saviour am happy and blessed;
watching and waiting, looking above,
filled with his goodness, lost in his love.

53   Kevin Prosch and Danny Daniels

Blessed be the name of the Lord.
Blessed be the name of the Lord.
Blessed be the name of the Lord.
Blessed be the name of the Lord.
For he is our Rock, for he is our Rock,
he is the Lord.
For he is our Rock, for he is our Rock,
he is the Lord.

Jesus reigns on high in all the earth.
Jesus reigns on high in all the earth.
Jesus reigns on high in all the earth.
Jesus reigns on high in all the earth.
The universe is in the hands of the Lord.
The universe is in the hands of the Lord.

54   Gary Sadler and Jamie Harvill

Blessing and honour, glory and power
be unto the Ancient of Days;
from every nation, all of creation
bow before the Ancient of Days.

Every tongue in heaven and earth
shall declare your glory,
every knee shall bow at your throne
in worship;
you will be exalted, O God,
and your kingdom shall not pass away,
O Ancient of Days.

Your kingdom shall reign over all the earth:
sing unto the Ancient of Days.
For none shall compare to your matchless worth:
sing unto the Ancient of Days.

55   Geoff Bullock and Dave Reidy

Blessing, honour, glory to the Lamb.
Holy, righteous, worthy is the Lamb.
Blessing, honour, glory to the Lamb.
Holy, righteous, worthy is the Lamb.

Death could not hold him down
for he is risen.
Seated upon the throne
he is the Lamb of God.

56   Taizé Community

Bless the Lord, my soul,
and bless God's holy name.
Bless the Lord, my soul,
who leads me into life.

57   Edwin Hatch

Breathe on me, Breath of God,
fill me with life anew,
that I may love what thou dost love,
and do what thou wouldst do.

Breathe on me, Breath of God,
until my heart is pure:
until with thee I have one will
to do and to endure.

Breathe on me, Breath of God,
till I am wholly thine,
until this earthly part of me
glows with thy fire divine.

Breathe on me, Breath of God,
so shall I never die,
but live with thee the perfect life
of thine eternity.

58   Janet Lunt

Broken for me, broken for you,
the body of Jesus, broken for you.

He offered his body, he poured out his soul;
Jesus was broken, that we might be whole.

Come to my table and with me dine;
eat of my bread and drink of my wine.

This is my body given for you;
eat it remembering I died for you.

This is my blood I shed for you,
for your forgiveness, making you new.

59 Steven Fry

By his grace I am redeemed,
by his blood I am made clean,
and I now can know him face to face.
By his pow'r I have been raised,
hidden now in Christ by faith.
I will praise the glory of his grace.

60 Noel and Tricia Richards

By your side I would stay;
in your arms I would lay.
Jesus, lover of my soul,
nothing from you I withhold.

Lord, I love you, and adore you;
what more can I say?
You cause my love to grow stronger
with every passing day.
(Repeat)

61 Noel and Tricia Richards

Called to a battle, heavenly war;
though we may struggle, victory is sure.
Death will not triumph, though we may die;
Jesus has promised our eternal life.

> *By the blood of the Lamb*
> *we shall overcome,*
> *see the accuser thrown down.*
> *By the word of the Lord*
> *we shall overcome,*
> *raise a victory cry,*
> *like thunder in the skies,*
> *thunder in the skies.*

Standing together, moving as one;
we are God's army, called to overcome.
We are commissioned, Jesus says go;
in every nation, let his love be known.

62 Matt Redman

Can a nation be changed?
Can a nation be saved?
Can a nation be turned back to you?
(Repeat)

> *We're on our knees,*
> *we're on our knees again.*
> *We're on our knees,*
> *we're on our knees again.*

Let this nation be changed,
let this nation be saved,
let this nation be turned back to you.
(Repeat)

63 Matt Redman

Can I ascend the hill of the Lord?
Can I stand in that holy place?
There to approach the glory of my God;
come towards to seek your face.
Purify my heart,
and purify my hands,
for I know it is on holy ground I'll stand.

> *I'm coming up the mountain, Lord;*
> *I'm seeking you and you alone.*
> *I know that I will be transformed,*
> *my heart unveiled before you.*
> *I'm longing for your presence, Lord;*
> *envelop me within the cloud.*
> *I'm coming up the mountain, Lord,*
> *my heart unveiled before you, I will come.*

I'm coming to worship,
I'm coming to bow down,
I'm coming to meet with you.

64 Matt Redman

Can we walk upon the water
if our eyes are fixed on you?
There's an air of faith within us
for a time of breaking through.
Can we fly a little higher,
can we soar on eagle's wings?
Come and fan the flames of fire
that are flickering within.

> *Lead us to the promised land,*
> *all that's purposed, all that's planned;*
> *give us eyes of faith again.*
> *Take us on to higher ground*
> *and the greater things to come –*
> *where the eagles soar,*
> *and where we're finding more of you.*

Can we walk into the promise
of abundance in the land?
Take us on, beyond the river,
for the harvest you have planned:
let us see your kingdom coming
in a measure we've not seen.
There has been a time of sowing,
could this be a time to reap?

And can we sing the songs of heaven
while we're standing on the earth:
sing within the coming kingdom,
sing and live and breathe and move?

Can we fly a little higher,
can we fly a little higher,
can we fly a little higher,
can we fly a little higher?

© 1996 Kingsway's Thankyou Music

65 Graham Kendrick

Can you see what we have made
for this very special day?
An orange for our planet home,
circling around the sun.

Count the seasons as we sing,
summer, autumn, winter, spring.
Sing to God who sends the rain,
making all things new again.

Candlelight, burning bright,
chase the darkness of the night.
Christ the light, light our way,
live inside our hearts today.

See the food with colours bright,
tastebuds tingle at the sight.
Let's be thankful as we share,
God's good gifts are everywhere.

Why then is the world we made,
wrapped around with ribbon red?
Red is for the ransom paid,
when our Lord was crucified.

There's a world I'm dreaming of,
where there's peace and joy and love.
Light of Jesus everywhere,
this is my Christingle prayer.

© 1997 Make Way Music

66 Graham Kendrick

> *Celebrate, celebrate, celebrate,*
> *O celebrate Jesus.*

Leader   From the far corners of earth
          we hear music.
All   O celebrate.
Leader   Echoing over the land and sea.
All   O celebrate.
Leader   Sound of the drums
          awakes a new morning.
All   O celebrate.
Leader   Calling our feet
          to the rhythms of praise.
All   O celebrate Jesus.

Leader   Out of the West
          come shouts of rejoicing.
All   O celebrate.
Leader   Out of the East a loud reply.
All   O celebrate.
Leader   Over the nations
          a voice is calling.
All   O celebrate.

Leader	Worship the maker
	of earth and sky.
All	O celebrate Jesus.

Leader	We have millions of reasons
	to celebrate Jesus;
	and I'll sing you seven
	if you count from one.
	Everybody count:
All	One!
Leader	He gave up the glory of heaven.
All	Two!
Leader	Humbly became one of us.
All	Three!
Leader	Show us the love of the Father.
All	Four!
Leader	Paid for our sins on a cross.
All	Five!
Leader	Rose from the dead victorious.
All	Six!
Leader	Ascended to heaven's throne.
All	Seven!
Leader	Poured out his Spirit upon us.
All	O celebrate Jesus.

67 Gary Oliver

Celebrate Jesus, celebrate!
Celebrate Jesus, celebrate!
Celebrate Jesus, celebrate!
Celebrate Jesus, celebrate!

He is risen, he is risen,
and he lives for evermore.
He is risen, he is risen,
come on and celebrate
the resurrection of our Lord.

68 Eddie Espinosa

Change my heart, O God,
make it ever true;
change my heart, O God,
make I be like you.

You are the potter,
I am the clay;
mould me and make me:
this is what I pray.

69 Sue McClellan, John Paculabo and Keith Ryecroft

Colours of day
dawn into the mind,
the sun has come up,
the night is behind.
Go down in the city,
into the street,
and let's give the message
to the people we meet.

So light up the fire
and let the flame burn,
open the door,
let Jesus return.
Take seeds of his Spirit,
let the fruit grow,
tell the people of Jesus,
let his love show.

Go through the park,
on into the town;
the sun still shines on;
it never goes down.
The light of the world
is risen again;
the people of darkness
are needing a friend.

Open your eyes,
look into the sky,
the darkness has come,
the sun came to die.
The evening draws on,
the sun disappears,
but Jesus is living,
his Spirit is near.

70 Graham Kendrick

Come and see, come and see,
come and see the King of love;
see the purple robe
and crown of thorns he wears.
Soldiers mock, rulers sneer
as he lifts the cruel cross;
lone and friendless now,
he climbs towards the hill.

We worship at your feet,
where wrath and mercy meet,
and a guilty world
is washed by love's pure stream.
For us he was made sin –
oh, help me take it in.
Deep wounds of love
cry out 'Father, forgive.'
I worship, I worship
the Lamb who was slain.

Come and weep, come and mourn
for your sin that pierced him there;
so much deeper
than the wounds of thorn and nail.
All our pride, all our greed,
all our fallenness and shame;
and the Lord has laid
the punishment on him.

Man of heaven, born to earth
to restore us to your heaven.
Here we bow in awe
beneath your searching eyes.
From your tears comes our joy,
from your death our life shall spring;
by your resurrection power
we shall rise.

71 Bianco da Siena trans. Richard F. Littledale

Come down, O Love divine,
seek thou this soul of mine,
and visit it with
thine own ardour glowing;

O Comforter, draw near,
within my heart appear,
and kindle it,
thy holy flame bestowing.

O let it freely burn,
till earthly passions turn
to dust and ashes
in its heat consuming;
and let thy glorious light
shine ever on my sight,
and clothe me round,
the while my path illuming.

Let holy charity
mine outward vesture be,
and lowliness become
mine inner clothing;
true lowliness of heart,
which takes the humbler part,
and o'er its own shortcomings
weeps with loathing.

And so the yearning strong,
with which the soul will long,
shall far outpass
the pow'r of human telling;
nor can we guess its grace,
till we become the place
wherein the Holy Spirit
makes his dwelling.

72 Graham Kendrick

(Leader)
Come, let us return to the Lord;
come, let us return to the Lord;
come, let us return to the Lord,
let us return to the Lord.

As surely as the sun rises,
he will appear, he will appear;
he will come to us like winter rains
and like the spring rains that water the earth.

Come, let us return to the Lord;
come, let us return to the Lord;
come, let us return to the Lord,
let us return to the Lord.

Though he tore us, he will heal us;
though he tore us, he will heal us;
let us return to the Lord.

Come, let us press on to know him,
walk in his ways, walk in his ways,
that we may live in his presence
all of our days, all of our days.

Seek him, find him, know him, love him;
seek him, find him, know him, love him;
let us return to the Lord.

73 Graham Kendrick

Come, let us worship Jesus,
King of nations, Lord of all.
Magnificent and glorious,
just and merciful.

Jesus, King of the nations,
Jesus, Lord of all.
Jesus, King of the nations,
Lord of all!

Lavish our heart's affection,
deepest love and highest praise.
Voice, race and language blending,
all the world amazed.

Bring tributes from the nations,
come in joyful cavalcades.
One thunderous acclamation,
one banner raised.

Come, Lord, and fill your temple,
glorify your dwelling-place,
till nations see your splendour
and seek your face.

Fear God and give him glory,
for his hour of judgement comes.
Creator, Lord Almighty,
worship him alone.

74 Martin Smith

Come on, all us singers, sing
that Jesus Christ is Lord.
Come on, all us singers, sing
that Jesus Christ is Lord.
(Repeat)

As your people, Lord,
we now stand before your throne.
A sacrifice of praise will be our song.
As your singers, Lord,
we will shout that 'he is good,
for his love endures for ever'.

Come on, all us singers, sing . . .

As your people, Lord,
we will sing with thankfulness.
We want our lives to be a song of praise.
Banners we will wave
to proclaim that 'he is good,
for his love endures for ever'.

Come on, all us dancers, dance
that Jesus Christ is Lord.
Come on, all us dancers, dance
that Jesus Christ is Lord.
(Repeat)

Help us, Lord, to realise
that our lips were made for praising you,
not for bringing others down,
but for boasting of your love.
Show us, Lord, that when we meet,
we have our feet on holy ground.
Come and purify our lives,
forgive us for the wrong we've done.
We desire to see your face
but teach us first to fear the Lord.
Let us not presume your grace
for the sin we bring is our disgrace.
In your mercy send your pow'r,
demons go in Jesus' name.
Heal the sick and save the lost,
reveal the power of the cross.

Continued overleaf

Open up the heavens, Lord,
open up the heavens, Lord.
Open up the heavens, Lord,
let us sing the song that Jesus saves us.

75 Patricia Morgan and Dave Bankhead

Come on and celebrate
his gift of love, we will celebrate
the Son of God who loved us
and gave us life.
We'll shout your praise, O King,
you give us joy nothing else can bring,
we'll give to you our offering
in celebration praise.

Come on and celebrate, celebrate,
celebrate and sing,
celebrate and sing to the King.
Come on and celebrate, celebrate,
celebrate and sing,
celebrate and sing to the King.

76 Elizabeth Bourbourze

Come, Spirit, come.
Come, holy wind,
blow through the temple of my life.
O come, Spirit, come,
all-pow'rful wind,
all-loving breeze and breath of life.
Breathe upon me, breathe upon me, Spirit.
Breathe upon me, blow, O wind of Spirit.
Breathe upon me, blow, O wind of God.

Come, Spirit, come.
Come, holy rain,
fall on the dry ground of my life.
O come, Spirit, come,
O mighty flood,
O loving stream and source of life.
Flow over me, flow over me, Spirit.
Flow over me, flow over me, Spirit.
Flow over me, flow, O rain of God.

Come, Spirit, come.
Come, holy fire,
consume the offering of my life.
O come, Spirit, come,
O blazing fire,
O burning love and flame of life.
Burn in my heart, burn in my heart, Spirit.
Burn in my heart, burn in my heart, Spirit.
Burn in my heart, burn, O fire of God.

77 Matthew Bridges

Crown him with many crowns,
the Lamb upon his throne;
hark, how the heav'nly anthem drowns
all music but its own:
awake, my soul, and sing
of him who died for thee,
and hail him as thy matchless King
through all eternity.

Crown him the Lord of life,
who triumphed o'er the grave,
and rose victorious in the strife
for those he came to save.
His glories now we sing,
who died and rose on high;
who died eternal life to bring,
and lives that death may die.

Crown him the Lord of love;
behold his hands and side,
rich wounds, yet visible above,
in beauty glorified:
no angel in the sky
can fully bear that sight,
but downward bends each burning eye
at mysteries so bright.

Crown him the Lord of peace,
whose pow'r a sceptre sways
from pole to pole, that wars may cease,
and all be prayer and praise:
his reign shall know no end,
and round his piercèd feet
fair flow'rs of paradise extend
their fragrance ever sweet.

Crown him the Lord of years,
the Potentate of time,
Creator of the rolling spheres,
ineffably sublime.
All hail, Redeemer, hail!
for thou hast died for me;
thy praise shall never, never fail
throughout eternity.

78 David Fellingham

Day of favour, day of grace;
this is the day of jubilee.
The Spirit of the sovereign Lord
is falling now on me.
Let the oil of heaven flow
from the presence of the King.
Jesus, let your power flow
as we worship, as we sing.
Set us free to make you known
to a world that's full of shame.
Jesus, let your glory fall,
give us pow'r to speak your name.

Day of favour, day of grace;
this is the day of jubilee.
The Spirit of the sovereign Lord
is falling now on me.
Open wide the prison doors,
where Satan's held the key.
Bring deliverance to the bound,
and set the captives free.
Bring the good news to the poor,
and cause the blind to see.
The Spirit of the Lord
is falling now on me.

79 John Greenleaf Whittier

Dear Lord and Father of mankind,
forgive our foolish ways!
Reclothe us in our rightful mind,
in purer lives thy service find,
in deeper reverence praise,
in deeper reverence praise.

In simple trust like theirs who heard,
beside the Syrian sea,
the gracious calling of the Lord,
let us, like them, without a word,
rise up and follow thee,
rise up and follow thee.

O Sabbath rest by Galilee!
O calm of hills above,
where Jesus knelt to share with thee
the silence of eternity,
interpreted by love,
interpreted by love!

Drop thy still dews of quietness,
till all our strivings cease;
take from our souls the strain and stress,
and let our ordered lives confess
the beauty of thy peace,
the beauty of thy peace.

Breathe through the heats of our desire
thy coolness and thy balm;
let sense be dumb, let flesh retire;
speak through the earthquake, wind and fire,
O still small voice of calm,
O still small voice of calm!

80 Martin Smith

Did you feel the mountains tremble?
Did you hear the oceans roar,
when the people rose to sing of
Jesus Christ, the risen one?

Did you feel the people tremble?
Did you hear the singers roar,
when the lost began to sing of
Jesus Christ, the saving one?

And we can see that God, you're moving,
a mighty river through the nations.
And young and old will turn to Jesus.
Fling wide, you heavenly gates,
prepare the way of the risen Lord.

Continued overleaf

Open up the doors and let the music play;
let the streets resound with singing.
Songs that bring your hope,
songs that bring your joy,
dancers who dance upon injustice.

Do you feel the darkness tremble,
when all the saints join in one song,
and all the streams flow as one river,
to wash away our brokenness?

And we can see that God, you're moving,
a time of jubilee is coming,
when young and old will turn to Jesus.
Fling wide, you heavenly gates,
prepare the way of the risen Lord.

81 Brian Doerksen

Don't let my love grow cold,
I'm calling out,
light the fire again.
Don't let my vision die,
I'm calling out,
light the fire again.

You know my heart, my deeds,
I'm calling out,
light the fire again.
I need your discipline,
I'm calling out,
light the fire again.

I am here to buy gold,
refined in the fire;
naked and poor,
wretched and blind,
I come.
Clothe me in white,
so I won't be ashamed:
Lord, light the fire again.

82 Chris Bowater

Do something new, Lord,
in my heart, make a start;
do something new, Lord,
do something new.

I open up my heart,
as much as can be known;
I open up my will
to conform to yours alone.

I lay before your feet
all my hopes and desires;
unreservedly submit
to what your Spirit may require.

I only want to live
for your pleasure now;
I long to please you, Father –
will you show me how?

83 Andy Park

Down the mountain the river flows,
and it brings refreshing wherever it goes.
Through the valleys and over the fields,
the river is rushing and the river is here.

The river of God sets our feet a-dancing,
the river of God fills our hearts with cheer;
the river of God fills our mouths with laughter,
and we rejoice for the river is here.

The river of God is teeming with life,
and all who touch it can be revived.
And those who linger on this river's shore
will come back thirsting for more of the Lord.

Up to the mountain we love to go
to find the presence of the Lord.
Along the banks of the river we run,
we dance with laughter, giving praise to
    the Son.

84 Stuart Devane and Glenn Gore

Draw me closer, Lord;
draw me closer, dear Lord,
so that I might touch you,
so that I might touch you,
Lord, I want to touch you.

Touch my eyes, Lord;
touch my eyes, dear Lord,
so that I might see you,
so that I might see you,
Lord, I want to see you.

Your glory and your love,
your glory and your love,
your glory and your love,
and your majesty.

85 Graham Kendrick

Earth lies spellbound in darkness,
sin's oppressive night;
yet in Bethlehem hope is burning bright.
Mysteries are unfolding,
but the only sign is a manger bed
where a baby cries.

Wake up, wake up, it's Christmas morning,
Christ's eternal day is dawning.
Angels sing in exultation,
fill the streets with celebration.
Now to God on high be glory,
to the earth proclaim the story.
Ring the bells in jubilation,
tell the news to every nation:
Christ has come! Christ has come!

Crowding stairways of starlight,
choirs of angels sing:
'Glory, glory to God in the highest heav'n.'
Peace is stilling the violence,
hope is rising high, God is watching us now
through a baby's eyes.

Weakness shatters the pow'rful,
meekness shames the proud,
vain imaginings come tumbling down.
Ancient mercies remembered,
hungry satisfied, lowly, humble hearts
are lifted high.

86 Russell Fragar

Every nation, pow'r and tongue
will bow down to your name;
every eye will see, every ear will hear
your name proclaimed.
This is gonna be our cry
until you come again.
Jesus is the only name
by which man can be saved.

All over the world people just like us
are calling your name,
living in your love;
all over the world people just like us
are calling on Jesus.
All over the world people just like us
are calling your name,
living in your love;
all over the world people just like us
are following Jesus.

(Last time)
We're worshipping Jesus,
we're following Jesus,
we're worshipping Jesus,
we're calling on Jesus.

Makes you wanna dance,
makes you wanna sing,
makes you wanna shout all about it,
shout all about it, shout it
that Jesus is King.

87 Mike and Claire McIntosh

*Exalt the Lord
who is clothed in majesty,
holy is he.
Exalt the Lord
who has girded himself with strength,
holy is he.
(Repeat)*

Rise up, O soul,
and praise him joyfully,
rise up, O heart,
and praise his name.
(Repeat)

88 Chris Bowater

Faithful God, faithful God,
all-sufficient one, I worship you.
Shalom my peace,
my strong deliverer,
I lift you up,
faithful God.

89 Brian Doerksen

Faithful One, so unchanging,
Ageless One, you're my rock of peace.
Lord of all, I depend on you,
I call out to you again and again,
I call out to you again and again.

You are my rock in times of trouble,
you lift me up when I fall down.
All through the storm your love is the anchor,
my hope is in you alone.

90 Graham Kendrick

Far and near hear the call,
worship him, Lord of all;
families of nations, come,
celebrate what God has done.

Deep and wide is the love
heaven sent from above;
God's own Son, for sinners died,
rose again – he is alive.

*Say it loud, say it strong,
tell the world what God has done;
say it loud, praise his name,
let the earth rejoice –
for the Lord reigns.*

At his name, let praise begin;
oceans roar, nature sing,
for he comes to judge the earth
in righteousness and in his truth.

91 Ian Smale

Father God, I wonder
how I managed to exist
without the knowledge of your parenthood
and your loving care.
But now I am your child,
I am adopted in your family
and I can never be alone
'cause, Father God, you're there beside me.

I will sing your praises,
I will sing your praises,
I will sing your praises,
for evermore.
I will sing your praises,
I will sing your praises,
I will sing your praises,
for evermore.

92 Graham Kendrick

Father God, we worship you,
make us part of all you do.
As you move among us now,
we worship you.

Jesus King, we worship you,
help us listen now to you.
As you move among us now,
we worship you.

Spirit pure, we worship you,
with your fire our zeal renew.
As you move among us now,
we worship you.

© 1981 Kingsway's Thankyou Music

93   Andy Piercy

Father, hear our prayer,
that our lives may be
consecrated only unto you.
Cleanse us with your fire,
fill us with your pow'r,
that the world may glorify your name.

Lord, have mercy on us.
Christ, have mercy on us.
Lord, have mercy on us.

© 1995 IQ Music Ltd

94   Danny Daniels

Father, here I am again,
in need of mercy, hurt from sin,
so by the blood of Jesus' love,
let forgiveness flow.

In my heart and in my mind,
in word and deed I've been so blind,
so by the blood of Jesus' love,
let forgiveness flow.

To me, from me,
so my heart will know;
fully and sweetly,
let forgiveness flow.

© Mercy/Vineyard Publishing/Music Services/CopyCare

95   John Barnett

Father, I come to you,
lifting up my hands
in the name of Jesus,
by your grace I stand.
Just because you love me
and I love your Son,
I know your favour,
unending love.

   Unending love,
   your unending love.

I receive your favour,
your unending love,
not because I've earned it,
not for what I've done,
just because you love me
and I love your Son,
I know your favour,
unending love.

It's the presence of your kingdom
as your glory fills this place,
and I see how much you love me
as I look into your face.
Nothing could be better,
there's nothing I would trade
for your favour,
unending love.

© 1989 Mercy/Vineyard Publishing/Music Services/CopyCare

96   Bob Fitts

Father in heaven, how we love you,
we lift your name in all the earth.
May your kingdom be established in our
      praises
as your people declare your mighty works.
Blessèd be the Lord God Almighty,
who was and is and is to come.
Blessèd be the Lord God Almighty,
who reigns for evermore.

© 1985 Scripture in Song/Integrity Music/Kingsway's Thankyou Music

97 Jenny Hewer

Father, I place into your hands
the things I cannot do.
Father, I place into your hands
the things that I've been through.
Father, I place into your hands
the way that I should go,
for I know I always can trust you.

Father, I place into your hands
my friends and family.
Father, I place into your hands
the things that trouble me.
Father, I place into your hands
the person I would be,
for I know I always can trust you.

Father, we love to see your face,
we love to hear your voice.
Father, we love to sing your praise
and in your name rejoice.
Father, we love to walk with you
and in your presence rest,
for we know we always can trust you.

Father, I want to be with you
and do the things you do.
Father, I want to speak the words
that you are speaking too.
Father, I want to love the ones
that you will draw to you,
for I know that I am one with you.

98 Brian Doerksen

Father, I want you to hold me,
I want to rest in your arms today.
Father, I want you to show me,
how much you care for me
in every way.
I bring all my cares
and I lay them at your feet.
You are always there,
and you love me as I am,
yes, you love me as I am.

Father, I know you will hold me,
I know I am your child, your own.
Father, I know you will show me,
I feel your arms holding me,
I'm not alone.
I bring all my fears
and I lay them at your feet.
You are always here,
and you love me as I am,
yes, you love me as I am.

99 David Ruis

Father of creation,
unfold your sovereign plan.
Raise up a chosen generation
that will march through the land.
All of creation is longing
for your unveiling of pow'r.
Would you release your anointing,
O God, let this be the hour.

Let your glory fall in this room,
let it go forth from here to the nations.
Let your fragrance rest in this place,
as we gather to seek your face.

Ruler of the nations,
the world has yet to see
the full release of your promise,
the church in victory.
Turn to us, Lord, and touch us,
make us strong in your might.
Overcome our weakness,
that we could stand up and fight.

Men	Let your kingdom come.
Women	Let your kingdom come.
Men	Let your will be done.
Women	Let your will be done.
Men	Let us see on earth,
Women	let us see on earth
All	the glory of your Son.

100 Darlene Zschech

Father of life, draw me closer,
Lord, my heart is set on you;
let me run the race of time
with your life enfolding mine
and let the peace of God, let it reign.

O Holy Spirit, Lord, my comfort,
strengthen me, hold my head up high;
and I'll stand upon your truth,
bringing glory unto you,
and let the peace of God, let it reign.

> *O Lord, I hunger for more of you,*
> *rise up within me,*
> *let me know your truth.*
> *O Holy Spirit, saturate my soul,*
> *and let the life of God*
> *fill me now, let your healing pow'r*
> *bring life and make me whole*
> *and let the peace of God, let it reign*

101 Philip Lawson Johnston

Father, we adore you,
we are your children gathered here;
to be with you is our delight,
a feast beyond compare.

Father, in your presence
there is such freedom to enjoy.
We find in you a lasting peace
that nothing can destroy.

> *You are the fountain of life,*
> *you are the fountain of life,*
> *and as we drink,*
> *we are more than satisfied by you,*
> *O Fountain of Life.*

102 Carl Tuttle

Father, we adore you,
you've drawn us to this place.
We bow down before you,
humbly on our face.

> *All the earth shall worship*
> *at the throne of the King.*
> *Of his great and awesome pow'r*
> *we shall sing!*
> (Repeat)

Jesus, we love you,
because you first loved us,
you reached out and healed us
with your mighty touch.

Spirit, we need you,
to lift us from this mire,
consume and empower us
with your holy fire.

Holy is he;
blessed is he;
worthy is he;
gracious is he;
faithful is he;
awesome is he;
Saviour is he;
Master is he;
mighty is he.
Have mercy on me.

103 Donna Adkins

Father, we love you,
we worship and adore you,
glorify your name in all the earth.
Glorify your name,
glorify your name,
glorify your name in all the earth.

Jesus, we love you . . .

Spirit, we love you . . .

104 Andy Park

Father, you are my portion in this life,
and you are my hope and my delight,
and I love you, yes, I love you.
Lord, I love you, my delight.

Jesus, you are my treasure in this life,
and you are so pure and so kind,
and I love you, yes, I love you,
Lord, I love you, my delight.

105 Noel and Tricia Richards

Filled with compassion for all creation,
Jesus came into a world that was lost.
There was but one way that he could save us,
only through suffering death on a cross.

God, you are waiting, your heart is breaking
for all the people who live on the earth.
Stir us to action, filled with your passion
for all the people who live on the earth.

Great is your passion for all the people
living and dying without knowing you.
Having no saviour, they're lost for ever,
if we don't speak out and lead them to you.

From every nation we shall be gathered,
millions redeemed shall be Jesus' reward.
Then he will turn and say to his Father:
'Truly my suffering was worth it all.'

106 Paul Oakley

Fire, there's a fire,
sweet fire burning in my heart.
(Repeat)

And I will run
with all of the passion you've put in me.
I will spread
the seed of the gospel everywhere.

And I can feel
the power of your hand upon me.
Now I know
I'll never be the same again.
For as long as you will give me breath,
my heart is so resolved,
O, to lay my life before you, Lord.
Let everything I do
be to your praise.

Let me feel your tongues of fire
resting upon me,
let me hear the sound
of your mighty rushing wind.
Let my life be like an offering of worship,
let me be a living sacrifice of praise.

107 Ian Smale

5 0 0 0 + hungry folk,
5 0 0 0 + hungry folk,
5 0 0 0 + hungry folk
came 4 2 listen 2 Jesus.

The 6 x 2 said 0 0 0,
the 6 x 2 said 0 0 0,
the 6 x 2 said 0 0 0,
where can I get some food from?

Just 1 had 1 2 3 4 5,
just 1 had 1 2 3 4 5,
just 1 had 1 2 3 4 5
loaves and 1 2 fishes.

When Jesus blessed the 5 + 2,
when Jesus blessed the 5 + 2,
when Jesus blessed the 5 + 2
they were increased many x over.

5 0 0 0 + 8 it up,
5 0 0 0 + 8 it up,
5 0 0 0 + 8 it up,
with 1 2 3 4 5 6 7 8 9 10 11 12
basketfuls left over.

108 Dennis Jernigan

For all that you've done
I will thank you.
For all that you're going to do.
For all that you've promised,
and all that you are
is all that has carried me through.
Jesus, I thank you.
And I thank you, thank you, Lord.
Thank you, thank you, Lord.

Thank you for loving and setting me free.
Thank you for giving your life just for me.
How I thank you.
Jesus, I thank you, gratefully thank you,
thank you.

© 1991 Shepherds Heart Music/Word Music/CopyCare

109 Dave Richards

For I'm building a people of power
and I'm making a people of praise,
that will move through this land by my Spirit,
and will glorify my precious name.
Build your church, Lord,
make us strong, Lord,
join our hearts, Lord,
through your Son.
Make us one, Lord, in your body,
in the kingdom of your Son.

© 1977 Kingsway's Thankyou Music

110 Graham Kendrick

For the joys and for the sorrows,
the best and worst of times,
for this moment, for tomorrow,
for all that lies behind;
fears that crowd around me,
for the failure of my plans,
for the dreams of all I hope to be,
the truth of what I am:

For this I have Jesus,
for this I have Jesus,
for this I have Jesus,
I have Jesus.

For the tears that flow in secret,
in the broken times,
for the moments of elation,
or the troubled mind;
for all the disappointments,
or the sting of old regrets,
all my prayers and longings,
that seem unanswered yet:

For the weakness of my body,
the burdens of each day,
for the nights of doubt and worry
when sleep has fled away;
needing reassurance
and the will to start again,
a steely-eyed endurance,
the strength to fight and win:

© 1994 Make Way Music

111 Graham Kendrick

For this purpose Christ was revealed
to destroy all the works of the evil one.
Christ in us has overcome,
so with gladness we sing
and welcome his kingdom in.

Over sin he has conquered,
hallelujah, he has conquered.
Over death victorious,
hallelujah, victorious.
Over sickness he has triumphed,
hallelujah, he has triumphed,
Jesus reigns over all!

In the name of Jesus we stand,
by the power of his blood we now claim
  this ground.
Satan has no authority here,
powers of darkness must flee,
for Christ has the victory.

© 1985 Kingsway's Thankyou Music

112 Pete Sanchez Jnr

For thou, O Lord,
art high above all the earth.
Thou art exalted far above all gods.
For thou, O Lord,
art high above all the earth.
Thou art exalted far above all gods.

I exalt thee, I exalt thee,
I exalt thee, O Lord.
I exalt thee, I exalt thee,
I exalt thee, O Lord.

113 David Hadden

For unto us a child is born,
unto us a son is giv'n,
and the government shall be upon his shoulders.
(Repeat)

> *And he will be called wonderful,*
> *wonderful Counsellor, mighty God,*
> *the everlasting Father,*
> *Prince of Peace, mighty God.*

And there shall be no end
to the increase of his rule,
to the increase of his government and peace.
For he shall sit on David's throne
upholding righteousness.
Our God shall accomplish this.

For he is the mighty God,
he is the Prince of Peace,
the King of kings and Lord of lords.
All honour to the King,
all glory to his name,
for now and evermore.

114 Graham Kendrick

From heav'n you came, helpless babe,
entered our world, your glory veiled;
not to be served but to serve,
and give your life that we might live.

This is our God, the Servant King,
he calls us now to follow him,
to bring our lives as a daily offering
of worship to the Servant King.

There in the garden of tears,
my heavy load he chose to bear;
his heart with sorrow was torn.
'Yet not my will but yours,' he said.

Come, see his hands and his feet,
the scars that speak of sacrifice,
hands that flung stars into space,
to cruel nails surrendered.

So let us learn how to serve,
and in our lives enthrone him;
each other's needs to prefer,
for it is Christ we're serving.

115 Don Harris and Gary Sadler

From the ends of the earth
(from the ends of the earth),
from the depths of the sea
(from the depths of the sea),
from the heights of the heavens
(from the heights of the heavens)
your name be praised;
from the hearts of the weak
(from the hearts of the weak),
from the shouts of the strong
(from the shouts of the strong),
from the lips of all people
(from the lips of all people),
this song we raise, Lord.

> *Throughout the endless ages*
> *you will be crowned with praises,*
> *Lord most high;*
> *exalted in every nation,*
> *sovereign of all creation,*
> *Lord most high, be magnified.*

116 Graham Kendrick

From the sun's rising
unto the sun's setting,
Jesus our Lord
shall be great in the earth;
and all earth's kingdoms
shall be his dominion,
all of creation
shall sing of his worth.

Let every heart, every voice,
every tongue join with spirits ablaze;
one in his love, we will circle the world
with the song of his praise.
O, let all his people rejoice,
and let all the earth hear his voice!

To every tongue, tribe
and nation he sends us,
to make disciples
to teach and baptise.
For all authority
to him is given;
now as his witnesses
we shall arise.

Come, let us join with
the church from all nations,
cross every border,
throw wide every door;
workers with him
as he gathers his harvest,
till earth's far corners
our Saviour adore.

© 1988 Make Way Music

117 Graham Kendrick

From where the sun rises,
even to the place it goes down –
we're giving you praise,
giving you praise.
From sun-kissed islands
and even where the cold wind blows –
we're giving you praise,
giving you praise.

Even in the night when the sun goes down,
we're giving you praise;
passing it along as the world goes round,
we're giving you praise.

We're lifting our faces,
looking at the One we all love –
we're giving you praise,
giving you praise.
All colours and races
joining with the angels above –
we're giving you praise,
giving you praise.

© 1996 Make Way Music

118 Henry Smith

Give thanks with a grateful heart.
Give thanks to the Holy One.
Give thanks because he's given
Jesus Christ, his Son.
Give thanks with a grateful heart.
Give thanks to the Holy One.
Give thanks because he's given
Jesus Christ, his Son.

And now let the weak say, 'I am strong',
let the poor say, 'I am rich',
because of what the Lord has done for us.
And now let the weak say, 'I am strong',
let the poor say, 'I am rich',
because of what the Lord has done for us.

© 1978 Integrity's Hosanna! Music/Kingsway's Thankyou Music

119 Taizé Community

Gloria, gloria in excelsis Deo!
Gloria, gloria, alleluia, alleluia.

© Ateliers et Presses de Taizé

120 Danny Daniels

Glory, glory in the highest;
glory to the Almighty;
glory to the Lamb of God,
and glory to the living Word;
glory to the Lamb!
(Repeat)

Continued overleaf

I give glory (glory),
glory (glory),
glory, glory to the Lamb!
I give glory (glory),
glory (glory),
glory, glory to the Lamb!
I give glory to the Lamb!

121　Geoff Bullock

Glory to the King of kings!
Majesty, pow'r and strength
to the Lord of lords!
(Repeat)

Holy One, all creation crowns you
King of kings.
Holy One, King of kings,
Lord of lords, Holy One.

Jesus, Lord, with eyes unveiled
we will see your throne.
Jesus, Prince of Peace,
Son of God, Emmanuel.

122　Graham Kendrick

God, be gracious and bless us
and make your face shine on us:
let your ways be known,
your salvation shown
all over the earth;
let your ways be known,
your salvation shown
all over the earth.

May the peoples praise you, O God,
may all the peoples praise you;
may the nations be glad and sing for joy,
for you come to rule them justly.
May the peoples praise you, O God,
for you guide the nations of the earth;
may the peoples praise you, O God,
the nations be glad and sing for joy.

123　Carol Owens

God forgave my sin in Jesus' name,
I've been born again in Jesus' name;
and in Jesus' name I come to you
to share his love as he told me to.

He said, 'Freely, freely you have received,
freely, freely give;
go in my name and because you believe
others will know that I live.'

All power is given in Jesus' name,
in earth and heaven in Jesus' name;
and in Jesus' name I come to you
to share his power as he told me to.

124　Graham Kendrick

God is good, we sing and shout it,
God is good, we celebrate.
God is good, no more we doubt it,
God is good, we know it's true.

And when I think of his love for me,
my heart fills with praise
and I feel like dancing.
For in his heart there is room for me
and I run with arms opened wide.

125　Don Moen and Paul Overstreet

God is good all the time!
He put a song of praise in this heart of mine;
God is good all the time!
Through the darkest night
his light will shine:
God is good, God is good all the time.

If you're walking
through the valley
and there are shadows all around,
do not fear,
he will guide you,

he will keep you safe and sound
'cause he has promised
to never leave you
nor forsake you,
and his word is true.

We were sinners,
so unworthy,
still for us he chose to die:
filled us with
his Holy Spirit,
now we can stand and testify
that his love
is everlasting
and his mercies
they will never end.

Though I may not understand
all the plans you have for me,
my life is in your hands,
and through the eyes of faith
I can clearly see:

126 Graham Kendrick and Steve Thompson

God is great, amazing!
Come, let his praises ring.
God is great, astounding!
the whole creation sings.

His clothing is splendour and majesty bright,
for he wraps himself in a garment of light.
He spreads out the heavens, his palace of
    stars,
and rides on the wings of the wind.

What marvellous wisdom the Maker displays,
the sea vast and spacious, the dolphins and
    whales.
The earth full of creatures, the great and the
    small,
he watches and cares for them all.

The rain forest canopies darken the skies,
cathedrals of mist that resound with the choirs
of creatures discordant, outrageous, ablaze
in colourful pageants of praise.

Above his creation the Father presides.
The pulse of the planets, the rhythm of tides.
The moon marks the seasons, the day follows
    night,
yet he knows every beat of my heart.

Let cannons of thunder salute their acclaim,
the sunsets fly glorious banners of flame,
the angels shout 'holy' again and again
as they soar in the arch of the heavens.

127 Ian Smale

God is here, God is present,
God is moving by his Spirit.
Can you hear what he is saying,
are you willing to respond?
God is here, God is present,
God is moving by his Spirit.
Lord, I open up my life to you,
please do just what you will.

Lord, I won't stop loving you,
you mean more to me
than anyone else.
(Repeat)

128 Arthur Campbell Ainger,
adapted by Michael Forster

God is working his purpose out
as year succeeds to year.
God is working his purpose out,
and the day is drawing near.
Nearer and nearer draws the time,
the time that shall surely be,
when the earth shall be filled
with the glory of God
as the waters cover the sea.

Continued overleaf

From the east to the utmost west
wherever foot has trod,
through the mouths of his messengers
echoes forth the voice of God:
'Listen to me, ye continents,
ye islands, give ear to me,
that the earth shall be filled
with the glory of God
as the waters cover the sea.'

March we forth in the strength of God,
his banner is unfurled;
let the light of the gospel shine
in the darkness of the world:
strengthen the weary, heal the sick
and set every captive free,
that the earth shall be filled
with the glory of God
as the waters cover the sea.

All our efforts are nothing worth
unless God bless the deed;
vain our hopes for the harvest tide
till he brings to life the seed.
Yet ever nearer draws the time,
the time that shall surely be,
when the earth shall be filled
with the glory of God
as the waters cover the sea.

129 John Wimber

God of all comfort,
God of all grace,
oh, we have come to seek you,
we have come to seek your face.
Because you have called us
we're gathered in this place,
oh, we have come to seek you,
we have come to seek your face.

130 David Fellingham

God of glory, we exalt your name,
you who reign in majesty.
We lift our hearts to you
and we will worship, praise and magnify
your holy name.

In pow'r resplendent (in pow'r resplendent)
you reign in glory (you reign in glory),
eternal King (eternal King),
you reign for ever.
Your word is mighty (your word is mighty),
releasing captives (releasing captives),
your love is gracious (your love is gracious),
you are my God.

131 Simon and Tina Triffitt

God of glory, you are worthy,
you ride above the heavens,
you are Lord,
God of fire, my desire
is to be a vessel in this end time move.

Fire of God's glory, fall on me,
burn away the chaff of self
and set me free;
make me pure and holy,
a light for all to see;
fire of God's glory, fall on me.

132 Chris Bowater

God of grace, I turn my face to you,
I cannot hide;
my nakedness, my shame, my guilt,
are all before your eyes.
Strivings and all anguished dreams
in rags lie at my feet;
and only grace provides the way
for me to stand complete.

And your grace
clothes me in righteousness,
and your mercy
covers me in love.
Your life adorns and beautifies,
I stand complete in you.

133 Unknown

God's not dead. No! He is alive.
God's not dead. No! He is alive.
God's not dead. No! He is alive.
Praise him with my mouth.
Praise him with my feet.
Praise him with my hands.
Love him in my life.
Jesus is alive in me.

134 Don Moen

God will make a way
where there seems to be no way.
He works in ways we cannot see.
He will make a way for me.
He will be my guide,
hold me closely to his side,
with love and strength for each new day.
He will make a way,
he will make a way.

By a roadway in the wilderness he'll lead me,
and rivers in the desert will I see;
heaven and earth will fade
but his Word will still remain,
he will do something new today.

135 Todd Pettygrove

Great and mighty is he,
great and mighty is he;
clothed in glory, arrayed in splendour,
great and mighty is he.
(Repeat)

Let us lift his name up high,
celebrate his grace;
for he has redeemed our lives
and he reigns on high.

136 Noel Richards and Gerald Coates

Great is the darkness that covers the earth,
oppression, injustice and pain.
Nations are slipping in hopeless despair,
though many have come in your name.
Watching while sanity dies,
touched by the madness and lies.

Come, Lord Jesus,
come, Lord Jesus,
pour out your Spirit, we pray.
Come, Lord Jesus,
come, Lord Jesus,
pour out your Spirit on us today.

May now your church rise with power and love,
this glorious gospel proclaim.
In every nation salvation will come
to those who believe in your name.
Help us bring light to this world
that we might speed your return.

Great celebrations on that final day
when out of the heavens you come.
Darkness will vanish, all sorrow will end,
and rulers will bow at your throne.
Our great commission complete,
then face to face we shall meet.

137 Steve McEwan

Great is the Lord and most worthy of praise,
the city of God, the holy place,
the joy of the whole earth.
Great is the Lord in whom we have the victory.
He aids us against the enemy,
we bow down on our knees.

Continued overleaf

And, Lord, we want to lift your name on high,
and, Lord, we want to thank you
for the works you've done in our lives;
and, Lord, we trust in your unfailing love,
for you alone are God eternal,
throughout earth and heaven above.

138 Thomas O. Chisholm

Great is thy faithfulness,
O God my Father,
there is no shadow
of turning with thee;
thou changest not,
thy compassions they fail not;
as thou hast been
thou for ever wilt be.

Great is thy faithfulness!
Great is thy faithfulness!
Morning by morning
new mercies I see;
all I have needed
thy hand has provided,
great is thy faithfulness,
Lord, unto me!

Summer and winter,
and springtime and harvest,
sun, moon and stars
in their courses above,
join with all nature
in manifold witness
to thy great faithfulness,
mercy and love.

Pardon for sin
and a peace that endureth,
thine own dear presence
to cheer and to guide;
strength for today
and bright hope for tomorrow,
blessings all mine,
with ten thousand beside!

139 Jarrod Cooper

Great is your name,
great are your deeds, O Lord.
Day after day
your mercies displayed to all.
There is none like you,
who loves the way you do, Jehovah.

Only you deserve the glory,
only you deserve the praise,
only you deserve the honour,
so great are your ways.
(Repeat)

Faithful and true
in all you do, O Lord.
Saviour and King,
my everything, my all.
There is none like you,
who loves the way you do, Jehovah.

140 Joseph Vogels

Leader	Hail, Jesus, you're my King.
All	Hail, Jesus, you're my King.
Leader	Your life frees me to sing.
All	Your life frees me to sing.
Leader	I will praise you all my days.
All	I will praise you all my days.
Leader	You're perfect in all your ways.
All	You're perfect in all your ways.

Leader	Hail, Jesus, you're my Lord.
All	Hail, Jesus, you're my Lord.
Leader	I will obey your word.
All	I will obey your word.
Leader	I want to see your kingdom come.
All	I want to see your kingdom come.
Leader	Not my will, but yours be done.
All	Not my will, but yours be done.

Leader	Glory, glory to the Lamb.
All	Glory, glory to the Lamb.
Leader	You take me into the land.
All	You take me into the land.

Leader	We will conquer in your name.
All	We will conquer in your name.
Leader	And proclaim that Jesus reigns!
All	And proclaim that Jesus reigns!
Leader	Hail, hail, Lion of Judah!
All	Hail, hail, Lion of Judah!
Leader	How powerful you are!
All	How powerful you are!
Leader	Hail, hail, Lion of Judah!
All	Hail, hail, Lion of Judah!
Leader	How wonderful you are!
All	How wonderful you are!
Leader	How wonderful you are!
All	How wonderful you are!
	How wonderful you are!

141 Terry Butler

Hallelujah, hallelujah,
hallelujah, the Lord reigns.
Hallelujah, hallelujah,
hallelujah, the Lord Almighty reigns.

He has showed his awesome power,
he has triumphed mightily,
he has triumphed over darkness and the grave.
He has broken chains that bound us,
he has set the prisoner free,
by his own great mercy we are saved.

142 Ron Kenoly

Hallelujah! Jesus is alive,
death has lost its victory
and the grave has been denied;
Jesus lives for ever,
he's alive, he's alive!

He's the Alpha and Omega,
the first and last is he,
the curse of sin is broken

and we have perfect liberty,
the Lamb of God has risen,
he's alive, he's alive!

(Last time)
Hallelujah! Jesus is alive!

143 Tim Cullen

Hallelujah, my Father,
for giving us your Son;
sending him into the world
to be given up for all.
Knowing we would bruise him
and smite him from the earth,
Hallelujah, my Father,
in his death is my birth;
hallelujah, my Father,
in his life is my life.

144 Charles Wesley, George Whitefield, Martin Madan and others

Hark, the herald-angels sing
glory to the new-born King;
peace on earth and mercy mild,
God and sinners reconciled:
joyful, all ye nations rise,
join the triumph of the skies,
with the angelic host proclaim,
'Christ is born in Bethlehem.'

Hark, the herald-angels sing
glory to the new-born King.

Christ, by highest heav'n adored,
Christ, the everlasting Lord,
late in time behold him come,
offspring of a virgin's womb!
Veiled in flesh the Godhead see,
hail the incarnate Deity!
Pleased as man with us to dwell,
Jesus, our Emmanuel.

Continued overleaf

Hail, the heav'n-born Prince of Peace!
Hail, the Sun of Righteousness!
Light and life to all he brings,
ris'n with healing in his wings;
mild he lays his glory by,
born that we no more may die,
born to raise us from the earth,
born to give us second birth.

Hark, the herald-angels sing
glory to the new-born King.

145 Mick Gisbey

Have you got an appetite?
Do you eat what is right?
Are you feeding on the word of God?
Are you fat or are you thin?
Are you really full within?
Do you find your strength in him
or are you starving?

You and me,
all should be
exercising regularly,
standing strong
all day long,
giving God the glory.
Feeding on the living Bread,
not eating crumbs but loaves instead;
standing stronger,
living longer,
giving God the glory.

If it's milk or meat you need,
why not have a slap-up feed,
and stop looking like a weed and start to grow?
Take the full of fitness food,
taste and see that God is good,
come on, feed on what you should
and be healthy.

146 Stuart Garrard

Have you heard the good news,
have you heard the good news?
We can live in hope
because of what the Lord has done.
(Repeat)

There is a way when there seems no other way,
there is a light in the darkness;
there is a hope, an everlasting hope,
there is a God who can help us.

A hope for justice and a hope for peace,
a hope for those in desperation:
we have a future if only we believe
he works in every situation.

147 Matt Redman

Have you not said
as we pass through water,
you will be with us?
And you have said
as we walk through fire,
we will not be burned.
We are not afraid,
for you are with us;
we will testify
to the honour of your name.
We are witnesses,
you have shown us,
you are the one who can save.

Fill us up and send us out
in the power of your name.
Fill us up and send us out
in the power of your name.

Bring them from the west,
sons and daughters,
call them for your praise.
Gather from the east
all your children,
coming home again.
Bring them from afar,
all the nations,
from the north and south,
drawing all the peoples in.
Corners of the earth,
come to see
there's only one Saviour and King.

148 Graham Kendrick

Hear, O Lord, our cry:
revive us, revive us again.
For the sake of your glory,
revive us, revive us again.
Lord, hear our cry.
Lord, hear our cry.

Hear, O Lord, our cry:
revive us, revive us again.
For the sake of the children
revive us, revive us again.
Lord, hear our cry.
Lord, hear our cry.

© 1989 Make Way Music

149 Graham Kendrick

Women Hear our cry, O hear our cry:
Men 'Jesus, come!'
Women Hear our cry, O hear our cry:
Men 'Jesus, come!'

The tide of prayer is rising,
a deeper passion burning –

> *Women* Hear our cry, O hear our cry:
> *Men* 'Jesus, come!'
> *Women* Hear our cry, O hear our cry:
> *Men* 'Jesus, come!'
> *Women* Whoever is thirsty, come now
> and drink the waters of life;
> *Men* whoever is thirsty, come now
> and drink the waters of life.
> *Women* Hear our cry, O hear our cry:
> *Men* 'Jesus, come!'
> *Women* Hear our cry, O hear our cry:
> *Men* 'Jesus, come!'

We lift our eyes with longing
to see your kingdom coming –

The streets of teeming cities
cry out for healing rivers –

Refresh them with your presence,
give grace for deep repentance –

Tear back the shroud of shadows
that covers all the peoples –

Revealing your salvation
in every tribe and nation –

© 1996 Make Way Music

150 Graham Kendrick

Heaven invites you to a party,
to celebrate the birth of a Son;
angels rejoicing in the starlight,
singing, 'Christ your Saviour has come.'
(Repeat)

And it's for you (and it's for you)
and it's for me (and it's for me),
for all your friends (for all your friends)
and family (and family).

Now heaven's door (now heaven's door)
is open wide (is open wide),
so come on in (so come on in),
come, step inside (come, step inside).

Angels from the realms of glory,
wing your flight o'er all the earth;
you who sang creation's story,
now proclaim Messiah's birth.

And it's for you . . .

Let trumpets blast (let trumpets blast),
let music play (let music play),
let people shout (let people shout),
let banners wave (let banners wave).

Come, all you people (come, all you people),
join hands together (join hands together),
bring all your neighbours
(bring all your neighbours),
everybody! (everybody!)

Send invitations (send invitations)
to every nation (to every nation),
come and adore him (come and adore him),
everybody! (everybody!)
everybody! (everybody!)

Continued overleaf

Heaven invites you to a party,
to celebrate the birth of a Son;
angels rejoicing in the starlight,
singing, 'Christ your Saviour has come.'

And it's for you (and it's for you)
and it's for me (and it's for me),
for all your friends (for all your friends)
and family (and family).

Let trumpets blast (let trumpets blast),
let music play (let music play),
let people shout (let people shout),
let banners wave (let banners wave).

© 1988 Make Way Music

151 John L. Bell and Graham Maule

Heav'n shall not wait
for the poor to lose their patience,
the scorned to smile,
the despised to find a friend:
Jesus is Lord;
he has championed the unwanted;
in him injustice
confronts its timely end.

Heav'n shall not wait
for the rich to share their fortunes,
the proud to fall,
the élite to tend the least:
Jesus is Lord;
he has shown his master's privilege –
to kneel and wash
servants' feet before they feast.

Heav'n shall not wait
for the dawn of great ideas,
thoughts of compassion
divorced from cries of pain:
Jesus is Lord;
he has married word and action;
his cross and company
make his purpose plain.

Heav'n shall not wait
for our legalised obedience,
defined by statute,
to strict conventions bound:
Jesus is Lord;
he has hallmarked true allegiance –
goodness appears
where his grace is sought and found.

Heav'n shall not wait
for triumphant hallelujahs,
when earth has passed
and we reach another shore:
Jesus is Lord
in our present imperfection;
his pow'r and love
are for now and then for evermore.

© 1987 WGRG

152 Kevin Prosch

He brought me to his banqueting table
(he brought me to his banqueting table),
he brought me to his banqueting table
(he brought me to his banqueting table),
and his banner over me is love.

I am my beloved's and he is mine
(I am my beloved's and he is mine),
I am my beloved's and he is mine
(I am my beloved's and he is mine),
and his banner over me is love.
Yes, his banner over me is love.

And we can feel the love of God in this place,
we believe your goodness, we receive your grace.
We delight ourselves at your table, O God,
you do all things well, just look at our lives.

© 1991 Mercy/Vineyard Publishing/Music Services/CopyCare

153 Steve and Vicki Cook

He has clothed us with his righteousness,
covered us with his great love.
He has showered us with mercy,
and we delight to know the glorious favour,
wondrous favour of God.

We rejoice in the grace of God
poured upon our lives,
loving kindness has come to us
because of Jesus Christ.
We rejoice in the grace of God,
our hearts overflow.
What a joy to know the grace of God.

He's brought us into his family,
made us heirs with his own Son.
All good things he freely gives us
and we cannot conceive what God's preparing,
God's preparing for us.

154 Andy Park

He has fire in his eyes
and a sword in his hand
and he's riding a white horse
across this land.
He has fire in his eyes
and a sword in his hand,
he's riding a white horse
all across this land.
And he's calling out to you and me,
'Will you ride with me?'

He has fire in his eyes
and a sword in his hand
and he's riding a white horse
across this land.
And he's calling out to you and me,
'Will you ride with me?'
and we say, 'Yes, yes, Lord,
we will ride with you.'

And we say, 'Yes, Lord,
we will ride with you.
We will stand up and fight.
We will ride with the armies of heaven,
we'll be dressed in white
(we'll be dressed in white).'
And we say, 'Yes, yes, Lord, we will ride.'

He has a crown on his head,
he carries a sceptre in his hand
and he's leading the armies
across this land.
And he's calling out to you and me,
'Will you ride with me?'
and we say, 'Yes, yes, Lord,
we will ride with you.'

And that fire in his eyes
is his love for his bride,
and he's longing that she be with him,
right by his side.
That fire in his eyes
is his burning desire
that his bride be with him,
right by his side.
And he's calling out to us right now,
'Will you ride with me?'

155 Gerald Coates, Noel Richards and Tricia Richards

He has risen, he has risen,
he has risen, Jesus is alive.

When the life flowed from his body,
seemed like Jesus' mission failed.
But his sacrifice accomplished,
victory over sin and hell.

In the grave God did not leave him,
for his body to decay;
raised to life, the great awakening,
Satan's pow'r he overcame.

If there were no resurrection,
we ourselves could not be raised;
but the Son of God is living,
so our hope is not in vain.

When the Lord rides out of heaven,
mighty angels at his side,
they will sound the final trumpet,
from the grave we shall arise.

Continued overleaf

He has given life immortal,
we shall see him face to face;
through eternity we'll praise him,
Christ the champion of our faith.

He has risen, he has risen,
he has risen, Jesus is alive.

156 Twila Paris

He is exalted,
the King is exalted on high,
I will praise him.
He is exalted, for ever exalted,
and I will praise his name.

He is the Lord,
for ever his truth shall reign.
Heaven and earth
rejoice in his holy name.
He is exalted,
the King is exalted on high.

157 Graham Kendrick

He is here,
and we have come to worship him,
in his presence opening
the treasures of our hearts.
He is here,
the centre of our longings,
all our restless journeyings
are ended in his peace.

And God is here with us,
our Saviour, Jesus;
his mercy covers us.
Immanuel is here,
so tender, so near.
We welcome you, Immanuel,
adore you more than words can tell,
we worship you.
Immanuel is here,
he is here.

He is here,
and we have come to worship him,
in his presence opening
the treasures of our hearts.
He is here,
the One for whom the angels sing.
Heav'n and earth are touching,
this is a holy place.

158 Unknown

He is Lord, he is Lord,
he is risen from the dead
and he is Lord.
Every knee shall bow,
every tongue confess
that Jesus Christ is Lord.

159 Kevin Prosch

He is the Lord, and he reigns on high;
he is the Lord.
Spoke into the darkness, created the light.
He is the Lord.
Who is like unto him, never ending in days;
he is the Lord.
And he comes in power when we call on his
    name.
He is the Lord.

Show your power,
O Lord our God,
show your power,
O Lord our God, our God.

Your gospel, O Lord, is the hope for our nation;
you are the Lord.
It's the power of God for our salvation.
You are the Lord.
We ask not for riches, but look to the cross;
you are the Lord.
And for our inheritance give us the lost.
You are the Lord.

Send your power.
O Lord our God,
send your power,
O Lord our God, our God.

160 Carol Owen

He is the mighty God,
he is the risen King,
he is the Lord of lords.
He is the first and last,
he is holy, he is true,
he is the Lord of lords.

    And we know he is coming back again
    in pow'r and glory.
    He is coming back again
    to claim his people;
    he is coming back again
    to bring his children home with him,
    home with him.

He is the One who gave
his life for all the world,
he is the Lord of lords,
who rose up from the grave,
defeated death and hell;
he is the Lord of lords.

He's coming in the clouds
and every eye shall see
he is the Lord of lords;
then every knee shall bow
and every tongue proclaim
he is the Lord of lords.

161 Chris Bowater

    Here I am, wholly available.
    As for me, I will serve the Lord.
    Here I am, wholly available.
    As for me, I will serve the Lord.

The fields are white unto harvest,
but O, the labourers are so few,
so, Lord, I give myself to help the reaping,
to gather precious souls unto you.

The time is right in the nation
for works of power and authority;
God's looking for a people who are willing
to be counted in his glorious victory.

As salt are we ready to savour,
in darkness are we ready to be light?
God's seeking out a very special people
to manifest his truth and his might.

162 Don Moen

Here in your presence,
beholding your glory,
bowing in reverence
we worship you only.

    Standing before you,
    we love and adore you, O Lord,
    there is none like you.

Name above all names,
beholding your glory,
to Jesus, our Saviour
our lives we surrender.

Worthy of glory,
worthy of honour,
we give you blessing,
glory and power.

163 Graham Kendrick

Here is bread, here is wine,
Christ is with us, he is with us.
Break the bread, taste the wine,
Christ is with us here.

Continued overleaf

Here is grace, here is peace,
Christ is with us, he is with us;
know his grace, find his peace,
feast on Jesus here.

In this bread there is healing,
in this cup is life for ever.
In this moment, by the Spirit,
Christ is with us here.

Here we are, joined in one,
Christ is with us, he is with us;
we'll proclaim till he comes
Jesus crucified.

© 1993 Make Way Music

164   William Rees

Here is love vast as the ocean,
loving kindness as the flood.
When the Prince of Life, our ransom,
shed for us his precious blood.
Who his love will not remember?
Who can cease to sing his praise?
He can never be forgotten,
throughout heav'n's eternal days.

On the mount of crucifixion
fountains opened deep and wide;
through the floodgates of God's mercy
flowed a vast and gracious tide.
Grace and love, like mighty rivers,
poured incessant from above,
and heaven's peace and perfect justice
kissed a guilty world in love.

165   C. Groves and A. Piercy

Here we stand
in total surrender,
lifting our voices,
abandoned to your cause;
here we stand,
praying in the glory
of the one and only
Jesus Christ, the Lord.

This time revival;
Lord, come and heal our land,
bring to completion
the work that you've begun.
This time revival;
stir up your church again,
pour out your Spirit
on your daughters and your sons.

Here we stand
in need of your mercy,
Father, forgive us
for the fire that we have lost.
Once again
make us an army
to conquer this nation
with the message of the cross.

© 1995 IQ Music

166   David Hadden

He's given me a garment of praise
instead of a spirit of despair.
He's given me a garment of praise
instead of a spirit of despair.
(Repeat)

A crown of beauty,
instead of ashes.
The oil of gladness,
instead of mourning.
My soul rejoices
as I delight myself in God.
He's given me a garment of praise
instead of a spirit of despair

© 1994 Restoration Music/Sovereign Music UK

167   Graham Kendrick

He that is in us is greater
than he that is in the world.
He that is in us is greater
than he that is in the world.

Therefore I will sing and I will rejoice
for his Spirit lives in me.
Christ the living one has overcome
and we share in his victory.

All the powers of death and hell and sin
lie crushed beneath his feet.
Jesus owns the name above all names,
crowned with honour and majesty.

168 Graham Kendrick

He walked where I walk
(he walked where I walk).
He stood where I stand
(he stood where I stand).
He felt what I feel
(he felt what I feel).
He understands
(he understands).
He knows my frailty
(he knows my frailty),
shared my humanity
(shared my humanity),
tempted in every way
(tempted in every way),
yet without sin
(yet without sin).

> *God with us, so close to us,*
> *God with us, Immanuel.*

One of a hated race
(one of a hated race),
stung by the prejudice
(stung by the prejudice),
suffering injustice
(suffering injustice),
yet he forgives
(yet he forgives).
Wept for my wasted years
(wept for my wasted years),
paid for my wickedness
(paid for my wickedness),

he died in my place
(he died in my place),
that I might live
(that I might live).

169 Maggi Dawn

He was pierced for our transgressions,
and bruised for our iniquities;
and to bring us peace he was punished,
and by his stripes we are healed.

He was led like a lamb to the slaughter,
although he was innocent of crime;
and cut off from the land of the living,
he paid for the guilt that was mine.

> *We like sheep have gone astray,*
> *turned each one to his own way,*
> *and the Lord has laid on him*
> *the iniquity of us all.*

170 Unknown

Higher, higher, higher, higher, higher,
higher, higher, lift up Jesus higher.
Higher, higher, higher, higher, higher,
higher, higher, lift up Jesus higher.

Lower, lower, lower, lower, lower,
lower, lower, lower Satan lower.
Lower, lower, lower, lower, lower,
lower, lower, lower Satan lower.

Cast your burdens on to Jesus,
he cares for you.
Cast your burdens on to Jesus,
he cares for you.

171 David Ruis

His love is higher
than the highest of mountains.
His love goes deeper
than the deepest of seas.
His love, it stretches
to the farthest horizon,
and his love, it reaches to me.

His love is stronger
than the angels and demons.
His love, it keeps me
in my life's darkest hour.
His love secures me
on the pathway to heaven,
and his love is my strength and power.

His love is sweeter
than the sweetest of honey.
His love is better
than the choicest of wine.
His love, it satisfies
the deepest of hunger,
and his love, in Jesus it's mine.

Your love . . .

© 1992 Mercy/Vineyard Publishing/Music Services/CopyCare

172 Noel and Tricia Richards

Hold me closer to you each day;
may my love for you never fade.
Keep my focus on all that's true;
may I never lose sight of you.

In my failure, in my success,
if in sadness or happiness,
be the hope I am clinging to,
for my heart belongs to you.

You are only a breath away,
watching over me every day;
in my heart I am filled with peace
when I hear you speak to me.

No one loves me in the way you do,
no one cares for me like you do.
Feels like heaven has broken through;
God, you know how I love you.

© 1996 Kingsway's Thankyou Music

173 Danny Daniels

Hold me, Lord (hold me, Lord),
in your arms (in your arms).
Fill me, Lord (fill me, Lord),
with your Spirit.
Touch my heart (touch my heart),
with your love (with your love).
Let my life (let my life)
glorify your name.

Singing alleluia, singing alleluia,
singing alleluia, singing alleluia.
Alleluia (alleluia),
allelu (allelu),
alleluia (alleluia),
allelu (allelu).

© 1982 Mercy/Vineyard Publishing/Music Services/CopyCare

174 Brian Doerksen

Holiness is your life in me,
making me clean through your blood.
Holiness is your fire in me,
purging my heart like a flood.
I know you are perfect in holiness.
Your life in me, setting me free,
making me holy.

Only the blood of Jesus covers all of my sin.
Only the life of Jesus renews me from within.
Your blood is enough, your mercy complete,
your work of atonement paid for my debts,
making me holy.
Only the blood of Jesus.

© 1990 Mercy/Vineyard Publishing/Music Services/CopyCare

175 Danny Daniels

Holiness unto the Lord,
unto the King.
Holiness unto your name
I will sing.

Holiness unto Jesus,
holiness unto you, Lord.
Holiness unto Jesus,
holiness unto you, Lord.

I love you, I love your ways,
I love your name.
I love you, and all my days
I'll proclaim:

© 1989 Mercy/Vineyard Publishing/Music Services/CopyCare

176 Reginald Heber

Holy, holy, holy!
Lord God Almighty!
Early in the morning
our song shall rise to thee;
holy, holy, holy!
merciful and mighty!
God in three persons,
blessed Trinity!

Holy, holy, holy!
all the saints adore thee,
casting down their golden crowns
around the glassy sea;
cherubim and seraphim
falling down before thee,
which wert, and art,
and evermore shall be.

Holy, holy, holy!
though the darkness hide thee,
though the eye made blind by sin
thy glory may not see,
only thou art holy,
there is none beside thee,
perfect in pow'r,
in love, and purity.

Holy, holy, holy!
Lord God Almighty!
All thy works shall praise thy name,
in earth, and sky, and sea;
holy, holy, holy!
merciful and mighty!
God in three persons,
blessèd Trinity!

177 Richard Lewis

Holy, holy, Lord God Almighty,
who was and who is and is to come.
Holy, holy, Lord God Almighty,
who was and who is and is to come.
All the angels cry, 'Holy',
all the angels cry, 'Holy',
all the angels cry, 'Holy is your name.'
Holy is your name. Holy is your name.
Holy is your name. Holy is your name.

© 1997 Kingsway's Thankyou Music

178 Ron Kenoly and Louis Smith

Holy, holy, Lord, you're worthy
and I'm honoured to sing your praise.
King of glory, God Almighty,
hallowed be your name.

All creation, every nation,
has its being by your word;
as your will is done up in heaven,
let it be done here on earth,
let it be done on earth.

Hallowed be your name,
hallowed be your name,
hallowed be your name,
Lord and Majesty,
divine Authority.
hallowed be your name.

Holy, holy, Lord, you're worthy
and I'm honoured to sing your praise.
King of glory, God Almighty,
hallowed be your name,
hallowed be your name.

© 1992 Integrity's Hosanna! Music/Kingsway's Thankyou Music

179 Geoff Bullock

Holy One of God,
the Son of Righteousness,
risen Lamb of God,
Prince of Peace.
Rejected and despised,
suffered, crucified.
This risen Lamb of God,
Jesus Christ,
suffered hell and death
in the pow'r of righteousness;
death is swallowed up in victory.
He's risen from the grave,
salvation has been made.
Worthy is the Lamb that was slain.

180 Geoff Bullock

Holy Spirit, come,
Holy Spirit, come.
Heal our hearts, our lives,
cleanse our thoughts, our minds.
Holy Spirit, come,
O come to us.

Holy Spirit, fall,
Holy Spirit, fall.
drench us with your love,
fill our lives with peace.
Holy Spirit, fall,
O fall on us.

Holy Spirit, flow,
Holy Spirit, flow.
Lead us in your will,
empowered to proclaim.
Holy Spirit, flow,
O flow through us.

181 Chris Bowater

Holy Spirit, we welcome you.
Holy Spirit, we welcome you.
Move among us with holy fire,
as we lay aside all earthly desires,
hands reach out and our hearts aspire.
Holy Spirit, Holy Spirit,
Holy Spirit, we welcome you.

Holy Spirit, we welcome you.
Holy Spirit, we welcome you.
Let the breeze of your presence blow,
that your children here might truly know
how to move in the Spirit's flow.
Holy Spirit, Holy Spirit,
Holy Spirit, we welcome you.

Holy Spirit, we welcome you.
Holy Spirit, we welcome you.
Please accomplish in me today
some new work of loving grace, I pray;
unreservedly have your way.
Holy Spirit, Holy Spirit,
Holy Spirit, we welcome you.-

182 Carl Tuttle

Hosanna, hosanna, hosanna in the highest!
Hosanna, hosanna, hosanna in the highest!
Lord, we lift up your name,
with hearts full of praise;
be exalted, O Lord, my God!
Hosanna in the highest!

Glory, glory, glory to the King of kings!
Glory, glory, glory to the King of kings!
Lord, we lift up your name,
with hearts full of praise;
be exalted, O Lord, my God!
Glory to the King of kings!

183 Graham Kendrick and Steve Thompson

How can I be free from sin?
lead me to the cross of Jesus,
from the guilt, the pow'r, the pain,
lead me to the cross of Jesus.

There's no other way,
no price that I could pay,
simply to the cross I cling.
This is all I need,
this is all I plead,
that his blood was shed for me.

How can I know peace within?
lead me to the cross of Jesus,
sing a song of joy again,
lead me to the cross of Jesus.

Flowing from above,
all-forgiving love,
from the Father's heart to me.
What a gift of grace,
his own righteousness,
clothing me in purity.

How can I live day by day?
lead me to the cross of Jesus,
following his narrow way,
lead me to the cross of Jesus.

© 1991 Make Way Music

184 Wes Sutton

How can I not love you
when I see all that you've given me?
How can I not love you,
Jesus, my Lord?

I love you, first and last,
in your love I've come to rest.
I will dwell before your throne.
you are my eternal home.

How can I not serve you,
when I see all that you've done for me?
How can I not serve you,
Jesus, my Lord.

I draw near by your grace,
I desire to seek your face.
In your presence there is light,
you are my eternal life.

© 1997 Sovereign Lifestyle Music

185 Stuart Townend

How deep the Father's love for us,
how vast beyond all measure,
that he should give his only Son
to make a wretch his treasure.
How great the pain of searing loss,
the Father turns his face away,
as wounds which mar the Chosen One
bring many sons to glory.

Behold the man upon a cross,
my sin upon his shoulders;
ashamed, I hear my mocking voice
call out among the scoffers.
It was my sin that held him there
until it was accomplished;
his dying breath has brought me life –
I know that it is finished.

I will not boast in anything,
no gifts, no pow'r, no wisdom;
but I will boast in Jesus Christ,
his death and resurrection.
Why should I gain from his reward?
I cannot give an answer,
but this I know with all my heart,
his wounds have paid my ransom.

© 1995 Kingsway's Thankyou Music

186 Richard Keen

How firm a foundation,
you saints of the Lord,
is laid for your faith
in his excellent word;
what more can he say
than to you he has said,
you who unto Jesus
for refuge have fled?

Continued overleaf

Fear not, I am with you,
O be not dismayed;
for I am your God,
and will still give you aid;
I'll strengthen you, help you,
and cause you to stand,
upheld by my righteous,
omnipotent hand.

In every condition,
in sickness, in health,
in poverty's vale,
or abounding in wealth;
at home and abroad,
on the land, on the sea,
as your days may demand
shall your strength ever be.

When through the deep waters
I call you to go,
the rivers of grief
shall not you overflow;
for I will be with you
in trouble to bless,
and sanctify to you
your deepest distress.

When through fiery trials
your pathway shall lie,
my grace all-sufficient
shall be your supply;
the flame shall not hurt you,
my only design
your dross to consume
and your gold to refine.

The soul that on Jesus
has leaned for repose
I will not, I cannot,
desert to its foes;
that soul, though all hell
should endeavour to shake,
I never will leave,
I will never forsake.

187 Graham Kendrick

How good and how pleasant it is
when we all live in unity,
refreshing as dew at the dawn,
like rare anointing oil upon the head.

It's so good, so good
when we live together
in peace and harmony;
it's so good, so good
when we live together
in his love.

How deep are the rivers that run
when we are one in Jesus
and share with the Father and Son
the blessings of his everlasting life.

188 Matt Redman

How lovely is your dwelling place,
O Lord Almighty.
My soul longs and even faints for you.
For here my heart is satisfied,
within your presence.
I sing beneath the shadow of your wings.

Better is one day in your courts,
better is one day in your house,
better is one day in your courts
than thousands elsewhere.
(Repeat)

One thing I ask and I would seek;
to see your beauty:
to find you in the place your glory dwells.

My heart and flesh cry out
for you, the living God.
Your Spirit's water for my soul.
I've tasted and I've seen,
come once again to me;
I will draw near to you,
I will draw near to you.

189 Leonard E. Smith Jnr

How lovely on the mountains
are the feet of him
who brings good news, good news,
proclaiming peace,
announcing news of happiness:
our God reigns, our God reigns,
our God reigns, our God reigns,
our God reigns, our God reigns!

You watchmen, lift your voices
joyfully as one,
shout for your King, your King.
See eye to eye
the Lord restoring Zion:
your God reigns, your God reigns!

Waste places of Jerusalem,
break forth with joy,
we are redeemed, redeemed.
The Lord has saved
and comforted his people:
your God reigns, your God reigns!

Ends of the earth,
see the salvation of your God,
Jesus is Lord, is Lord.
Before the nations
he has bared his holy arm:
your God reigns, your God reigns!

190 John Newton

How sweet the name of Jesus sounds
in a believer's ear!
It soothes our sorrows, heals our wounds,
and drives away our fear.

It makes the wounded spirit whole,
and calms the troubled breast;
'tis manna to the hungry soul,
and to the weary rest.

Dear name! the rock on which I build,
my shield and hiding-place,
my never-failing treasury filled
with boundless stores of grace.

Jesus! my Shepherd, Saviour, Friend,
my Prophet, Priest and King,
my Lord, my life, my way, my end,
accept the praise I bring.

Weak is the effort of my heart,
and cold my warmest thought;
but when I see thee as thou art,
I'll praise thee as I ought.

Till then I would thy love proclaim
with every fleeting breath;
and may the music of thy name
refresh my soul in death.

191 Dave Bilbrough

I am a new creation,
no more in condemnation,
here in the grace of God I stand.
My heart is overflowing,
my love just keeps on growing,
here in the grace of God I stand.

And I will praise you, Lord,
yes, I will praise you, Lord,
and I will sing of all that you have done.

A joy that knows no limit,
a lightness in my spirit,
here in the grace of God I stand.

192 Loren Bieg

I am so thankful
for the fullness of your love.
I am so thankful
for the shedding of your blood.
I am so thankful
you died in my place
Oh, Lord, I'm thankful for your love.

Continued overleaf

I am so thankful
that you came into my life.
I am so thankful
that you love me like a child.
I am so thankful
I'll be with you for all time.
Oh, Lord, I'm thankful for your love.

193 Andy Park

I am standing beneath your wings,
I am resting in your shelter,
your great faithfulness has been my shield
and it makes me want to sing.

Blessed be the name of the Lord,
blessed be the name of the Lord.
I will bless your holy name
for all my days;
blessed be the name of the Lord.

I sing praises to your name, O Lord,
for you daily bear my burdens.
Your great faithfulness is my reward
and it makes me want to sing.

194 Don Moen

I am the God that healeth thee,
I am the Lord, your healer;
I sent my word and healed your disease,
I am the Lord, your healer.

You are the God that healeth me,
you are the Lord, my healer;
you sent your word and healed my disease,
you are the Lord, my healer.

195 Marc Nelson

I believe in Jesus;
I believe he is the Son of God.
I believe he died and rose again,
I believe he paid for us all.

And I believe he's here now
(I believe that he's here),
standing in our midst;
here with the power to heal now
(with the power to heal),
and the grace to forgive.

I believe in you, Lord;
I believe you are the Son of God.
I believe you died and rose again,
I believe you paid for us all.

And I believe you're here now
(I believe that you're here),
standing in our midst;
here with the power to heal now
(with the power to heal),
and the grace to forgive.

196 Russell Fragar

I believe the promise
about the visions and the dreams
that the Holy Spirit will be poured out
and his power will be seen.
Well, the time is now
and the place is here
and his people have come in faith;
there's a mighty sound and a touch of fire
when we're gathered in once place.

I believe that the presence of God is here;
there's not one thing that can't be changed
when the Spirit of God is near.
I believe that the presence of God is here;
when two or three are gathered,
when people rise in faith,
I believe God answers
and his presence is in this place.

Nothing in earth or heaven
can stop the power of God;
into our hands is given
the call to take it on;

no ocean can contain it,
no star can rise above;
into our hearts is given
the power of his love.

197 Bonnie Deuschle

I bow my knee before your throne,
I know my life is not my own;
I offer up a song of praise
to bring you pleasure, Lord.

I seek the giver, not the gift,
my heart's desire is to lift you
high above all earthly kings;
to bring you pleasure, Lord.

> *Hallelujah, hallelujah,*
> *hallelujah, glory to the King.*
> *Hallelujah, hallelujah,*
> *hallelujah, glory to the King.*

198 Debbie and Rob Eastwood

I bow my knee,
I give myself
as a living sacrifice for you.
I lay me down
before your throne.
Take my past; I will stand for you.
Let your blood wash over me,
let your blood wash over me;
you have cleansed my heart
and set my spirit free.

> *You are my Lord,*
> *I'll love you more,*
> *I'll follow you,*
> *no matter when,*
> *no matter where.*

199 William Young Fullerton

I cannot tell
how he whom angels worship
should stoop to love
the peoples of the earth,
or why as shepherd
he should seek the wanderer
with his mysterious promise
of new birth.
But this I know,
that he was born of Mary,
when Bethlehem's manger
was his only home,
and that he lived at
Nazareth and laboured,
and so the Saviour,
Saviour of the world, is come.

I cannot tell
how silently he suffered,
as with his peace
he graced this place of tears,
or how his heart
upon the cross was broken,
the crown of pain
to three and thirty years.
But this I know,
he heals the broken-hearted,
and stays our sin,
and calms our lurking fear,
and lifts the burden
from the heavy laden,
for yet the Saviour,
Saviour of the world, is here.

I cannot tell
how he will win the nations,
how he will claim
his earthly heritage,
how satisfy
the needs and aspirations
of east and west,
of sinner and of sage.
But this I know,
all flesh shall see his glory,

Continued overleaf

and he shall reap
the harvest he has sown,
and some glad day
his sun shall shine in splendour
when he the Saviour,
Saviour of the world, is known.

I cannot tell
how all the lands shall worship,
when, at his bidding,
every storm is stilled,
or who can say
how great the jubilation
when every heart
with perfect love is filled.
But this I know,
the skies will thrill with rapture,
and myriad, myriad
human voices sing,
and earth to heav'n,
and heav'n to earth, will answer:
'At last the Saviour,
Saviour of the world, is King!'

200 Martin Smith

O, I could sing unending songs
of how you saved my soul.
Well, I could dance a thousand miles
because of your great love.

My heart is bursting, Lord,
to tell of all you've done.
Of how you changed my life
and wiped away the past.
I wanna shout it out,
from every roof-top sing.
For now I know that God
is for me, not against me.

Everybody's singing now,
'cos we're so happy!
Everybody's dancing now,
'cos we're so happy!

If only we could see your face
and see you smiling over us
and unseen angels celebrate,
for joy is in this place.

201 Craig Musseau

I cry out for your hand of mercy to heal me.
I am weak, I need your love to free me.
Oh, Lord, my rock, my strength in weakness,
come rescue me, oh, Lord.

You are my hope, your promise never fails me.
And my desire is to follow you for ever.

For you are good, for you are good,
for you are good to me.
For you are good, for you are good,
for you are good to me.

202 Graham Kendrick

If you are encouraged
in our union with Christ,
finding consolation in his love,
compassion, warmth and friendship
in the Spirit's flow of life;
this is how you make my joy complete:

By being of the same mind,
and loving with the same love,
united in the Spirit,
with the same goal in sight.
By being of the same mind,
and loving with the same love,
united in the Spirit
to the glory of Christ.

Be sure you do nothing
out of selfishness or pride,
never seeing past your own concerns;
but humbly keep the interests
of each other in your hearts,
seeing them as better than yourselves:

203   Carl Tuttle

I give you all the honour
and praise that's due your name,
for you are the King of Glory,
the Creator of all things.

And I worship you,
I give my life to you,
I fall down on my knees.
Yes, I worship you,
I give my life to you,
I fall down on my knees.

As your Spirit moves upon me now,
you meet my deepest need,
and I lift my hands up to your throne,
your mercy I've received.

You have broken chains that bound me,
you've set this captive free,
I will lift my voice to praise your name
for all eternity.

© 1982 Mercy/Vineyard Publishing/Music Services/CopyCare

204   Matt Redman

I have come to love you,
I have come to love you today.
(Repeat)

And today and for evermore
I'll love your name.
Lord, today and for evermore
I'll love your name.

I have come to worship,
I have come to worship today.
(Repeat)

I have come to thank you,
I have come to thank you today.
(Repeat)

© 1995 Kingsway's Thankyou Music

205   Lynn DeShazo

I have made you too small in my eyes,
O Lord, forgive me;
and I have believed in a lie
that you were unable to help me,
but now, O Lord, I see my wrong:
heal my heart and show yourself strong,
and in my eyes and with my song,
O Lord, be magnified,
O Lord, be magnified.

Be magnified, O Lord,
you are highly exalted;
and there is nothing you can't do,
O Lord, my eyes are on you.
Be magnified,
O Lord, be magnified.

I have leaned on the wisdom of men,
O Lord, forgive me;
and I have responded to them
instead of your light and your mercy.
But now, O Lord, I see my wrong:
heal my heart and show yourself strong,
and in my eyes and with my song,
O Lord, be magnified,
O Lord, be magnified.

© 1992 Integrity's Hosanna! Music/Kingsway's Thankyou Music

206   Horatius Bonar

I heard the voice of Jesus say,
'Come unto me and rest;
lay down, thou weary one,
lay down thy head upon my breast.'
I came to Jesus as I was,
so weary, worn and sad;
I found in him a resting-place,
and he has made me glad.

I heard the voice of Jesus say,
'Behold, I freely give
the living water, thirsty one;
stoop down and drink and live.'
I came to Jesus, and I drank
of that life-giving stream;
my thirst was quenched, my soul revived,
and now I live in him.

Continued overleaf

I heard the voice of Jesus say,
'I am this dark world's light;
look unto me, thy morn shall rise,
and all thy day be bright.'
I looked to Jesus, and I found
in him my star, my sun;
and in that light of life I'll walk
till travelling days are done.

207 Don Moen

I just want to be where you are,
dwelling daily in your presence;
I don't want to worship from afar:
draw me near to where you are.
I just want to be where you are,
in your dwelling-place for ever;
take me to the place where you are:
I just want to be with you.

I want to be where you are,
dwelling in your presence,
feasting at your table,
surrounded by your glory,
in your presence,
that's where I always want to be:
I just want to be,
I just want to be with you.

I just want to be where you are,
to enter boldly in your presence;
I don't want to worship from afar,
draw me near to where you are.

O my God, you are my strength and my song
and when I'm in your presence,
though I'm weak, you're always strong.
I just want to be where you are,
in your dwelling-place for ever.
Take me to the place where you are:
I just want to be,
I just want to be with you;
I just want to be,
I just want to be with you.

© 1989 Integrity's Hosanna! Music/Kingsway's Thankyou Music

208 Arthur Tannous

I just want to praise you,
lift my hands and say, 'I love you.'
You are everything to me
and I exalt your holy name on high.
I just want to praise you,
lift my hands and say, 'I love you.'
You are everything to me
and I exalt your holy name,
I exalt your holy name,
I exalt your holy name on high.

© 1984 Acts Music/Kingsway's Thankyou Music

209 Randy and Terry Butler

I know a place, a wonderful place,
where accused and condemned
find mercy and grace,
where the wrongs we have done
and the wrongs done to us
were nailed there with him,
there on the cross.

At the cross (at the cross),
he died for our sin.
At the cross (at the cross),
he gave us life again.

© 1993 Mercy/Vineyard Publishing/Music Services/CopyCare

210 Darlene Zschech

I know it, I know it,
his blood has set me free,
I've been delivered, forgiven,
fear has got no hold on me.
I'm set apart,
not living life my own way,
no holding back
till I see him face to face
because I know it,
oh yes, I know it,
I know it,
the blood of Jesus has set me free!

There is healing in the name of Jesus,
salvation in the name of Jesus,
forgiveness in the name of Jesus.
I've never known it like I know it today;
there is power in the name of Jesus,
fullness of joy I've found in Jesus,
strength in the name of Jesus.
I know it, I know it,
oh, I've got to tell you that
I know it . . .

211 Brian Doerksen

I lift my eyes up to the mountains,
where does my help come from?
My help comes from you,
maker of heaven, creator of the earth.

O how I need you, Lord,
you are my only hope;
you're my only prayer.
So I will wait for you
to come and rescue me,
come and give me life.

212 Andre Kempen

I lift my hands to the coming King,
to the great 'I Am',
to you I sing,
for you're the One
who reigns within my heart.

And I will serve no foreign god,
or any other treasure;
you are my heart's desire,
Spirit without measure.
Unto your name
I would bring my sacrifice.

213 Paul Baloche and Ed Kerr

I love to be in your presence
with your people singing praises;
I love to stand and rejoice,
lift my hands and raise my voice.
(Repeat)

You set my feet to dancing,
you fill my heart with song,
you give me reason to rejoice, rejoice.

(Last time)
Lift my hands, lift my hands,
lift my hands and raise my voice.

214 Laurie Klein

I love you, Lord,
and I lift my voice to worship you,
O my soul rejoice.
Take joy, my King, in what you hear.
May it be a sweet, sweet sound in your ear.

215 Mike Day and Dave Bell

I love you, Lord, with all of my heart.
I love you, Lord, with all of my soul.
Let all that is within me
cry, 'Holy is your name.'
Let all that is within me
cry, 'Holy is your name.'

I love you, Lord, with all of my mind.
I love you, Lord, with all of my strength.
Let all that is within me
cry, 'Holy is your name.'
Let all that is within me
cry, 'Holy is your name.'

And we cry, 'Holy, holy is your name.'
We sing, 'Glory to the Lamb that was slain.'
We cry, 'Holy, holy is your name,
holy is your name,
holy is your name.'

216

Fabienne Pons trans. Judith Robertson

I love your presence, Jesus;
I love your presence, beloved Lord.
I love your presence, Jesus;
I love your presence, beloved Lord.

I know your love is here, powerful and real;
yes, your love is here, with the grace to heal.
I know your love is here, flowing from Calvary;
yes, your love is here, stirring faith in me.

Your Holy Spirit's here, mighty Counsellor;
yes, your Spirit's here, with releasing pow'r.
Your Holy Spirit's here, poured out from above;
yes, your Spirit's here, showing Father's love.

217

Rob Hayward

I'm accepted, I'm forgiven,
I am fathered by the true and living God.
I'm accepted, no condemnation,
I am loved by the true and living God.
There's no guilt or fear as I draw near
to the Saviour and Creator of the world.
There is joy and peace as I release
my worship to you, O Lord.

218

Capt. Alan J. Price

I'm gonna click, click, click,
I'm gonna clap, clap, clap,
I'm gonna click, I'm gonna clap
and praise the Lord!
Because of all he's done
I'm gonna make him 'number one',
I'm gonna click, I'm gonna clap
and praise the Lord!

I'm gonna zoom, zoom, zoom,
around the room, room, room,
I'm gonna zoom around the room
and praise the Lord!

Because of all he's done,
I'm gonna make him 'number one',
I'm gonna zoom around the room
and praise the Lord!

I'm gonna sing, sing, sing,
I'm gonna shout, shout, shout,
I'm gonna sing, I'm gonna shout
and praise the Lord!
Because of all he's done,
I'm gonna make him 'number one',
I'm gonna sing, I'm gonna shout
and praise the Lord!

I'm gonna click, click, click,
I'm gonna clap, clap, clap,
I'm gonna zoom around the room
and praise the Lord!
Because of all he's done,
I'm gonna make him 'number one',
I'm gonna sing, I'm gonna shout
and praise the Lord!

219

Graham Kendrick

Immanuel, O Immanuel,
bowed in awe I worship at your feet,
and sing Immanuel,
God is with us,
sharing my humanness, my shame,
feeling my weaknesses, my pain,
taking the punishment, the blame,
Immanuel.
And now my words cannot explain,
all that my heart cannot contain,
how great are the glories of your name,
Immanuel.

Immanuel, O Immanuel,
bowed in awe I worship at your feet,
and sing Immanuel . . .

220 Walter Chalmers Smith

Immortal, invisible,
God only wise,
in light inaccessible
hid from our eyes,
most blessed, most glorious,
the Ancient of Days,
almighty, victorious,
thy great name we praise.

Unresting, unhasting,
and silent as light,
nor wanting, nor wasting,
thou rulest in might;
thy justice like mountains
high soaring above
thy clouds which are fountains
of goodness and love.

To all life thou givest,
to both great and small;
in all life thou livest,
the true life of all;
we blossom and flourish
as leaves on the tree,
and wither and perish;
but naught changeth thee.

Great Father of glory,
pure Father of light,
thine angels adore thee,
all veiling their sight;
all laud we would render,
O help us to see,
'tis only the splendour
of light hideth thee.

Immortal, invisible,
God only wise,
in light inaccessible
hid from our eyes,
most blessed, most glorious,
the Ancient of Days,
almighty, victorious,
thy great name we praise.

221 Reuben Morgan

I'm so secure,
you're here with me;
you stay the same,
your love remains
here in my heart.

So close I believe
you're holding me now,
in your hands I belong.
You'll never let me go.
So close I believe
you're holding me now,
in your hands I belong.
You'll never let me go.

You gave your life
in your endless love;
you set me free
and showed the way:
now I am found.

All along, you were beside me,
even when I couldn't tell.
Through the years you showed me
more of you, more of you.

© 1996 Reuben Morgan/Hillsongs Australia/Kingsway's Thankyou Music

222 Graham Kendrick

I'm special because God has loved me,
for he gave the best thing that he had
    to save me;
his own Son, Jesus,
crucified to take the blame,
for all the bad things I have done.
Thank you, Jesus,
thank you, Lord,
for loving me so much.
I know I don't deserve anything;
help me feel your love right now
to know deep in my heart
that I'm your special friend.

© 1986 Kingsway's Thankyou Music

223 Kevin Prosch

I'm standing here to testify
(O, the Lord is good),
to sing of how he changed my heart
(O, the Lord is good).
I was bound by hate and pride
(O, the Lord is good),
never knowing of his light
(O, the Lord is good).
I did not think I could have peace,
(O, the Lord is good)
trapped inside by fear and shame
(O, the Lord is good).
He wiped away all of my grief
(O, the Lord is good)
when I believed upon his name.

Come to the light,
come as you are;
you can be a friend of God.
Humble yourself,
give him your heart,
he will meet you where you are.
Come to the light,
just as you are;
fall on the Rock for the wasted years.
He will restore
all that was lost,
surrender now, his power is here.

Clap your hands, O God.
Clap your hands, O God.
Clap your hands, O God.
Clap your hands, O God.

224 Richard Hubbard

I'm your child and you are my God.
I thank you, Father, for your loving care.
I'm your child and you are my God.
You've made me special and you're always there.

I'm your child and you are my God.
I love you, Jesus, you're close to me.
I'm your child and you are my God.
I give you worship, I bow the knee.

I'm your child and you are my God.
Holy Spirit, flow out to me.
I'm your child and you are my God.
You give me power and authority.

225 Shawn Craig and Don Koch

In Christ alone I place my trust,
and find my glory in the power of the cross;
in every victory let it be said of me
my source of strength, my source of hope
is Christ alone.

226 Lindell Cooley and Bruce Haynes

I need you more,
more than yesterday,
I need you more,
more than words can say.
I need you more
than ever before,
I need you, Lord,
I need you, Lord.

More than the air I breathe,
more than the song I sing,
more than the next heartbeat,
more than anything.
And, Lord, as time goes by,
I'll be by your side
'cause I never want to go
back to my old life.

Right here in your presence
is where I belong;
this old broken heart
has finally found a home
and I'll never be alone.

227 David Fellingham

In every circumstance of life
you are with me, glorious Father.
And I have put my trust in you,
that I may know the glorious hope
to which I'm called.

And by the pow'r that works in me,
you've raised me up and set me free;
and now in every circumstance
I'll prove your love without a doubt;
your joy shall be my strength,
your joy shall be my strength.

© 1994 Kingsway's Thankyou Music

228 Jamie Owens-Collins

In heav'nly armour we'll enter the land,
the battle belongs to the Lord.
No weapon that's fashioned against us will
    stand,
the battle belongs to the Lord.

And we sing glory, honour,
power and strength to the Lord.
We sing glory, honour,
power and strength to the Lord.

When the power of darkness comes like a
    flood,
the battle belongs to the Lord.
He'll raise up a standard, the power of his
    blood,
the battle belongs to the Lord.

When your enemy presses in hard,
    do not fear,
the battle belongs to the Lord.
Take courage, my friend, your redemption
    is near,
the battle belongs to the Lord.

© 1984 Fairhill Music/CopyCare

229 David Graham

In moments like these
I sing out a song,
I sing out a love song to Jesus.
In moments like these
I lift up my hands,
I lift up my hands to the Lord.

Singing, 'I love you, Lord',
singing, 'I love you, Lord';
singing, 'I love you, Lord,
I love you.'

© 1980 CA Music/Word Music/CopyCare

230 Bob Kilpatrick

In my life, Lord,
be glorified, be glorified.
In my life, Lord,
be glorified today.

In your church, Lord,
be glorified, be glorified.
In your church, Lord,
be glorified, today.

© 1978 Bob Kilpatrick Music

231 Andy Park

In the morning when I rise
expectantly I lift my eyes
and I see you (and I see you).
Gazing on your heav'nly throne,
in your presence I'm at home,
here with you (here with you).
And all I want
is more and more of you.

Earthly cares and passions pale
when you take away the veil
and I see you (and I see you).
When you open heaven's door
all I want is to have more,
more of you (more of you).
And all I want
is more and more of you.

Continued overleaf

The earth and all its glory will fade,
but the word of our God will stand.
The earth and all its glory will fade,
but the kingdom of God I will seek.

Nothing in the world compares
to the love that I can share
alone with you (alone with you).
There is nothing else so real
as the things that you reveal
when I'm with you (when I'm with you).
And all I want
is more and more of you.

232 Mark Altrogge

In the presence of a holy God
there's new meaning now to grace;
you took all my sins upon yourself,
I can only stand amazed.

And I cry holy, holy, holy God,
how awesome is your name.
Holy, holy, holy God,
how majestic is your name,
and I am changed
in the presence of a holy God.

In the presence of your infinite might,
I'm so small and frail and weak;
when I see your pow'r and wisdom, Lord,
I have no words left to speak.

In the presence of your glory
all my crowns lie in the dust.
You are righteous in your judgements, Lord,
you are faithful, true and just.

233 Andy Park

In the secret, in the quiet place,
in the stillness you are there.
In the secret, in the quiet hour I wait
only for you
'cause I want to know you more.

I want to know you,
I want to hear your voice,
I want to know you more.
I want to see you,
I want to see your face,
I want to know you more.

I am reaching for the highest goal,
that I might receive the prize.
Pressing onward, pushing every hindrance aside,
out of my way,
'cause I want to know you more.

234 Graham Kendrick

In the tomb so cold they laid him,
death its victim claimed.
Pow'rs of hell, they could not hold him;
back to life he came!

Christ is risen!
(Christ is risen!)
Death has been conquered.
(Death has been conquered.)
Christ is risen!
(Christ is risen!)
He shall reign for ever.

Hell had spent its fury on him,
left him crucified.
Yet, by blood, he boldly conquered,
sin and death defied.

Now the fear of death is broken,
love has won the crown.
Prisoners of the darkness listen,
walls are tumbling down.

Raised from death to heav'n ascending,
love's exalted King.
Let his song of joy, unending,
through the nations ring!

235 Judy Bailey

I reach up high, I touch the ground,
I stomp my feet and turn around.
I've got to (woo woo) praise the Lord.
I jump and dance with all my might,
I might look funny, but that's all right,
I've got to (woo woo) praise the Lord.

I'll do anything just for my God
'cos he's done everything for me.
It doesn't matter who is looking on,
Jesus is the person that I want to please.

May my whole life be a song of praise
to worship God in every way.
In this song the actions praise his name,
I want my actions every day to do the same.

236 Paul Armstrong

I receive your love,
I receive your love,
in my heart I receive your love, O Lord.
I receive your love
by your Spirit within me,
I receive, I receive your love.

I confess your love,
I confess your love,
from my heart I confess your love, O Lord.
I confess your love
by your Spirit within me,
I confess, I confess your love.

237 Graham Kendrick

Is anyone thirsty? – (yes!) – anyone?
Is anyone thirsty? (Yes!)
Is anyone thirsty? – (yes!) – anyone?
Is anyone thirsty? (Yes!)
Jesus said, 'Let them come to me and drink,
let them come to me.'

O let the living waters flow,
O let the living waters flow,
let the river of your Spirit flow through me;
O let the living waters flow,
O let the living waters flow,
let the river of your Spirit flow through me.

(Last time)
Flow through me.
Flow through me.

Let the living waters flow,
let the living waters flow.
Let the living waters flow,
let the living waters flow.

238 Chris Falson

I see the Lord
seated on the throne, exalted;
and the train of his robe
fills the temple with glory:
the whole earth is filled,
the whole earth is filled,
the whole earth is filled
with your glory.

Holy, holy, holy, holy,
yes, holy is the Lord;
holy, holy, holy, holy,
yes, holy is the Lord of lords.

239 Craig Musseau

I sing a simple song of love
to my Saviour, to my Jesus.
I'm grateful for the things you've done,
my loving Saviour, O precious Jesus.
My heart is glad
that you've called me your own;
there's no place I'd rather be than

in your arms of love,
in your arms of love,
holding me still,
holding me near,
in your arms of love.

(Last time)
Holding me still,
holding me near,
holding me still,
holding me near
in your arms of love.

240 Terry MacAlmon

I sing praises to your name, O Lord,
praises to your name, O Lord,
for your name is great
and greatly to be praised.
(Repeat)

I give glory to your name, O Lord,
glory to your name, O Lord,
for your name is great
and greatly to be praised.
(Repeat)

241 Martin Smith

Is it true today
that when people pray
cloudless skies will break,
kings and queens will shake?
Yes, it's true and I believe it,
I'm living for you.

Well, it's true today
that when people pray
we'll see dead men rise
and the blind set free.
Yes, it's true and I believe it,
I'm living for you.

> *I'm going to be a history maker*
> *in this land.*
> *I'm going to be a speaker of truth*
> *to all mankind.*
> *I'm going to stand,*
> *I'm going to run into your arms,*
> *into your arms again,*
> *into your arms, into your arms again.*

Well, it's true today
that when people stand
with the fire of God
and the truth in hand,
we'll see miracles,
we'll see angels sing,
we'll see broken hearts
making history.
Yes it's true and I believe it,
I'm living for you.

242 John Wimber

Isn't he beautiful, beautiful, isn't he?
Prince of Peace, Son of God, isn't he?
Isn't he wonderful, wonderful, isn't he?
Counsellor, Almighty God, isn't he,
isn't he, isn't he?

Yes, you are beautiful, beautiful, yes, you are.
Prince of Peace, Son of God, yes, you are.
Yes, you are wonderful, wonderful, yes, you are.
Counsellor, Almighty God, yes, you are,
yes, you are, yes, you are.

243 Charles H. Gabriel

I stand amazed in the presence
of Jesus the Nazarene,
and wonder how he could love me,
a sinner, condemned, unclean.

O, how marvellous! O, how wonderful,
and my song shall ever be:
O, how marvellous! O, how wonderful!
is my Saviour's love for me.

For me it was in the garden
he prayed – 'Not my will, but thine';
he had no tears for his own griefs,
but sweat drops of blood for mine.

In pity angels beheld him,
and came from the world of light,
to comfort him in the sorrows
he bore for my soul that night.

He took my sins and my sorrows,
he made them his very own;
he bore the burden to Calvary,
and suffered, and died alone.

When with the ransomed in glory
his face I at last shall see,
'twill be my joy through the ages
to sing of his love for me.

© The Rodeheaver Company/Word Music/CopyCare

244 Mavis Ford

I stand before the presence
of the Lord God of hosts,
a child of my Father
and an heir of his grace,
for Jesus paid the debt for me,
the veil was torn in two,
and the Holy of Holies
has become my dwelling-place.

© 1980 Springtide/Word Music/CopyCare

245 Matthew Ling

I stand before your throne,
the beauty of your holiness amazes me.
From you and you alone
comes the word of life
and pow'r that changes me.
You are bounteous in mercy,
abundant in your grace.
You make your face to shine upon me.

I will seek your face,
draw me closer to embrace your glory.
I will seek your face,
I run into your secret place
with all my heart and all my strength.
I will seek your face.

In adoration now,
my spirit soars upon the breeze of mercy.
The rapture of my heart
poured out in songs of love
for you are worthy;
worth the price of sacrifice,
surrendering my all,
changed from glory into glory.

© 1995 Restoration Music/Sovereign Music UK

246 Dan Schutte

I, the Lord of sea and sky,
I have heard my people cry.
All who dwell in dark and sin
my hand will save.
I who made the stars of night,
I will make their darkness bright.
Who will bear my light to them?
Whom shall I send?

Here I am, Lord.
Is it I, Lord?
I have heard you calling in the night.
I will go, Lord,
if you lead me.
I will hold your people in my heart.

Continued overleaf

I, the Lord of snow and rain,
I have borne my people's pain.
I have wept for love of them.
They turn away.
I will break their hearts of stone,
give them hearts for love alone.
I will speak my word to them.
Whom shall I send?

> *Here I am, Lord.*
> *Is it I, Lord?*
> *I have heard you calling in the night.*
> *I will go, Lord,*
> *if you lead me.*
> *I will hold your people in my heart.*

I, the Lord of wind and flame,
I will tend the poor and lame.
I will set a feast for them.
My hand will save.
Finest bread I will provide
till their hearts be satisfied.
I will give my life to them.
Whom shall I send?

© 1981 Daniel L. Schutte/New Dawn Music

247 Duke Kerr

It is to you I give the glory,
it is to you I give the praise,
because you have done so much for me,
I will magnify your name.
It is to you, Holy Father,
no one else but you,
and I will praise your name,
praise your name,
and I will praise your name
for evermore.

© Duke Kerr and Remission Music UK

248 David Ruis

It's our confession, Lord,
that we are weak,
so very weak,
but you are strong.

And though we've nothing, Lord,
to lay at your feet,
we come to your feet
and say, 'Help us along'.

A broken heart and a contrite spirit
you have yet to deny.
Your heart of mercy beats
with love's strong current;
let the river flow by your Spirit now,
Lord, we cry:

> *Let your mercies fall from heaven,*
> *sweet mercies flow from heaven,*
> *new mercies for today,*
> *O shower them down, Lord, as we pray.*
> (Repeat)

© 1995 Mercy/Vineyard Publishing/Music Services/CopyCare

249 Matt Redman and Martin Smith

It's rising up from coast to coast,
from north to south, and east to west;
the cry of hearts that love your name,
which with one voice we will proclaim.

The former things have taken place.
Can this be the new day of praise?
A heav'nly song that comes to birth,
and reaches out to all the earth.
O let the cry to nations ring,
that all may come and all may sing:

> *Holy is the Lord.*
> *Holy is the Lord.*
> *Holy is the Lord.*
> *Holy is the Lord.*

And we have heard the lion's roar,
that speaks of heaven's love and pow'r.
Is this the time, is this the call
that ushers in your kingdom rule?
O let the cry to nations ring,
that all may come and all may sing:

> *Jesus is alive!*
> *Jesus is alive!*
> *Jesus is alive!*
> *Jesus is alive!*

© 1995 Kingsway's Thankyou Music

250 Michael Christ

It's your blood that cleanses me,
it's your blood that gives me life,
it's your blood that took my place
in redeeming sacrifice,
and washes me whiter than the snow,
than the snow.
My Jesus, God's precious sacrifice.

251 Russell Fragar

I've found a friend, O such a friend,
he made my heart his home.
God himself is with me
and I know I'm never alone.
I know all my tomorrows
will be better than all my hopes;
we've got love! grace! peace and pow'r and
joy in the Holy Ghost.

My God is never wrong
and he makes time for me.
It blew apart my chains
and set this sinner free.
It's like a river
and you'll never run it dry.
We've got power over fear and death
and hearts filled up with joy.

The Holy Spirit fills me up
and I need him every day
for fire, faith and confidence
and knowing what to say.
I gave my heart and all I am
to the one who loves me most;
we've got love! grace! peace and pow'r and
joy in the Holy Ghost.

252 Matt Redman

I've got a love song in my heart.
(I've got a love song in my heart.)
It is for you, Lord, my God.
(It is for you, Lord, my God.)
(Repeat)

I've got a passion in my heart.
(I've got a passion in my heart.)
It is for you, Lord, my God.
(It is for you, Lord, my God.)
(Repeat)

La la la, la la, la la,
la la la, la la, la la,
la la la, la la, la la
(Repeat)

I've got rejoicing in my heart.
(I've got rejoicing in my heart.)
It is for you, Lord, my God.
(It is for you, Lord, my God.)
(Repeat)

And there is dancing in my heart.
(And there is dancing in my heart.)
It is for you, Lord, my God.
(It is for you, Lord, my God.)
(Repeat)

La la la, la la, la la . . .

I've never known a love like this.
(I've never known a love like this.)
I've never known a love like this.
(I've never known a love like this.)
(Repeat)

253 Chris Falson

I walk by faith, each step by faith,
to live by faith, I put my trust in you.
I walk by faith, each step by faith,
to live by faith, I put my trust in you.

Every step I take is a step of faith;
no weapon formed against me shall prosper.
And every prayer I make is a prayer of faith;
and if my God is for me,
then who can be against me?

254 Doug Horley

I want to be a tree that's bearing fruit,
that God has pruned and caused to shoot,
O, up in the sky, so very, very high.
I want to be, I want to be a blooming tree.

God has promised his Holy Spirit
will water our roots and help us grow.
Listen and obey, and before you know it
your fruit will start to grow, grow, grow, grow,
    grow.

You'll be a tree that's bearing fruit,
with a very, very, very strong root,
bright colours like daisies, more fruit than
    Sainsbury's,
you'll be a blooming tree.

255 Doug Horley and Noel Richards

I want to be out of my depth in your love,
feeling your arms so strong around me.
Out of my depth in your love,
out of my depth in you.
(Repeat)

Learning to let you lead,
putting all trust in you;
deeper into your arms,
surrounded by you.
Things I have held so tight,
made my security;
give me the strength I need
to simply let go.

256 Mark Altrogge

I want to serve the purpose of God
in my generation.
I want to serve the purpose of God
while I am alive.
I want to give my life for something
that'll last for ever,
oh, I delight, I delight to do your will.

What is on your heart?
Show me what to do.
Let me know your will
and I will follow you.
(Repeat)

I want to build with silver and gold
in my generation . . .

I want to see the kingdom of God
in my generation . . .

I want to see the Lord come again
in my generation . . .

257 Richard Black

I went to the enemy's camp
and I took back what he stole from me,
I took back what he stole from me,
I took back what he stole from me.
I went to the enemy's camp
and I took back what he stole from me.
He's under my feet, he's under my feet,
he's under my feet, he's under my feet,
he's under my feet, he's under my feet,
Satan is under my feet.

258 Brian Doerksen

I will be yours, you will be mine,
together in eternity.
Our hearts of love will be entwined,
together in eternity,
for ever in eternity.
(Repeat)

No more tears of pain in our eyes;
no more fear or shame,
for we will be with you,
for we will be with you.

259 Graham Kendrick

Men	I will build my church
Women	I will build my church
Men	and the gates of hell
Women	and the gates of hell
Men	shall not prevail
Women	shall not prevail
All	against it.

(Repeat)

So you pow'rs in the heavens above,
bow down!
And you pow'rs on the earth below,
bow down!
And acknowledge that Jesus, Jesus,
Jesus is Lord, is Lord.

© 1988 Make Way Music

260 D. J. Butler

I will change your name,
you shall no longer be called
wounded outcast,
lonely or afraid.
I will change your name,
your new name shall be
confidence, joyfulness,
overcoming one.
Faithfulness,
friend of God,
one who seeks my face.

© 1987 Mercy/Vineyard Publishing/Music Services/CopyCare

261 Matt Redman

I will dance, I will sing,
to be mad for my King.
Nothing, Lord, is hindering
the passion in my soul.
(Repeat)

And I'll become
even more undignified than this.
I'll become
even more undignified than this.

Na, na, na, na, na, na! Hey!
Na, na, na, na, na, na! Hey!
(Repeat)

© 1995 Kingsway's Thankyou Music

262 Leona von Brethorst

I will enter his gates with thanksgiving in my
    heart,
I will enter his courts with praise,
I will say this is the day that the Lord has
    made,
I will rejoice for he has made me glad.
He has made me glad,
he has made me glad,
I will rejoice for he has made me glad.
He has made me glad,
he has made me glad,
I will rejoice for he has made me glad.

© 1976 Maranatha! Music/CopyCare

263 Geoff Bullock

I will lift my voice to the King of kings
as an offering to him.
I will lift my heart to the King of kings
as an offering to him.

Jesus, how I love you,
I will worship you alone.
Jesus, precious Jesus,
I will serve you, you alone.

I will lift my hands to the Lord of lords
as an offering to him.
I will lift my life to the Lord of lords
as an offering to him.

© 1988 Word Music Inc./CopyCare

264 Geoff Bullock

I will never be the same again,
I can never return,
I've closed the door.
I will walk the path,
I'll run the race
and I will never be the same again.

Continued overleaf

Fall like fire, soak like rain,
flow like mighty waters again and again:
sweep away the darkness,
burn away the chaff
and let a flame burn
to glorify your name.

There are higher heights,
there are deeper seas:
whatever you need to do,
Lord, do in me;
the glory of God fills my life
and I will never be the same again,
and I will never be the same again.

265   Matt Redman

I will offer up my life
in spirit and truth,
pouring out the oil of love
as my worship to you.
In surrender I must give
my every part;
Lord, receive the sacrifice
of a broken heart.

Jesus, what can I give,
what can I bring
to so faithful a friend,
to so loving a King?
Saviour, what can be said,
what can be sung
as a praise of your name
for the things you have done?
O my words could not tell,
not even in part,
of the debt of love that is owed
by this thankful heart.

You deserve my every breath
for you've paid the great cost;
giving up your life to death,
even death on a cross.
You took all my shame away,
there defeated my sin,
opened up the gates of heav'n,
and have beckoned me in.

266   Mark Altrogge

I will praise you all my life;
I will sing to you with my whole heart.
I will trust in you, my hope and my help,
my Maker and my faithful God.

O faithful God, O faithful God,
you lift me up and you uphold my cause;
you give me life, you dry my eyes,
you're always near, you're a faithful God.

267   Matthew Lockwood

I will seek you with all of my heart,
I will trust you with all of my life,
I will hope in all that you say,
for you are my Lord.
I will give you my hopes and my dreams,
I will fix my thoughts on your word,
I will speak of all you have done for me,
for you are my Lord.

For you are the rock on which I stand,
and you are the friend who holds my hand,
and you are the bright morning star,
the light in my darkest hour.

268   Noel and Tricia Richards

I will seek your face, O Lord;
I will seek your face, O Lord;
I will seek your face, O Lord;
I will seek your face, O Lord.

Lord, how awesome is your presence.
Who can stand in your light?
Those who by your grace and mercy
are made holy in your sight.

I will dwell in your presence
all the days of my life;
there to gaze upon your glory,
and to worship only you.

269   Ian Smale

I will wave my hands
in praise and adoration,
I will wave my hands
in praise and adoration,
I will wave my hands
in praise and adoration,
praise and adoration to the living God.

For he's given me hands
that just love clapping:
one, two, one, two, three,
and he's given me a voice
that just loves shouting:
'Hallelujah!'
He's given me feet
that just love dancing:
one, two, one, two, three,
and he's put me in a being
that has no trouble seeing
that whatever I am feeling
he is worthy to be praised.

270   David Ruis

I will worship (I will worship)
with all of my heart (with all of my heart).
I will praise you (I will praise you)
with all of my strength (all my strength).
I will seek you (I will seek you)
all of my days (all of my days).
I will follow (I will follow)
all of your ways (all your ways).

I will give you all my worship,
I will give you all my praise.
You alone I long to worship,
you alone are worthy of my praise.

I will bow down (I will bow down),
hail you as King (hail you as King).
I will serve you (I will serve you),
give you everything (give you everything).

I will lift up (I will lift up)
my eyes to your throne (my eyes to your
   throne).
I will trust you (I will trust you),
I will trust you alone (trust in you alone).

271   Sondra Corbett

I worship you, Almighty God,
there is none like you.
I worship you, O Prince of Peace,
that is what I love to do.
I give you praise,
for you are my righteousness.
I worship you, Almighty God,
there is none like you.

272   Graham Kendrick

I worship you (I worship you),
O Lamb of God,
who takes away (who takes away)
the sin of the world.
(Repeat)

   Alleluia, alleluia,
   alleluia, alleluia.

I kneel before (I kneel before)
the Lamb of God,
who takes away (who takes away)
the sin of the world.
(Repeat)

273   Chris Bowater

Jesus, at your name we bow the knee.
Jesus, at your name we bow the knee.
Jesus, at your name we bow the knee,
and acknowledge you as Lord.
(Repeat)

Continued overleaf

You are the Christ, you are the Lord.
Through your Spirit in our lives
we know who you are.
(Repeat)

274 Matt Redman

Jesus Christ, I think upon your sacrifice;
you became nothing, poured out to death.
Many times I've wondered at your gift of life,
and I'm in that place once again,
I'm in that place once again.

> *And once again I look upon*
> *the cross where you died.*
> *I'm humbled by your mercy*
> *and I'm broken inside.*
> *Once again I thank you,*
> *once again I pour out my life.*

Now you are exalted to the highest place,
King of the heavens, where one day I'll bow.
But for now I marvel at this saving grace,
and I'm full of praise once again,
I'm full of praise once again.

Thank you for the cross, thank you for the cross,
thank you for the cross, my friend.
Thank you for the cross, thank you for the cross,
thank you for the cross, my friend.

275 Graham Kendrick

Jesus Christ is Lord of all
(Jesus Christ is Lord of all),
King of kings and Lord of lords
(King of kings and Lord of lords),
he will reign for evermore
(he will reign for evermore),
from East to West and shore to shore
(from East to West and shore to shore).

Jesus (Jesus),
King of kings (King of kings),
Jesus (Jesus),
Lord of all (Lord of all),
Jesus (Jesus),
King of kings (King of kings),
Jesus (Jesus),
Lord of all,
(Lord of all, Lord of all,
Lord of all).

Jesus is our battle cry
(Jesus is our battle cry),
King of justice, peace and joy
(King of justice, peace and joy).
We want Jesus more and more
(we want Jesus more and more).
He's the one we're marching for
(he's the one we're marching for).

276 From *Lyra Davidica*

Jesus Christ is ris'n today, alleluia!
our triumphant holy day, alleluia!
who did once, upon the cross, alleluia!
suffer to redeem our loss, alleluia!

Hymns of praise then let us sing, alleluia!
unto Christ, our heav'nly King, alleluia!
who endured the cross and grave, alleluia!
sinners to redeem and save, alleluia!

But the pains that he endured, alleluia!
our salvation have procured; alleluia!
now above the sky he's King, alleluia!
where the angels ever sing, alleluia!

277 Steve Israel and Gerrit Gustafson

> *Jesus Christ is the Lord of all,*
> *Lord of all the earth.*
> *Jesus Christ is the Lord of all,*
> *Lord of all the earth.*
> (Repeat)

Only one God,
over the nations,
only one Lord of all;
in no other name
is there salvation,
Jesus is Lord of all.

Jesus Christ is Lord of all,
Jesus Christ is Lord of all.
Jesus Christ is Lord of all,
Jesus Christ is Lord of all.

278 Geoff Bullock

Jesus, God's righteousness revealed,
the Son of Man, the Son of God,
his kingdom comes.
Jesus, redemption's sacrifice,
now glorified, now justified,
his kingdom comes.

And his kingdom will know no end,
and its glory shall know no bounds,
for the majesty and power
of this kingdom's King has come,
and this kingdom's reign,
and this kingdom's rule,
and this kingdom's power and authority,
Jesus, God's righteousness revealed.

Jesus, the expression of God's love,
the grace of God, the word of God,
revealed to us;
Jesus, God's holiness displayed,
now glorified, now justified,
his kingdom comes.

279 Dave Bolton

Jesus, how lovely you are,
you are so gentle, so pure and kind.
You shine as the morning star,
Jesus, how lovely you are.

Hallelujah, Jesus is my Lord and King;
hallelujah, Jesus is my everything.

Hallelujah, Jesus died and rose again;
hallelujah, Jesus forgave all my sin.

Hallelujah, Jesus is meek and lowly;
hallelujah, Jesus is pure and holy.

Hallelujah, Jesus is the Bridegroom;
hallelujah, Jesus will take his bride soon.

280 Jean Sophia Pigott

Jesus! I am resting, resting
in the joy of what thou art;
I am finding out the greatness
of thy loving heart.
Thou hast bid me gaze upon thee,
and thy beauty fills my soul,
for, by thy transforming power,
thou hast made me whole.

O how great thy loving kindness,
vaster, broader than the sea!
O how marvellous thy goodness,
lavished all on me!
Yes, I rest in thee, beloved,
know what wealth of grace is thine,
know thy certainty of promise,
and have made it mine.

Simply trusting thee, Lord Jesus,
I behold thee as thou art,
and thy love so pure, so changeless,
satisfies my heart,
satisfies its deepest longings,
meets, supplies its every need,
compasses me round with blessings;
thine is love indeed!

Ever lift thy face upon me,
as I work and wait for thee;
resting 'neath thy smile, Lord Jesus,
earth's dark shadows flee.
Brightness of my Father's glory,
sunshine of my Father's face,
keep me ever trusting, resting,
fill me with thy grace.

281 Don Harris and Martin J. Nystrom

Jesus, I am thirsty,
won't you come and fill me?
Earthly things have left me dry,
only you can satisfy,
all I want is more of you.

All I want is more of you,
all I want is more of you;
nothing I desire, Lord,
but more of you.
(Repeat)

282 Gill Hutchinson

Jesus is greater than the greatest heroes,
Jesus is closer than the closest friends.
He came from heaven and he died to save us,
to show us love that never ends.
(Repeat)

Son of God, and the Lord of glory,
he's the light, follow in his way.
He's the truth that we can believe in,
and he's the life, he's living today.
(Repeat)

283 Wendy Churchill

Jesus is King and I will extol him,
give him the glory and honour his name.
He reigns on high, enthroned in the heavens,
Word of the Father, exalted for us.

We have a hope that is steadfast and certain,
gone through the curtain and touching the
    throne.
We have a Priest who is there interceding,
pouring his grace on our lives day by day.

We come to him, our Priest and Apostle,
clothed in his glory and bearing his name,
laying our lives with gladness before him;
filled with his Spirit we worship the King.

O holy One, our hearts do adore you;
thrilled with your goodness we give you our
    praise.
Angels in light with worship surround him,
Jesus, our Saviour, for ever the same.

284 David Mansell

Jesus is Lord! creation's voice proclaims it,
for by his pow'r each tree and flow'r
was planned and made.
Jesus is Lord! the universe declares it,
sun, moon and stars in heaven
cry, 'Jesus is Lord!'

Jesus is Lord! Jesus is Lord!
Praise him with hallelujahs
for Jesus is Lord!

Jesus is Lord! yet from his throne eternal
in flesh he came to die in pain
on Calvary's tree.
Jesus is Lord! from him all life proceeding,
yet gave his life a ransom
thus setting us free.

Jesus is Lord! o'er sin the mighty conqueror,
from death he rose, and all his foes
shall own his name.
Jesus is Lord! God sent his Holy Spirit
to show by works of power
that Jesus is Lord.

285 Philip Lawson Johnston

Jesus is the name we honour;
Jesus is the name we praise.
Majestic Name above all other names,
the highest heav'n and earth proclaim
that Jesus is our God.

We will glorify,
we will lift him high,
we will give him honour and praise.
We will glorify,
we will lift him high,
we will give him honour and praise.

Jesus is the name we worship;
Jesus is the name we trust.
He is the King above all other kings,
let all creation stand and sing
that Jesus is our God.

Jesus is the Father's splendour;
Jesus is the Father's joy.
He will return to reign in majesty,
and every eye at last will see
that Jesus is our God.

286 John Barnett

Jesus, Jesus,
holy and anointed One, Jesus.
Jesus, Jesus,
risen and exalted One, Jesus.

Your name is like honey on my lips,
your Spirit like water to my soul.
Your word is a lamp unto my feet.
Jesus, I love you, I love you.

287 Chris Bowater

Jesus, Jesus, Jesus,
your love has melted my heart.
Jesus, Jesus, Jesus,
your love has melted my heart.

288 David Hadden

Jesus (Jesus), Jesus (Jesus).
You have the name
that's higher than all other names.
Jesus (Jesus), Jesus (Jesus).
You are the King,
the mighty God, the one who reigns.
Glorious in splendour and majesty,
clothed with the robe of authority.
Jesus, my King, you will always be
my deepest joy,
my one desire.
O Prince of Peace,
you set my heart on fire.

289 Graham Kendrick

Jesus' love has got under our skin,
Jesus' love has got under our skin.
Deeper than colour oh;
richer than culture oh;
stronger than emotion oh;
wider than the ocean oh.
Don't you want to celebrate
and congratulate somebody,
talk about a family!
It's under our skin, under our skin.

Leader	Everybody say love:
All	love.
Leader	Everybody say love:
All	love,
Leader	love,
All	love.

Isn't it good to be
living in harmony.
Jesus in you and me;
he's under our skin,
under our skin,
he's under our skin,
under our skin.

290 John Ezzy, Daniel Grul and Stephen McPherson

Jesus, lover of my soul,
Jesus, I will never let you go;
you've taken me from the miry clay,
you've set my feet upon the rock
and now I know

> I love you, I need you,
> though my world will fall,
> I'll never let you go.
> My Saviour, my closest friend,
> I will worship you until the very end.

291 Naida Hearn

Jesus, name above all names,
beautiful Saviour, glorious Lord;
Emmanuel, God is with us,
blessed Redeemer, Living Word.

292 Graham Kendrick

Jesus put this song into our hearts,
Jesus put this song into our hearts,
it's a song of joy no one can take away,
Jesus put this song into our hearts.

Jesus taught us how to live in harmony,
Jesus taught us how to live in harmony,
different faces, different races, he made us one,
Jesus taught us how to live in harmony.

Jesus taught us how to be a family,
Jesus taught us how to be a family,
loving one another with the love that he gives,
Jesus taught us how to be a family.

Jesus turned our sorrow into dancing,
Jesus turned our sorrow into dancing,
changed our tears of sadness into rivers of joy,
Jesus turned our sorrow into a dance.

293 Colin Owen

> Jesus reigns over sin,
> Jesus reigns deep within,
> Jesus is the King of kings.
> Jesus brings life and breath,
> Jesus rules over death
> Jesus is the King of kings.

Jesus, holy Lamb of God,
who triumphed over sin;
gentle, humble Lamb of God
with a lion's heart within,
you are Messiah
and you're coming back again.

Jesus, mighty living Lord,
whose face shines like the sun;
awesome in your majesty,
you are God's Holy One,
you are Messiah
and you're coming back again.

Jesus, Name above all names,
the most exalted One;
you are the Way, the Truth, the Life,
God's precious living Son,
you are Messiah
and you're coming back again.

294 Taizé Community

Jesus, remember me
when you come into your kingdom.
Jesus, remember me
when you come into your kingdom.

295 Graham Kendrick

Jesus, restore to us again
the gospel of your holy name,
that comes with pow'r, not words alone,
owned, signed and sealed from heaven's throne.
Spirit and word in one agree;
the promise to the power wed.

The word is near,
here in our mouths
and in our hearts,
the word of faith;
proclaim it on the Spirit's breath:
Jesus.

Your word, O Lord, eternal stands,
fixed and unchanging in the heav'ns.
The Word made flesh, to earth came down
to heal our world with nail-pierced hands.
Among us here you lived and breathed,
you are the message we received.

Spirit of truth, lead us, we pray,
into all truth as we obey.
And as God's will we gladly choose,
your ancient pow'r again will prove
Christ's teaching truly comes from God,
he is indeed the living Word.

Upon the heights of this dark land
with Moses and Elijah stand.
Reveal your glory once again,
show us your face, declare your name.
Prophets and law, in you, complete
where promises and power meet.

Grant us in this decisive hour
to know the Scriptures and the pow'r;
the knowledge in experience proved,
the pow'r that moves and works by love.
May words and works join hands as one,
the word go forth, the Spirit come.

296   Chris Bowater

Jesus shall take the highest honour,
Jesus shall take the highest praise;
let all earth join heav'n in exalting
the Name which is above all other names.
Let's bow the knee in humble adoration,
for at his name every knee must bow.
Let every tongue confess
he is Christ, God's only Son,
Sovereign Lord, we give you glory now.

For all honour and blessing and power
belongs to you, belongs to you.
All honour and blessing and power
belongs to you, belongs to you,
Lord Jesus Christ, Son of the living God.

297   Dave Bryant

Jesus, take me as I am,
I can come no other way.
Take me deeper into you,
make my flesh life die away.
Make me like a precious stone,
crystal clear and finely honed.
Life of Jesus shining through,
giving glory back to you.

298   Charles Wesley

Jesus! The name high over all,
in hell, or earth, or sky;
Angels and mortals prostrate fall
and devils fear and fly.

Jesus, the name to sinners dear,
the name to sinners giv'n;
it scatters all their guilty fear,
it turns their hell to heav'n.

Jesus, the prisoner's fetters breaks,
and bruises Satan's head;
pow'r into strengthless souls he speaks,
and life into the dead,
and life into the dead.

O, that the world might taste and see
the riches of his grace!
The arms of love that compass me,
hold all the human race.

His only righteousness I show,
his saving grace proclaim:
'tis all my business here below
to cry: 'Behold the Lamb!'

Happy, if with my latest breath
I may but gasp his name:
preach him to all, and cry in death:
'Behold, behold the Lamb!'

299 John Gibson

Jesus, we celebrate your victory;
Jesus, we revel in your love.
Jesus, we rejoice you've set us free;
Jesus, your death has brought us life.

It was for freedom that Christ has set us free,
no longer to be subject to a yoke of slavery;
so we're rejoicing in God's victory,
our hearts responding to his love.

His Spirit in us releases us from fear,
the way to him is open, with boldness we
   draw near.
And in his presence our problems disappear;
our hearts responding to his love.

300 Paul Kyle

Jesus, we enthrone you,
we proclaim you our King,
standing here in the midst of us,
we raise you up with our praise.
And as we worship, build a throne,
and as we worship, build a throne,
and as we worship, build a throne;
come, Lord Jesus, and take your place.

301 Tanya Riches

Jesus, what a beautiful name.
Son of God, Son of Man,
Lamb that was slain.
Joy and peace, strength and hope,
grace that blows all fear away.
Jesus, what a beautiful name.

Jesus, what a beautiful name.
Truth revealed, my future sealed,
healed my pain.
Love and freedom, life and warmth,
grace that blows all fear away.
Jesus, what a beautiful name.

Jesus, what a beautiful name.
Rescued my soul, my stronghold,
lifts me from shame.
Forgiveness, security, power and love,
grace that blows all fear away.
Jesus, what a beautiful name.

302 Nancy Gordon and Jamie Harvill

Jesus, you're my firm foundation,
I know I can stand secure;
Jesus, you're my firm foundation,
I put my hope in your holy word,
I put my hope in your holy word.

I have a living hope
(I have a living hope),
I have a future
(I have a future);
God has a plan for me
(God has a plan for me),
of this I'm sure
(of this I'm sure).

Your word is faithful
(your word is faithful),
mighty in power
(mighty in power);
God will deliver me
(God will deliver me),
of this I'm sure
(of this I'm sure).

303 Reuben Morgan

Jesus, your loving kindness,
I'm so blessed by all that you've done,
this life that you give.
Jesus, your loving kindness
is life that's changing my heart,
drawing me near to you.

Your love is better than life,
I know it well
and I'll find all that I need in you, in you.
Your love is better than life,
I know it well
and I'll find all that I need in you.

304 Claire Cloninger

Jesus, your name is power,
Jesus, your name is might.
Jesus, your name will break every stronghold,
Jesus, your name is life.

Jesus, your name is healing,
Jesus, your name gives sight.
Jesus, your name will free every captive,
Jesus, your name is life.

Jesus, your name is holy,
Jesus, your name brings light.
Jesus, your name above every other,
Jesus, your name is life.

Jesus, your name is power,
Jesus, your name is might.
Jesus, your name will break every stronghold,
Jesus, your name is life.

305 Isaac Watts

Joy to the world! The Lord is come;
let earth receive her King;
let every heart prepare him room
and heav'n and nature sing,
and heav'n and nature sing,
and heav'n, and heav'n and nature sing.

Joy to the earth! The Saviour reigns;
let us our songs employ;
while fields and floods, rocks, hills and plains
repeat the sounding joy,
repeat the sounding joy,
repeat, repeat the sounding joy.

He rules the world with truth and grace,
and makes the nations prove
the glories of his righteousness,
and wonders of his love,
and wonders of his love,
and wonders, wonders of his love.

306 Charlotte Elliott

Just as I am, without one plea
but that thy blood was shed for me,
and that thou bid'st me come to thee,
O Lamb of God, I come.

Just as I am, though tossed about
with many a conflict, many a doubt,
fightings and fears within, without,
O Lamb of God, I come.

Just as I am, poor, wretched, blind;
sight, riches, healing of the mind,
yea, all I need, in thee to find,
O Lamb of God, I come.

Just as I am, thou wilt receive,
wilt welcome, pardon, cleanse, relieve:
because thy promise I believe,
O Lamb of God, I come.

Just as I am, thy love unknown
has broken every barrier down,
now to be thine, yea, thine alone,
O Lamb of God, I come.

Just as I am, of that free love
the breadth, length, depth and height to prove,
here for a season, then above,
O Lamb of God, I come.

307 Naomi Batya and Sophie Conty

King of kings and Lord of lords,
glory, hallelujah.
King of kings and Lord of lords,
glory, hallelujah.
Jesus, Prince of Peace,
glory, hallelujah.
Jesus, Prince of Peace,
glory, hallelujah.

308 Graham Kendrick

King of kings, Lord of lords,
Lion of Judah, Word of God.
King of kings, Lord of lords,
Lion of Judah, Word of God.
Word of God.
And here he comes,
the King of glory comes!
In righteousness he comes to judge the earth.
And here he comes,
the King of glory comes!
With justice he'll rule the earth.

(Shout)
Almighty God, you are the Rock;
all your works are perfect,
and all your ways are just.
You are a faithful God who does no wrong.
Yet we your people,
both church and nation,
are covered with shame
because of our unfaithfulness to you.
We have sinned so seriously against you,
and against one another –
therefore the foundations of our society crumble.
Have mercy, Lord,
forgive us, Lord,
restore us, Lord,
revive your church again;
let justice flow
like rivers,
and righteousness like a never-failing stream.

© 1988 Make Way Music

309 Jarrod Cooper

King of kings, majesty,
God of heaven living in me,
gentle Saviour, closest friend,
strong deliverer, beginning and end,
all within me falls at your throne.

Your majesty, I can but bow.
I lay my all before you now.
In royal robes I don't deserve
I live to serve your majesty.

Earth and heav'n worship you,
love eternal, faithful and true,
who bought the nations, ransomed souls,
brought this sinner near to your throne;
all within me cries out in praise.

© 1998 Sovereign Lifestyle Music

310 Chris Bowater

Lamb of God, Holy One,
Jesus Christ, Son of God,
lifted up willingly to die;
that I the guilty one may know
the blood once shed still freely flowing,
still cleansing, still healing.

I exalt you, Jesus, my sacrifice,
I exalt you, my Redeemer and my Lord.
I exalt you, worthy Lamb of God,
and in honour I bow down
before your throne.

© 1988 Sovereign Lifestyle Music Ltd.

311 James Edmeston

Lead us, heav'nly Father, lead us
o'er the world's tempestuous sea;
guard us, guide us, keep us, feed us,
for we have no help but thee;
yet possessing every blessing
if our God our Father be.

Saviour, breathe forgiveness o'er us:
all our weakness thou dost know;
thou didst tread this earth before us,
thou didst feel its keenest woe;
lone and dreary, faint and weary,
through the desert thou didst go.

Spirit of our God, descending,
fill our hearts with heav'nly joy,
love with every passion blending,
pleasure that can never cloy:
thus provided, pardoned, guided,
nothing can our peace destroy.

312 Graham Kendrick

Led like a lamb to the slaughter
in silence and shame,
there on your back you carried
a world of violence and pain.
Bleeding, dying, bleeding, dying.

You're alive, you're alive,
you have risen, alleluia!
And the pow'r and the glory is given,
alleluia! Jesus to you.

At break of dawn, poor Mary,
still weeping she came,
when through her grief she heard your voice
now speaking her name.
(Men) Mary, *(Women)* Master,
(Men) Mary, *(Women)* Master.

At the right hand of the Father
now seated on high
you have begun your eternal reign
of justice and joy.
Glory, glory, glory, glory.

© 1983 Kingsway's Thankyou Music

313 Graham Kendrick

Let it be to me
according to your word.
Let it be to me
according to your word.

I am your servant,
no rights shall I demand.
Let it be to me,
let it be to me,
let it be to me
according to your word.
(Repeat)

© 1988 Make Way Music

314 Joel Pott

Let it rain, let it rain, let it rain,
let it rain on every nation.
Let it rain, let it rain, let it rain,
let it rain on every nation.
(Repeat)

Take our hearts as fuel for the fire,
now is the time to see your power.
Take our prayers as abundant rain,
open up the floodgates of heaven.
Let the trumpet sound
and the rain come down.

Love rain down, down on me.
Love rain down, down on me.
Love rain down, down on me.
Love rain down on me.
(Repeat)

© 1995 Joel Pott

315 Daniel Gardner

Let me be a sacrifice,
holy and acceptable,
let me be a sacrifice,
consumed in your praise;
let me be a sacrifice,
holy and acceptable,
let me be a sacrifice,
worshipping your name.

© 1981 Integrity's Hosanna! Music/ Kingsway's Thankyou Music

316 Bryn Haworth

Let the righteous sing,
come, let the righteous dance,
rejoice before your God,
be happy and joyful.
Give him your praise.
We give you our praise.
Shout for joy to God
who rides upon the clouds;
how awesome are his deeds,
so great is his power.
Give him your praise.
We give you our praise.

He gives the desolate a home.
He leads the prisoners out with singing.
Father to the fatherless,
defender of the widow,
is God in his holy place.

© 1991 Kingsway's Thankyou Music

317 Dave Bilbrough

Let there be love shared among us,
let there be love in our eyes.
May now your love sweep this nation,
cause us, O Lord, to arise.
Give us a fresh understanding
of brotherly love that is real.
Let there be love shared among us,
let there be love.

318 John Watson

Let your living water flow over my soul.
Let your Holy Spirit come and take control
of every situation that has troubled my mind.
All my cares and burdens on to you I roll.

Jesus, Jesus, Jesus.
Father, Father, Father.
Spirit, Spirit, Spirit.

Come now, Holy Spirit, and take control.
Hold me in your loving arms and make me
    whole.
Wipe away all doubt and fear and take my pride.
Draw me to your love and keep me by your side.

Give your life to Jesus, let him fill your soul.
Let him take you in his arms and make you
    whole.
As you give your life to him, he'll set you free.
You will live and reign with him eternally.

Let your living water flow over my soul.
Let your Holy Spirit come and take control
of every situation that has troubled my mind.
All my cares and burdens on to you I roll.

319 Noel and Tricia Richards

Oh, oh, oh,
let your love come down.
(Repeat)

There is violence in the air.
Fear touches all our lives.
How much pain can people bear?
Are we reaping what we've sown,
voices silent for too long?
We are calling, let your love come down.

There is power in your love,
bringing laughter out of tears.
It can heal the wounded soul.
In the streets where anger reigns,
love will wash away the pain.
We are calling, heaven's love come down.

320 Robin Mark

Let your word go forth among the nations,
let your voice be heard among the people.
May they know our God, the only true God,
reigns on earth as you reign in heaven.

May your church be bold and speak with one
    voice,
may our hearts be strong and never failing.
May we know no fear
except a holy fear of you, my King.

321 Graham Kendrick

Lift up your heads, O you gates,
swing wide, you everlasting doors.
Lift up your heads, O you gates,
swing wide, you everlasting doors.

That the King of glory may come in,
that the King of glory may come in.
That the King of glory may come in,
that the King of glory may come in.

Up from the dead he ascends,
through every rank of heav'nly power.
Let heaven prepare the highest place,
throw wide the everlasting doors.

With trumpet blast and shouts of joy,
all heaven greets the risen King.
With angel choirs come line the way,
throw wide the gates and welcome him.

322 Graham Kendrick

Like a candle flame,
flick'ring small
in our darkness.
Uncreated light
shines through infant eyes.

> God is with us,
> alleluia,
> come to save us,
> alleluia,
> alleluia!

Stars and angels sing,
yet the earth
sleeps in shadows;
can this tiny spark
set a world on fire?

Yet his light shall shine
from our lives,
spirit blazing,
as we touch the flame
or his holy fire.

323 David Hadden and Bob Silvester

Living under the shadow of his wing
we find security.
Standing in his presence we will bring
our worship, worship, worship to the King.

Bowed in adoration at his feet
we dwell in harmony.
Voices joined together that repeat,
worthy, worthy, worthy is the Lamb.

Heart to heart embracing in his love
reveals his purity.
Soaring in my spirit like a dove,
holy, holy, holy is the Lord.

324 Charles Wesley, John Cennick and Martin Madan

Lo, he comes with clouds descending,
once for mortal sinners slain;
thousand, thousand saints attending
swell the triumph of his train.
Alleluia! Alleluia! Alleluia!
Christ appears on earth to reign.

Every eye shall now behold him
robed in glorious majesty;
we who set at naught and sold him,
pierced and nailed him to the tree,
deeply wailing, deeply wailing, deeply wailing,
shall the true Messiah see.

Those dear tokens of his passion
still his dazzling body bears,
cause of endless exultation
to his ransomed worshippers:
with what rapture, with what rapture, with
    what rapture
gaze we on those glorious scars!

Yea, amen, let all adore thee,
high on thine eternal throne;
Saviour, take the pow'r and glory,
claim the kingdom for thine own.
Alleluia! Alleluia! Alleluia!
Thou shalt reign, and thou alone.

325 Graham Kendrick

Look what God has done for us,
over all the years we've shared,
ever since the day
he joined our flickering lights into one flame.
Look at all the lives he's changed,
by his grace we're not the same;
all the fruit that's grown,
all that's yet to come,
look what God has done.
And his love goes on and on for ever.

Continued overleaf

Look at all we've shared in him,
joy and laughter, tears and pain,
grace to carry on when darks were dark
and all our strength was gone.
Look at all the prayers he's heard,
all the times he's proved his word;
blessing on our homes,
children that have grown,
look what God has done.
And his love goes on and on for ever.

Freely we have all received,
freely we must also give,
thinking of the price he paid
that we might be his very own.
Born for such a time as this,
chosen for the harvest years,
we have just begun,
the best is yet to come,
look what God has done.
And his love goes on and on for ever.

326 Mark David Hanby

Look what the Lord has done,
look what the Lord has done,
he healed my body,
he touched my mind,
he saved me just in time.
Oh I'm gonna praise his name,
each day he's just the same.
Come on and praise him,
look what the Lord has done.

327 Timothy Dudley-Smith

Lord, for the years
your love has kept and guided,
urged and inspired us,
cheered us on our way,
sought us and saved us,
pardoned and provided,
Lord of the years,
we bring our thanks today.

Lord, for that Word,
the Word of life which fires us,
speaks to our hearts
and sets our souls ablaze,
teaches and trains,
rebukes us and inspires us:
Lord of the Word,
receive your people's praise.

Lord, for our land,
in this our generation,
spirits oppressed by pleasure,
wealth and care;
for young and old,
for commonwealth and nation,
Lord of our land,
be pleased to hear our prayer.

Lord, for our world;
when we disown and doubt him,
loveless in strength,
and comfortless in pain,
hungry and helpless,
lost indeed without him:
Lord of the world,
we pray that Christ may reign.

Lord for ourselves;
in living pow'r remake us –
self on the cross
and Christ upon the throne,
past put behind us,
for the future take us:
Lord of our lives,
to live for Christ alone.

328 Graham Kendrick

Lord, have mercy on us,
come and heal our land.
Cleanse with your fire,
heal with your touch.
Humbly we bow
and call upon you now.
O Lord, have mercy on us,
O Lord, have mercy on us.

329 Geoff Bullock

Lord, I come to you,
let my heart be changed, renewed,
flowing from the grace
that I found in you.
And, Lord, I've come to know
the weaknesses I see in me
will be stripped away
by the pow'r of your love.

Hold me close,
let your love surround me,
bring me near,
draw me to your side;
and as I wait,
I'll rise up like an eagle,
and I will soar with you;
your Spirit leads me on
in the pow'r of your love.

Lord, unveil my eyes,
let me see you face to face,
the knowledge of your love
as you live in me.
Lord, renew my mind
as your will unfolds in my life,
in living every day
in the pow'r of your love.

© 1992 Word Music Inc./CopyCare

330 Rick Founds

Lord, I lift your name on high;
Lord, I love to sing your praises.
I'm so glad you're in my life;
I'm so glad you came to save us.
(Repeat)

You came from heaven to earth
to show the way,
from the earth to the cross,
my debt to pay,
from the cross to the grave,
from the grave to the sky,
Lord, I lift your name on high.

© 1989 Maranatha! Music/CopyCare

331 Darlene Zschech

Lord, my heart cries out,
glory to the King,
my greatest love in life.
I hand you everthing.
Glory, glory, I hear the angels sing.

Open my ears,
let me hear your voice
to know that sweet sound.
O, my soul, rejoice.
Glory, glory, I hear the angels sing.

You're the Father to the fatherless,
the answer to my dreams.
I see you crowned in righteousness.
We cry glory to the King.
Comforter to the lonely,
the lifter of my head,
I see you veiled in majesty,
we cry glory, glory,
we cry glory, to the King.
We cry glory, glory,
we cry glory, to the King.

© 1997 Darlene Zschech/Hillsongs Australia/Kingsway's Thankyou Music

332 Jessy Dixon, Randy Scruggs and John Thompson

Lord of lords, King of kings,
maker of heaven and earth
and all good things.
We give you glory.
Lord Jehovah, Son of Man,
precious Prince of Peace and the great 'I Am'.
We give you glory.

Glory to God! Glory to God!
Glory to God Almighty in the highest!

Lord, you're righteous in all your ways.
We bless your holy name
and we will give you praise.
We give you glory.
You reign for ever in majesty.
We praise you and lift you up for eternity.
We give you glory.

© 1983 Windswept Pacific Music

333 Lucy Fisher

Lord of the heavens and the earth,
my Saviour, Redeemer, risen Lord,
all honour and glory, pow'r and strength
to him upon the throne.
(Repeat)

Holy, holy, you are worthy,
praises to the Son of God.
Jesus, you alone are worthy,
crowned in righteousness and peace.
Glory, glory, hallelujah,
praises to the great 'I Am'.
Hosanna, join with angels singing,
worthy is the Lamb of God.

(Last time)
Worthy is the Lamb of God,
worthy is the Lamb of God,
worthy is the Lamb of God.

© 1996 Lucy Fisher/Hillsongs Australia/Kingsway's Thankyou Music

334 John Thompson and Randy Scruggs

Lord, prepare me
to be a sanctuary
pure and holy, tried and true,
with thanksgiving.
I'll be a living sanctuary
for you.

© 1982 Windswept Pacific Music

335 Graham Kendrick

Lord, the light of your love is shining,
in the midst of the darkness, shining;
Jesus, Light of the World, shine upon us,
set us free by the truth you now bring us.
Shine on me, shine on me.

Shine, Jesus, shine,
fill this land with the Father's glory;
blaze, Spirit, blaze,
set our hearts on fire.

Flow, river, flow,
flood the nations with grace and mercy;
send forth your word, Lord,
and let there be light.

Lord, I come to your awesome presence,
from the shadows into your radiance;
by the blood I may enter your brightness,
search me, try me, consume all my darkness.
Shine on me, shine on me.

As we gaze on your kingly brightness,
so our faces display your likeness,
ever changing from glory to glory;
mirrored here may our lives tell your story.
Shine on me, shine on me.

© 1987 Make Way Music

336 Judy Bailey

Lord, we lift you high
when we praise your name,
when we worship you
and our hands are raised,
that is how we lift you up.
Lord, we lift you high
when we tell the truth,
when we give our best
in everything we do,
that is how we lift you up.

By our voices be lifted, lifted,
by our actions, Lord, be lifted high.
By our love, Lord, be lifted, lifted,
by our lives, O Lord, be lifted high.

Lord, we lift you high
when we're good and kind,
when we turn from wrong
and we do what's right,
that is how we lift you up.
Lord, we lift you high
when we shine like stars,
when we tell our friends
just how good you are,
that is how we lift you up.

You are God, Jesus the Lord of all,
we place you above all else.
So shine through me
and keep drawing the world
to your heart.

Lord, we lift you high
when we praise your name,
when we worship you
and our hands are raised,
that is how we lift you up.
Lord, we lift you high
when we tell the truth,
when we give our best
in everything we do,
that is how we lift you up.

© Ice Music Ltd

337 Trish Morgan, Ray Goudie, Ian Townend and
Dave Bankhead

Lord, we long for you to move in power.
There's a hunger deep within our hearts
to see healing in our nation.
Send your Spirit to revive us.

Heal our nation!
Heal our nation!
Heal our nation!
Pour out your Spirit on this land!

Lord, we hear your Spirit coming closer,
a mighty wave to break upon our land,
bringing justice and forgiveness.
God, we cry to you, 'Revive us!'

© 1986 Kingsway's Thankyou Music

338 Richard Lewis

Lord, we long to see your glory,
gaze upon your lovely face.
Holy Spirit, come among us,
lead us to that secret place.
Holy God, we long to see your glory,
to touch your holy majesty, O Lord.
Holy God, let us stay in your presence,
and worship at your feet for evermore.
Holy God. Holy God.

© 1997 Kingsway's Thankyou Music

339 Lynn DeShazo

Lord, you are more precious than silver,
Lord, you are more costly than gold.
Lord, you are more beautiful than diamonds,
and nothing I desire compares with you.

© 1982 Integrity's Hosanna! Music/Kingsway's Thankyou Music

340 Graham Kendrick

Lord, you are so precious to me,
Lord, you are so precious to me
and I love you, yes, I love you
because you first loved me.

Lord, you are so gracious to me . . .

Lord, you are a father to me . . .

Lord, you are so faithful to me . . .

Lord, you are so loving to me . . .

© 1986 Kingsway's Thankyou Music

341 Martin Smith

Lord, you have my heart,
and I will search for yours;
Jesus, take my life and lead me on.
Lord, you have my heart,
and I will search for yours;
let me be to you a sacrifice.

And I will praise you, Lord
(I will praise you, Lord).
And I will sing of love come down
(I will sing of love come down).
And as you show your face
(show your face),
we'll see your glory here.

© 1992 Kingsway's Thankyou Music

342 Ian Smale

Lord, you put a tongue in my mouth
and I want to sing to you.
Lord, you put a tongue in my mouth
and I want to sing to you.
Lord, you put a tongue in my mouth
and I want to sing only to you.
Lord Jesus, free us in our praise;
Lord Jesus, free us in our praise.

Lord, you put some hands on my arms
which I want to raise to you . . .

Lord, you put some feet on my legs
and I want to dance to you . . .

© 1983 Kingsway's Thankyou Music

343 Charles Wesley

Love divine, all loves excelling,
joy of heav'n, to earth come down,
fix in us thy humble dwelling,
all thy faithful mercies crown.

Jesu, thou art all compassion,
pure unbounded love thou art;
visit us with thy salvation,
enter every trembling heart.

Breathe, O breathe thy loving Spirit
into every troubled breast;
let us all in thee inherit,
let us find thy promised rest.

Take away the love of sinning,
Alpha and Omega be;
end of faith, as its beginning,
set our hearts at liberty.

Come, almighty to deliver,
let us all thy grace receive;
suddenly return, and never,
never more thy temples leave.

Thee we would be always blessing,
serve thee as thy hosts above;
pray, and praise thee without ceasing,
glory in thy perfect love.

Finish then thy new creation,
pure and spotless let us be;
let us see thy great salvation
perfectly restored in thee.

Changed from glory into glory,
till in heav'n we take our place,
till we cast our crowns before thee,
lost in wonder, love, and praise.

344 Graham Kendrick

Love of Christ, come now,
like a mighty ocean.
Flow through here,
with mercy and grace;
love of Christ, come now.

© 1989 Make Way Music

345 Robert Lowry

Low in the grave he lay,
Jesus, my Saviour;
waiting the coming day,
Jesus, my Lord.

Up from the grave he arose,
with a mighty triumph o'er his foes;
he arose a victor from the dark domain,
and he lives for ever with his saints to reign.
He arose! He arose!
Hallelujah! Christ arose!

Vainly they watch his bed,
Jesus, my Saviour;
vainly they seal the dead,
Jesus, my Lord.

Death cannot keep its prey,
Jesus, my Saviour;
he tore the bars away,
Jesus, my Lord.

346   Jack W. Hayford

Majesty, worship his majesty,
unto Jesus be glory, honour and praise.
Majesty, kingdom authority
flows from his throne unto his own,
his anthem raise.
So exalt, lift up on high the name of Jesus;
magnify, come glorify Christ Jesus the King.
Majesty, worship his majesty,
Jesus who died, now glorified,
King of all kings.

347   Edwin Hawkins

Make a joyful noise, all ye people,
sing a song to the Lord
of his goodness and his mercy,
of his faithfulness and love.
(Repeat)

> *Worship the Lord,*
> *let's praise his holy name.*
> *Worship the Lord,*
> *let's magnify his name.*
> (Repeat)

348   Sebastian Temple

Make me a channel of your peace.
Where there is hatred, let me bring your love.
Where there is injury, your pardon, Lord,
and where there's doubt, true faith in you.

> *O Master, grant that I may never seek*
> *so much to be consoled as to console,*
> *to be understood, as to understand,*
> *to be loved, as to love with all my soul.*

Make me a channel of your peace.
Where there's despair in life, let me bring hope.
Where there is darkness, only light,
and where there's sadness, ever joy.

Make me a channel of your peace.
It is in pardoning that we are pardoned,
in giving of ourselves that we receive,
and in dying that we're born to eternal life.

349   Graham Kendrick

Make way, make way, for Christ the King
in splendour arrives;
fling wide the gates and welcome him
into your lives.

> *Make way (make way),*
> *make way (make way),*
> *for the King of kings*
> *(for the King of kings);*
> *make way (make way),*
> *make way (make way),*
> *and let his kingdom in!*

He comes the broken hearts to heal,
the prisoners to free;
the deaf shall hear, the lame shall dance,
the blind shall see.

And those who mourn with heavy hearts,
who weep and sigh,
with laughter, joy and royal crown
he'll beautify.

We call you now to worship him
as Lord of all,
to have no gods before him,
their thrones must fall.

350   Philipp Bliss

Man of sorrows! What a name
for the Son of God who came
ruined sinners to reclaim!
Alleluia! What a Saviour!

Bearing shame and scoffing rude,
in my place condemned he stood;
sealed my pardon with his blood:
Alleluia! What a Saviour!

Continued overleaf

Guilty, vile and helpless we;
spotless Lamb of God was he:
full atonement – can it be?
Alleluia! What a Saviour!

Lifted up was he to die:
'It is finished!' was his cry;
now in heav'n exalted high:
Alleluia! What a Saviour!

When he comes, our glorious King,
all his ransomed home to bring,
then anew this song we'll sing:
Alleluia! What a Saviour!

351 Chris Bowater

May our worship
be as fragrance,
may our worship
be as incense poured forth,
may our worship
be acceptable as a living sacrifice,
as a living sacrifice.

We are willing
to pay the price,
we are willing
to lay down our lives
as an offering of obedience,
as a living sacrifice,
as a living sacrifice.

© 1992 Sovereign Lifestyle Music

352 Graham Kendrick

May the fragrance of Jesus fill this place
(may the fragrance of Jesus fill this place).
May the fragrance of Jesus fill this place
(lovely fragrance of Jesus),
rising from the sacrifice
of lives laid down in adoration.

May the glory of Jesus fill his church
(may the glory of Jesus fill his church).
May the glory of Jesus fill his church
(radiant glory of Jesus),
shining from our faces
as we gaze in adoration.

May the beauty of Jesus fill my life
(may the beauty of Jesus fill my life).
May the beauty of Jesus fill my life
(perfect beauty of Jesus),
fill my thoughts, my words, my deeds;
may I give in adoration.
Fill my thoughts, my words, my deeds;
may I give in adoration.

© 1986 Kingsway's Thankyou Music

353 Graham Kendrick

Meekness and majesty,
manhood and deity,
in perfect harmony,
the Man who is God.
Lord of eternity
dwells in humanity,
kneels in humility
and washes our feet.

O what a mystery,
meekness and majesty.
Bow down and worship
for this is your God,
this is your God.

Father's pure radiance,
perfect in innocence,
yet learns obedience
to death on a cross.
Suffering to give us life,
conquering through sacrifice,
and as they crucify
prays: 'Father, forgive.'

Wisdom unsearchable,
God the invisible,
love indestructible
in frailty appears.
Lord of infinity,
stooping so tenderly,
lifts our humanity
to the heights of his throne.

© 1986 Kingsway's Thankyou Music

354 Martin Smith

Men of faith, rise up and sing
of the great and glorious King.
You are strong when you feel weak,
in your brokenness complete.

Shout to the north and the south,
sing to the east and the west.
Jesus is Saviour to all,
Lord of heaven and earth.

Rise up, women of the truth,
stand and sing to broken hearts.
Who can know the healing pow'r
of our awesome King of love.

We've been through fire,
we've been through rain,
we've been refined by the pow'r of his name.
We've fallen deeper in love with you,
you've burned the truth on our lips.

Rise up, church with broken wings,
fill this place with songs again
of our God who reigns on high,
by his grace again we'll fly.

© 1995 Curious? Music UK/Kingsway's Thankyou Music

355 David Ruis

Mercy is falling, is falling, is falling,
mercy it falls like the sweet spring rain.
Mercy is falling, is falling all over me.
(Repeat)

Hey O, I receive your mercy.
Hey O, I receive your grace.
Hey O, I will dance for evermore.
(Repeat)

© 1994 Mercy/Vineyard Publishing/Music Services/CopyCare

356 Mark Johnson, Helen Johnson and Chris Bowater

Mighty God,
everlasting Father,
wonderful Counsellor,
you're the Prince of Peace.
(Repeat)

You are Lord of heaven,
you are called Emmanuel;
God is now with us,
ever-present to deliver.
You are God eternal,
you are Lord of the all the earth;
love has come to us,
bringing us new birth.

A light to those in darkness,
and a guide to paths of peace;
love and mercy dawns,
grace, forgiveness and salvation.
Light for revelation,
glory to your people;
Son of the Most High,
God's love-gift to all.

© 1991 Sovereign Lifestyle Music

357 Eugene Greco, Gerrit Gustafson and Don Moen

Mighty is our God,
mighty is our King;
mighty is our Lord,
ruler of everything.
(Repeat)

His name is higher,
higher than any other name;
his pow'r is greater
for he has created everything.

Glory to our God,
glory to our King,
glory to our Lord,
ruler of everything.
(Repeat)

His name is higher . . .

Mighty is our God . . .

© 1989 Integrity's Hosanna! Music/Kingsway's Thankyou Music

358 E. E. Hewitt

More about Jesus would I know,
more of his grace to others show;
more of his saving fullness see,
more of his love who died for me.

More, more about Jesus,
more, more about Jesus;
more of his saving fullness see,
more of his love who died for me.

More about Jesus let me learn,
more of his holy will discern;
Spirit of God my teacher be,
showing the things of Christ to me.

More about Jesus; in his word,
holding communion with my Lord;
hearing his voice in every line,
making each faithful saying mine.

More about Jesus; on his throne,
riches in glory all his own;
more of his kingdom's sure increase;
more of his coming, Prince of Peace.

359 Jude del Hierro

More love (more love),
more power (more power),
more of you in my life.
(Repeat)

And I will worship you with all of my heart,
and I will worship you with all of my mind,
and I will worship you with all of my strength,
for you are my Lord.

And I will seek your face with all of my heart,
and I will seek your face with all of my mind,
and I will seek your face with all of my strength,
for you are my Lord.

(Last time)
For you are my Lord; you are my Lord.

360 Lindell Cooley and Bruce Haynes

More of your glory,
more of your power,
more of your Spirit in me.
Speak to my heart
and change my life,
manifest yourself in me.

It's been a long time,
you have stayed on my mind.
There's a stirring in my soul
that causes me to know
how much I need you.

Send your glory
(send your glory),
send your power
(send your power),
send your Spirit
(send your Spirit),
come and change me
(come and change me).

361 Brian Doerksen

More than oxygen
I need your love.
More than life-giving food
the hungry dream of.
More than an eloquent word
depends on the tongue.
More than a passionate song
needs to be sung.

More than a word could ever say,
more than a song could ever convey.
I need you more than all of these things.
Father, I need you more.

More than magnet and steel
are drawn to unite.
More than poets love words
to rhyme as they write.

More than the comforting warmth
of the sun in the spring.
More than the eagle loves wind
under its wings.

More than a blazing fire
on a winter's night.
More than the tall evergreens
reach for the light.
More than the pounding waves
long for the shore.
More than these gifts you give,
I love you more.

362 Stuart Townend

My first love is a blazing fire,
I feel his pow'rful love in me;
for he has kindled a flame of passion,
and I will let it grow in me.
And in the night I will sing your praise, my love.
And in the morning I'll seek your face, my love.

And like a child I will dance in your presence.
O let the joy of heaven pour down on me.
I still remember the first day I met you,
and I don't ever want to lose that fire,
*   my first love.*

My first love is a rushing river,
a waterfall that will never cease;
and in the torrent of tears and laughter,
I feel a healing power released.
And I will draw from your well of life, my love.
And in your grace I'll be satisfied, my love.

Restore the years of the church's slumber,
revive the fire that has grown so dim;
renew the love of those first encounters,
that we may come alive again.
And we will rise like the dawn throughout
    the earth,
until the trumpet announces your return.

363 Graham Kendrick

My heart is full of admiration
for you, my Lord, my God and King.
Your excellence, my inspiration,
your words of grace have made my spirit sing.

All the glory, honour and pow'r
belong to you, belong to you.
Jesus, Saviour, anointed One,
I worship you, I worship you.

You love what's right and hate what's evil,
therefore your God sets you on high,
and on your head pours oil of gladness,
while fragrance fills your royal palaces.

Your throne, O God, will last for ever,
justice will be your royal decree.
In majesty, ride out victorious,
for righteousness, truth and humility.

364 Robin Mark

My heart will sing to you because of your
    great love,
a love so rich, so pure, a love beyond compare;
the wilderness, the barren place,
become a blessing in the warmth of your
    embrace.

When earthly wisdom dims the light of
    knowing you,
or if my search for understanding clouds
    your way,
to you I fly, my hiding-place,
where revelation is beholding face to face.

May my heart sing your praise for ever,
may my voice lift your name, my God;
may my soul know no other treasure
than your love, than your love.

365   Edward Mote

My hope is built on nothing less
than Jesus' blood and righteousness.
I dare not trust the sweetest frame,
but wholly lean on Jesus' name.

On Christ the solid Rock I stand;
all other ground is sinking sand,
all other ground is sinking sand.

When darkness veils his lovely face,
I rest on his unchanging grace;
in every high and stormy gale
my anchor holds within the veil.

His oath, his covenant, his blood
support me in the 'whelming flood;
when all around my soul gives way,
he then is all my hope and stay.

When he shall come with trumpet sound,
O may I then in him be found;
dressed in his righteousness alone,
faultless to stand before the throne.

366   William R. Featherston and Adoniram J. Gordon

My Jesus, I love thee, I know thou art mine.
For thee all the follies of sin I resign.
My gracious Redeemer, my Saviour art thou.
If ever I loved thee, my Jesus, 'tis now.

I love thee because thou has first lovèd me,
and purchased my pardon on Calvary's tree.
I love thee for wearing the thorns on thy brow.
If ever I loved thee, my Jesus, 'tis now.

In mansions of glory and endless delight,
I'll ever adore thee in heaven so bright.
I'll sing with a glittering crown on my brow.
If ever I loved thee, my Jesus, 'tis now.

© 1995 Latter Rain Music/Universal Songs/CopyCare

367   Darlene Zschech

My Jesus, my Saviour,
Lord, there is none like you.
All of my days
I want to praise
the wonders of your mighty love.

My comfort, my shelter,
tower of refuge and strength,
let every breath,
all that I am,
never cease to worship you.

Shout to the Lord,
all the earth, let us sing
power and majesty, praise to the King.
Mountains bow down and the seas will roar
at the sound of your name.
I sing for joy
at the work of your hands.
For ever I'll love you, for ever I'll stand.
Nothing compares to the promise
I have in you.

© 1993 Darlene Zschech/Hillsongs Australia/Kingsway's Thankyou Music

368   Daniel Gardner

My life is in you, Lord,
my strength is in you, Lord,
my hope is in you, Lord,
in you, it's in you.
(Repeat)

I will praise you with all of my life,
I will praise you with all of my strength,
with all of my life,
with all of my strength.
All of my hope is in you.

© 1986 Integrity's Hosanna! Music/Kingsway's Thankyou Music

369   Noel and Tricia Richards

My lips shall praise you, my great Redeemer;
my heart will worship, Almighty Saviour.

You take all my guilt away,
turn the darkest night to brightest day;
you are the restorer of my soul.

Love that conquers every fear,
in the midst of trouble you draw near;
you are the restorer of my soul.

You're the source of happiness,
bringing peace when I am in distress;
you are the restorer of my soul.

© 1991 Kingsway's Thankyou Music

370 Graham Kendrick

My Lord, what love is this,
that pays so dearly,
that I, the guilty one,
may go free!

Amazing love, O what sacrifice,
the Son of God, giv'n for me.
My debt he pays, and my death he dies,
that I might live,
that I might live.

And so they watched him die,
despised, rejected;
but O, the blood he shed
flowed for me!

And now this love of Christ
shall flow like rivers;
come, wash your guilt away,
live again!

© 1989 Make Way Music

371 Reuben Morgan

My spirit rests in you alone,
you're all I know.
Embrace and touch me
like a child,
I'm safe in you.

You're my shelter through it all,
you're my refuge and my strength,
Lord, I hide in the shadow of your wings.
(Repeat)

My Lord, you're faithful,
you supply all good things,
you know completely
all my thoughts,
my deepest needs.

© 1997 Reuben Morgan/Hillsongs Australia/Kingsway's Thankyou Music

372 Sarah Flower Adams

Nearer, my God, to thee,
nearer to thee!
And though it be
a cross that raises me:
still all my song would be,
'Nearer, my God, to thee.
Nearer, my God, to thee,
nearer to thee.'

Though, like the wanderer,
the sun gone down,
darkness be over me,
my rest a stone;
yet in my dreams I'd be
nearer, my God, to thee.
Nearer, my God, to thee,
nearer to thee!

There let the way appear,
steps unto heav'n;
all that thou sendest me
in mercy giv'n:
angels to beckon me
nearer, my God, to thee.
Nearer, my God, to thee,
nearer to thee!

Then, with my waking thoughts
bright with thy praise,
out of my stony griefs
Bethel I'll raise;
so by my woes to be
nearer, my God, to thee.
Nearer, my God, to thee,
nearer to thee.

Or if on joyful wing
cleaving the sky,
sun, moon and stars forgot,
upwards I fly,
still all my song shall be,
'Nearer, my God, to thee.
Nearer, my God, to thee,
nearer to thee.'

373 Andy Park

No one but you, Lord,
can satisfy the longing in my heart.
Nothing I do, Lord,
can take the place of drawing near to you.

Only you can fill my deepest longing,
only you can breathe in me new life;
only you can fill my heart with laughter,
only you can answer my heart's cry.

Father, I love you,
come satisfy the longing in my heart.
Fill me, overwhelm me,
until I know your love deep in my heart.

374 Robert Gay

No other name but the name of Jesus,
no other name but the name of the Lord;
no other name but the name of Jesus
is worthy of glory,
and worthy of honour,
and worthy of power and all praise.
(Repeat)

His name is exalted far above the earth.
His name is high above the heavens;
his name is exalted far above the earth;
give glory and honour and praise unto his name.

375 Graham Kendrick

No scenes of stately majesty
for the King of kings.
No nights aglow with candle flame
for the King of love.
No flags of empire hung in shame
for Calvary.
No flowers perfumed the lonely way
that led him to
a borrowed tomb for Easter Day.

No wreaths upon the ground were laid
for the King of kings.
Only a crown of thorns remained
where he gave his love.
A message scrawled in irony –
King of the Jews –
lay trampled where they turned away,
and no one knew
that it was the first Easter Day.

Yet nature's finest colours blaze
for the King of kings.
And stars in jewelled clusters say,
'Worship heaven's King.'
Two thousand springtimes more have bloomed –
is that enough?
Oh, how can I be satisfied
until he hears
the whole world sing of Easter love.

My prayers shall be a fragrance sweet
for the King of kings.
My love the flowers at his feet
for the King of love.
My vigil is to watch and pray
until he comes.
My highest tribute to obey
and live to know
the pow'r of that first Easter Day.

I long for scenes of majesty
for the risen King.
For nights aglow with candle flame
for the King of love.
A nation hushed upon its knees
at Calvary,
where all our sins and griefs were nailed
and hope was born
of everlasting Easter Day.

376 Robin Mark

No, not by might,
nor even power,
but by your Spirit, O Lord.
Healer of hearts, binder of wounds.

Lives that are lost, restored.
Flow through this land
till everyone praises your name
once more.

377 Noel and Tricia Richards

Nothing shall separate us
from the love of God.
Nothing shall separate us
from the love of God.

God did not spare his only Son,
gave him to save us all.
Sin's price was met by Jesus' death
and heaven's mercy falls.

Up from the grave Jesus was raised
to sit at God's right hand;
pleading our cause in heaven's courts,
forgiven we can stand.

Now by God's grace we have embraced
a life set free from sin;
we shall deny all that destroys
our union with him.

378 Joey Holder

Now unto the King eternal,
unto the King immortal,
unto the King invisible,
the only wise God,
the only wise God.
(Repeat)

Unto the King be glory and honour,
unto the King for ever.
Unto the King be glory and honour
for ever and ever, Amen. Amen.

379 Elizabeth Ann Porter Head

O Breath of Life, come sweeping through us,
revive your church with life and pow'r;
O Breath of Life, come cleanse, renew us,
and fit your church to meet this hour.

O Breath of Love, come breathe within us,
renewing thought and will and heart;
come, love of Christ, afresh to win us,
revive your church in every part!

O Wind of God, come bend us, break us,
till humbly we confess our need;
then, in your tenderness remake us,
revive, restore – for this we plead.

Revive us, Lord; is zeal abating
while harvest fields are vast and white?
Revive us, Lord, the world is waiting –
equip thy church to spread the light.

380 John Francis Wade, trans. Frederick Oakeley
and others

O come, all ye faithful,
joyful and triumphant,
O come ye, O come ye to Bethlehem;
come and behold him,
born the king of angels:

O come, let us adore him,
O come, let us adore him,
O come, let us adore him,
Christ the Lord.

God of God,
Light of Light,
lo, he abhors not the Virgin's womb;
very God,
begotten not created:

See how the shepherds,
summoned to his cradle,
leaving their flocks, draw nigh with lowly fear;
we too will thither
bend our joyful footsteps:

Continued overleaf

Lo, star-led chieftains,
Magi, Christ adoring,
offer him incense, gold and myrrh;
we to the Christ-child
bring our hearts' oblations:

O come, let us adore him,
O come, let us adore him,
O come, let us adore him,
Christ the Lord.

Sing, choirs of angels,
sing in exultation,
sing, all ye citizens of heav'n above;
glory to God
in the highest:

Yea, Lord, we greet thee,
born this happy morning,
Jesu, to thee be glory giv'n;
Word of the Father,
now in flesh appearing:

381 Graham Kendrick

O come and join the dance
that all began so long ago,
when Christ the Lord was born in Bethlehem.
Through all the years of darkness
still the dance goes on and on,
oh, take my hand and come and join the song.

Rejoice! (Rejoice!)
Rejoice! (Rejoice!)
O lift your voice and sing,
and open up your heart to welcome him.
Rejoice! (Rejoice!)
Rejoice! (Rejoice!)
and welcome now your King,
for Christ the Lord was born in Bethlehem.

Come, shed your heavy load
and dance your worries all away,
for Christ the Lord was born in Bethlehem.
He came to break the pow'r of sin
and turn your night to day,
oh, take my hand and come and join the song.

Let laughter ring and angels sing
and joy be all around,
for Christ the Lord was born in Bethlehem.
And if you seek with all your heart
he surely can be found,
oh, take my hand and come and join the song.

© Copyright 1988 Make Way Music

382 Graham Kendrick

O Father of the fatherless,
in whom all families are blessed,
I love the way you father me.
You gave me life, forgave the past,
now in your arms I'm safe at last;
I love the way you father me.

Father me,
for ever you'll father me,
and in your embrace
I'll be for ever secure;
I love the way you father me.
I love the way you father me.

When bruised and broken I draw near,
you hold me close and dry my tears;
I love the way you father me.
At last my fearful heart is still,
surrendered to your perfect will;
I love the way you father me.

If in my foolishness I stray,
returning empty and ashamed,
I love the way you father me.
Exchanging for my wretchedness
your radiant robes of righteousness,
I love the way you father me.

And when I look into your eyes,
from deep within my spirit cries,
I love the way you father me.
Before such love I stand amazed
and ever will through endless days;
I love the way you father me.

© 1992 Make Way Music

383 Charles Wesley

O for a thousand tongues to sing
my dear Redeemer's praise,
my dear Redeemer's praise,
the glories of my God and King,
the triumphs of his grace.

Jesus! the name that charms our fears,
that bids our sorrows cease,
that bids our sorrows cease;
'tis music in the sinner's ears,
'tis life and health and peace.

He breaks the pow'r of cancelled sin,
he sets the prisoner free,
he sets the prisoner free;
his blood can make the foulest clean;
his blood availed for me.

He speaks; and listening to his voice,
new life the dead receive,
new life the dead receive,
the mournful broken hearts rejoice,
the humble poor believe.

Hear him, ye deaf; his praise, ye dumb,
your loosened tongues employ,
your loosened tongues employ;
ye blind, behold your Saviour come;
and leap, ye lame, for joy!

My gracious Master and my God,
assist me to proclaim,
assist me to proclaim,
and spread through all the earth abroad
the honours of thy name.

384 Graham Kendrick

*O give thanks to the Lord,
for his love will never end.
O give thanks to the Lord,
for his love it never will end.*
(Repeat)

Sing to him, sing your praise to him.
Tell the world of all he has done.
Fill the nations with celebrations,
to welcome him as he comes.

Give him thanks for the fruitful earth,
for the sun, the seasons, the rain.
For the joys of his good creation,
the life and breath he sustains.

Let the heavens rejoice before him,
the earth and all it contains.
All creation in jubilation,
join in the shout, 'The Lord reigns!'

Let the hearts of those who seek him
be happy now in his love.
Let their faces look up and gaze
at his gracious smile from above.

385 Jamie Owens-Collins

O God, Most High, Almighty King,
the champion of heaven, Lord of everything;
you've fought, you've won, death's lost its
     sting,
and standing in your victory we sing.

*You have broken the chains
that held our captive souls.
You have broken the chains
and used them on your foes.
All your enemies are bound,
they tremble at the sound of your name;
Jesus, you have broken the chains.*

The pow'r of hell has been undone,
captivity held captive by the risen One,
and in the name of God's great Son,
we claim the mighty victory you've won.

(Last time)
*Jesus, you have broken the chains.
Jesus, you have broken the chains.*

386

William Booth

O God of burning, cleansing flame:
send the fire!
Your blood-bought gift today we claim:
send the fire today!
Look down and see this waiting host,
and send the promised Holy Ghost;
we need another Pentecost!
Send the fire today!
Send the fire today!

God of Elijah, hear our cry:
send the fire!
and make us fit to live or die:
send the fire today!
To burn up every trace of sin,
to bring the light and glory in,
the revolution now begin!
Send the fire today!
Send the fire today!

It's fire we want, for fire we plead:
send the fire!
The fire will meet our every need:
send the fire today!
For strength to always to do what's right,
for grace to conquer in the fight,
for pow'r to walk the world in white.
Send the fire today!
Send the fire today!

To make our weak heart strong and brave:
send the fire!
To live, a dying world to save:
send the fire today!
O, see us on your altar lay,
we give our lives to you today,
so crown the offering now we pray:
send the fire today!
Send the fire today!
Send the fire today!

© 1994 Kingsway's Thankyou Music

387

Philip Doddridge

O happy day! that fixed my choice
on thee, my Saviour and my God!
Well may this glowing heart rejoice,
and tell its raptures all abroad.

O happy day! O happy day!
when Jesus washed my sins away;
he taught me how to watch and pray,
and live rejoicing every day;
O happy day! O happy day!
when Jesus washed my sins away.

'Tis done, the work of grace is done!
I am the Lord's, and he is mine!
He drew me, and I followed on,
glad to confess the voice divine.

Now rest, my long-divided heart,
fixed on this blissful centre, rest;
nor ever from thy Lord depart,
with him of every good possessed.

High heav'n, that heard the solemn vow,
that vow renewed shall daily hear;
till in life's latest hour I bow,
and bless in death a bond so dear.

388

Graham Kendrick

O, heaven is in my heart.
O, heaven is in my heart.
(Repeat)

Leader	The kingdom of our God is here,
All	heaven is in my heart.
Leader	The presence of his majesty,
All	heaven is in my heart.
Leader	And in his presence joy abounds,
All	heaven is in my heart.
Leader	The light of holiness surrounds,
All	heaven is in my heart.

Leader	His precious life on me he spent,
All	heaven is in my heart.
Leader	To give me life without an end,
All	heaven is in my heart.
Leader	In Christ is all my confidence,
All	heaven is in my heart.
Leader	The hope of my inheritance,
All	heaven is in my heart.

Leader	We are a temple for his throne,
All	heaven is in my heart.
Leader	And Christ is the foundation stone,
All	heaven is in my heart.
Leader	He will return to take us home,
All	heaven is in my heart.
Leader	The Spirit and the Bride say, 'Come!',
All	heaven is in my heart.

389 Graham Kendrick

Oh, I was made for this,
to know your tender kiss,
to know a love divine,
to know this love is mine.
And I was made to laugh,
and I was made to sing,
given the gift of life,
you gave me everything.
(Repeat)

> *So I will celebrate*
> *and drink your cup of joy,*
> *I will give thanks each day and sing.*
> *My joy is found in you*
> *and you are all my joy.*
> *Oh, I was made for this.*

My feet were made to dance,
my spirit made to soar;
my life is not by chance,
you give me more and more.
For I was made for you,
and I have made my choice,
and all that stole my joy,
I left it at the cross.

When I was far away,
you ran to welcome me;
I felt your warm embrace,
I saw your smiling face.
And when you rescued me,
I saw my destiny:
to worship you, my Lord,
to be a friend of God.

I was made to love you, Jesus,
I was made for this.
I was made to love you, Jesus,
I was made for this.

390 Martin Smith

Oh, lead me
to the place where I can find you,
oh, lead me
to the place where you'll be.
Lead me to the cross
where we first met,
draw me to my knees
so we can talk;
let me feel your breath,
let me know you're here with me.

391 John Ernest Bode

O Jesus, I have promised
to serve thee to the end;
be thou for ever near me,
my Master and my friend:
I shall not fear the battle
if thou art by my side,
nor wander from the pathway
if thou wilt be my guide.

O let me feel thee near me:
the world is ever near;
I see the sights that dazzle,
the tempting sounds I hear;
my foes are ever near me,
around me and within;
but, Jesus, draw thou nearer,
and shield my soul from sin.

O let me hear thee speaking
in accents clear and still,
above the storms of passion,
the murmurs of self-will;
O speak to reassure me,
to hasten or control;
O speak and make me listen,
thou guardian of my soul.

Continued overleaf

O Jesus, thou hast promised
to all that follow thee,
that where thou art in glory
there shall thy servants be;
and, Jesus, I have promised
to serve thee to the end:
O give me grace to follow,
my Master and my friend.

O let me see thy footmarks,
and in them plant my own;
my hope to follow duly
is in thy strength alone:
O guide me, call me, draw me,
uphold me to the end;
and then in heav'n receive me,
my Saviour and my friend,
and then in heav'n receive me,
my Saviour and my friend.

392 John Wimber

O let the Son of God enfold you
with his Spirit and his love,
let him fill your heart and satisfy your soul.
O let him have the things that hold you,
and his Spirit like a dove
will descend upon your life and make you whole.

Jesus, O Jesus,
come and fill your lambs.
Jesus, O Jesus,
come and fill your lambs.

O come and sing this song with gladness
as your hearts are filled with joy,
lift your hands in sweet surrender to his name.
O give him all your tears and sadness,
give him all your years of pain,
and you'll enter into life in Jesus' name.

© 1979 Mercy/Vineyard Publishing/Music Services/CopyCare

393 Phillips Brooks

O little town of Bethlehem,
how still we see thee lie!
Above thy deep and dreamless sleep
the silent stars go by.

Yet in thy dark streets shineth
the everlasting light;
the hopes and fears of the all the years
are met in thee tonight.

O morning stars, together
proclaim the holy birth,
and praises sing to God the King,
and peace upon the earth.
For Christ is born of Mary;
and, gathered all above,
while mortals sleep, the angels keep
their watch of wondering love.

How silently, how silently,
the wondrous gift is giv'n!
So God imparts to human hearts
the blessings of his heav'n.
No ear may hear his coming;
but in this world of sin,
where meek souls will receive him, still
the dear Christ enters in.

O holy child of Bethlehem,
descend to us, we pray;
cast out our sin, and enter in,
be born in us today.
We hear the Christmas angels
the great glad tidings tell:
O come to us, abide with us,
our Lord Emmanuel.

394 Traditional

O Lord, hear my prayer,
O Lord, hear my prayer:
when I call, answer me.
O Lord, hear my prayer,
O Lord, hear my prayer.
Come and listen to me.

395 Ben Lindquist and Don Moen

O Lord, how majestic is your name,
O Lord, how majestic is your name,
you are high and lifted up
and your glory fills the temple,
you are high and lifted up
and we worship you.

You are high and lifted up
and your glory fills the temple.
We worship you in spirit and truth,
we worship you in spirit and truth.
(Repeat)

You are exalted on high,
you reign in wisdom,
in power and in might.

396   Karl Boberg trans. Stuart K. Hine

O Lord, my God, when I, in awesome wonder,
consider all the works thy hand has made,
I see the stars, I hear the rolling thunder,
thy pow'r throughout the universe displayed.

Then sings my soul, my Saviour God, to thee:
how great thou art, how great thou art.
Then sings my soul, my Saviour God, to thee:
how great thou art, how great thou art.

When through the woods and forest glades I
    wander,
and hear the birds sing sweetly in the trees;
when I look down from lofty mountain grandeur,
and hear the brook, and feel the gentle breeze.

And when I think that God, his Son not sparing,
sent him to die, I scarce can take it in
that on the cross, my burden gladly bearing,
he bled and died to take away my sin.

When Christ shall come with shout of
    acclamation,
and take me home, what joy shall fill my heart;
then I shall bow in humble adoration,
and there proclaim: my God, how great thou
    art.

397   Psalm 131

O Lord, my heart is not proud,
nor haughty my eyes.
I have not gone after things too great,
nor marvels beyond me.

Truly I have set my soul
in silence and peace;
at rest, as a child in its mother's arms,
so is my soul.

398   Philip Lawson Johnston

O Lord our God, how majestic is your name;
the earth is filled with your glory.
O Lord our God, you are robed in majesty;
you've set your glory above the heavens.

We will magnify, we will magnify
the Lord enthroned in Zion.
We will magnify, we will magnify
the Lord enthroned in Zion.

O Lord our God, you have established a throne,
you reign in righteousness and splendour.
O Lord our God, the skies are ringing with
    your praise;
soon those on earth will come to worship.

O Lord our God, the world was made at your
    command,
in you all things now hold together.
Now to him who sits on the throne and to the
    Lamb
be praise and glory and pow'r for ever.

399   Graham Kendrick

O Lord, the clouds are gathering,
the fire of judgement burns,
how we have fallen!
O Lord, you stand appalled
to see your laws of love so scorned
and lives so broken.

Have mercy, Lord (have mercy, Lord),
forgive us, Lord (forgive us, Lord),
restore us, Lord,
revive your church again.
Let justice flow (let justice flow)
like rivers (like rivers)
and righteousness like a never-failing stream.

Continued overleaf

O Lord, over the nations now,
where is the dove of peace?
Her wings are broken.
O Lord, while precious children starve,
the tools of war increase;
their bread is stolen.

Have mercy, Lord (have mercy, Lord),
forgive us, Lord (forgive us, Lord),
restore us, Lord,
revive your church again.
Let justice flow (let justice flow)
like rivers (like rivers)
and righteousness like a never-failing stream.

O Lord, dark pow'rs are poised to flood
our streets with hate and fear;
we must awaken!
O Lord, let love reclaim the lives
that sin would sweep away,
and let your kingdom come.

Yet, O Lord, your glorious cross shall tower
triumphant in this land,
evil confounding.
Through the fire your suffering church displays
the glories of her Christ:
praises resounding.

© 1987 Make Way Music

400 Geoff Bullock

O Lord, you lead me
by the still waters,
quietly restoring my soul.
You speak words of wisdom,
the promise of glory,
the pow'r of the presence of God.

Have faith in God,
let your hope rest
on the faith he has placed in your heart.
Never give up,
never let go
of the faith he has placed in your heart.

O Lord, you guide me
through all the darkness,
turning my night into day;
you'll never leave me,
never forsake me
the pow'r of the presence of God.

© 1993 Word Music Inc./CopyCare

401 Keith Green

O Lord, you're beautiful,
your face is all I seek,
for when your eyes are on this child,
your grace abounds to me.

O Lord, please light the fire
that once burned bright and clear,
replace the lamp of my first love
that burns with holy fear!

I wanna take your word
and shine it all around,
but first help me just to live it, Lord!
And when I'm doing well,
help me to never seek a crown,
for my reward is giving glory to you.

O Lord, you're beautiful,
your face is all I seek,
for when your eyes are on this child,
your grace abounds to me.

© Birdwing Music/BMG Songs Inc./Universal Songs/CopyCare

402 Graham Kendrick

O Lord, your tenderness,
melting all my bitterness,
O Lord, I receive your love.
O Lord, your loveliness,
changing all my ugliness,
O Lord, I receive your love.
O Lord, I receive your love,
O Lord, I receive your love.

© 1986 Kingsway's Thankyou Music

403 George Bennard

On a hill far away,
stood an old rugged cross,
the emblem of suffering and shame;
and I loved that old cross
where the dearest and best
for a world of lost sinners was slain.

So I'll cherish the old rugged cross,
till my trophies at last I lay down;
I will cling to the old rugged cross
and exchange it some day for a crown.

O, that old rugged cross,
so despised by the world,
has a wondrous attraction for me:
for the dear Lamb of God
left his glory above
to bear it to dark Calvary.

In the old rugged cross,
stained with blood so divine,
a wondrous beauty I see.
For 'twas on that old cross
Jesus suffered and died
to pardon and sanctify me.

To the old rugged cross
I will ever be true,
its shame and reproach gladly bear.
Then he'll call me some day
to my home far away;
there his glory for ever I'll share.

404 Cecil Frances Alexander (v. 4: Michael Forster)

Once in royal David's city
stood a lowly cattle shed,
where a mother laid her baby
in a manger for his bed:
Mary was that mother mild,
Jesus Christ her little child.

He came down to earth from heaven,
who is God and Lord of all,
and his shelter was a stable,
and his cradle was a stall;
with the poor and meek and lowly,
lived on earth our Saviour holy.

And through all his wondrous childhood
day by day like us he grew;
he was little, weak and helpless,
tears and smiles like us he knew;
and he feeleth for our sadness,
and he shareth in our gladness.

Still among the poor and lowly
hope in Christ is brought to birth,
with the promise of salvation
for the nations of the earth;
still in him our life is found
and our hope of heav'n is crowned.

And our eyes at last shall see him
through his own redeeming love,
for that child so dear and gentle
is our Lord in heav'n above;
and he leads his children on
to the place where he is gone.

Not in that poor lowly stable,
with the oxen standing by,
we shall see him, but in heaven,
set at God's right hand on high;
when like stars his children crowned,
all in white shall wait around.

405 David Hadden

One heart, one voice, one mind.
One in Spirit, and one in love.
This will be the hope that we long for,
this will be the covenant we live,
one heart, one voice, one mind.

Heirs of God, and children of the kingdom.
Living proof that he's alive.
We're reconciled, sinners now forgiven.
One in heart, and one in voice and mind.

406 Graham Kendrick

One shall tell another,
and he shall tell his friend,
husbands, wives and children
shall come following on.
From house to house in families
shall more be gathered in,
and lights will shine in every street,
so warm and welcoming.

Come on in and taste the new wine,
the wine of the kingdom,
the wine of the kingdom of God.
Here is healing and forgiveness,
the wine of the kingdom,
the wine of the kingdom of God.

Compassion of the Father
is ready now to flow,
through acts of love and mercy
we must let it show.
He turns now from his anger
to show a smiling face,
and longs that all should stand beneath
the fountain of his grace.

He longs to do much more than
our faith has yet allowed,
to thrill us and surprise us
with his sovereign power.
Where darkness has been darkest
the brightest light will shine;
his invitation comes to us,
it's yours and it is mine.

407 Andy Park

One thing I ask, one thing I seek,
that I may dwell in your house, O Lord.
All of my days, all of my life,
that I may see you, Lord.

Hear me, O Lord, hear me when I cry;
Lord, do not hide your face from me.
You have been my strength,
you have been my shield,
and you will lift me up.

One thing I ask, one thing I desire,
is to see you, is to see you.

408 Gerrit Gustafson

Only by grace can we enter,
only by grace can we stand;
not by our human endeavour,
but by the blood of the Lamb.
Into your presence you call us,
you call us to come.
Into your presence you draw us,
and now by your grace we come,
now by your grace we come.

Lord, if you mark our transgressions,
who would stand?
Thanks to your grace we are cleansed
by the blood of the Lamb.
(Repeat)

409 Wes Sutton

On this day we now come
to stand before the Father,
enveloped in his love.
Humbly now offering all
to live for the glory of God.

It is so good to know,
Lord, you are faithful,
you love without end.
We pledge our heart and soul
to live for the glory of God.

On this day we now come
to kneel before the Saviour,
Jesus Christ the Lord.
With his word in our hearts
we will live for the glory of God.

On this day we now come
walking in the Spirit –
the holy fire of God.
Anointed with the living flame
we will live for the glory of God.

410 Graham Kendrick

On this day of happiness,
we have gathered here to bless
the union of two lives in holy love.
Love's blossoming is now expressed
in solemn vows and promises,
with flowers and golden rings, a wedding dress.
We look around with joy to see
the smiles of friends and family
as witness to this day.
But, best of all, a friend unseen
is here with us, and once again,
water turns to wine.

On this, their wedding day,
we ask you, Lord, to stay,
and by your Spirit join these hearts together.
And from this moment on,
teach them your lover's song,
that all the world may hear
a three-part harmony,
a three-part harmony.

Oh, may this song of love ring clear
though health or sickness, joy or tears,
for as long as both of them shall live.
May they harmonise with heaven above,
stay tuned into the key of love,
keep their eyes on Jesus day by day.
And may the music of their days
become a symphony of praise
in honour of their Lord.
And may the song become a dance
to celebrate the great romance
of Jesus and his bride.

© 1991 Make Way Music

411 Ian White

Open the doors of praise.
Open the doors of praise.
Open the doors of praise
and let the Lord come in.

In the spirit world
there's a battle going on,
and it rages endlessly.

But in the name of the Lord,
we can stand on his word,
for in him we have the victory.
Leader   For he lives in the praises of his
people.
All   For he lives in the praises of his
people.
Here among us to empow'r us!

And the demons will flee,
as he said it would be,
and the skies will ring
with shouts of praise.
And the Lord Jesus Christ
will be lifted high,
the Holy One who truly saves!
Leader   For he lives in the praises of his
people.
All   For he lives in the praises of his
people.
Here among us to empow'r us!

© 1997 Little Misty Music/Kingsway's Thankyou Music

412 Unknown

O the blood of Jesus,
O the blood of Jesus,
O the blood of Jesus,
it washes white as snow.

413 Colin Owen

O the blood of my Saviour,
O the blood of the Lamb,
O the blood of God's only Son
has paid the price for my sin.

It's the blood, it's the blood,
the blood that my Lord shed for me.
It's the blood, it's the blood,
the blood of my Lord set me free.

O the blood shed at Calvary,
O the blood spilled for me,
O the blood of God's only Son,
Jesus, your blood set me free.

Continued overleaf

O the blood from the nail prints,
O the blood from the thorns,
O the blood from the spear in his side
has given me life evermore.

It's the blood, it's the blood,
the blood that my Lord shed for me.
It's the blood, it's the blood,
the blood of my Lord set me free.

414 Samuel Trevor Francis

O the deep, deep love of Jesus!
Vast, unmeasured, boundless, free;
rolling as a mighty ocean
in its fullness over me.
Underneath me, all around me,
is the current of thy love;
leading onward, leading homeward,
to my glorious rest above.

O the deep, deep love of Jesus!
Spread his praise from shore to shore,
how he loveth, ever loveth,
changeth never, nevermore;
how he watches o'er his loved ones,
died to call them all his own;
how for them he intercedeth,
watcheth o'er them from the throne.

O the deep, deep love of Jesus!
Love of every love the best;
'tis an ocean vast of blessing,
'tis a haven sweet of rest.
O the deep, deep love of Jesus!
'Tis a heav'n of heav'ns to me;
and it lifts me up to glory,
for its lifts me up to thee.

415 Steven Fry

O the glory of your presence,
we, your temple, give you reverence.
So arise to your rest
and be blessed by our praise
as we glory in your embrace,
as your presence now fills this place.

416 Charles Wesley

O thou who camest from above
the pure celestial fire to impart,
kindle a flame of sacred love
on the mean altar of my heart.

There let it for thy glory burn
with inextinguishable blaze,
and trembling to its source return
in humble prayer and fervent praise.

Jesus, confirm my heart's desire
to work and speak and think for thee;
still let me guard the holy fire
and still stir up thy gift in me.

Ready for all thy perfect will,
my acts of faith and love repeat,
till death thy endless mercies seal,
and make the sacrifice complete.

417 Noel and Tricia Richards

Our confidence is in the Lord,
the source of our salvation.
Rest is found in him alone,
the Author of creation.
We will not fear the evil day,
because we have a refuge;
in every circumstance we say,
our hope is built on Jesus.

He is our fortress,
we will never be shaken.
He is our fortress,
we will never be shaken.
He is our fortress,
we will never be shaken.
He is our fortress,
we will never be shaken.
We will put our trust in God.
We will put our trust in God.

418 Rich Mullins

Our God is an awesome God,
he reigns from heaven above
with wisdom, pow'r and love.
Our God is an awesome God.
(Repeat)

419 Noel and Tricia Richards

Our God is awesome in power,
scatters his enemies;
our God is mighty in bringing
the powerful to their knees.
He has put on his armour,
he is prepared for war;
mercy and justice triumph
when the Lion of Judah roars.

> *The Lord is a warrior,*
> *we will march with him.*
> *The Lord is a warrior,*
> *leading us to win.*
> (Repeat)

Waken the warrior spirit,
army of God, arise;
challenge the powers of darkness,
there must be no compromise.
We shall attack their strongholds,
our hands are trained for war;
we shall advance the kingdom,
for the victory belongs to God.

420 Unknown

Our God is so great,
so strong and so mighty,
there's nothing that he cannot do.
(Repeat)

The rivers are his,
the mountains are his,
the stars are his handiwork too.

Our God is so great,
so strong and so mighty,
there's nothing that he cannot do.

421 Martin Smith

Over the mountains and the sea
your river runs with love for me,
and I will open up my heart
and let the Healer set me free.
I'm happy to be in the truth,
and I will daily lift my hands,
for I will always sing of
when your love came down.

> *I could sing of your love for ever,*
> *I could sing of your love for ever,*
> *I could sing of your love for ever,*
> *I could sing of your love for ever.*

O, I feel like dancing,
it's foolishness, I know;
but when the world has seen the light,
they will dance with joy
like we're dancing now.

422 Noel Richards

Overwhelmed by love,
deeper than oceans,
high as the heavens.
Ever-living God,
your love has rescued me.

All my sin was laid
on your dear Son,
your precious One.
All my debt he paid,
great is your love for me.

> *No one could ever earn your love,*
> *your grace and mercy is free.*
> *Lord, these words are true,*
> *so is my love for you.*

423 Steven Fry

O, we are more than conquerors,
O, we are more than conquerors,
and who can separate us from the love,
the love of God?
O yes, we are,
we are more than conquerors,
O, we are more than conquerors.

For he has promised to fulfil his will in us,
he said that he would guide us with his eye;
for he has blessed us with all gifts in Christ
and we are his delight.

For he's within to finish what's begun in me,
he opens doors that no one can deny,
he makes a way where there's no other way
and gives me wings to fly.

424 Graham Kendrick

O, what a morning, O, how glorious,
O, what a light has broken through!
Out of the tomb of death and dark despair,
angels in white announce incredible news.

Christ is risen!
He's alive, alleluia!
Yes, he's risen,
he's alive, alleluia!

Suddenly hope has filled our darkest night,
suddenly life has blossomed here;
suddenly joy has rushed like rivers,
he is alive and love has conquered our fear.

425 Robert Grant

O worship the King
all glorious above;
O gratefully sing
his pow'r and his love:

our shield and defender,
the Ancient of Days,
pavilioned in splendour,
and girded with praise.

O tell of his might,
O sing of his grace,
whose robe is the light,
whose canopy space;
his chariots of wrath
the deep thunder-clouds form,
and dark is his path
on the wings of the storm.

This earth with its store
of wonders untold,
almighty, thy pow'r
hath founded of old:
hath stablished it fast
by a changeless decree,
and round it hath cast,
like a mantle, the sea.

Thy bountiful care
what tongue can recite?
It breathes in the air,
it shines with the light;
it streams from the hills,
it descends to the plain,
and sweetly distils
in the dew and the rain.

Frail children of dust,
and feeble as frail,
in thee do we trust,
nor find thee to fail;
thy mercies how tender,
how firm to the end!
Our maker, defender,
redeemer, and friend.

O measureless might,
ineffable love,
while angels delight
to hymn thee above,
thy humbler creation,
though feeble their lays,
with true adoration
shall sing to thy praise.

426 John Samuel Bewley Monsell

O worship the Lord
in the beauty of holiness;
bow down before him,
his glory proclaim;
with gold of obedience,
and incense of lowliness,
kneel and adore him:
the Lord is his name.

Low at his feet lay
thy burden of carefulness:
high on his heart
he will bear it for thee,
comfort thy sorrows,
and answer thy prayerfulness,
guiding thy steps
as may best for thee be.

Fear not to enter
his courts in the slenderness
of the poor wealth
thou wouldst reckon as thine:
truth in its beauty,
and love in its tenderness,
these are the offerings
to lay on his shrine.

These, though we bring them
in trembling and fearfulness,
he will accept
for the name that is dear;
mornings of joy give
for evenings of tearfulness,
trust for our trembling
and hope for our fear.

O worship the Lord
in the beauty of holiness;
bow down before him,
his glory proclaim;
with gold of obedience,
and incense of lowliness,
kneel and adore him:
the Lord is his name.

427 Graham Kendrick

Peace be to these streets,
peace be to these streets,
Peace be to these streets
in the name of Jesus.

Walk here, Lord,
draw near, Lord,
pass through these streets today.
Bring healing, forgiveness;
here let your living waters flow.

Peace be to these streets . . .

Love come to these streets . . .

Joy come to these streets . . .

© 1996 Make Way Music

428 Graham Kendrick

Peace I give to you,
I give to you my peace.
Peace I give to you,
I give to you my peace.

Let it flow to one another,
let it flow, let it flow.
Let it flow to one another,
let it flow, let it flow.

Love I give to you . . .

Hope I give to you . . .

Joy I give to you . . .

Grace I give to you . . .

Pow'r I give to you . . .

© 1979 Kingsway's Thankyou Music

429 John Watson

Peace like a river,
love like a mountain,
the wind of your Spirit
is blowing everywhere.
Joy like a fountain,
healing spring of life;
come, Holy Spirit,
let your fire fall.

© 1989 Ampelos Music/CopyCare

430 Kevin Mayhew

Peace, perfect peace,
is the gift of Christ our Lord.
Peace, perfect peace,
is the gift of Christ our Lord.
Thus, says the Lord,
will the world know my friends.
Peace, perfect peace,
is the gift of Christ our Lord.

Love, perfect love . . .

Faith, perfect faith . . .

Hope, perfect hope . . .

Joy, perfect joy . . .

© 1976 Kevin Mayhew Ltd

431 Graham Kendrick

Peace to you.
We bless you now
in the name of the Lord.
Peace to you.
We bless you now
in the name of the Prince of Peace.
Peace to you.

© 1988 Make Way Music

432 Andy Piercy and Dave Clifton

Praise God, from whom all blessings flow,
praise him, all creatures here below.
Praise him above, you heav'nly host,
praise Father, Son and Holy Ghost.
(Repeat)

Give glory to the Father,
give glory to the Son,
give glory to the Spirit
while endless ages run.
'Worthy the Lamb,' all heaven cries,
'to be exalted thus.'
'Worthy the Lamb,' our hearts reply,
'for he was slain for us.'

Praise God, from whom all blessings flow.
Praise God, from whom all blessings flow.
Praise God, from whom all blessings flow.
Praise God, from whom all blessings flow.

© 1993 IQ Music Ltd

433 Henry Francis Lyte

Praise, my soul, the King of heaven!
To his feet thy tribute bring;
ransomed, healed, restored, forgiven,
who like me his praise should sing?
Praise him! Praise him!
Praise him! Praise him!
Praise the everlasting King!

Praise him for his grace and favour
to our fathers in distress;
praise him still the same as ever,
slow to chide and swift to bless.
Praise him! Praise him!
Praise him! Praise him!
Glorious in his faithfulness.

Father-like, he tends and spares us;
well our feeble frame he knows;
in his hands he gently bears us,
rescues us from all our foes.
Praise him! Praise him!
Praise him! Praise him!
Widely as his mercy flows.

Angels, help us to adore him;
ye behold him face to face;
sun and moon, bow down before him,
dwellers all in time and space.
Praise him! Praise him!
Praise him! Praise him!
Praise with us the God of grace!

434 Jeannie Hall and Carol Owen

Praise the Lord, O my soul,
praise his holy name.
Praise the Lord, O my soul,
praise his holy name.

All of my inmost being,
praise his holy name . . .

Forget not all his benefits,
praise his holy name . . .

He forgives me all my sins,
praise his holy name . . .

He heals all my diseases,
praise his holy name . . .

He redeems my life from the pit,
praise his holy name . . .

He crowns me with love and compassion,
praise his holy name . . .

He satisfies your desires with good things,
praise his holy name . . .

So my youth is renewed like the eagles',
praise his holy name . . .

© 1991 Kingsway's Thankyou Music

435   Roy Hicks

Praise the name of Jesus,
praise the name of Jesus,
he's my rock, he's my fortress,
he's my deliverer, in him will I trust.
Praise the name of Jesus.

© 1976 Latter Rain Music/CopyCare

436   Brian Doerksen

Purify my heart,
let me be as gold and precious silver.
Purify my heart,
let me be as gold, pure gold.

Refiner's fire,
my heart's one desire
is to be holy,
set apart for you, Lord.
I choose to be holy,
set apart for you, my master,
ready to do your will.

Purify my heart,
cleanse me from within and make me holy.
Purify my heart,
cleanse me from my sin, deep within.

© 1990 Mercy/Vineyard Publishing/Music Services/CopyCare

437   Chris Bowater

Reign in me, Sovereign Lord,
reign in me.
Reign in me, Sovereign Lord,
reign in me.

Captivate my heart,
let your kingdom come,
establish there your throne,
let your will be done.

© 1985 Sovereign Lifestyle Music

438   Graham Kendrick

Rejoice! Rejoice! Christ is in you,
the hope of glory in our hearts.
He lives! He lives! His breath is in you,
arise a mighty army, we arise.

Now is the time for us
to march upon the land,
into our hands
he will give the ground we claim.
He rides in majesty
to lead us into victory,
the world shall see that Christ is Lord!

God is at work in us
his purpose to perform,
building a kingdom
of power not of words,
where things impossible
by faith shall be made possible;
let's give the glory to him now.

Though we are weak, his grace
is everything we need;
we're made of clay
but this treasure is within.
He turns our weaknesses
into his opportunities,
so that the glory goes to him.

© 1983 Kingsway's Thankyou Music

439

Graham Kendrick and Chris Rolinson

Restore, O Lord,
the honour of your name,
in works of sovereign power
come shake the earth again,
that all may see,
and come with reverent fear
to the living God,
whose kingdom shall outlast the years.

Restore, O Lord,
in all the earth your fame,
and in our time revive
the church that bears your name.
And in your anger,
Lord, remember mercy,
O living God,
whose mercy shall outlast the years.

Bend us, O Lord,
where we are hard and cold,
in your refiner's fire:
come purify the gold.
Though suffering comes
and evil crouches near,
still our living God
is reigning, he is reigning here.

440

Helena Barrington

Righteousness, peace, joy in the Holy Ghost,
righteousness, peace, and joy in the Holy
    Ghost:
    that's the kingdom of God.
    (Repeat)

Don't you want to be a part of the kingdom,
don't you want to be a part of the kingdom,
don't you want to be a part of the kingdom?
Come on, everybody.
(Repeat)

There's love in the kingdom,
so much love in the kingdom;
there's love in the kingdom.
Come on, everybody!

There's peace in the kingdom . . .

There's joy in the kingdom . . .

I'm an heir of the kingdom,
I'm an heir of the kingdom,
I'm an heir of the kingdom.
Come on, everybody!

441

Dougie Brown

River, wash over me,
cleanse me and make me new.
Bathe me, refresh me and fill me anew.
River, wash over me.

Spirit, watch over me,
lead me to Jesus' feet.
Cause me to worship and fill me anew.
Spirit, watch over me.

Jesus, rule over me,
reign over all my heart.
Teach me to praise you and fill me anew.
Jesus, rule over me.

442

David Fellingham

Ruach, Ruach,
holy wind of God, blow on me.
Touch the fading embers,
breathe on me.
Fan into a flame
all that you've placed in me.
Let the fire burn more pow'rfully.
Ruach, Ruach,
holy wind of God,
holy wind of God, breathe on me.

443 Adrian Howard and Pat Turner

Salvation belongs to our God,
who sits on the throne,
and to the Lamb.
Praise and glory, wisdom and thanks,
honour and power and strength.

Be to our God for ever and ever,
be to our God for ever and ever,
be to our God for ever and ever. Amen.

And we, the redeemed, shall be strong
in purpose and unity,
declaring aloud,
praise and glory, wisdom and thanks,
honour and power and strength.

444 Graham Kendrick

Save the people, save the people now. (x4)
Lord, have mercy. Christ, have mercy.
Father, hear our prayer: save the people now.

Save the children, save the children now. (x4)
Lord, have mercy. Christ, have mercy.
Father, hear our prayer: save the children now.

Send your Spirit, send your Spirit now. (x4)
Lord, have mercy. Christ, have mercy.
Father, hear our prayer: send your Spirit now.

Send revival, send revival now. (x4)
Lord, have mercy. Christ, have mercy.
Father, hear our prayer: send revival now.

445 Stuart Townend

Say the word, I will be healed;
you are the great Physician,
you meet every need.
Say the word, I will be free;
where chains have held me captive,
come, sing your songs to me,
say the word.

Say the word, I will be filled;
my hands reach out to heaven,
where striving is stilled.
Say the word, I will be changed;
where I am dry and thirsty,
send cool, refreshing rain,
say the word.

His tears have fallen like rain on my life,
each drop a fresh revelation.
I will return to the place of the cross,
where grace and mercy pour from heaven's
    throne.

Say the word, I will be poor,
that I might know the riches
that you have in store.
Say the word, I will be weak;
your strength will be the power
that satisfies the meek,
say the word.

The Lord will see the travail of his soul,
and he and I will be satisfied.
Complete the work you have started in me:
O come, Lord Jesus, shake my life again.

446 Chris Bowater

See his glory, see his glory,
see his glory now appear.
See his glory, see his glory,
see his glory now appear.
God of light, holiness and truth,
pow'r and might,
see his glory, see it now appear.

Now we declare our God is good,
and his mercies endure for ever.
Now we declare our God is good,
and his mercies endure for ever.

447 Karen Lafferty

Seek ye first the kingdom of God
and his righteousness,
and all these things shall be added unto you,
hallelu, hallelujah!

Hallelujah! hallelujah!
Hallelujah! Hallelu, hallelujah!

You shall not live by bread alone,
but by every word
that proceeds from the mouth of God,
hallelu, hallelujah!

Ask and it shall be given unto you,
seek and you shall find.
Knock, and it shall be opened unto you,
hallelu, hallelujah.

If the Son shall set you free,
you shall be free indeed.
You shall know the truth and the truth shall
    set you free,
hallelu, hallelujah!

Let your light so shine before men
that they may see your good works
and glorify your Father in heaven,
hallelu, hallelujah!

Trust in the Lord with all your heart,
he shall direct your paths,
in all your ways acknowledge him,
hallelu, hallelujah!

© 1972 Maranatha! Music/CopyCare

448 Graham Kendrick

See, your Saviour comes;
see, your Saviour comes.

Desolate cities, desolate homes,
desolate lives on the streets,
angry and restless. When will you know
the things that would make for your peace?

Father of mercy, hear as we cry
for all who live in this place;
show here your glory, come satisfy
your longing that all should be saved.

Where lives are broken, let there be hope,
where there's division bring peace;
where there's oppression, judge and reprove,
and rescue the crushed and the weak.

Lord, let your glory dwell in this land,
in mercy restore us again:
pour out salvation, grant us your peace,
and strengthen the things that remain.

© 1996 Make Way Music

449 Dave Bilbrough

Shout for joy and sing,
let your praises ring;
see that God is building a kingdom for a King.
His dwelling-place with men,
the new Jerusalem;
where Jesus is Lord over all.

And we will worship, worship,
we will worship Jesus the Lord.
We will worship, worship,
we will worship Jesus the Lord.

A work so long concealed,
in time will be revealed,
as the sons of God shall rise and take their
    stand.
Clothed in his righteousness,
the church made manifest,
where Jesus is Lord over all.

Sovereign over all,
hail him risen Lord.
He alone is worthy of our praise.
Reigning in majesty,
ruling in victory,
Jesus is Lord over all.

© 1983 Kingsway's Thankyou Music

450 David Fellingham

Shout for joy and sing your praises to the King,
lift your voice and let your hallelujahs ring;
come before his throne to worship and adore,
enter joyfully now the presence of the Lord.

You are my Creator, you are my Deliverer,
you are my Redeemer, you are Lord,
and you are my Healer.
You are my Provider,
you are now my Shepherd, and my Guide,
Jesus, Lord and King, I worship you.

451 Dave Bell

Shout, shout for joy,
shout, shout for joy,
for the Lord has given you the victory.
Shout, shout for joy,
shout, shout for joy,
for the Lord has given you the victory.

No weapon formed against you shall prosper.
No kingdom raised against you shall stand.
For the Lord is the rock of our salvation,
and we have overcome by the blood of the
  Lamb.

452 Graham Kendrick

Shout! The Lord is risen!
His work on earth is done.
Shout! We are forgiven!
This is the day of his power,
(woa-oh) his power.

Shout together in the day of his power.
Sing together in the day of his power.
Walk together in the day of his power.
Serve together in the day of his power.
Pray together in the day of his power.

Work together in the day of his power.
Come together in the day of his power.
This is the day of his power,
(woa-oh) his power, (woa-oh) his power.
Shout!

Shout! He has ascended,
he reigns at God's right hand.
Shout! Till death is ended.
This is the day of his power,
(woa-oh) his power.

Shout! With fire from heaven,
he sends his Spirit down.
Shout! And gifts were given.
This is the day of his power,
(woa-oh) his power.

Shout! Proclaim the kingdom!
Announce the Jubilee.
Shout! The year of freedom!
This is the day of his power,
(woa-oh) his power.

Shout! A new generation
rises across this land.
Shout! A new demonstration.
This is the day of his power,
(woa-oh) his power.

Go! Tell every nation.
Our hearts are willing now.
Go! He is our passion.
This is the day of his power,
(woa-oh) his power.

Come! O come, Lord Jesus.
We cry, O Lord, how long?
Come! And end injustice.
This is the day of his power,
(woa-oh) his power.

Come! If you are thirsty,
while living waters flow.
Come! And taste his mercy.
This is the day of his power,
(woa-oh) his power.

Continued overleaf

Shout! In expectation
the whole creation yearns.
Shout! For liberation.
This is the day of his power,
(woa-oh) his power.

Shout together in the day of his power.
Sing together in the day of his power.
Walk together in the day of his power.
Serve together in the day of his power.
Pray together in the day of his power.
Work together in the day of his power.
Come together in the day of his power.
This is the day of his power,
(woa-oh) his power, (woa-oh) his power.
Shout!

453   Collette Dallas and Deborah Page

Shout unto God with a voice of triumph,
sing and proclaim his mighty name.
Shout unto God with a voice of triumph,
sing and proclaim that our God reigns.
(Repeat)

He is Lord over all the nation,
he is Lord over all the earth.
With high praises we shall sing
all the honour to the King.
With a two-edged sword in our hand
we are marching on to take the land.

He is Lord over all the nation,
he is Lord over all the earth.
We shall go out in one accord,
in the power of God's Word.
We proclaim liberty,
in Christ Jesus the victory.

454   Graham Kendrick

Show your pow'r, O Lord,
demonstrate the justice of your kingdom.
Prove your mighty word,
vindicate your name
before a watching world.
Awesome are your deeds, O Lord;
renew them for this hour.
Show your pow'r, O Lord,
among the people now.

Show your pow'r, O Lord,
cause your church to rise and take action.
Let all fear be gone,
powers of the age to come
are breaking through.
We your people are ready to serve,
to arise and to obey.
Show you pow'r, O Lord,
and set the people free.

(Last time)
Show your pow'r, O Lord,
and set the people –
show your pow'r, O Lord,
and set the people –
show your pow'r, O Lord,
and set the people free.

455   Joseph Mohr trans. John Freeman Young

Silent night, holy night.
All is calm, all is bright,
round yon virgin mother and child;
holy infant, so tender and mild,
sleep in heavenly peace,
sleep in heavenly peace.

Silent night, holy night.
Shepherds quake at the sight,
glories stream from heaven afar,
heav'nly hosts sing alleluia:
Christ the Saviour is born,
Christ the Saviour is born.

Silent night, holy night.
Son of God, love's pure light,
radiant beams from thy holy face,
with the dawn of redeeming grace:
Jesus, Lord, at thy birth,
Jesus, Lord, at thy birth.

456 Pamela Hayes

Silent, surrendered, calm and still,
open to the word of God.
Heart humbled to his will,
offered is the servant of God.

Come, Holy Spirit, calm and still,
teach us, heal us, give us life.
Come, Lord, O let our hearts
flow with love and all that is true.

© Sister Pamela Hayes RSCJ

457 David Ruis

Sing a song of celebration,
lift up a shout of praise,
for the Bridegroom will come,
the glorious One.
And O, we will look on his face;
we'll go to a much better place.

Dance with all your might,
lift up your hands and clap for joy:
the time's drawing near
when he will appear.
And O, we will stand by his side;
a strong, pure, spotless bride.

> O, we will dance on the streets that are
>   golden,
> the glorious bride and the great Son of man,
> from every tongue and tribe and nation
> will join in the song of the Lamb.

Sing aloud for the time of rejoicing is near
(sing aloud for the time of rejoicing is near).
The risen King, our Groom, is soon to appear
(the risen King, our Groom, is soon to appear).

The wedding feast to come is now near at
   hand
(the wedding feast to come is now near at
   hand).
Lift up your voice, proclaim the coming Lamb
(lift up your voice, proclaim the coming Lamb).

© 1993 Mercy/Vineyard Publishing/Music Services/CopyCare

458 Taizé Community

Sing, praise and bless the Lord.
Sing, praise and bless the Lord,
peoples! nations!
Alleluia!

© 1982 Ateliers et Presses de Taizé

459 Graham Kendrick

Soften my heart, Lord,
soften my heart.
From all indifference set me apart.
To feel your compassion,
to weep with your tears,
come soften my heart, O Lord,
soften my heart.

© 1988 Make Way Music

460 Andraé Crouch

Soon and very soon
we are going to see the King,
soon and very soon
we are going to see the King,
soon and very soon
we are going to see the King,
hallelujah, hallelujah,
we're going to see the King.

No more crying there,
we are going to see the King . . .

No more dying there,
we are going to see the King . . .

© 1978 Bud John Songs/Crouch Music/Universal Songs/CopyCare

461 Dave Bilbrough

Sound the trumpet, strike the drum,
see the King of glory come,
join the praises rising from the people
   of the Lord.
Let your voices now be heard,
unrestrained and unreserved,
prepare a way for his return,
   you people of the Lord.
Sing Jesus is Lord, Jesus is Lord.
Bow down to his authority,
for he has slain the enemy.
Of heav'n and hell he holds the key.
Jesus is Lord, Jesus is Lord.

© 1991 Kingsway's Thankyou Music

462 Daniel Iverson

Spirit of the living God,
fall afresh on me.
Spirit of the living God,
fall afresh on me.
Melt me, mould me,
fill me, use me,
Spirit of the living God,
fall afresh on me.

© 1963 Birdwing Music/Universal Songs/CopyCare

463 Paul Armstrong

Spirit of the living God,
fall afresh on me.
Spirit of the living God,
fall afresh on me.
Fill me anew,
fill me anew.
Spirit of the Lord,
fall afresh on me.

© 1984 Restoration Music/Sovereign Music UK

464 David Hadden

Streams of worship
and rivers of praise,
ascending to the One who is
the Ancient of Days:
to him who is worthy,
to him who was slain,
to him who sits upon the throne
and to the Lamb:

Thousands upon thousands
encircle the throne,
singing a new song
to the One who is to come:
to him who is worthy,
to him who was slain,
to him who sits upon the throne
and to the Lamb:

   You are worthy,
   you are holy –
   the Lord who was,
   the Lord who is,
   the Lord who is to come;
   you are mighty,
   you are awesome,
   be praise and honour and glory
   for evermore.

Streams of worship
and rivers of praise
flowing from the lips of those
who never cease to be amazed
with him who is worthy,
with him who was slain,
with him who sits upon the throne
and with the Lamb:

© 1994 Restoration Music/Sovereign Music UK

465 Graham Kendrick

Such love, pure as the whitest snow;
such love weeps for the shame I know;
such love, paying the debt I owe;
O Jesus, such love.

Such love, stilling my restlessness;
such love, filling my emptiness;
such love, showing me holiness;
O Jesus, such love.

Such love springs from eternity;
such love, streaming through history;
such love, fountain of life to me;
O Jesus, such love.

466 David and Liz Morris

*Surely our God is the God of gods
and the Lord of kings,
a revealer of mysteries.
Surely our God is the God of gods
and the Lord of kings,
a revealer of mysteries.*

He changes the times and the seasons,
he gives rhythm to the tides;
he knows what is hidden in the darkest
    of places,
brings the shadows into his light.

I will praise you always, my Father,
you are Lord of heaven and earth,
you hide your secrets from the wise and
    the learnèd
and reveal them to this your child.

Thank you for sending your only Son,
we may know the myst'ry of God;
he opens the treasures of wisdom and
    knowledge
to the humble, not to the proud.

467 Dave Browning

Take me past the outer courts,
and through the holy place,
past the brazen altar, Lord,
I want to see your face.

Pass me by the crowds of people,
and the priests who sing their praise;
I hunger and thirst for your righteousness,
but it's only found one place.

*So take me in to the Holy of holies,
take me in by the blood of the Lamb;
so take me in to the Holy of holies,
take the coal, cleanse my lips, here I am.*

468 Frances Ridley Havergal

Take my life, and let it be
consecrated, Lord, to thee;
take my moments and my days,
let them flow in ceaseless praise.

Take my hands, and let them move
at the impulse of thy love;
take my feet, and let them be
swift and beautiful for thee.

Take my voice, and let me sing
always, only, for my King;
take my lips, and let them be
filled with messages from thee.

Take my silver and my gold;
not a mite would I withhold;
take my intellect, and use
every pow'r as thou shalt choose.

Take my will, and make it thine:
it shall be no longer mine;
take my heart: it is thine own;
it shall be thy royal throne.

Take my love; my Lord, I pour
at thy feet its treasure-store;
take myself, and I will be
ever, only, all for thee.

468a Frances Ridley Havergal

Take my life, and let it be
consecrated, Lord, to thee;
take my hands, and let them move
at the impulse of thy love,
at the impulse of thy love.

Continued overleaf

Take my feet, and let them be
swift and beautiful for thee.
Take my voice, and let me sing
always, only, for my King,
always, only, for my King.

Take my lips, and let them be
filled with messages from thee.
Take my silver and my gold,
not a mite would I withhold,
not a mite would I withhold.

Take my love; my God I pour
at thy feet its treasure-store.
Take myself, and I will be
ever, only, all for thee,
ever, only, all for thee.

Take my life, and let it be
consecrated, Lord, to thee.
Take myself, and I will be
ever, only, all for thee,
ever, only, all for thee.

469 Graham Kendrick and Steve Thompson

*Teach me to dance
to the beat of your heart,
teach me to move
in the pow'r of your Spirit,
teach me to walk
in the light of your presence,
teach me to dance
to the beat of your heart.
Teach me to love
with your heart of compassion,
teach me to trust
in the word of your promise,
teach me to hope
in the day of your coming,
teach me to dance
to the beat of your heart.*

You wrote the rhythm of life,
created heaven and earth,
in you is joy without measure.

So, like a child in your sight,
I dance to see your delight,
for I was made for your pleasure,
pleasure.

Let all my movements express
a heart that loves to say 'yes',
a will that leaps to obey you.
Let all my energy blaze
to see the joy in your face;
let my whole being praise you,
praise you.

470 Eugene Greco

Teach me your ways,
O Lord, my God,
and I will walk in your truth.
Give me a totally undivided heart
that I may fear your name.

*Purify my heart,
cleanse me, Lord, I pray,
remove from me all
that is standing in the way.
Purify my heart,
cleanse me, Lord, I pray,
remove from me all
that is standing in the way
of your love.*

471 Timothy Dudley-Smith

Tell out, my soul,
the greatness of the Lord:
unnumbered blessings
give my spirit voice;
tender to me
the promise of his word;
in God my Saviour
shall my heart rejoice.

Tell out, my soul,
the greatness of his name:
make known his might,
the deeds his arm has done;
his mercy sure,
from age to age the same;
his holy name:
the Lord, the Mighty One.

Tell out, my soul,
the greatness of his might:
pow'rs and dominions
lay their glory by;
proud hearts and stubborn wills
are put to flight,
the hungry fed,
the humble lifted high.

Tell out, my soul,
the glories of his word:
firm is his promise,
and his mercy sure.
Tell out, my soul,
the greatness of the Lord
to children's children
and for evermore.

© Copyright Timothy Dudley-Smith

472 Martin Smith

Thank you for saving me;
what can I say?
You are my everything,
I will sing your praise.
You shed your blood for me;
what can I say?
You took my sin and shame,
a sinner called by name.

Great is the Lord.
Great is the Lord.
For we know your truth has set us free;
you've set your hope in me.

Mercy and grace are mine,
forgiv'n is my sin;
Jesus, my only hope,
the Saviour of the world.

'Great is the Lord,' we cry;
God, let your kingdom come.
Your word has let me see,
thank you for saving me.

© 1993 Curious? Music UK/Kingsway's Thankyou Music

473 Graham Kendrick

Thank you for the cross,
the price you paid for us,
how you gave yourself so completely,
precious Lord (precious Lord).
Now our sins are gone,
all forgiven,
covered by your blood,
all forgotten,
thank you, Lord (thank you, Lord).

O I love you, Lord,
really love you, Lord.
I will never understand
why you love me.
You're my deepest joy,
you're my heart's delight,
and the greatest thing of all, O Lord, I see:
you delight in me.

For our healing there,
Lord, you suffered,
and to take our fear
you poured out your love,
precious Lord (precious Lord).
Calvary's work is done,
you have conquered,
able now to save
so completely,
thank you, Lord (thank you, Lord).

© 1985 Kingsway's Thankyou Music

474 Don Moen

Thank you for your mercy,
thank you for your grace;
thank you for your blood
that's made a way
to come into your presence
and glorify your name.
Lord, I stand amazed at what I see.

Continued overleaf

Great is your mercy toward me,
your loving kindness toward me,
your tender mercies I see
day after day.
For ever faithful to me,
always providing for me,
great is your mercy toward me
great is your grace.

Your promises are ageless,
your love will never end,
for a thousand generations
your covenant will stand;
showing grace and mercy
to those who fear your name,
establishing your righteousness and praise.

475 Unknown

Thank you, Jesus, thank you, Jesus,
thank you, Lord, for loving me.
Thank you, Jesus, thank you, Jesus,
thank you, Lord, for loving me.

You went to Calvary,
and there you died for me.
Thank you, Lord, for loving me.
(Repeat)

You rose up from the grave,
to me new life you gave,
thank you, Lord, for loving me.
(Repeat)

You're coming back again,
and we with you shall reign.
Thank you, Lord, for loving me.
(Repeat)

476 Matt Redman

The angels, Lord, they sing around your throne;
and we will join their song: praise you alone.
(Repeat)

Holy, holy, holy, Lord our God,
who was and is and is to come.
Holy, holy, holy, Lord our God,
who was and is and is to come.

(Last time)
Amen. Amen.

The living creatures, Lord, speak endless praise;
and joining at your throne, we'll sing their sweet
    refrain.
(Repeat)

The elders, Lord, they fall before your throne;
our hearts we humbly bow to you alone.
(Repeat)

477 Samuel John Stone

The church's one foundation
is Jesus Christ, her Lord;
she is his new creation,
by water and the word;
from heav'n he came and sought her
to be his holy bride,
with his own blood he bought her,
and for her life he died.

Elect from every nation,
yet one o'er all the earth,
her charter of salvation,
one Lord, one faith, one birth;
one holy name she blesses,
partakes one holy food,
and to one hope she presses,
with every grace endued.

'Mid toil and tribulation,
and tumult of her war,
she waits the consummation
of peace for evermore;
till with the vision glorious
her longing eyes are blest,
and the great church victorious
shall be the church at rest.

Yet she on earth hath union
with God the Three in One,
and mystic sweet communion
with those whose rest is won:
O happy ones and holy!
Lord, give us grace that we
like them, the meek and lowly,
on high may dwell with thee.

478 Matt Redman and Martin Smith

The cross has said it all,
the cross has said it all.
I can't deny what you have shown,
the cross speaks of a God of love;
there displayed for all to see,
Jesus Christ, our only hope,
a message of the Father's heart,
'Come, my children, come on home.'

As high as the heavens are above the earth,
so high is the measure of your great love,
as far as the east is from the west,
so far have you taken our sins from us.
(Repeat)

The cross has said it all,
the cross has said it all.
I never recognised your touch,
until I met you at the cross.
We are fallen, dust to dust,
how could you do this for us?
Son of God shed precious blood,
who can comprehend this love?

How high, how wide, how deep.
How high, how wide, how deep.
How high, how wide, how deep.
How high, how wide, how deep.
How high!

© 1995 Kingsway's Thankyou Music

479 Martin Smith

The crucible for silver
and the furnace for gold,
but the Lord tests the heart of this child.

Standing in all purity, God,
our passion is for holiness,
lead us to the secret place of praise.

Jesus, Holy One, you are my heart's desire.
King of kings, my everything,
you've set this heart on fire.
(Repeat)

Father, take our offering,
with our song we humbly praise you.
You have brought your holy fire to our lips.
Standing in your beauty, Lord,
your gift to us is holiness;
lead us to the place where we can sing:

© 1993 Kingsway's Thankyou Music

480 Geoff Bullock

The heavens shall declare
the glory of his name,
all creation bows
at the coming of the King.
Every eye shall see,
every heart will know,
every knee shall bow,
every tongue confess:
Holy, holy, holy is the Lord.
See the coming of the King,
holy is the Lord.

© 1990 Word Music Inc./CopyCare

481 Graham Kendrick

Men	The Lord is a mighty King,
Women	the Maker of everything.
Men	The Lord, he made the earth,
Women	he spoke and it came at once to birth.
Men	He said, 'Let us make mankind',
Women	the crown of his design,
Men	'in our own likeness',
Women	his image in every human face.

Continued overleaf

And he made us for his delight,
gave us the gift of life,
created us family to be his glory,
to be his glory.

Men	And yet we were deceived,
Women	in pride the lie believed,
Men	to sin and death's decay –
Women	the whole creation fell that day.
Men	Now all creation
Women	yearns for liberation;
Men	all things in Christ restored –
Women	the purchase of his precious blood.

Shout:
For by him
all things were created.
Things in heaven
and on earth.
Visible and invisible.
Whether thrones
or powers
or rulers
or authorities;
all things were created by him,
and for him.

482 Graham Kendrick

The Lord is marching out in splendour,
in awesome majesty he rides,
for truth, humility and justice,
his mighty army fills the skies.

>*O give thanks to the Lord*
>*for his love endures,*
>*O give thanks to the Lord*
>*for his love endures,*
>*O give thanks to the Lord*
>*for his love endures*
>*for ever, for ever.*

His army marches out with dancing
for he has filled our hearts with joy.
Be glad the kingdom is advancing,
the love of God, our battle cry!

483 Colin Owen

The Lord is moving across this land,
it's time to rise up and take our stand
behind the banner of Jesus Christ
and claim the victory that's ours by right;
we're in God's army,
we're in God's army.

The Spirit's leading us out to war,
but we're not the same as we were before,
we are anointed to multiply;
the Lord has called us and that is why
we're in God's army,
we're in God's army.

>*We are marching out to take the land,*
>*strongholds fall beneath our feet.*
>*Satan, we proclaim your time's at hand;*
>*we're marching on to victory.*

The Devil's shakin', his time has come,
the powers of darkness are on the run;
we're standing firm by faith in our authority,
defeating all our foes and bringing liberty;
we're in God's army,
we're in God's army.

484 Carol Owen

The Lord is our strength,
the Lord is our song,
with joy we draw
from the wells of salvation today.
(Repeat)

>*So let's sing to the Lord,*
>*he's done glorious things,*
>*let's shout aloud and dance for joy*
>*for great is the Holy One.*
>*So let's sing to the Lord,*
>*he's done glorious things,*
>*let's rejoice in our God*
>*for the things he has done.*

We give thanks to you, Lord,
and call on your name;
we proclaim that your name is exalted on high.
(Repeat)

So we sing to you, Lord,
you've done glorious things,
we shout aloud and dance for joy,
for great is the Holy One.
So we sing to you, Lord,
you've done glorious things,
we rejoice in our God
for the things you have done.

485 Dan C. Stradwick

The Lord reigns, the Lord reigns,
the Lord reigns,
let the earth rejoice, let the earth rejoice,
let the earth rejoice,
let the people be glad that our God reigns.
(Repeat)

A fire goes before him
and burns up all his enemies;
the hills melt like wax at the presence of the
    Lord,
at the presence of the Lord.

The heav'ns declare his righteousness,
the peoples see his glory;
for you, O Lord, are exalted over all the earth,
over all the earth.

486 The Scottish Psalter

The Lord's my shepherd, I'll not want.
He makes me down to lie
in pastures green. He leadeth me
the quiet waters by.

My soul he doth restore again,
and me to walk doth make
within the paths of righteousness,
e'en for his own name's sake.

Yea, though I walk in death's dark vale,
yet will I fear none ill.
For thou art with me, and thy rod
and staff me comfort still.

My table thou hast furnishèd
in presence of my foes:
my head thou dost with oil anoint,
and my cup overflows.

Goodness and mercy all my life
shall surely follow me.
And in God's house for evermore
my dwelling-place shall be.

487 Graham Kendrick

The price is paid,
come, let us enter in
to all that Jesus died
to make our own.
For every sin
more than enough he gave,
and bought our freedom
from each guilty stain.

The price is paid,
alleluia,
amazing grace,
so strong and sure,
and so with all my heart,
my life in every part,
I live to thank you
for the price you paid.

The price is paid,
see Satan flee away;
for Jesus crucified
destroys his pow'r.
No more to pay,
let accusation cease,
in Christ there is
no condemnation now.

The price is paid
and by that scourging cruel
he took our sicknesses
as if his own.
And by his wounds
his body broken there,
his healing touch may now
by faith be known.

Continued overleaf

The price is paid,
'Worthy the Lamb!' we cry,
eternity shall never
cease his praise.
The church of Christ
shall rule upon the earth,
in Jesus' name
we have authority.

The price is paid,
alleluia,
amazing grace,
so strong and sure,
and so with all my heart,
my life in every part,
I live to thank you
for the price you paid.

488 Richard Hubbard

The promise of the Holy Spirit
is for you.
The promise of the Holy Spirit
is for your children.
The promise of the Holy Spirit
is for all who are far off,
even as many as the Lord your God shall call.
O yeah!
Acts, chapter two, verse thirty-nine.

489 Unknown

Therefore we lift our hearts in praise,
sing to the living God who saves,
for grace poured out for you and me.

There for everyone to see,
there on the hill at Calvary,
Jesus died for you and me.

For our sad and broken race,
he arose with life and grace,
and reigns on high for you and me.

There for such great pain and cost
the Spirit came at Pentecost
and comes in pow'r for you and me.

Therefore we lift our hearts in praise,
sing to the living God who saves,
for grace poured out for you and me.

490 Matt Redman

There is a louder shout to come,
there is a sweeter song to hear;
all the nations with one voice,
all the people with one fear.
Bowing down before your throne,
every tribe and tongue will be;
all the nations with one voice,
all the people with one King.
And what a song we'll sing upon that day!

O what a song we'll sing
and O what a tune we'll bear;
you deserve an anthem of the highest praise.
O what a joy will rise
and O what a sound we'll make;
you deserve an anthem of the highest praise.

Now we see a part of this,
one day we shall see in full;
all the nations with one voice,
all the people with one love.
No one else will share your praise,
nothing else can take your place;
all the nations with one voice,
all the people with one Lord.
And what a song we'll sing upon that day!

Even now upon the earth
there's a glimpse of all to come;
many people with one voice,
harmony of many tongues.
We will all confess your name,
you will be our only praise;
all the nations with one voice,
all the people with one God.
And what a song we'll sing upon that day!

491 David Ruis

There is a place of commanded blessing
where brethren in unity dwell,
a place where anointing oil is flowing,
where we live as one.

You have called us to be a body,
you have called us as friends,
joined together in the bond of the Spirit,
unto the end.

Father, we join with the prayer of Jesus;
as you are, so let us be one,
joined together in unity and purpose,
all for the love of your Son.

We will break dividing walls,
we will break dividing walls,
we will break dividing walls
in the name of your Son.
We will break dividing walls,
we will break dividing walls
and we will be one.
(Repeat)

© 1994 Mercy/Vineyard Publishing/Music Services/CopyCare

492 Melody Green

There is a Redeemer,
Jesus, God's own Son,
precious Lamb of God, Messiah,
Holy One.

Thank you, O my Father,
for giving us your Son,
and leaving your Spirit
till the work on earth is done.

Jesus, my Redeemer,
Name above all names,
precious Lamb of God, Messiah,
O for sinners slain.

When I stand in glory,
I will see his face.
And there I'll serve my King for ever,
in that Holy Place.

© 1982 Birdwing Music/Ears to Hear Music/BMG Songs Inc./CopyCare

493 Lenny LeBlanc

There is none like you,
no one else can touch my heart like you do.
I could search for all eternity long
and find there is none like you.
(Repeat)

Your mercy flows like a river wide,
and healing comes from your hands.
Suffering children are safe in your arms;
there is none like you.

© 1991 Integrity's Hosanna! Music/Kingsway's Thankyou Music

494 Morris Chapman and Claire Cloninger

There is only one Lord that we cling to,
there is only one truth that we claim;
there is only one way that we walk in,
there is only power in one name.

And in the strong name of Jesus,
by the blood of the Lamb,
we are able to triumph,
we are able to stand.
In the power of his Spirit,
by the strength of his hand,
in the strong name of Jesus,
by the precious blood of the Lamb.

Though apart from him we can do nothing,
by his Spirit we can do all things;
covered by his blood we are made righteous,
lifting up the name of Christ, our King!

© 1991 Word Music Inc./CopyCare

495 Noel Richards

There is pow'r in the name of Jesus;
we believe in his name.
We have called on the name of Jesus;
we are saved! We are saved!
At his name the demons flee.
At his name captives are freed,
for there is no other name that is higher
than Jesus!

Continued overleaf

There is pow'r in the name of Jesus,
like a sword in our hands.
We declare in the name of Jesus
we shall stand! We shall stand!
At his name God's enemies
shall be crushed beneath our feet,
for there is no other name that is higher
than Jesus!

496 J. B. Vaughn

There's a blessed time that's coming, coming
    soon,
it may be evening, morning or at noon.
There'll be a wedding of the Bride,
united with the Groom.
We shall see the King when he comes.

We shall see the King,
we shall see the King,
we shall see the King when he comes.
He is coming in pow'r,
he'll hail the blessed hour.
We shall see the King when he comes.

Are you ready should the Saviour call today?
Would Jesus say, 'Well done' or 'Go away'?
He's building a home for the pure,
the vile can never stay.
We shall see the King when he comes.

O my brother, are you ready for the call?
We'll crown our Saviour King and Lord of all.
All the kingdoms of this world
shall soon before him fall.
We shall see the King when he comes.

497 Richard Lewis

There's an awesome sound
    on the winds of heaven,
mighty thunder-clouds in the skies above.
The immortal King who will reign for ever
is reaching out with his arms of love,
his arms of love, his arms of love.

All creation sings of the Lamb of glory
who laid down his life for all the world.
What amazing love, that the King of heaven
should be crucified, stretching out his arms,
his arms of love, his arms of love.

Send revival to this land,
fill this nation with your love.
Send revival to this land,
fill this nation with your love.

498 Paul Oakley

There's a place where the streets shine
with the glory of the Lamb.
There's a way, we can go there,
we can live there beyond time.

Because of you, because of you,
because of your love,
because of your blood.

No more pain, no more sadness,
no more suffering, no more tears.
No more sin, no more sickness,
no injustice, no more death.

Because of you . . .

All our sins are washed away,
and we can live for ever,
now we have this hope,
because of you.
O, we'll see you face to face,
and we will dance together
in the city of our God,
because of you.

There is joy everlasting,
there is gladness, there is peace.
There is wine everflowing,
there's a wedding, there's a feast.

Because of you . . .

All our sins are washed away . . .

499

Taran Ash, James Mott and Matthew Pryce

There's a river of joy
that flows from your throne,
O river of joy, flow through me.
There's a river of joy
that flows from your throne,
come, Holy Spirit, with joy,
come, Holy Spirit, with joy.
(Repeat)

I will rise up on the wings of an eagle;
with joy I receive your love.
I will praise you with a song everlasting.
Thank you, Lord, for your love,
thank you, Lord, for your love.

500

Matt Redman and Paul Donnelly

There's a sound of singing in our midst,
there's an offering of praise.
We set our hearts towards you, Lord,
with our lips our songs we raise.
There is jubilation in the camp
for your promises are true,
and by your grace salvation comes
to bring us home to you.

We rejoice in you,
give our lives to you.
We rejoice in you
and we testify
that this love is true
with the sound of singing.

With our lives we humbly bow to you,
and standing in this place
our songs express our hearts' desire
to serve you all our days.
We will honour you and magnify
your name above all names,
for we know there is no other God,
yes, you are the King of kings.

Our hearts are filled with gladness
and a sacrifice of praise,
for you have done great things for us.

So glad that you have called us
and what else can we say,
you've saved us by your grace.

501

David Ruis

There's a wind a-blowing
all across the land;
fragrant breeze of heaven
blowing once again.
Don't know where it comes from,
don't know where it goes,
but let it blow over me.
O, sweet wind,
come and blow over me.

There's a rain a-pouring
showers from above;
mercy drops are coming,
mercy drops of love.
Turn your face to heaven,
let the water pour,
well, let it pour over me.
O, sweet rain,
come and pour over me.

There's a fire burning,
falling from the sky;
awesome tongues of fire,
consuming you and I.
Can you feel it burning,
burn the sacrifice?
Well, let it burn over me.
O, sweet fire,
come and burn over me.

502

Eddie Espinosa

There's no one like you, my Lord,
no one could take your place;
my heart beats to worship you,
I live just to seek your face.
There's no one like you, my Lord,
no one could take your place;
there's no one like you, my Lord,
no one like you.

Continued overleaf

You are my God.
You're everything to me,
there's no one like you, my Lord,
no one like you.
(Repeat)

There's no one like you, my Lord,
no one could take your place;
I long for your presence, Lord,
to serve you is my reward.
There's no one like you, my Lord,
no one could take your place;
there's no one like you, my Lord,
no one like you.

© 1990 Mercy/Vineyard Publishing/Music Services/CopyCare

503 Robin Mark

These are the days of Elijah,
declaring the word of the Lord;
and these are the days of your servant, Moses,
righteousness being restored.
And though these are days of great trial,
of famine and darkness and sword,
still we are the voice in the desert crying,
'Prepare ye the way of the Lord.'

Behold, he comes riding on the clouds,
shining like the sun at the trumpet call;
lift your voice, it's the year of jubilee,
out of Zion's hill salvation comes.

These are the days of Ezekiel,
the dry bones becoming as flesh;
and these are the days of your servant, David,
rebuilding a temple of praise.
These are the days of the harvest,
the fields are as white in the world,
and we are the labourers in your vineyard,
declaring the word of the Lord.

© 1996 Daybreak Music

504 Andy Park

The Spirit of the sovereign Lord is upon you
because he has anointed you
to preach good news;

the Spirit of the sovereign Lord is upon you
because he has anointed you
to preach good news.

He has sent you to the poor
(this is the year),
to bind up the broken-hearted
(this is the day);
to bring freedom to the captives
(this is the year),
and to release the ones in darkness.

This is the year
of the favour of the Lord,
this is the day
of the vengeance of our God;
this is the year,
of the favour of the Lord,
this is the day
of the vengeance of our God.

The Spirit of the sovereign Lord is upon us
because he has anointed us
to preach good news;
the Spirit of the sovereign Lord is upon us
because he has anointed us
to preach good news.

He will comfort all who mourn
(this is the year),
he will provide for those who grieve in Zion
(this is the day);
he will pour out the oil of gladness
(this is the year),
instead of mourning we will praise.

This is the year . . .

© 1994 Mercy/Vineyard Publishing/Music Services/CopyCare

505 Edith McNeil

The steadfast love of the Lord never ceases,
his mercies never come to an end.
They are new every morning,
new every morning;
great is thy faithfulness, O Lord,
great is thy faithfulness.

© 1974 Celebration/Kingsway's Thankyou Music

506 Graham Kendrick

The trumpets sound, the angels sing,
the feast is ready to begin;
the gates of heav'n are open wide,
and Jesus welcomes you inside.

Tables are laden with good things,
O taste the peace and joy he brings;
he'll fill you up with love divine,
he'll turn your water into wine.

Sing with thankfulness songs of pure delight,
come and revel in heaven's love and light;
take your place at the table of the King,
the feast is ready to begin,
the feast is ready to begin.

The hungry heart he satisfies,
offers the poor his paradise;
now hear all heav'n and earth applaud
the amazing goodness of the Lord.

Leader Jesus,
All Jesus,
Leader we thank you,
All we thank you,
Leader for your love,
All for your love,
Leader for your joy,
All for your joy.
Leader Jesus,
All Jesus,
Leader we thank you,
All we thank you,
Leader for the good things,
All for the good things,
Leader you give to us,
All you give to us.

© 1989 Make Way Music

507 Wes Sutton

The Word made flesh, full of truth and grace,
the light of men, God incarnate came.
He lived, he loved, a servant, humble, meek,
and in his voice we hear the Father speak.

We await a Saviour from heaven,
and he will surely come,
in his glory and with the angels
and the power of this throne.
The Christ from heaven returning,
his promise to fulfil
before the splendour of his presence,
let the earth be still.

Such hate, such scorn, and a traitor's kiss
led to the cross for such a world as this.
The death he died, the grave in which he laid
could not hold him; to life again he came.

Now death destroyed, the grave left open wide,
our Saviour reigns at the Father's side.
Where death your sting, where your power,
 O grave?
The Son of God prepares to come again.

© 1997 Sovereign Lifestyle Music

508 Noel and Tricia Richards

The world is looking for a hero;
we know the greatest one of all:
the mighty ruler of the nations,
King of kings and Lord of lords,
who took the nature of a servant,
and gave his life to save us all.

We will raise a shout,
we will shout it out,
he is the Champion of the world.
(Repeat)

The Lord Almighty is our hero,
he breaks the stranglehold of sin.
Through Jesus' love we fear no evil;
pow'rs of darkness flee from him.
His light will shine in every nation,
a sword of justice he will bring.

© 1994 Kingsway's Thankyou Music

509 Kevin Prosch

They that wait on the Lord
will renew their strength.
Run and not grow weary,
walk and not faint.
(Repeat)

Do you not know, have you not heard?
My Father does not grow weary.
He'll give passion to a willing heart.
Even the youths get tired and faint,
but strength will come for those who wait.

I will wait, I will wait,
I will wait on you.
I will run, I will run,
I will run with you.
My love, my love,
my love for you.

510 Edmond Louis Budry trans. Richard Birch Hoyle

Thine be the glory,
risen, conquering Son,
endless is the victory
thou o'er death hast won;
angels in bright raiment
rolled the stone away,
kept the folded grave-clothes
where thy body lay.

Thine be the glory,
risen, conquering Son,
endless is the victory
thou o'er death hast won.

Lo! Jesus meets us,
risen from the tomb;
lovingly he greets us,
scatters fear and gloom.
Let the church with gladness
hymns of triumph sing,
for her Lord now liveth;
death hast lost its sting.

No more we doubt thee,
glorious Prince of Life;
life is naught without thee:
aid us in our strife.
Make us more than conquerors
through thy deathless love;
bring us safe through Jordan
to thy home above.

511 Graham Kendrick

This Child, secretly comes in the night,
O this Child, hiding a heavenly light,
O this Child, coming to us like a stranger,
this heavenly Child.

This Child, heaven come down now
to be with us here,
heavenly love and mercy appear,
softly in awe and wonder come near –
to this heavenly Child.

This Child, rising on us like the sun,
O this Child, given to light everyone,
O this Child, guiding our feet on the pathway
to peace on earth.

This Child, raising the humble and poor,
O this Child, making the proud ones to fall;
O this child, filling the hungry with good things,
this heavenly Child.

512 Geoff Bullock

This grace is mine,
this glory, earth-bound heaven sent
this plan divine,
this life, this light that breaks my night,
the Spirit of God
heaven falls like a dove to my heart.

This love is mine,
so undeserved, this glorious name,
this Son, this God,
this life, this death, this victory won,
forgiveness has flowed and
this grace that is mine finds my heart.

The power and the glory of your name.
The power and the glory of your name.
The power and the glory of your name,
the name of the Lord, the Son of God.

This life is mine,
so perfect and so pure, this God in me,
this glorious hope
from earth to heaven, death to life,
this future assured and secured
by this love in my heart.

© 1994 Word Music Inc./CopyCare

513 Gary Sadler and Lynn DeShazo

This, in essence, is the message
we heard from Christ.
This, in essence, is the message
we heard from Christ
and are passing on to you.
God is light, God is light,
pure light, pure light.
God is light, pure light.
There's not a trace of darkness in him.

© 1997 Integrity's Hosanna! Music/Kingsway's Thankyou Music

514 Graham Kendrick

This is my beloved Son
who tasted death
that you, my child, might live.
See the blood he shed for you,
what suffering,
say what more could he give?
Clothed in his perfection
bring praise, a fragrant sweet,
garlanded with joy,
come worship at his feet.

That the Lamb who was slain
might receive the reward,
might receive the reward
of his suffering.

Look, the world's great harvest fields
are ready now
and Christ commands us: 'Go!'
Countless souls are dying
so hopelessly,
his wondrous love unknown.
Lord, give us the nations
for the glory of the King.
Father, send more labourers
the lost to gather in.

Come the day when we will stand
there face to face,
what joy will fill his eyes.
For at last his bride appears
so beautiful,
her glory fills the skies.
Drawn from every nation,
people, tribe and tongue;
all creation sings,
the wedding has begun.

© 1985 Kingsway's Thankyou Music

515 Reuben Morgan

This is my desire, to honour you.
Lord, with all my heart,
I worship you.
All I have within me I give you praise.
All that I adore is in you.

Lord, I give you my heart,
I give you my soul;
I live for you alone.
Every breath that I take,
every moment I'm awake,
Lord, have your way in me.

© 1995 Reuben Morgan/Hillsongs Australia/Kingsway's Thankyou Music

516 Bob Fitts

This is the day that the Lord has made;
I will rejoice and celebrate.
This is the day that the Lord has made;
I will rejoice, I will rejoice and celebrate.
(Repeat)

He goes before me (he goes before me),
he walks beside me (he walks beside me),
he lives within me,
he's the lover of my soul.
He's my defender (he's my defender),
he's my provider (he's my provider),
his overflowing mercies
are brand new every day.

517 Les Garrett

This is the day,
this is the day that the Lord has made,
that the Lord has made;
we shall rejoice,
we shall rejoice and be glad in it,
and be glad in it.
This is the day that the Lord has made,
we shall rejoice and be glad in it;
this is the day,
this is the day that the Lord has made.

518 Martin Smith

This is the message of the cross,
that we can be free,
to live in the victory
and turn from our sin.
My precious Lord Jesus,
with sinners you died,
for there you revealed your love
and you laid down your life.

This is the message of the cross,
that we can be free,
to lay all our burdens here,
at the foot of the tree.
The cross was the shame of the world,
but the glory of God,
for Jesus you conquered sin
and you gave us new life.

You set me free
when I came to the cross,
poured out your blood
for I was broken and lost.
There I was healed
and you covered my sin.
It's there you saved me.
This is the message of the cross.

This is the message of the cross,
that we can be free,
to hunger for heaven,
to hunger for thee.
The cross is such foolishness
to the perishing,
but to us who are being saved,
it is the power of God.

You set us free
when we come to the cross,
you pour out your blood
for we are broken and lost.
Here we are healed
and you cover our sin.
It's here you save us.
You set me free
when I come to the cross,
pour out your blood
for I am broken and lost.
Here I am healed
and you cover my sin.
It's here you save me.
This is the message of the cross.

Let us rejoice at the foot of the cross;
we can be free, glory to God.
Let us rejoice at the foot of the cross;
we can be free, Glory to God.

Thank you, Lord, thank you, Lord,
you've set us free, glory to God.
Thank you, Lord, thank you, Lord,
you've set us free, glory to God.

519 Philip Lawson Johnston and Chris Bowater

This is the mystery,
that Christ has chosen you and me,
to be the revelation of his glory;
a chosen, royal, holy people
set apart and loved,
a bride preparing for her King.

Let the Bride say, 'Come',
let the Bride say, 'Come',
let the Bride of the Lamb say,
'Come, Lord Jesus!'
Let the Bride say, 'Come',
let the Bride say, 'Come',
let the Bride of the Lamb say,
'Come, Lord Jesus, come!'

She's crowned in splendour
and a royal diadem,
the King is enthralled by her beauty.
Adorned in righteousness,
arrayed in glorious light,
the Bride is waiting for her King.

Now hear the Bridegroom call,
'Beloved, come aside;
the time of betrothal is at hand.
Lift up your eyes and see
the dawning of the day,
when as King, I'll return to claim my Bride.'

520 Andy Piercy and Dave Clifton

This is the sweetest mystery
that you, O Lord, are One in Three;
majestic, glorious Trinity
of Father, Spirit, Son.

The heav'nly Father, great 'I Am',
the Son of God, the Son of Man,
and yet within this wondrous plan
the Spirit with us here.

Lord, may this truth become a flame
that burns within our hearts again,
that we may glorify your name
in all we do and say.
And so, dear Lord, we gladly come
to stand before the Three in One,
and worship Father, Spirit, Son;
accept the praise we bring.

521 Geoff Bullock

This love, this hope,
this peace of God, this righteousness,
this faith, this joy,
this life, complete in me.
Now healed and whole
and risen in his righteousness;
I live in him, he lives in me.
And filled with this hope in God,
reflecting his glory.

Now is the time to worship you,
now is the time to offer you
all of my thoughts, my dreams and plans;
I lay it down.
Now is the time to live for you,
now is the time I'm found in you,
now is the time your kingdom comes.

522 Ian White

Though I feel afraid
of territory unknown,
I know that I can say
that I do not stand alone.
For Jesus, you have promised
your presence in my heart;
I cannot see the ending,
but it's here that I must start.

Continued overleaf

And all I know is you have called me,
and that I will follow is all I can say.
I will go where you will send me,
and your fire lights my way.

What lies across the waves
may cause my heart to fear;
will I survive the day,
must I leave what's known and dear?
A ship that's in the harbour
is still and safe from harm,
but it was not built to be there,
it was made for wind and storm.

523 Mark Altrogge

Though the earth should tremble
and the oceans roar
and the mountains slip into the sea,
I shall not fear any harm
with your powerful arms around me.

I worship you, eternal God,
I worship you, the unchanging One.
Before the angels ever sang one song,
before the morning stars had ever shone,
you were on the throne, eternal God.

Though earth's kingdoms crumble
and the nations rage
and rulers and kings come and go,
yours is the kingdom unshaken,
and you've never forsaken your own.

524 Noel Richards

To be in your presence,
to sit at your feet,
where your love surrounds me,
and makes me complete.

This is my desire,
O Lord, this is my desire.
This is my desire,
O Lord, this is my desire.

To rest in your presence,
not rushing away,
to cherish each moment,
here would I stay.

525 Bob Fitts

To every good thing God is doing
within me that I cannot see, amen.
And to the healing virtue of Jesus
that's flowing in me, amen.
For every hope that is still just a dream,
by trusting in you, Lord, becomes reality.
I stake my claim, seal it in faith,
I say amen.

Amen (amen), amen (amen).
So be it, Lord, your word endures, I say 'amen'.
Amen (amen), amen (amen).
So be it, Lord, amen.
So be it, Lord, amen.

526 Frances Jane van Alstyne

To God be the glory!
great things he hath done;
so loved he the world
that he gave us his Son;
who yielded his life
an atonement for sin,
and opened the life-gate
that all may go in.

Praise the Lord, praise the Lord!
let the earth hear his voice;
praise the Lord, praise the Lord!
let the people rejoice:
O come to the Father,
through Jesus the Son,
and give him the glory;
great things he hath done.

O perfect redemption,
the purchase of blood!
to every believer
the promise of God;

the vilest offender
who truly believes
that moment from Jesus
a pardon receives.

Great things he hath taught us,
great things he hath done,
and great our rejoicing
through Jesus the Son;
but purer, and higher,
and greater will be
our wonder, our rapture,
when Jesus we see.

527 Graham Kendrick

To keep your lovely face
ever before my eyes,
this is my prayer,
make it my strong desire;
that in my secret heart
no other love competes,
no rival throne survives,
and I serve only you.

© 1983 Kingsway's Thankyou Music

528 Graham Kendrick

Tonight, while all the world was sleeping,
a light exploded in the skies.
And then, as glory did surround us,
a voice, an angel did appear!

Glory to God in the highest,
and on the earth all peace from heav'n!
Glory to God in the highest,
and on the earth all peace from heav'n!

Afraid, we covered up our faces,
amazed at what our ears did hear.
Good news of joy for all the people –
today a Saviour has appeared!

And so to Bethlehem
to find it all was true;
despised and worthless shepherds,
we were the first to know.

© 1988 Make Way Music

529 Craig Musseau

To you, O Lord, I bring my worship,
an offering of love to you.
Surrounded in your holy presence,
all I can say is that I love you.

Give ear to the groaning in my spirit.
Hear the crying in my heart.
Release my soul to freely worship,
for I was made to give you honour.

Holy, holy, holy, holy.
Holy, holy, holy, holy.

© 1990 Mercy/Vineyard Publishing/Music Services/CopyCare

530 Graham Kendrick

To you, O Lord, I lift up my soul.
In you I trust, O my God.
Do not let me be put to shame,
nor let my enemies triumph over me.

No one whose hope is in you
will ever be put to shame;
that's why my eyes are on you, O Lord.
Surround me, defend me,
O how I need you.
To you I lift up my soul,
to you I lift up my soul.

Show me your ways and teach me your paths.
Guide me in truth, lead me on;
for you're my God, you are my Saviour.
My hope is in you each moment of the day.

Remember, Lord, your mercy and love
that ever flow from of old.
Remember not the sins of my youth
or my rebellious ways.
According to your love, remember me.
According to your love, for you are good,
O Lord.

© 1997 Make Way Music

531 *Graham Kendrick*

Turn our hearts, turn our hearts.

Turn our hearts to one another,
let your kindness show:
where our words or deeds have wounded,
let forgiveness flow.

Turn our hearts from pride and anger
to your ways of peace,
for you died and shed your blood
that enmity may cease.

Turn the hearts of generations
that we may be one:
make us partners in the kingdom
till your work is done.

As we all have been forgiven,
so must we forgive;
as we all have found acceptance,
so let us receive.

Turn our hearts, change our hearts,
join our hearts, turn our hearts.

532 *Graham Kendrick*

Turn to me and be saved,
all you nations.
Turn to me and be saved,
all you nations.

Turn to me (turn to me)
and be saved (and be saved),
all you nations.
Turn to me (turn to me)
and be saved (and be saved)
all you nations.
For I am God, and there is no other.
For I am God, and there is no other.
Turn to me (turn to me)
and be saved (and be saved),
all you people.

Turn to me (turn to me)
and be saved (and be saved),
all you people.
For he is God, and there is no other.
For he is God, and there is no other.
For you are God, and there is no other.
For you are God, and there is no other.

Shout:

Leader	Now, Lord, send your Holy Spirit.
All	Now, Lord, send your Holy Spirit.
Leader	Drench this land with your awesome presence.
All	Drench this land with your awesome presence.
Leader	Send your Holy Spirit more powerfully.
All	Send your Holy Spirit more powerfully.
Leader	Let grace and mercy flood this land.
All	Let grace and mercy flood this land.
Leader	Let mercy triumph over judgement.
All	Let mercy triumph over judgement.
Leader	Let mercy triumph over judgement.
All	Let mercy triumph over judgement.

533 *Helen H. Lemmel*

Turn your eyes upon Jesus,
look full in his wonderful face,
and the things of earth
will grow strangely dim
in the light of his glory and grace.

534 *Matt Redman*

Wake up, my soul,
worship the Lord of truth and life.
Have strength, my heart,
press on as one who seeks the prize.
I'll run for you, my God and King,
I'll run as one who runs to win.
I'm pressing on, not giving in.
I will run, I will run for you, my King.

And Spirit, come, give life to us,
come breathe the Father's love in us.
Won't you fill us once again?
And we will run and run with him.
We'll run with strength, with all our might,
we'll fix our eyes on Jesus Christ;
he has conquered death and sin.
And we will run and run and run with him.

535 Graham Kendrick

Wake up, O sleeper,
and rise from the dead,
and Christ will shine on you.
Wake up, O sleeper,
and rise from the dead,
and Christ will shine on you.

Once you were darkness, but now you are light,
now you are light in the Lord.
So as true children of light you must live,
showing the glory of God.

This is the beautiful fruit of the light,
the good, the righteous, the true.
Let us discover what pleases the Lord
in everything we do.

As days get darker, take care how you live,
not as unwise, but as wise,
making the most of each moment he gives,
and pressing on for the prize.

536 Trevor King

We are a people of power,
we are a people of praise;
we are a people of promise,
Jesus has risen, he's conquered the grave!
Risen, yes, born again,
we walk in the power of his name;
power to be the sons of God,
the sons of God! the sons of God!
we are the sons, sons of God!

537 Graham Kendrick

We are his children,
the fruit of his suffering,
saved and redeemed by his blood;
called to be holy, a light to the nations:
clothed with his power,
filled with his love.

Go forth in his name,
proclaiming, 'Jesus reigns!'
Now is the time for the church to arise
and proclaim him
'Jesus, Saviour, Redeemer and Lord'.
(Repeat)

Countless the souls
that are stumbling in darkness;
why do we sleep in the light?
Jesus commands us to go make disciples,
this is our cause,
this is our fight.

Listen, the wind
of the Spirit is blowing,
the end of the age is so near;
powers in the earth and heavens are shaking,
Jesus our Lord
soon shall appear.

538 Kevin Prosch

We are his people,
he gives us music to sing.
There is a sound now,
like the sound of the Lord
when his enemies flee.
But there is a cry in our hearts,
like when deep calls unto the deep,
for your breath of deliverance,
to breathe on the music we so desperately
    need.
But without your power
all we have are these simple songs.
If you'd step down from heaven,
then the gates of hell would surely fall.

Continued overleaf

So we shout to the Lord,
shout to the Lord,
shout to the Lord of hosts.
Shout to the Lord, shout to the Lord,
shout to the Lord of hosts.
And it breaks the heavy yoke,
breaks the heavy yoke,
when you shout, you shout to the Lord.
It breaks the heavy yoke,
breaks the heavy yoke,
when you shout, you shout to the Lord.
Woa, you shout to the Lord,
yeah, you shout to the Lord,
woa, you shout to the Lord.

539   Traditional African

We are marching in the light of God,
we are marching in the light of God.
We are marching in the light of God,
we are marching in the light of God.

We are marching, marching,
we are marching, oh, we are marching
in the light of God.
(Repeat)

We are living in the love of God . . .

We are moving in the pow'r of God . . .

540   Kevin Prosch

We are the army of God,
children of Abraham,
we are a chosen generation.
Under a covenant,
washed by his precious blood,
filled with the mighty Holy Ghost.
And I hear the sound of the coming rain,
as we sing the praise to the great 'I Am'.

And the sick are healed,
and the dead shall rise,
and your church is the army
that was prophesied.

(Last time)
Your church is the army.
Your church is the army.
Your church is the army.
Your church is the army.

541   Graham Kendrick

We believe in God the Father,
Maker of the universe,
and in Christ his Son, our Saviour,
come to us by virgin birth.
We believe he died to save us,
bore our sins, was crucified.
Then from death he rose victorious,
ascended to the Father's side.

Jesus, Lord of all, Lord of all,
Jesus, Lord of all, Lord of all,
Jesus, Lord of all, Lord of all,
Jesus, Lord of all, Lord of all.
Name above all names.
Name above all names.

We believe he sends his Spirit
on his church with gifts of pow'r.
God, his word of truth affirming,
sends us to the nations now.
He will come again in glory,
judge the living and the dead.
Every knee shall bow before him,
then must every tongue confess.

542   Kirk Dearman

We bring the sacrifice of praise
into the house of the Lord.
We bring the sacrifice of praise
into the house of the Lord.

We bring the sacrifice of praise
into the house of the Lord.
We bring the sacrifice of praise
into the house of the Lord.

And we offer up to you
the sacrifices of thanksgiving,
and we offer up to you
the sacrifices of joy.

543 Robert Eastwood

We come into your presence
to sing a song to you,
a song of praise and honour
for all the things you've helped us through;
you gave a life worth living,
a life in love with you,
and now I just love giving
all my praises back to you.

You're the Father of creation,
the risen Lamb of God,
you're the One who walked away
from the empty tomb that day;
and you set your people free
with love and liberty,
and I can walk with you
every night and every day.

544 Malcolm du Plessis

We declare your majesty,
we proclaim that your name is exalted;
for you reign magnificently,
rule victoriously
and your pow'r is shown throughout the earth.
And we exclaim our God is mighty,
lift up your name, for you are holy.
Sing it again, all honour and glory,
in adoration we bow before your throne.

545 Andy Piercy

We do not presume
to come to your table
trusting in our own righteousness.
For we are not worthy so much
as to gather the crumbs
from under your table.
But trusting, O Lord,
in your great and manifold mercies.
For you are the same Lord
whose nature's always to have mercy.

So cleanse us and feed us
with the body and blood of your Son.
That we may live in him,
that he may live in us
for ever and ever. Amen.

546 Dave Clifton

We have a great priest
over the house of God.
So let us draw near to God
with a sincere heart,
in full assurance,
assurance of our faith,
having our hearts touched
to cleanse us from our guilt.

For he who promised is faithful,
for he who promised is faithful,
is faithful to me.

Give me a pure heart,
holding to your hope,
the hope I profess, Lord,
lead me in your way;
be now my strength, Lord,
and all of my trust, Lord,
I will fear no one,
for you are with me.

547 Paul Oakley

We have prayed that you would have mercy;
we believe from heaven you've heard.
Heal our land, so dry and so thirsty;
we have strayed so far from you, Lord.
Your cloud appeared on the horizon,
small as a man's hand.
But now you're near, filling our vision,
pour out your Spirit again.
I felt the touch of your wind on my face:
I feel the first drops of rain.

> *Let it rain, let it rain.*
> *I will not be the same.*
> *Let it rain, rain on me.*
> *Let it pour down on me,*
> *let it rain, let it rain,*
> *let it rain, let it rain, let it rain on me.*

548 Noel Richards

> *Welcome, King of kings!*
> *How great is your name.*
> *You come in majesty*
> *for ever to reign.*

You rule the nations, they shake
at the sound of your name.
To you is given all pow'r
and you shall reign.

Let all creation bow down
at the sound of your name.
Let every tongue now confess,
the Lord God reigns.

549 Graham Kendrick

Welcome the King, welcome the King,
welcome the King, welcome the King,
welcome the King
who comes in the name of the Lord.
(Repeat)

Clear the road before him,
open the ancient doors,
let every heart receive him:
welcome the King
who comes in the name of the Lord.

Who is this King, who is this King,
who is this King, who is this King,
who is this King
who comes in the name of the Lord?
(Repeat)

He is the King of Glory,
crucified and risen;
he is the Lord Almighty:
welcome the King
who comes in the name of the Lord;
welcome the King
who comes in the name of the Lord.

550 Martin Smith

Well, I hear they're singing in the streets
that Jesus is alive,
and all creation shouts aloud
that Jesus is alive;
now surely we can all be changed
'cos Jesus is alive;
and everybody here can know
that Jesus is alive.

And I will live for all my days
to raise a banner of truth and light,
to sing about my Saviour's love
and the best thing that happened –
it was the day I met you.

> *I've found Jesus, I've found Jesus,*
> *I've found Jesus, I've found Jesus.*

Well, I feel like dancing in the streets
'cos Jesus is alive,
to join with all who celebrate
that Jesus is alive.
The joy of God is in this town
'cos Jesus is alive;
for everybody's seen the truth
that Jesus is alive.

And I will live for all my days . . .

Well, you lifted me from where I was,
set my feet upon a rock,
humbled that you even know 'bout me.
Now I have chosen to believe,
believing that you've chosen me;
I was lost but now I've found –

551 Graham Kendrick

We'll walk the land with hearts on fire;
and every step will be a prayer.
Hope is rising, new day dawning;
sound of singing fills the air.

Two thousand years, and still the flame
is burning bright across the land.
Hearts are waiting, longing, aching,
for awakening once again.

Let the flame burn brighter
in the heart of the darkness,
turning night to glorious day.
Let the song grow louder,
as our love grows stronger;
let it shine! Let it shine!

We'll walk for truth, speak out for love;
in Jesus' name we shall be strong,
to lift the fallen, to save the children,
to fill the nation with your song.

552 Steven Fry

We march to the tune of a love-song,
singing the King's jubilee;
anointed to enter the hell-gate,
anointed to set captives free.
We lift up our banner of worship
and Jesus our Champion we praise;
an army of worshippers stand by his side,
baptised in his fire,
revealing his glorious light.

We lift up a shout,
a victory shout,
for we've overcome
by the blood of the Lamb
and the word of our mouth.
We've declared war
in the name of the Lord,
we've laid down our lives
that the triumph of Christ
may resound in the earth.

We sing the high praises of heaven
and fight with the sword of the Word;
to bind every stronghold of Satan,
preparing the way of the Lord.
We lift up a standard of worship
that shatters the darkness with light,
and God will arise on the wings of our praise
and march as a Warrior
who's mighty and able to save.

553 Ian Mizen and Andy Pressdee

We must work together,
bringing in the kingdom,
bringing heaven here on earth.
Start a new world order,
start a revolution,
let all people know their worth.

We'll see it all (we'll see it all),
we'll see it all (we'll see it all),
we'll see it all (we'll see it all),
we'll see it all,

when the kingdom comes,
when Jesus comes,
when the kingdom comes,
when Jesus comes,
when the kingdom comes.
When Jesus comes,
when the kingdom comes,
when Jesus comes.

Your kingdom come,
your will be done,
your kingdom come,
your will be done.

Continued overleaf

When the kingdom comes,
when Jesus comes . . .

We will see the dawning,
in this generation
see the start of a new day.
We'll know peace and freedom.
We will know true laughter,
we'll see sickness blown away.

554 Carol Owen

We rejoice in the goodness of our God,
we rejoice in the wonders of your favour.
You've set the captives free,
you've caused the blind to see,
hallelujah, you give us liberty,
hallelujah.

Always the same, you never change,
and your mercies are new every day.
Compassionate and gracious,
our faithful, loving God,
slow to anger, rich in love.

You give us hope, you give us joy,
you give us fullness of life to enjoy.
Our shepherd and provider,
our God who's always there,
never failing, always true.

555 Mark Altrogge

We serve a God of miracles,
you heal the sick and open blinded eyes;
we serve a God of miracles,
the demons flee the moment you arise,
arise, and show yourself strong,
arise, arise, and show yourself strong.
(Repeat)

We serve a God of power,
we serve a God of might,
we serve a God of signs and wonders;

we serve a God of power,
we serve a God of might.
You speak and all creation thunders.

556 Graham Kendrick

We shall stand
with our feet upon the Rock.
Whatever they may say,
we'll lift your name up high.
And we shall walk
through the darkest night;
setting our faces like flint,
we'll walk into the light.

Lord, you have chosen me
for fruitfulness,
to be transformed
into your likeness.
I'm gonna fight on through
till I see you face to face.

Lord, as your witnesses
you've appointed us.
And with your Holy Spirit
anointed us.
And so I'll fight on through
till I see you face to face.

557 Matt Redman

We've had a light shine in our midst,
we've felt your presence, we've known your
    peace,
and though this blessing comes to us free,
it carries a challenge to go.
We've had a feast laid on for us,
you have commanded, 'Bring in the lost',
there's food for all, any who'd come,
any who would know your Son.

We know it's time to go,
we've heard the cries of all of the earth.
Send us with pow'r,
we cannot do it alone.

With passion for the lost
we'll take the truth,
whatever the cost;
time is so short,
we cannot squander this love.

*Surely the time has come
to bring the harvest home.
Surely the time has come
to bring the harvest home.*

558 Andy Piercy and Dave Clifton

We want to remain in your love,
we want to remain in your love.
O Lord, O Lord, we need you so.
I want to remain in your love,
I want to remain in your love.
O Lord, don't ever let us go.
(Repeat)

Love is patient, love is kind,
does not envy, does not boast,
is not proud, is not rude;
love does not rejoice in evil,
but rejoices with the truth.
Love protects, always trusts,
always hopes, and perseveres,
is slow to anger, never fails;
love does not delight in evil,
but rejoices with the truth.
Love does not delight in evil,
but rejoices with the truth.

I want to remain in your love,
I want to remain in your love.
O Lord, don't ever let us go.

559 Doug Horley

We want to see Jesus lifted high,
a banner that flies across this land,
that all men might see the truth
and know he is the way to heaven.
(Repeat)

*We want to see, we want to see,
we want to see Jesus lifted high.
We want to see, we want to see,
we want to see Jesus lifted high.*

Step by step we're moving forward,
little by little taking ground,
every prayer a powerful weapon,
strongholds come tumbling down,
and down, and down, and down.

We're gonna see . . .

560 Graham Kendrick

We will cross every border,
throw wide every door,
joining our hands across the nations,
we'll proclaim Jesus is Lord.

We will break sin's oppression,
speak out for the poor,
announce the coming of Christ's kingdom
from east to west and shore to shore.

We will gather in the harvest,
and work while it's day,
though we may sow with tears of sadness,
we will reap with shouts of joy.

Soon our eyes shall see his glory,
the Lamb, our risen Lord,
when he receives from every nation
his blood-bought Bride, his great reward.
Then we'll proclaim Jesus is Lord.
We shall proclaim Jesus is Lord.

561 Tricia Allen and Martin J. Nystrom

We will run and not grow weary,
we will walk and will not faint,
for the Lord will go before us
and his joy will be our strength.
Mounting up with wings as eagles,
as our spirits start to soar;
when we come into his presence,
and we wait upon the Lord.

Continued overleaf

We will wait upon the Lord,
for in his presence is fullness of joy;
and our strength will be restored,
as we wait upon the Lord.

562 Kath Hall

We will turn the hearts of the fathers
so they will look again to their children.
We will turn the hearts of the children
so that together we can look to you.
(Repeat)

The young and the old now,
standing together,
looking to Jesus to carry us through.
All different races, all different ages,
all of us here for your glory.
And we call on your Spirit,
keep us together and pour in your power.

563 Dennis Jernigan

We will worship the Lamb of glory,
we will worship the King of kings;
we will worship the Lamb of glory,
we will worship the King.

And with our hands lifted high
we will worship and sing,
and with our hands lifted high
we come before you rejoicing.
With our hands lifted high to the sky,
when the world wonders why,
we'll just tell them
we're loving our King.
Oh, we'll just tell them
we're loving our King.
Yes, we'll just tell them
we're loving our King.

Bless the name of the Lamb of glory,
I bless the name of the King of kings;
bless the name of the Lamb of glory,
bless the name of the King.

564 Andy Piercy (v. 3 Cecil Frances Alexander)

We worship and adore you, Lord,
hear us when we call,
for there is no god above you,
you are the Lord of all.

But how can we begin to express
what's on our hearts?
There are no words enough, Lord,
for us to even start.

The tongues of men and angels
we need, to sing your praise,
so that we may glorify your name
through heav'n's eternal days.

There was no other good enough
to pay the price of sin;
you only could unlock the gate
of heav'n, and let us in.

So, we worship and adore you . . .

565 Martin Smith

What a friend I've found,
closer than a brother.
I have felt your touch,
more intimate than lovers.

Jesus, Jesus,
Jesus, friend for ever.

What a hope I've found,
more faithful than a mother.
It would break my heart
to ever lose each other.

566 Joseph Medlicott Scriven

What a friend we have in Jesus,
all our sins and griefs to bear!
What a privilege to carry
everything to him in prayer!
O what peace we often forfeit,
O what needless pain we bear,
all because we do not carry
everything to God in prayer!

Have we trials and temptations?
Is there trouble anywhere?
We should never be discouraged:
take it to the Lord in prayer!
Can we find a friend so faithful,
who will all our sorrows share?
Jesus knows our every weakness –
take it to the Lord in prayer!

Are we weak and heavy-laden,
cumbered with a load of care?
Jesus only is our refuge,
take it to the Lord in prayer!
Do thy friends despise, forsake thee?
Take it to the Lord in prayer!
In his arms he'll take and shield thee,
thou wilt find a solace there.

567 Graham Kendrick

What kind of greatness can this be,
that chose to be made small?
Exchanging untold majesty
for a world so pitiful.
That God should come as one of us,
I'll never understand.
The more I hear the story told,
the more amazed I am.

O what else can I do
but kneel and worship you,
and come just as I am,
my whole life an offering.

The One in whom we live and move
in swaddling clothes lies bound.
The voice that cried, 'Let there be light',
asleep without a sound.
The One who strode among the stars,
and called each one by name,
lies helpless in a mother's arms
and must learn to walk again.

What greater love could he have shown
to shamed humanity,
yet human pride hates to believe
in such deep humility.
But nations now may see his grace
and know that he is near,
when his meek heart, his words, his works
are incarnate in us.

© 1994 Make Way Music

568 Bryn and Sally Haworth

What kind of love is this
that gave itself for me?
I am the guilty one,
yet I go free.
What kind of love is this,
a love I've never known?
I didn't even know his name.
What kind of love is this?

What kind of man is this
that died in agony?
He who had done no wrong
was crucified for me.
What kind of man is this
who laid aside his throne,
that I may know the love of God?
What kind of man is this?

By grace I have been saved;
it is the gift of God.
He destined me to be his child,
such is his love.
No eye has ever seen,
no ear has ever heard,
nor has the heart of man conceived
what kind of love is this.

© 1983 Signalgrade/Kingsway's Thankyou Music

569   Lucy East

What noise shall we make
to say that God is great?
What noise shall we make
unto the Lord?

Let's make a loud noise
to say that God is great.
Let's make a loud noise
unto the Lord.
Here is my loud noise,
here is my loud noise,
here is my loud noise
unto the Lord.

Let's make a quiet noise . . .
Here is my quiet noise . . .

Let's make a fast noise . . .
Here is my fast noise . . .

Let's make a slow noise . . .
He is my slow noise . . .

Let's make a joyful noise . . .
Here is my joyful noise . . .

Let's make a praising noise . . .
Here is my praising noise . . .

We love making noise
to say that God is great.
We love making noise
unto the Lord.

570   Keri Jones and David Matthew

When I feel the touch
of your hand upon my life,
it causes me to sing a song
that I love you, Lord.
So from deep within
my spirit singeth unto thee,
you are my King,
you are my God,
and I love you, Lord.

571   Wayne and Cathy Perrin

When I look into your holiness,
when I gaze into your loveliness,
when all things that surround
become shadows in the light of you;
when I've found the joy
of reaching your heart,
when my will becomes enthralled
in your love,
when all things that surround
become shadows in the light of you:

> *I worship you, I worship you,*
> *the reason I live is to worship you.*
> *I worship you, I worship you,*
> *the reason I live is to worship you.*

572   Isaac Watts

When I survey the wondrous cross
on which the Prince of Glory died,
my richest gain I count but loss,
and pour contempt on all my pride.

Forbid it, Lord, that I should boast,
save in the death of Christ, my God:
all the vain things that charm me most,
I sacrifice them to his blood.

See from his head, his hands, his feet,
sorrow and love flow mingling down:
did e'er such love and sorrow meet,
or thorns compose so rich a crown?

Were the whole realm of nature mine,
that were an offering far too small;
love so amazing, so divine,
demands my soul, my life, my all.

573   Lynn DeShazo

When my heart is overwhelmed,
hear my cry, give heed to my prayer;
and my eyes are dim with tears,
O Father, make them clear;

from the ends of all the earth,
when my heart is fainting,
let me know that you have heard,
lead me into safety.

> And lead me to the rock,
> the rock that's higher,
> lead me to the rock
> that's higher than I.
> Lead me to the rock
> the rock that's higher, higher than I.
> (Repeat)

You, O Lord, have been for me
a refuge from my enemies,
let me live within your strength,
in the shelter of your wings;
from the ends of all the earth,
when my heart is fainting,
let me know that you have heard,
lead me into safety.

© 1984 Integrity's Hosanna! Music/Kingsway's Thankyou Music

574 Horatio G. Spafford

When peace like a river
attendeth my way,
when sorrows like sea-billows roll,
whatever my lot,
thou hast taught me to know,
it is well, it is well with my soul.

> It is well (it is well)
> with my soul (with my soul),
> it is well, it is well with my soul.

Though Satan should buffet,
though trials should come,
let this blest assurance control,
that Christ hath regarded
my helpless estate,
and hath shed his own blood for my soul.

For me be it Christ,
be it Christ, hence to live!
If Jordan above me shall roll,

no pang shall be mine,
for in death as in life,
thou wilt whisper thy peace to my soul.

But, Lord, 'tis for thee,
for thy coming we wait,
the sky, not the grave, is our goal;
oh, trump of the angel!
O voice of the Lord!
Blessed hope! Blessed rest of my soul!

575 Graham Kendrick

When the Lord brought us back
and restored our freedom,
we felt so good, we felt so strong,
at first we thought we were dreaming.
How we laughed! How we sang,
we were overflowing;
then we heard the nations say,
'Look what the Lord has done.'

The Lord has done great things for us,
and we are filled with joy.
The Lord has done great things for us,
and we are filled with joy,
with joy, with joy, with joy.

© 1995 Make Way Music

576 Matt Redman

When the music fades,
all is stripped away,
and I simply come.
Longing just to bring
something that's of worth
that will bless your heart.

I'll bring you more than a song,
for a song in itself
is not what you have required.
You search much deeper within,
through the way things appear;
you're looking into my heart.

Continued overleaf

I'm coming back to the heart of worship,
and it's all about you,
all about you, Jesus.
I'm sorry, Lord,
for the thing I've made it,
when it's all about you,
all about you, Jesus.

King of endless worth,
no one could express
how much you deserve.
Though I'm weak and poor,
all I have is yours,
every single breath.

I'll bring you . . .

577 Tommy Walker

Where there once was only hurt,
he gave his healing hand.
Where there once was only pain,
he brought comfort like a friend.
I feel the sweetness of his love
piercing my darkness.
I see the bright and morning sun
as it ushers in his joyful gladness.

> *He's turned my mourning*
> *into dancing again,*
> *he's lifted my sorrow.*
> *I can't stay silent,*
> *I must sing for his joy has come.*
> (Repeat)

His anger lasts for a moment in time;
but his favour is here
and will be on me for all my lifetime.

578 Graham Kendrick

Where two or three of you gather in my name,
I am there, I am there with you;
and if just two of you stand in agreement,
as you pray gathered in my name,

my Father will hear your prayer,
hear your prayer,
and answer and will give you
anything you ask in my name.

579 Graham Kendrick

Who can sound the depths of sorrow
in the Father heart of God,
for the children we've rejected,
for the lives so deeply scarred?
And each light that we've extinguished
has brought darkness to our land:
upon our nation, upon our nation
have mercy, Lord.

We have scorned the truth you gave us,
we have bowed to other lords.
We have sacrificed the children
on the altar of our gods.
O let truth again shine on us,
let your holy fear descend:
upon our nation, upon our nation
have mercy, Lord.

(Men)
Who can stand before your anger?
Who can face your piercing eyes?
For you love the weak and helpless,
and you hear the victims' cries.
(All)
Yes, you are a God of justice,
and your judgement surely comes:
upon our nation, upon our nation
have mercy, Lord.

(Women)
Who will stand against the violence?
Who will comfort those who mourn?
In an age of cruel rejection,
who will build for love a home?
(All)
Come and shake us into action,
come and melt our hearts of stone:
upon your people, upon your people
have mercy, Lord.

Who can sound the depths of mercy
in the Father heart of God?
For there is a Man of sorrows
who for sinners shed his blood.
He can heal the wounds of nations,
he can wash the guilty clean:
because of Jesus, because of Jesus
have mercy, Lord.

580 Graham Kendrick

Who sees it all, before whose gaze
is darkest night bright as the day;
watching as in the secret place
his likeness forms upon a face?

Who sees it all, the debt that's owed
of lives unlived, of love unknown?
Who weighs the loss of innocence,
or feels the pain of our offence?

God sees, God knows,
God loves the broken heart;
and holds, and binds,
and heals the broken heart.

Who knows the fears that drive a choice,
unburies pain and gives it a voice?
And who can wash a memory,
or take the sting of death away?

God sees, God knows . . .

Whose anger burns at what we've done,
then bears our sin as if his own?
Who will receive us as we are,
whose arms are wide and waiting now?

Whose broken heart upon a cross
won freedom, joy and peace for us?
Whose blood redeems, who ever lives
and all because of love forgives?

God sees, God knows . . .

581 Steve McGregor

With all my heart,
I will put my trust in you.
With all my heart,
I will put my trust in you.
I will lean on you,
depend on you,
I will look to the one I love
with all my heart.

When in despair,
and no one else cares,
storms all around,
no friends can be found;
you're always there,
you're always there for me.

Nothing compares
to your faithfulness,
no greater love
in earth or above:
so I'll declare,
my heart is safe in your arms.

582 Graham Kendrick

With my whole heart I will praise you,
holding nothing back, hallelujah!
You have made me glad and now
I come with open arms to thank you,
with my heart embrace, hallelujah!
I can see your face is smiling.
With my whole life I will serve you,
captured by your love, hallelujah!
O amazing love! O amazing love!

Lord, your heart is overflowing
with a love divine, hallelujah!
And this love is mine for ever.
Now your joy has set you laughing
as you join the song, hallelujah!
Heaven sings along, I hear the
voices swell to great crescendos,
praising your great love, hallelujah!
O amazing love! O amazing love!

Continued overleaf

Come, O Bridegroom, clothed in splendour,
my Beloved One, hallelujah!
How I long to run and meet you.
You're the fairest of ten thousand,
you're my life and breath, hallelujah!
Love as strong as death has won me.
All the rivers, all the oceans
cannot quench this love, hallelujah!
O amazing love! O amazing love!

583 Geoff Baker

With this bread we will remember him,
Son of God, broken and suffering;
for our guilt – innocent offering.
As we eat, remember him.

With this wine we will remember him,
on the cross, paying the price for sin –
blood of Christ cleansing us deep within.
As we drink, remember him.

584 Eddie Espinosa

Worthy is the Lamb,
worthy is the Lamb,
worthy is the Lamb
that was slain.
(Repeat)

To receive wisdom and honour,
to receive power and strength,
to receive wealth and all glory,
worthy is the Lamb.

Jesus is the Lamb,
Jesus is the Lamb,
Jesus is the Lamb
that was slain.
Worthy is the Lamb,
worthy is the Lamb,
worthy is the Lamb
that was slain.

585 Mark S. Kinzer

Worthy, O worthy are you, Lord,
worthy to be thanked and praised
and worshipped and adored.
(Repeat)

Singing hallelujah,
Lamb upon the throne,
we worship and adore you,
make your glory known.
Hallelujah, glory to the King:
you're more than a conqueror,
you're Lord of everything.

586 Andy Park

Yahweh, Yahweh, Ancient One,
yet you're here today.
Ageless One, Changeless One,
showing love to all generations.
Show us your glory, O Lord,
let your goodness pass before us,
right before our eyes.

And we will worship,
and we will bow down,
and we will call you Lord.
And we will kneel
before the Maker of the universe,
and we will call you Lord.

Yahweh, Yahweh, Faithful One,
you have shown us the way.
Through the years, through all our lives,
you have shown you are faithful to the end.
Show us your glory, O Lord,
let your goodness pass before us,
right before our eyes.

587 Carl Tuttle

Yet this will I call to mind,
and therefore I will hope,
because of the Lord's great love
I've been redeemed.

The Lord is gracious and kind
to all who call on his name,
because of the Lord's great love
I've been redeemed.

Because of the Lord's great love,
because of the Lord's great love,
because of the Lord's great love,
I've been redeemed.

I know of his steadfast love,
his mercy renewed each day,
because of the Lord's great love
I've been redeemed.
Washed in the blood of the Lamb,
guiltless for ever I stand,
because of the Lord's great love
I've been redeemed.

588 Carol Owen

You alone, Lord, are wonderful.
Father, you alone are wise.
Your love, Lord, is eternal,
your faithfulness reaches to the skies.

And I adore you, Lord.
I stand in awe of you,
for all of your ways are so great.
Yes, I adore you, Lord.
I stand in awe of you,
for all of your ways are so great.

And I exalt you, my Lord,
I exalt you, my Lord,
I exalt you, my Lord and my King.
I exalt you, my Lord,
I exalt you, my Lord,
for you are my God and King.

589 Mark Altrogge

You are beautiful beyond description,
too marvellous for words,
too wonderful for comprehension,
like nothing ever seen or heard.

Who can grasp your infinite wisdom?
Who can fathom the depth of your love?
You are beautiful beyond description,
majesty, enthroned above.

And I stand, I stand in awe of you.
I stand, I stand in awe of you.
Holy God, to whom all praise is due,
I stand in awe of you.

590 John Sellers

You are crowned with many crowns,
and rule all things in righteousness.
You are crowned with many crowns,
upholding all things by your word.
You rule in power and reign in glory!
You are Lord of heaven and earth!
You are Lord of all.
You are Lord of all.

591 Carol Owen

You are God, you are great,
you are Lord over all.
You are good, you are kind,
you are Lord over all.
You are God, you are great,
you are Lord over all.
You are good, you are kind,
you are Lord over all.
My God, my Friend, my King.

Nothing can compare with all your mighty
  ways.
You sustain the heavens and the earth.
You've revealed your glory
to the sons of men through Jesus.

You're the God of wisdom and of majesty,
the earth is like a footstool at your feet,
yet you came down and dwelt
among the sons of men in Jesus.

592
Trish Morgan

You are Lord of our hearts,
you are Lord of our lives,
and you reign, and you reign.

His wave of love will wash away
our prejudice and shame,
our brokenness and pain.
Faith will rise,
faith instead of fear,
connected in his love,
anointed from above.

593
Ian White

You are merciful to me,
you are merciful to me,
you are merciful to me, my Lord.
You are merciful to me,
you are merciful to me,
you are merciful to me, my Lord.

Every day my disobedience
grieves your loving heart,
but then redeeming love breaks through,
and causes me to worship you.

Redeemer (Redeemer),
Saviour (Saviour),
Healer (Healer)
and Friend (and Friend).
Every day (every day)
renew my ways (renew my ways),
fill me with love (fill me with love)
that never ends (that never ends).

594
Craig Musseau

You are mighty,
you are holy,
you are awesome in your power;
you have risen,
you have conquered,
you have beaten the power of death.

Hallelujah, we will rejoice;
hallelujah, we will rejoice!

595
Brian Doerksen

You are my King (you are my King),
and I love you.
You are my King (you are my King)
and I worship you,
kneeling before you now,
all of my life I gladly give to you.

You are my King (you are my King),
and I love you.
You are my King (you are my King)
and I worship you,
kneeling before you now,
all of my life I gladly give to you,
placing my hopes and dreams in your hands,
I give my heart to you.

I love you, love you, Jesus.
Yes, I love you, love you, Jesus, my King.

596
Noel and Tricia Richards

You are my passion, love of my life,
friend and companion, my Lover.
All of my being longs for your touch;
with all my heart I love you.
Now will you draw me close to you,
gather me in your arms;
let me hear the beating of your heart,
O my Jesus, O my Jesus.

597
Jarrod Cooper and Sharon Pearce

You are my rock, you are my fortress,
you are my strength, I will not fear.
You are my shield and my strong tower,
you are my refuge in the storm.

You are the invincible God,
mighty in power and great in splendour.
You are the invincible God,
mighty in power and great in splendour.
King of kings,
Lord of lords,
God of all the earth.

You are my light and my salvation,
I run to you, my hiding-place.
Your name is Jesus and you are mighty.
You are my stronghold, you are my life.

598   Lynn DeShazo and Martin J. Nystrom

You have called us out of darkness,
out of darkness into your glorious light.
You have saved us from the darkness,
we rejoice in your power and might.
(Repeat)

We are a chosen race,
a royal priesthood by your grace.
We are a holy nation
set apart for you.

We are to take your light
to every nation, tongue and tribe;
so they may see your glory
shining through our lives.

599   Brian Thiessen

You have shown me favour unending;
you have given your life for me.
And my heart knows of your goodness,
your blood has covered me.

I will arise and give thanks to you,
Lord, my God,
and your name I will bless
with my whole heart.
You have shown mercy,
you have shown mercy to me.
I give thanks to you, Lord.

You have poured out your healing upon us;
you have set the captives free.
And we know it's not what we've done,
but by your hand alone.

We will arise and give thanks to you,
Lord, our God,
and your name we will bless
with all our hearts.
You have shown mercy,
you have shown mercy to us.
We give thanks to you, Lord.

You, O Lord, are the healer of my soul.
You, O Lord, are the gracious Redeemer,
you come to restore us again.
Yes, you come to restore us again, and again.

600   Kevin Prosch and Tom Davis

You have taken the precious
from the worthless
and given us beauty for ashes, love for hate.
You have chosen the weak things of the world
to shame that which is strong,
and the foolish things to shame the wise.

You are help to the helpless,
strength to the stranger,
and a father to the child that's left alone.
And the thirsty are invited
to come to the waters,
and those who have no money come and buy.

So come, so come.

Behold, the days are coming,
for the Lord has promised
that the ploughman will overtake the reaper.
And our hearts shall be the threshing floor,
and the move of God we've cried out for
will come, it will surely come.

Continued overleaf

For you will shake the heavens,
and fill your house with glory,
and turn the shame of the outcast into praise.
And all creation groans and waits
for the Spirit and the bride to say
the word that your heart has longed to hear.

So come, so come.

© 1991 Mercy/Vineyard Publishing/Music Services/CopyCare

601 Noel Richards

You laid aside your majesty,
gave up everything for me,
suffered at the hands of those you had created.
You took all my guilt and shame,
when you died and rose again;
now today you reign,
in heav'n and earth exalted.

I really want to worship you, my Lord,
you have won my heart and I am yours
for ever and ever;
I will love you.
You are the only one who died for me,
gave your life to set me free,
so I lift my voice to you in adoration.

© 1985 Kingsway's Thankyou Music

602 Russell Fragar

You love me as you found me;
your love keeps following me.
You wrapped your arms around me,
your love keeps following me.
By grace I'm what I should be;
your love keeps following me.
You saw me as I could be;
your love keeps following me.

And it's higher (reaches from heaven to man),
it's wider (anyone can come in),
it's deeper (it covers any sin),
and I know this one thing:
wherever I go I know
your love keeps following me.

© 1993 Russell Fragar/Hillsongs Australia/Kingsway's Thankyou Music

603 Patricia Morgan and Sue Rinaldi

You make my heart feel glad,
you make my heart feel glad;
Jesus, you bring me joy,
you make my heart feel glad.

Lord, your love brings healing
and a peace into my heart;
I want to give myself in praise to you.
Though I've been through heartache,
you have understood my tears:
O Lord, I will give thanks to you.

When I look around me
and I see the life you made,
all creation shouts aloud in praise;
I realise your greatness –
how majestic is your name!
O Lord, I love you more each day.

© 1990 Kingsway's Thankyou Music

604 Darlene Zschech and Russell Fragar

You make your face to shine on me,
and that my soul knows very well.
You lift me up, I'm cleansed and free,
and that my soul knows very well.

When mountains fall I'll stand
by the power of your hand
and in your heart of hearts I'll dwell,
and that my soul knows very well.

Joy and strength each day I find,
and that my soul knows very well.
Forgiveness, hope, I know is mine,
and that my soul knows very well.

© Darlene Zschech and Russell Fragar/Hillsongs Australia/Kingsway's Thankyou Music

605 Geoff Bullock

You rescued me, and picked me up,
a living hope of grace revealed
a life transformed in righteousness.
O Lord, you have rescued me.

Forgiving me, you healed my heart,
and set me free from sin and death.
You brought me life, you made me whole,
O Lord, you have rescued me.

And you loved me before I knew you,
and you knew me for all time.
I've been created in your image, O Lord.
And you bought me, and you sought me,
your blood poured out for me;
a new creation in your image, O Lord.
You rescued me, you rescued me.

606   Robin Mark

You're the Lion of Judah,
the Lamb that was slain,
you ascended to heaven
and evermore will reign;
at the end of the age
when the earth you reclaim,
you will gather the nations before you.
And the eyes of all men
will be fixed on the Lamb
who was crucified,
for with wisdom and mercy
and justice he reigns
at the Father's side.

And the angels will cry:
'Hail the Lamb who was slain
for the world – rule in pow'r.'
And the earth will reply:
'You shall reign
as the King of all kings
and the Lord of all lords.'

There's a shield in our hand
and a sword at our side,
there's a fire in our spirit
that cannot be denied;
as the Father has told us:
for these you have died,
for the nations that gather before you.

And the ears of all men
need to hear of the Lamb
who was crucified,
who descended to hell
yet was raised up to reign
at the Father's side.

607   Scott and Michele Brenner

Your love flows like a river,
flows like a fountain into the sea.
Your love washes me over,
filling my spirit, making me clean.

As I worship you,
come fill me with your love,
flow over me.
As I lift your name
for all the world to see,
flow over me.
As I bless you, Lord,
with all that's in my heart.
Jesus, my King,
O eternal One,
my sacrificial Lamb,
flow over me.

Your touch, taking me over,
leading me gently into your arms.
Your touch, holding me closer,
healing my spirit, restoring my soul.

Flow over me,
river, flow over me,
river, flow over me,
flow over me.
Jesus, wash over me,
wash over me,
wash over me,
flow over me.
Fill me with your love,
Spirit, fill me with your love,
fill me with your love,
flow over me.

608 Wes Sutton

Your mercy flows upon us like a river.
Your mercy stands unshakable and true.
Most holy God, of all good things the giver,
we turn and lift our fervent prayer to you.

Hear our cry (hear our cry),
O Lord (O Lord),
be merciful (be merciful)
once more (once more).
Let your love (let your love)
your anger stem (your anger stem),
remember mercy, O Lord, again.

Your Church once great, though standing
    clothed in sorrow,
is even still the bride that you adore;
revive your church, that we again may honour
our God and King, our Master and our Lord.

As we have slept, this nation has been taken
by every sin we have ever known,
so at its gates, though burnt by fire and broken,
in Jesus' name we come to take our stand.

© 1987 Sovereign Lifestyle Music

609 Steffi Geiser Rubin and Stuart Dauermann

You shall go out with joy
and be led forth with peace,
and the mountains and the hills
shall break forth before you.
There'll be shouts of joy
and the trees of the field
shall clap, shall clap their hands.
And the trees of the field
shall clap their hands,
and the trees of the field
shall clap their hands,
and the trees of the field
shall clap their hands,
and you'll go out with joy.

© 1975 Lillenas Publishing Co./CopyCare

610 David Palmer

This is the time,
this is the place;
we're living in a season of amazing grace.
We are the people,
born for this hour,
and we will be willing in the day of his pow'r.
Can you hear him saying
that the prophecy's fulfilled.
Now a Holy Ghost revival
is gonna gather every field.

I hear the sound of a distant thunder,
I hear the sound of a coming rain.
I hear the wind blowing through the harvest,
he's coming, he's coming again.

Though the mountains tremble,
though the oceans roar,
all the earth will be filled
with the glory of the Lord.

© 1997 David Palmer/City Church Sunderland

611 Lenny LeBlanc and Paul Baloche

Above all powers, above all kings,
above all nature and all created things;
above all wisdom and all the ways of man,
you were here before the world began.
Above all kingdoms, above all thrones,
above all wonders the world has ever known;
above all wealth and treasures of the earth,
there's no way to measure what you're worth.
Crucified, laid behind the stone;
you lived to die, rejected and alone;
like a rose, trampled on the ground,
you took the fall, and thought of me, above all.

612 Isaac Watts and Ralph E. Hudson

Alas! and did my Saviour bleed
and did my Sov'reign die?
Would he devote that sacred head
for sinners such as I?

At the cross, at the cross where I first saw
the light
and the burden of my heart rolled away.
It was there by faith I received my sight,
and now I am happy all the day!

Was it for crimes that I have done
he groaned upon the tree?
Amazing pity! Grace unknown!
And love beyond degree!

But drops of grief can ne'er repay
the debt of love I owe:
here, Lord, I give myself away,
'tis all that I can do!

613 Paul Oakley

All around the world there's a new day
dawning,
there's a sound coming round,
there's a new song rising up,
ah, it's a new day!

Ev'rywhere you go you can hear this story,
there's a power coming down,
there's a glimpse of glory now,
ah, it's a new day!

There's a sound of praise, there's a sound
of war, yeah;
lift the banner high, let the Lion roar.
Can you hear the sound in the tops of the
trees, yeah?
Heaven's armies come! Crush the enemy!

Let the lame run, let the blind see, yeah!
Let your power come, set the captives free!
Let the lost return to the Lover of our
souls, yeah!
Let the prodigal find the way back home.

Lift your hands before the King,
the sov'reign Ruler of the earth;
let the nations come to him,
let the cry of hearts be heard.
Revive us! Revive us! Revive us again!
Revive us! Revive us! Revive us again!

All around the world there's a new day
dawning,
there's a sound coming round,
there's a new song rising up,
ah, it's a new day!
Ev'rywhere you go you can hear this story,
there's a power coming down,
there's a glimpse of glory now,
ah, it's a new day!

614 William Henry Draper, alt.

All creatures of our God and King,
lift up your voice and with us sing
alleluia, alleluia!
Thou burning sun with golden beam,
thou silver moon with softer gleam:

O praise him, O praise him,
alleluia, alleluia, alleluia!

Continued overleaf

Thou rushing wind that art so strong,
ye clouds that sail in heav'n along,
O praise him, alleluia!
Thou rising morn, in praise rejoice,
ye lights of evening, find a voice:

O praise him, O praise him,
alleluia, alleluia, alleluia!

Thou flowing water, pure and clear,
make music for thy Lord to hear,
alleluia, alleluia!
Thou fire so masterful and bright,
that givest us both warmth and light:

And all ye men of tender heart,
forgiving others, take your part,
O sing ye, alleluia!
Ye who long pain and sorrow bear,
praise God and on him cast your care:

Let all things their Creator bless,
and worship him in humbleness,
O praise him, alleluia!
Praise, praise the Father, praise the Son,
and praise the Spirit, Three in One.

615 Michael W. Smith

Alleluia, alleluia, for the Lord God Almighty
    reigns.
Alleluia, alleluia, for the Lord God Almighty
    reigns.
Alleluia. Holy, holy are you, Lord God Almighty.
Worthy is the Lamb; worthy is the Lamb.
You are holy. Holy are you, Lord God
    Almighty.
Worthy is the Lamb; worthy is the Lamb.

Amen.

616 William Chatterton Dix, alt.

Alleluia, sing to Jesus,
his the sceptre, his the throne;
alleluia, his the triumph,
his the victory alone:
hark, the songs of peaceful Sion
thunder like a mighty flood:
Jesus, out of ev'ry nation,
hath redeemed us by his blood.

Alleluia, not as orphans
are we left in sorrow now;
alleluia, he is near us,
faith believes, nor questions how;
though the cloud from sight received him
when the forty days were o'er,
shall our hearts forget his promise,
'I am with you evermore'?

Alleluia, bread of angels,
here on earth our food, our stay;
alleluia, here the sinful
come to you from day to day.
Intercessor, friend of sinners,
earth's redeemer, plead for me,
where the songs of all the sinless
sweep across the crystal sea.

Alleluia, King eternal,
he the Lord of lords we own;
alleluia, born of Mary,
earth his footstool, heav'n his throne;
he within the veil has entered
robed in flesh, our great High Priest;
he on earth both priest and victim
in the Eucharistic Feast.

617 Mark Altrogge

All I have is by your mercy,
and all I have is all of grace.
All I am is what your love has made of me.
Now I am your new creation,
your workmanship in Jesus Christ.
Made to walk in works you have prepared
for me.

I rejoice in all your kindness,
and I rejoice in all your goodness.
I rejoice in your great love for me.

All I have is from you, Father,
the Author of each perfect gift.
You gladly give me all things
to enjoy in you.
You who did not spare your Son
but freely gave him for us all,
will you not with joy supply
my ev'ry need?

618 Martin Smith

All I have in this world
is more than a king could ever wish for.
All these crowns leave me cold
for I was born to kiss your feet.

All I have in this life
is all for a King you know I live for.
And your crown bears my name
for I was born to give you praise.

Isn't he beautiful? *(x3)*

Take this life; take it all
I'm breathing the dirt,
but I have clean hands
so I'll run with my boots on
for I was born to give you fame.

Isn't he beautiful? *(x3)*

Yes, you are beautiful. *(x3)*

619 Scott Underwood

All I want is to know you, Jesus.
All I want is to know I belong to you.
Show me all of the things that are worthless,
that I thought were so valuable to you.

Nothing is as lovely, nothing is as worthy,
nothing is as wonderful as knowing you.
Nothing is as lovely, nothing is as worthy,
nothing is as wonderful as knowing you.

All I want is to know you, Jesus,
and the power that raised you from the dead.
Help me forget all the things that I've done.
Set my heart on what lies ahead.

620 Joachim Neander

All my hope on God is founded;
he doth still my trust renew,
me through change and chance he guideth,
only good and only true.
God unknown, he alone
calls my heart to be his own.

Pride of man and earthly glory,
sword and crown betray his trust;
what with care and toil he buildeth,
tower and temple, fall to dust.
But God's pow'r, hour by hour,
is my temple and my tower.

God's great goodness aye endureth,
deep his wisdom, passing thought:
splendour, life, and light attend him,
beauty springeth out of naught.
Evermore from his store
new-born worlds rise and adore.

Daily doth th'almighty giver
bounteous gifts on us bestow;
his desire our soul delighteth,
pleasure leads us where we go.
Love doth stand at his hand;
joy doth wait on his command.

Still from man to God eternal
sacrifice of praise be done,
high above all praises praising
for the gift of Christ his Son.
Christ doth call one and all:
ye who follow shall not fall.

621
Wayne and Libby Huirua

All my life I'll praise you.
There's no other like you.
You alone are Lord,
Lord Jesus.

Who controls the rushing of the mighty wind,
who holds the power of the seas?
Who by his word, formed the heavens and
the earth?
Almighty God, the Lord Jesus is his name.

He is the one who holds the universe,
the pow'r of life is in his hands.
His strength is in me, helping me to do his will.
He is my Lord, in his power I will stand.

You alone are Lord,
you alone are Lord,
you alone are Lord, Lord Jesus.

622
James Wright

All praise, all honour,
all strength, wisdom and power:
Jesus, be enthroned upon
our worship and our praise.

Jesus, the Name above all names.
Jesus, let all the earth proclaim.
Jesus, the risen Lamb of God,
exalted above all creation.
Jesus, the Name above all names.
Jesus, let all the earth proclaim.
Jesus, the Name at which creation
shall bow the knee and confess.

All praise, all praise, all praise
to the risen Lord.

All praise.

623
Claire Cloninger and Don Moen

All that I am, all that I have,
I lay them down before you, O Lord;
all my regrets, all my acclaim,
the joy and the pain, I'm making them yours.

Lord, I offer my life to you,
ev'rything I've been through,
use it for your glory;
Lord, I offer my days to you,
lifting my praise to you,
as a pleasing sacrifice;
Lord, I offer you my life.

Things in the past, things yet unseen,
wishes and dreams that are yet to come true;
all of my hopes, all of my plans,
my heart and my hands are lifted to you.

What can we give that you have not given;
and what do we have that is not already
yours?
All we possess are these lives we're living,
and that's what we give to you, Lord.

624
Darlene Zschech

All that is within me, Lord,
will bless your holy name,
I live my life to worship you alone.
You brought me out of darkness
and into your glorious light.
For ever I will sing of your great love,
For ever I will sing of your great love.

I love to see you glorified,
to see you lifted high.
I yearn to see all nations bow their knee.
It's you alone, Lord Jesus,
who can cause the coldest heart
to find your love and everlasting peace,
to find your love and everlasting peace.

Holy, holy, holy is the Lord.

And your trumpet will sound
and all of heaven will know,
that the time has fin'lly come
for the bride to take her place
and we'll hear the angels sing.

625 Frances Jane van Alstyne (Fanny J. Crosby)

All the way, my Saviour leads me,
what have I to ask beside?
Can I doubt his tender mercy,
who through life has been my guide?
Heavenly peace, divinest comfort,
here by faith in him to dwell,
for I know whate'er befall me,
Jesus doeth all things well.

All the way, my Saviour leads me,
cheers each winding path I tread.
Gives me grace for ev'ry trial,
feeds me with the Living Bread.
Though my weary steps may falter
and my soul a-thirst may be,
gushing from a Rock before me,
lo! a spring of joy I see.

And all the way, my Saviour leads me,
oh the fullness of his love.
Perfect rest to me is promised
in my Father's house above.
And when my spirit clothed immortal
wings its flight to realms of day,
this my song through endless ages,
Jesus led me all the way.

626 Colin Hardy

All the world can offer,
none of it compares with you.
All the gold and silver
can't replace the God I love.

All the world sees precious,
one day it will fade away,
and all its greatest treasures,
they are worth nothing
compared to you.

Because you love me,
because you called me,
because you saved me
I'm not living for this world,
'cause I'm living for you.

Don't know what I'd do without your love,
don't know what I'd do without you;
don't know what I'd do without your love,
your love is the only answer.
(Repeat)

All the world's wisdom,
chose to crucify the truth.
But when you called I followed,
I have given ev'rything for you.
Jesus, my treasure,
you are my heart's desire.
I'm glad to be your servant,
I'm glad to seek your kingdom first.

627 Brenton Brown and Glenn Robertson

All who are thirsty,
all who are weak,
come to the fountain,
dip your heart in the stream of life.
Let the pain and the sorrow
be washed away
in the waves of his mercy
as deep cries out to deep.
(We sing)

Come, Lord Jesus, come.
Come, Lord Jesus, come.
Holy Spirit, come.
Holy Spirit, come.

As deep cries out to deep.
As deep cries out to deep.
(We sing)

628 Charles Wesley

All ye that pass by,
to Jesus draw nigh;
to you is it nothing
that Jesus should die?
Your ransom and peace,
your surety he is:
come, see if there ever
was sorrow like his.

He dies to atone
for sins not his own;
your debt he hath paid,
and your work he hath done.
Ye all may receive
the peace he did leave,
who made intercession:
my Father, forgive!

For you and for me
he prayed on the tree:
the pray'r is accepted,
the sinner is free.
That sinner am I,
who on Jesus rely,
and come for the pardon
God cannot deny.

My pardon I claim;
for a sinner I am,
a sinner believing
in Jesus's name.
He purchased the grace
which now I embrace:
O Father, thou know'st
he hath died in my place.

629 *The Alternative Service Book (1980)*

Almighty God,
to whom all hearts are open,
all desires known,
and from whom no secrets are hidden:
cleanse the thoughts of our hearts
by the inspiration of your Holy Spirit,
that we may perfectly love you,
and worthily magnify,
that we may perfectly love you,
and worthily magnify
your holy name;
through Christ our Lord,
amen.
Through Christ our Lord,
amen.

© 1980 Central Board of Finance of the CofE

630 Claire Cloninger and Don Moen

And here we are,
lifting our hands to you;
here we are, giving our thanks
for all you do;
and as we praise
and worship your holy name,
you are here,
dwelling within our praise.

For ev'ry answered pray'r,
for always being there,
for love that hears us when we call,
for arms that lift us when we fall.
You have always been right beside us,
leading us all along the way,
and we've made it through,
because of you.

For days we cannot see,
for all that's yet to be,
the trials we may have to face,
when we'll be leaning on your grace.
It will be your strength that saves us,
your love that makes us strong,
and through it all,
we'll sing this song.

© 2000 Juniper Landing Music/CopyCare and Integrity's Hosanna!
Music/Kingsway's Thank you Music

631 James Montgomery

Angels from the realms of glory,
wing your flight o'er all the earth;
ye who sang creation's story
now proclaim Messiah's birth:

Come and worship
Christ, the new-born King;
come and worship,
worship Christ, the new-born King.

Shepherds, in the field abiding,
watching o'er your flocks by night,
God with us is now residing,
yonder shines the infant Light:

Sages, leave your contemplations;
brighter visions beam afar:
seek the great Desire of Nations;
ye have seen his natal star:

Saints before the altar bending,
watching long in hope and fear,
suddenly the Lord, descending,
in his temple shall appear:

Though an infant now we view him,
he shall fill his Father's throne,
gather all the nations to him;
ev'ry knee shall then bow down:

632 John Newton

Approach, my soul, the mercy-seat,
where Jesus answers pray'r;
there humbly fall before his feet,
for none can perish there.

Thy promise is my only plea,
with this I venture nigh;
thou callest burdened souls to thee
and such, O Lord, am I!

Bowed down beneath the load of sin,
by Satan sorely pressed,
by wars without and fears within,
I come to thee for rest.

Be thou my shield and hiding-place,
that, sheltered near thy side,
I may my fierce accuser face
and tell him thou hast died.

O wondrous love! to bleed and die,
to bear the cross and shame,
that guilty sinners, such as I,
might plead thy gracious name.

633 Aran Puddle

A rising generation,
set apart for liberty.
A royal, loving people,
chosen to be mighty,
mighty in the land.

A people who are hungry,
hungry for the bread of life.
A people who are thirsty,
thirsty for the river,
the river of joy.

And all across this nation,
a cry is ringing out,
the church of the King's breaking out.

In freedom, in power, in healing,
salvation to the ends of the earth.

© 1998 Hillsong Publishing/Kingsway's Thankyou Music

634 Bill Drake

As I come into your presence,
and am moved with humble rev'rence,
I'm enamoured by the beauty
of the One who died to save me.
I've been bought with blood as ransom
to be a child of your kingdom;
I'm a debtor to your gospel,
but an heir of ev'ry promise.

I will worship you,
give my life to you,
I bow down to you,
fall before your throne.
I will worship you,
give my life to you,
I bow down to you,
fall before your throne. Precious Lord.

Continued overleaf

When I come into your presence
you will make my life a fragrance,
I will see the One who's worthy,
now displayed in awesome glory.
I will hear the angels singing,
see the nations humbly kneeling;
clouds of witnesses surrounding,
bring a symphony of praise!

635   David Klassen

As long as there is air to breathe,
as long as there is life in me,
while the river runs into the sea
I will give you praise.
while the raindrops fall down from the sky
and the sunlight beams down from on high,
while the lion roars and birds can fly
I will give you praise.

From the rising of the sun
to the setting of the same,
Lord, I lift my voice.
I'll sing praises to your name,
King of Glory, I'll worship you endlessly
for that's what you created me to be.

As long as there is air to breathe,
as long as there is life in me,
while the river runs into the sea
I will give you praise.
And, though my days on earth will pass,
the praise in me will always last;
for however long forever lasts,
I will give you praise.

636   Robin Mark

As sure as gold is precious, and the honey
    sweet,
so you love this city, and you love these
    streets.
Ev'ry child out playing by their own front
    door,
ev'ry baby lying on the bedroom floor.

I hear that thunder in the distance,
like a train on the edge of town,
I can feel the brooding of your Spirit:
lay your burdens down, lay your burdens
    down.
Revive us, revive us, revive us with your
    fire.
Revive us, revive us, revive us with your
    fire.

From the preacher preaching when the well
    is dry,
to the lost soul reaching for a higher high.
From the young man working through his
    hopes and fears,
to the widow walking through the vale of
    tears.

Ev'ry man and woman, ev'ry old and young,
ev'ry father's daughter, ev'ry mother's son;
I feel it in my spirit, feel it in my bones,
you're going to send revival, bring them all
    back home.

I hear that thunder in the distance,
like a train on the edge of town,
I can feel the brooding of your Spirit:
lay your burdens down, lay your burdens
    down.
Revive us, revive us, revive us with your
    fire.
Revive us, revive us, revive us with your
    fire.

637   David Baroni and Wayne Tate

As the sun is reborn, and a beautiful
    morning
reminds me of your faithfulness to me.
Through the long, lonely night,
when the darkness hid the light,
you gave me grace to trust and now I see.
Even when it's hard to believe,
even when our hope seems all gone,
there has never been a night without a
    dawn.

Faithful God, unfailing love,
for ever you are worthy of our praise.
Faithful God, unfailing love,
we can always trust the wisdom of your
ways,
faithful God.

The heavens, they are telling
of the glory of our King,
so we join with all creation now and sing:

638 Tommy Walker

As we worship you,
let all the world come and see
how the mercy we've received
from you can set them free.
As we worship you,
let all this joy that fills our hearts
bring a hunger and a hope
to those who've strayed so far.

As we bow in adoration
and stand in rev'rent awe,
show your majesty and glory,
let your anointing fall.
As we declare your name, Lord Jesus,
as the only one who saves,
may the pow'r of your salvation
fill each heart, we pray.

As we worship you,
let all the nations hear our song,
the song of Jesus and his blood
that proved his love for all.
As we worship you,
may all the lost and broken come;
may they hear your still small voice
call out their names, each one.

As we bow in adoration
and stand in rev'rent awe,
show your majesty and glory,
let your anointing fall.

As we declare your name, Lord Jesus,
as the only one who saves,
may the pow'r of your salvation
fill each heart, we pray.
As we worship you, as we worship you;
as we worship you, as we worship you.

639 William Chatterton Dix

As with gladness men of old
did the guiding star behold,
as with joy they hailed its light,
leading onward, beaming bright;
so, most gracious Lord, may we
evermore be led to thee.

As with joyful steps they sped,
to that lowly manger-bed,
there to bend the knee before
him whom heav'n and earth adore,
so may we with willing feet
ever seek thy mercy-seat.

As their precious gifts they laid,
at thy manger roughly made,
so may we with holy joy,
pure, and free from sin's alloy,
all our costliest treasures bring,
Christ, to thee our heav'nly King.

Holy Jesu, ev'ry day
keep us in the narrow way;
and, when earthly things are past,
bring our ransomed souls at last
where they need no star to guide,
where no clouds thy glory hide.

In the heav'nly country bright
need they no created light,
thou its light, its joy, its crown,
thou its sun which goes not down;
there for ever may we sing
alleluias to our King.

640 Darlene Zschech

Beautiful Lord, wonderful Saviour,
I know for sure all of my days
are held in your hand,
crafted into your perfect plan.
You gently call me into your presence,
guiding me by your Holy Spirit;
teach me, dear Lord, to live all of my life
through your eyes.
I'm captured by your holy calling,
set me apart, I know you're drawing me
    to yourself;
lead me, Lord, I pray.

Take me, mould me,
use me, fill me;
I give my life to the Potter's hand.
Call me, guide me,
lead me, walk beside me;
I give my life to the Potter's hand.

© 1997 Darlene Zschech/Hillsong Publishing/Kingsway's Thankyou
Music

641 Neil Bennetts

Beauty for ashes and garments of praise,
you come and adorn me with joy once again,
and pour oil of gladness in instead of
despair;
bringing your mercy again like sweet, spring
rain.

Sweet spring rain, mercy from heaven,
sweet spring rain, come fall down on me.
Jesus, your truth has come
to restore me in mercy, in mercy.

© 2000 Daybreak Music Ltd.

642 Capt. Alan Price

Because of who he is,
because of who he is,
because of all he's done,
because of all he's done,
because of all his love for us,
we worship the Three in One.

We have come to God the Father,
we have come to God the Father,
in the name of God the Son,
in the name of God the Son,
by the power of the Spirit,
we worship the Three in One.

Because of who you are,
because of who you are,
because of all you've done,
because of all you've done,
because of all your love for us,
we worship the Three in One.

© 1994 Daybreak Music Ltd.

643 Charitie L. Bancroft

Before the throne of God above
I have a strong, a perfect plea,
a great High Priest whose name is Love,
who ever lives and pleads for me.
My name is graven on his hands,
my name is written on his heart;
I know that while in heav'n he stands
no tongue can bid me thence depart,
no tongue can bid me thence depart.

When Satan tempts me to despair,
and tells me of the guilt within,
upward I look and see him there,
who made an end to all my sin.
Because the sinless Saviour died,
my sinful soul is counted free;
for God the Just is satisfied
to look on him and pardon me,
to look on him and pardon me.

Behold him there! The risen Lamb,
my perfect, spotless righteousness;
the great unchangeable I Am,
the King of glory and of grace!
One with himself I cannot die,
my soul is purchased with his blood;
my life is hid with Christ on high,
with Christ, my Saviour and my God,
with Christ, my Saviour and my God.

644 Mark Altrogge

Behold the Lamb,
silent before his accusers
as thorns are pressed into his brow.
They lift him up,
oh see the spikes that hold him,
redeeming blood flows down.
But look again,
the cross stands empty now
and he is risen.

Behold the Lamb,
see him crowned with glory.
Behold the Lamb,
cast your crowns before him
crying, 'Holy, holy is the Lamb.'

Behold the Lamb,
carrying all our transgressions,
he freely takes our place;
endures the lash,
the mocking and the laughter
of those he dies to save.
But look again,
the cross stands empty now
and he is risen.

© 2000 PDI Praise/CopyCare

645 Mark Altrogge

Better by far is your presence.
Better by far is your Spirit.
Nothing compares to your love
poured out in my heart.
Better by far is your presence.
Better by far is your Spirit.
Nothing compares to your love
poured out in my heart,
it's better by far.

Better by far to be near you
than be freed from all of my trials.
Better by far that you make me like Christ
than to give me all I desire.

Better by far just to know you
than be blessed in all other ways.
Better by far that you work in my life
to the praise of your glory and grace.

© 1997 PDI Praise/CopyCare

646 Graham Kendrick

Blessed are the humble in spirit,
for theirs is the Kingdom of heaven.
And blessed are the mourners,
they will find comfort.
And blessed are the lowly,
they shall reign (they shall reign)
on the earth (on the earth).

Oh how you bless us, Lord!
Blessing upon blessing, Lord!
Making us a blessing,
a blessing for the world.
Oh how you bless us, Lord!
Blessing upon blessing, Lord!
Making us a blessing,
a blessing for the world.

And blessed are those who hunger,
who thirst for justice,
for surely you'll fill them completely.
And those who show mercy,
will be shown mercy.
And blessed are the pure hearts,
they'll see God (they'll see God),
they'll see God (they'll see God).

And blessed are peace-makers,
called the sons of God.
Blessed are those oppressed for
righteousness' sake,
for theirs shall be, shall always be,
yes, theirs shall be heaven's kingdom.

© 2001 Make Way Music

647 Don Moen

Blessèd be the name of the Lord,
he is worthy to be praised and adored;
so we lift up holy hands in one accord,
singing, 'Blessèd be the name,
blessèd be the name,
blessèd be the name of the Lord!'

648 Unknown

Bless the Lord, O my soul;
bless the Lord, O my soul;
and all that is within me
bless his holy name.

649 Andraé Crouch

Bless the Lord, O my soul,
and all that is within me,
bless his holy name.
(Repeat)

He has done great things,
he has done great things,
he has done great things;
bless his holy name.
Bless the Lord, O my soul,
and all that is within me,
bless his holy name.

650 Loulita Di Somma

Break the fallow ground
in my hardened heart,
soften me again;
take me to the place,
where I know your love,
Father, I draw near.

Lord, consume my soul,
take my life, it's yours;
breathe on me again;
in the secret place,
where I feel your touch,
Father, I draw near.

I draw near,
where mercy's waiting for me,
I draw near,
surrounded by your glory.
I draw near,
where holiness enfolds me,
Father, I draw near.

651 Henry Hinn

Breathe upon me, breath of God,
breathe upon me, Spirit of the Lord,
as I lift my hands in surrender to your name,
    Most High.
Yielding to your Spirit, walking in your grace,
Jesus, I adore, Jesus, I adore,
Jesus, I adore your holy name.

652 John Chisum and George Searcy

Christ above me, Christ beside me,
Christ within me ever-guiding;
Christ behind me, Christ before,
Christ, my love, my life, my Lord.

Bread of life from heaven,
lover of my soul;
peace of God so ever-present,
I surrender my control to

Mercy everlasting,
tenderness divine;
word of God so ever-healing,
I surrender heart and mind to

653 John Byrom, alt.

Christians, awake! Salute the happy morn,
whereon the Saviour of the world was born;
rise to adore the mystery of love,
which hosts of angels chanted from above:
with them the joyful tidings first begun
of God incarnate and the Virgin's Son.

Then to the watchful shepherds it was told,
who heard th' angelic herald's voice, 'Behold,
I bring good tidings of a Saviour's birth
to you and all the nations on the earth:
this day hath God fulfilled his promised
   word,
this day is born a Saviour, Christ the Lord.'

He spake; and straightway the celestial choir
in hymns of joy, unknown before, conspire;
the praises of redeeming love they sang,
and heav'n's whole orb with alleluias rang:
God's highest glory was their anthem still,
peace on the earth, in ev'ry heart good will.

To Bethl'em straight th'enlightened
   shepherds ran,
to see, unfolding, God's eternal plan,
and found, with Joseph and the blessèd
   maid,
her Son, the Saviour, in a manger laid:
then to their flocks, still praising God, return,
and their glad hearts with holy rapture burn.

O may we keep and ponder in our mind
God's wondrous love in saving lost mankind;
trace we the babe, who hath retrieved our
   loss,
from his poor manger to his bitter cross;
tread in his steps, assisted by his grace,
till our first heav'nly state again takes place.

Then may we hope, th'angelic hosts among,
to sing, redeemed, a glad triumphal song:
he that was born upon this joyful day
around us all his glory shall display;
saved by his love, incessant we shall sing
eternal praise to heav'n's almighty King.

654 'Urbs beata Jerusalem'
trans. John Mason Neale, alt.

Christ is made the sure foundation,
Christ the head and cornerstone,
chosen of the Lord, and precious,
binding all the Church in one,
holy Zion's help for ever,
and her confidence alone.

To this temple, where we call you,
come, O Lord of hosts, today;
you have promised loving kindness,
hear your servants as we pray,
bless your people now before you,
turn our darkness into day.

Hear the cry of all your people,
what they ask and hope to gain;
what they gain from you, for ever
with your chosen to retain,
and hereafter in your glory
evermore with you to reign.

Praise and honour to the Father,
praise and honour to the Son,
praise and honour to the Spirit,
ever Three and ever One,
One in might and One in glory,
while unending ages run.

655 Michael Saward

Christ triumphant, ever-reigning,
Saviour, Master, King.
Lord of heav'n, our lives sustaining,
hear us as we sing:

Yours the glory and the crown,
the high renown, the eternal name.

Word incarnate, truth revealing,
Son of Man on earth!
Pow'r and majesty concealing
by your humble birth:

Continued overleaf

Suff'ring servant, scorned, ill-treated,
victim crucified!
Death is through the cross defeated,
sinners justified:

> Yours the glory and the crown,
> the high renown, the eternal name.

Priestly King, enthroned for ever
high in heav'n above!
Sin and death and hell shall never
stifle hymns of love:

So, our hearts and voices raising
through the ages long,
ceaselessly upon you gazing,
this shall be our song:

© Michael Saward/Jubilate Hymns

656 Steve James

> Christ, your glory fills the heavens,
> your truth the world must know;
> Morning Star, you triumph over darkness –
> you are Jesus the Lord.

You are the sun of righteousness dawning
that shall cause our hearts to sing;
shine upon our faithless shadows
bringing healing in your wings.

> Christ, your glory fills the heavens,
> your truth the world must know;
> Morning Star, you triumph over darkness –
> you are Jesus the Lord.

You are the final word to be given,
you're the hope that sets us free;
let the earth be filled with your glory
as the waters fill the sea!

> Christ, your glory fills the heavens,
> your truth the world must know;
> Morning Star, you triumph over darkness –
> you are Jesus the Lord.

The light of your face is all we desire;
now walk by our side
and turn our hearts to burn with fire.

> Christ, your glory fills the heavens,
> your truth the world must know;
> Morning Star, you triumph over darkness –
> you are Jesus the Lord.
> Christ, your glory fills the heavens,
> your truth the world must know;
> Morning Star, you triumph over darkness –
> you are Jesus the Lord.

© Steve James/Jubilate Hymns

657 Andrew Bromley

Clothed with splendour and majesty,
you wear light like a robe,
you stretch out the heavens like a curtain,
awesome God.
You laid the earth on its foundation;
at the sound of your voice,
the mountains and oceans took their places,
awesome God.

All the earth displays your glory,
all creation calls your name.
As all of heaven is standing in awe,
all the nations shout your praise.

> Creation's anthem will rise to you,
> all the universe is crying out for you,
> in adoration to the Holy One,
> in higher praises to the awesome God.

© 1999 Sovereign Lifestyle Music

658 Geoff Bullock

Come, let's lift our praise,
Lord, to you our song we raise,
we will shout and sing with joy
to you our God.
For you are our coming King,
let us raise our voice and sing,
Lord, we magnify your name on high.

How good it is to praise and sing,
with thanksgiving we lift our hearts.
All the heavens above
will declare his love
and his enemies will depart.

Let us praise his name,
people now proclaim
his victorious majesty.
Shout your praises high,
all the earth and sky.
Joy that lasts for eternity.

659 Danny Antill

Come, let us rejoice before him
and make a joyful noise.
Come, let us bow down before him
and sing a song of praise!

Hosanna! You are glorious.
Hosanna! You are righteousness.
Hosanna! You're victorious,
Lord, we thank you for your name.
Hosanna! You are glorious.
Hosanna! You are righteousness.
Hosanna! You're victorious,
Lord, we thank you for your name.

Come, let us proclaim his greatness,
he healed the blind and lame.
He is the Lord and Saviour
and Jesus is his name.

Hosanna . . .

Come, let us dance before him
and bless his holy name.
He is the first and last
and he always stays the same!

Hosanna! You are glorious.
Hosanna! You are righteousness.
Hosanna! You're victorious,
Lord, we thank you for your name.
Lord, we praise your name,
Lord, we bless your holy name.
Hosanna!

660 Robert Walmsley

Come, let us sing of a wonderful love,
tender and true;
out of the heart of the Father above,
streaming to me and to you:
wonderful love
dwells in the heart of the Father above.

Jesus, the Saviour, this gospel to tell,
joyfully came;
came with the helpless and hopeless to
    dwell,
sharing their sorrow and shame;
seeking the lost,
saving, redeeming at measureless cost.

Jesus is seeking the wanderers yet;
why do they roam?
Love only waits to forgive and forget;
home! weary wanderer, home!
Wonderful love
dwells in the heart of the Father above.

Come to my heart, O thou wonderful love,
come and abide,
lifting my life till it rises above
envy and falsehood and pride;
seeking to be
lowly and humble, a learner of thee.

661 Dave Doherty

Come, let us worship and bow down,
let us kneel before the Lord,
our God, our maker.
(Repeat)

For he is our God,
and we are the people of his pasture,
and the sheep of his hand,
just the sheep of his hand.

662 Brian Doerksen

Come, now is the time to worship.
Come, now is the time to give your heart.
Come, just as you are to worship.
Come, just as you are before your God, come.

One day ev'ry tongue will confess you
    are God,
one day ev'ry knee will bow.
Still, the greatest treasure remains for those
who gladly choose you now.

663 Robert Robinson

Come, thou fount of ev'ry blessing,
tune my heart to sing thy grace;
streams of mercy, never ceasing,
call for songs of loudest praise.
Teach me some melodious sonnet,
sung by flaming tongues above;
praise the mount, I'm fixed upon it,
mount of thy redeeming love.

O to grace, how great a debtor,
daily I'm constrained to be,
let thy grace, Lord, like a fetter,
bind my wand'ring heart to thee.
Prone to wander, Lord, I feel it,
prone to leave the God I love;
here's my heart, Lord, take and seal it;
seal it for thy courts above.

664 Eric Nuzum and Chris Springer

Come to me, Lord (come to me, Lord),
here is my heart (here is my heart);
can't live on my own (can't live on my own),
can't live without you.

I want more, more of you, Lord
more, more of you, Lord;
wanna hold you, love you,
not let you go,
renew this fire that's within my soul,
I want more, more of you, Lord,
more, more of you, Lord.

665 Richard Lewis

Come to the power, the power of the
    living God.
His name is higher, higher than any
    other name:
mighty Jehovah, awesome deliverer,
his pow'r is greater, greater than any
    principality.
A mighty fortress is our God;
he sits enthroned in the heavens,
the Lord of hosts is he.
A mighty fortress is our God;
he sits enthroned in the heavens,
he reigns in majesty.
A mighty fortress is our God;
he sits enthroned in the heavens,
the Lord of hosts is he.
A mighty fortress is our God;
he sits enthroned in the heavens,
he reigns in majesty, in majesty.

666 Arthur Tannous

Come worship, come bow down,
in rev'rence to him crowned
our Saviour, who encompassed
all favour and compassion.
Worship his tender love and mercy,
worship his holiness.
Worship his grace and loving kindness,
worship his awesome pow'r.
Glory, praise and honour,
glory, praise and beauty,
glory, praise and power be to you.

667 Joseph Hart

Come, ye sinners, poor and needy,
weak and wounded, sick and sore;
Jesus ready stands to serve you,
full of pity, love and pow'r.

I will arise and go to Jesus,
he will embrace me in his arms;
in the arms of my dear Saviour,
O, there are ten thousand charms.

Come, ye thirsty, come and welcome,
God's free bounty glorify;
true belief and true repentance,
ev'ry grace that brings you nigh.

I will arise . . .

Let not conscience make you linger,
nor of fitness fondly dream;
all the fitness he requireth,
is to feel you need of him.

I will arise . . .

Come, ye weary, heavy laden,
lost and ruined by the fall;
if you tarry till you're better,
you will never come at all.

668 David Clifton and Phil Baggaley

Could I bring you words of comfort,
offer peace where there is war?
Could I bless the ones who curse me,
can I forgive the ones who hurt me most?
Would I weep if you were weeping,
walk with those the world disowns?
Can I break the bread of heaven
with ev'ry lost, lost and hungry soul?

Lord, I will, so hear my prayer.
Let your Spirit lead me on
to where I stand with the broken,
it's what Jesus would have done.

Would I stand against injustice,
speak for those who cannot speak?
Be the hands that help the helpless,
and be your arms, the arms that hold the
weak?

Lord, I will . . .

Could I lose the life you gave me,
lay it down with all I own?
Will I walk with ev'ry pilgrim who walks this
road,
this narrow way of love?

Lord, I will . . .

© 1999 Little Room Music/IQ Music Ltd.

669 Keith Green

Create in me a clean heart O God,
and renew a right spirit within me.
Create in me a clean heart O God,
and renew a right spirit within me.
Cast me not away from thy presence O Lord,
and take not thy Holy Spirit from me.
Restore unto me the joy of my salvation
and renew a right spirit within me.

© Shepherd Music/EMI Christian Music Publishing/CopyCare

670 Sue Howson

Create in me a pure heart that's yours
    for ever,
yielded and steadfast, secure in your love.
Restore to me joy in belonging to you.
Make me yours, Lord, make me yours,
I long to be devoted to you.
Oh may my life be one that's willing to
    live for you,
bearing the marks of sacrifice,
living to die, laying all down for your name.
Make me yours, Lord, make me yours,
I long to be devoted to you.

© 1995 Daybreak Music Ltd.

671 Chris Bowater and Ian Taylor

Creation is awaiting the return of the King.
The trees are poised to clap their hands
    for joy.
The mountains stand majestic to salute
    their God;
the desert lies in wait to burst into bloom.

The King is coming, the King is coming,
the King is coming to set creation free.
(Repeat)

The church is awaiting the return of the
    King.
The people joined together in his love.
Redeemed by his blood,
washed in his word.
As a bride longs for her bridegroom
the church looks to God.

The King is coming, the King is coming,
the King is coming to receive his bride.
(Repeat)

The world is awaiting the return of the King.
The earth is a footstool for his feet.
Ev'ry knee will bow down,
ev'ry tongue confess,
that Jesus Christ is Lord
of heaven and earth.

The King is coming, the King is coming,
the King is coming to reign in majesty.
(Repeat)

672 Sharon Damazio

Crown him King of kings,
crown him Lord of lords,
Wonderful Counsellor, the Mighty God;
Emmanuel, God is with us, and he shall reign,
he shall reign, he shall reign, for evermore.

673 Simon Goodall

Deep within my heart
is a longing to know you more.
I have searched for love unending
and have found you to be true.

You are the one that I live for,
there's no one else that I love more;
you're all I need, my all in all,
and I adore you, I adore you, Lord.

Once we were apart
then you found me
and made me your own.
All this world had to offer
couldn't match the love you've shown.

674 Kelly Carpenter

Draw me close to you,
never let me go.
I lay it all down again,
to hear you say that I'm your friend.

You are my desire,
no one else will do,
'cause nothing else could take your place,
to feel the warmth of your embrace.
Help me find the way,
bring me back to you.

You're all I want,
you're all I've ever needed.
You're all I want,
help me know you are near.

675 Bob McGee

Emmanuel, Emmanuel,
his name is called Emmanuel;
God with us, revealed in us;
his name is called Emmanuel.

676 Nick and Anita Haigh

Empty, broken, here I stand,
Kyrie eleison.
Touch me with your healing hand,
Kyrie eleison.
Take my arrogance and pride,
Kyrie eleison.
Wash me in your mercy's tide,

Kyrie eleison.
Kyrie eleison,
Christe eleison,
Kyrie eleison.

When my faith has all but gone,
Kyrie eleison,
give me strength to carry on,
Kyrie eleison.
When my dreams have turned to dust,
Kyrie eleison,
in you, O Lord, I put my trust,
Kyrie eleison.

When my heart is cold as ice,
your love speaks of sacrifice,
love that sets the captive free,
O pour compassion down on me.

You're the voice that calms my fears,
you're the laughter, dries my tears,
you're my music, my refrain,
help me sing your song again.

Humble heart of holiness,
kiss me with your tenderness,
Jesus, faithful friend and true,
all I am I give to you.

© 2000 Break of Day Music/Daybreak Music Ltd.

677 Thomas Binney

Eternal Light, eternal Light!
how pure the soul must be,
when, placed within thy searching sight,
it shrinks not, but with calm delight,
can live and look on thee.

The spirits that surround thy throne
may bear the burning bliss;
but that is surely theirs alone,
since they have never, never known
a fallen world like this.

O how shall I, whose native sphere
is dark, whose mind is dim,
before th'Ineffable appear,
and on my naked spirit bear
the uncreated beam?

There is a way for us to rise
to that sublime abode;
an off'ring and a sacrifice,
a Holy Spirit's energies,
an Advocate with God.

These, these prepare us for the sight
of holiness above;
the sons of ignorance and night
can dwell in the eternal light,
through the eternal love.

678 Graham Kendrick

Ev'rybody, ev'rywhere, bless his holy
name.
Ev'rybody, ev'rywhere, for ever.
Ev'rybody, ev'rywhere, sing about his
love.
Ev'rybody, ev'rywhere, for ever and ever.

I will praise you my God and King
and bless your name each day and for ever.
Great is the Lord, greatly praise him.
His greatness knows no boundaries.
Oh, let each generation stand in awe
and tell their children what he's done.
I will meditate upon your glory,
splendour and majesty, mighty miracles.
Let them be on ev'ry tongue,
tell the glorious things you've done.

Continued overleaf

God is kind and merciful,
he is slow to anger, always rich in love,
all that he does full of compassion.
Creatures and creation give you thanks,
your people bless your holy name
telling the glories of your reign.
They will tell the world about your glory,
splendour and majesty, mighty miracles,
and this glorious King shall reign
generations without end.

Ev'rybody, ev'rywhere, bless his holy
      name.
Ev'rybody, ev'rywhere, for ever.
Ev'rybody, ev'rywhere, sing about his
      love.
Ev'rybody, ev'rywhere, for ever and ever.

See him lift the fallen,
share the burden as we walk the weary road.
The eyes of all look up to heaven
for he is our helper, our provider
and the source that satisfies
the needs of ev'ry living thing.
The Lord is always fair and full of kindness,
close to all who call, seek him truly.
He fulfils their hearts' desire
but the wicked he destroys.

679 Ian Mizen and Andy Pressdee

Ev'rything I am,
and ev'rything I have
I give to you.

Ev'rything I want,
and ev'rything I dream
I give to you.

You are, you are ev'rything to me.
You are, you are ev'rything to me.

Take me on a journey
into your heart.
Take me on a journey
into your love.

680 Lilian Stevenson from the German

Fairest Lord Jesus;
ruler of all nature,
O thou of God and man the Son;
thee will I cherish,
thee will I honour,
thou, my soul's glory, joy, and crown.

Fair are the meadows;
fairer still the woodlands,
robed in the blooming garb of spring.
Jesus is fairer,
Jesus is purer;
who makes the woeful heart to sing.

Fair is the sunshine;
fairer still the moonlight
and all the twinkling starry host.
Jesus shines brighter,
Jesus shines purer;
than all the angels heav'n can boast.

Beautiful Saviour!
Lord of the nations!
Son of God and Son of Man!
Glory and honour,
praise, adoration,
now and for evermore be thine!

681 Mark Altrogge

Faithful are your mercies, Lord,
they drench me like the dew.
Pure and sweet your holy love;
I find my joy in you.

Your favour greets me like the dawn,
my burning heart must sing
to you who rises over me,
with healing in your,
healing in your wings.

Your faithfulness is higher than the
  heavens,
deeper than the sea;
great is your faithfulness.
Your faithfulness is higher than the
  heavens,
deeper than the sea;
great is your faithfulness to me,
great is your faithfulness to me.

You seat me at your table, Lord,
you've given me a place.
You robe me in your righteousness,
adorning me with grace.

You crown me with your victor's wreath
you gained upon the tree.
You take the oil of gladness
and pour it out on,
you pour it out on me.

© 1999 PDI Praise/CopyCare

682 Graham Kendrick

Father, to you with songs of love we come
into your presence in awe of all you've done,
brought here with joy before your throne of
  grace
and in the Son you love given our place.

What grace to be found in him,
heaven's glorious King.
Father, what grace!
Raising us to life,
choosing us in Christ,
Father, what grace!

Deep is the joy that fills your courts above,
while angels wonder at your redeeming love;
and, as you gaze with joy upon your Son,
your eyes are on the ones his love has won.

No higher call than to be heirs with him,
so let our passion burn for heavenly things.
Seated with Christ, for him alone to live,
our hearts for ever where our treasure is.

© 2001 Make Way Music

683 Horatius Bonar, alt.

Fill thou my life, O Lord, my God,
in ev'ry part with praise,
that my whole being may proclaim
thy being and thy ways.

Not for the lip of praise alone,
nor e'en the praising heart,
I ask, but for a life made up
of praise in ev'ry part.

Praise in the common things of life,
its goings out and in;
praise in each duty and each deed,
however small and mean.

Fill ev'ry part of me with praise;
let all my being speak
of thee and of thy love, O Lord,
poor though I be and weak.

So shalt thou, Lord, receive from me
the praise and glory due;
and so shall I begin on earth
the song for ever new.

So shall each fear, each fret, each care,
be turnèd into song;
and ev'ry winding of the way
the echo shall prolong.

So shall no part of day or night
unblest or common be;
but all my life, in ev'ry step,
be fellowship with thee.

684
William Walsham How

For all the saints
who from their labours rest,
who thee by faith
before the world confessed,
thy name, O Jesus,
be for ever blest.

Alleluia, alleluia!

Thou wast their rock,
their fortress and their might;
thou, Lord, their captain
in the well-fought fight;
thou in the darkness drear
their one true light.

O may thy soldiers,
faithful, true and bold,
fight as the saints
who nobly fought of old,
and win, with them,
the victor's crown of gold.

O blest communion!
fellowship divine!
we feebly struggle,
they in glory shine;
yet all are one in thee,
for all are thine.

And when the strife is fierce,
the warfare long,
steals on the ear
the distant triumph-song,
and hearts are brave again,
and arms are strong.

The golden evening
brightens in the west;
soon, soon to faithful
warriors cometh rest;
sweet is the calm of
paradise the blest.

But lo! There breaks
a yet more glorious day;
the saints triumphant
rise in bright array:
the King of glory
passes on his way.

From earth's wide bounds,
from ocean's farthest coast,
through gates of pearl
streams in the countless host,
singing to Father,
Son and Holy Ghost.

685
Fred Pratt Green

For the fruits of his creation,
thanks be to God;
for his gifts to ev'ry nation,
thanks be to God;
for the ploughing, sowing, reaping,
silent growth while we are sleeping,
future needs in earth's safe-keeping,
thanks be to God.

In the just reward of labour,
God's will is done;
in the help we give our neighbour,
God's will is done;
in our world-wide task of caring
for the hungry and despairing,
in the harvests we are sharing,
God's will is done.

For the harvests of his Spirit,
thanks be to God;
for the good we all inherit,
thanks be to God;
for the wonders that astound us,
for the truths that still confound us,
most of all, that love had found us,
thanks be to God.

686 Michael Battersby

Freedom and liberty,
now I got a revelation
what you did for me.
You broke the chains and you set me free
and I'm never going back again.
(Repeat)

You're my strong and mighty fortress,
you're my shelter.
You're the glory and the lifter of my head.
You're the joy of my salvation,
you're the rock on which I stand,
so I will not fear
what life may bring,
'cause God, I'm in your hand.

© 1996 Michael Battersby/Smart Productions

687 Matt Redman

Friend of sinners, Lord of truth,
I am falling in love with you.
Friend of sinners, Lord of truth,
I have fallen in love with you.
Jesus, I love your name,
the name by which we're saved.
Jesus, I love your name,
the name by which we're saved.

Friend of sinners, Lord of truth,
I am giving my life to you.
Friend of sinners, Lord of truth,
I have given my life to you.
Jesus, I love your name,
the name by which we're saved.
Jesus, I love your name,
the name by which we're saved.

© 1994 Kingsway's Thankyou Music

688 Chris Tomlin

Give thanks to the Lord,
our God and King:
his love endures for ever.
For he is good, he is above all things:
his love endures for ever.
Sing praise, sing praise.

With a mighty hand
and outstretched arm:
his love endures for ever.
For the life that's been reborn:
his love endures for ever.
Sing praise, sing praise,
sing praise, sing praise.

For ever, God is faithful,
for ever God is strong.
For ever God is with us,
for ever, for ever.

From the rising to the setting sun:
his love endures for ever.
By the grace of God, we will carry on:
his love endures for ever.
Sing praise, sing praise,
sing praise, sing praise.

© 2000 Rivermusic Songs/sixstepspublishing

689 Richard Lewis

Give us passion for the Lamb of God,
who takes away the sins of the world.
Lord, give us passion.
Greater love has no man than to lay
    down his life for his friends.
Lord, give us passion for Jesus,
passion for his love that's strong as death,
passion that burns with your holy fire,
    passion for you.
Let the Church rise up with new
    determination,
that the world might know the power of
    the cross,
and your gospel be preached in ev'ry
    nation,
salvation to the lost.
Passion for Jesus, passion for Jesus,
passion for Jesus, passion for you.

© 1996 Kingsway's Thankyou Music

690 Carol Mundy

Glorious Lord, wonderful King of kings
and Lord of Glory.
Faithful and true, worthy are you
of the honour, glory and praise.
Mighty, majestic, victorious Lord.
Jesus, Saviour, the One we adore.
Faithful and true, worthy are you
and we crown you Lord of all.

691 John Newton
based on Isaiah 33:20-21, alt.

Glorious things of thee are spoken,
Zion, city of our God;
he whose word cannot be broken
formed thee for his own abode.
On the Rock of Ages founded,
what can shake thy sure repose?
With salvation's walls surrounded,
thou may'st smile at all thy foes.

See, the streams of living waters,
springing from eternal love,
well supply thy sons and daughters,
and all fear of want remove.
Who can faint while such a river
ever flows their thirst to assuage?
Grace which, like the Lord, the giver,
never fails from age to age.

Round each habitation hov'ring,
see the cloud and fire appear
for a glory and a cov'ring,
showing that the Lord is near.
Thus they march, the pillar leading,
light by night and shade by day;
daily on the manna feeding
which he gives them when they pray.

Saviour, if of Zion's city
I through grace a member am,
let the world deride or pity,
I will glory in thy name.

Fading is the worldling's pleasure,
boasted pomp and empty show;
solid joys and lasting treasure
none but Zion's children know.

692 Larry Dempsey

Glory, glory, glory to the Lamb.
Glory, glory, glory to the Lamb.
For he is glorious and worthy to be praised,
the Lamb upon the throne;
and unto him we lift our voice in praise,
the Lamb upon the throne.

693 D. Klassen

Glory, glory, I give you glory
just because of who you are.
God Almighty, pure and holy,
Prince of Peace, Morning Star!
Lord of all, who compares to you,
with my lips singing praise to you,
no one else I'd rather bow down to but you.

Blessing and honour to you, Lord,
you are the only living God.
Worthy of all the praises flowing from my
*   heart.*
Name above ev'ry other name,
Jesus, you always will remain.
Heaven and earth will pass,
but you will stay the same!

694 Scott Wesley Brown

Glory, honour, power
belongs to you, Lord,
blessing, praises,
wisdom and strength are yours.
We cry, 'Holy, Lord, you are holy',
only you will we praise and adore.
We cry, 'Worthy, Lord, you are worthy',
for ever and ever,
for ever and evermore.

695 Scott Wesley Brown

Glory to you,
glory to you;
may all that we are,
and all that we do
bring glory, Lord, to you.

Honour to you,
honour to you;
may all that we are,
and all that we do
bring honour, Lord, to you.

Blessing to you,
blessing to you;
may all that we are,
and all that we do
bring blessing, Lord, to you.

696 Michael Battersby

God Almighty,
let your presence fill this place;
Lord, you're all I need
and you're all that I long for.
My desire
is to worship you alone
in this secret place;
let me dwell here for ever.

Rushing wind, consuming fire,
fill this place,
touch me now,
let your glory fall,
let your glory fall,
let your glory fall on me.
Let your glory fall,
let your glory fall,
let your glory fall on me.

697 David Bird, Richard Lacy and Sarah Lacy

God in the darkness and God in the
    morning,
God in the work and the pain, and the play,
Lord of all heaven and earth's great Creator,
God at beginning and end of the day.

God in the tiniest infinite detail,
God in the nearest and furthest away,
Lord of all heaven and earth's great Creator,
God at beginning and end of the day,
God at beginning and end of the day.

I lay down my fear and my hatred,
tear down the curtain of sin;
open my heart and let all that is good
    enter in.

God in the darkness and God in the
    morning,
God in the work and the pain and the play,
Lord of all heaven and earth's great Creator,
God at beginning and end of the day,
God at beginning and end of the day.

I lay down, my heart is so weary,
and gaze on his presence with awe.
There's nothing too small to entrust to the
    infinite God.

God in the darkness and God in the morning,
God in the work and the pain and the play,
Lord of all heaven and earth's great Creator,
God at beginning and end of the day.

God for the humble and weak and bewildered,
God for the nearest and furthest away,
Lord of all heaven and earth's great Creator,
God at beginning and end of the day,
God at beginning and end of the day.

698 David Clifton

God is our refuge and our strength,
an ever-present help in times of trouble.

The seas may rise up,
the nations may fall,
but there's a city, a holy place
where the Most High dwells.
There's a river, a fortress,
therefore we will not fear.

699 Richard Bewes

God is our strength and refuge,
our present help in trouble,
and we therefore will not fear,
though the earth should change!
Though mountains shake and tremble,
though swirling waters are raging,
God the Lord of hosts is with us evermore!

There is a flowing river,
within God's holy city;
God is in the midst of her,
she shall not be moved!
God's help is swiftly given,
thrones vanish at his presence,
God the Lord of hosts is with us evermore!

Come, see the works of our maker,
learn of his deeds all-pow'rful;
wars will cease across the world
when he shatters the spear!
Be still and know your creator,
uplift him in the nations,
God the Lord of hosts is with us evermore!

700 William Cowper

God moves in a mysterious way
his wonders to perform;
he plants his footsteps in the sea,
and rides upon the storm.

Deep in unfathomable mines
of never-failing skill,
he treasures up his bright designs,
and works his sov'reign will.

Ye fearful saints, fresh courage take;
the clouds ye so much dread
are big with mercy, and shall break
in blessings on your head.

Judge not the Lord by feeble sense,
but trust him for his grace;
behind a frowning providence
he hides a shining face.

His purposes will ripen fast,
unfolding ev'ry hour;
the bud may have a bitter taste,
but sweet will be the flow'r.

Blind unbelief is sure to err,
and scan his work in vain;
God is his own interpreter,
and he will make it plain.

701 Gloria and William J. Gaither

God sent his Son, they called him Jesus;
he came to love, heal and forgive.
He lived and died to buy my pardon;
an empty grave is there to prove my Saviour
lives.

Because he lives I can face tomorrow;
because he lives, all fear is gone.
Because I know he holds my future,
and life is worth the living just because he
lives.

How sweet to hold a new-born baby,
and feel the pride and joy he gives;
but greater still the calm assurance:
this child can face uncertain days
because he lives.

And then one day I'll cross the river;
I'll fight life's final war with pain.
And then, as death gives way to vict'ry,
I'll see the lights of glory and I'll know he
    reigns.

702 John Hartley and Gary Sadler

God, you keep us without falling,
as you watch us from above;
in our comings and our goings,
sheltered by your precious love.
In the pouring rain of mercy
comes the grace by which we're saved
for the glory of your name,
for the glory of your name.

You have touched our lives for ever,
can we be the same again?
May our hearts be ever faithful,
ever faithful as a friend.
Let us live that we may serve you,
overflowing with your praise,
for the glory of your name,
for the glory of your name.

We behold the man of sorrows
hanging there up on a cross,
where we wounded one so holy,
yet these wounds are life to us.
For the blood you shed was perfect
and your finished work remains
for the glory of your name,
for the glory of your name.

Now we lift our eyes to heaven,
see you seated on the throne;
still rejoicing in your promise,
this is where our hope is found.
For we know that you are coming,
ev'ry tongue will sing your fame,
for the glory of your name,
for the glory of your name.

703 Stuart Garrard

God, you're my God, you're my God;
God, you're my God, you're my God.
And I will seek you, yes, I will seek you;
and I will seek you, yes, I will seek you.

You satisfy my soul; you satisfy my soul.
So I will praise you as long as I live;
So I will praise you
as long as I live.

I've seen your power and your glory.
You've let me see you in the sanctuary,
because your love is better than my life,
I will lift up my hands in sacrifice.

We give you praise, give you praise;
we give you praise, give you praise.
For you are worthy, yes, you are worthy;
for you are worthy, yes, you are worthy.
So I will praise you,
as long as I live.

704 Chris Bowater

Greater grace, deeper mercy,
wider love, higher ways.
Perfect peace, complete forgiveness,
it's all found in you,
it's all found in you.

More than hope, full assurance,
joy that more than satisfies.
Comfort strength, pow'r and healing,
it's all found in you,
it's all found in you.

It's all found in you, Jesus,
it's all found in you.
All I desire and all I require,
it's all found in you.

Continued overleaf

Mercy triumphs over justice,
judgement is good, mercy is best.
Where sin abounds,
grace is more abounding,
it's all found in you.

705 Unknown

Great is he who's the King of kings
and the Lord of lords,
he is wonderful!

Alleluia, alleluia, alleluia,
he is wonderful!

Alleluia, salvation and glory,
honour and power,
he is wonderful!

706 Michael W. Smith and Deborah D. Smith

Great is the Lord and worthy of glory,
great is the Lord and worthy of praise;
great is the Lord, now lift up your voice,
now lift up your voice, great is the Lord,
great is the Lord.

Great is the Lord, he is holy and just,
by his power we trust in his love;
great is the Lord, he is faithful and true,
by his mercy he proves he is love.

Great are you, Lord, and worthy of glory,
great are you, Lord, and worthy of praise;
great are you, Lord, I lift up my voice,
I lift up my voice, great are you, Lord,
great are you, Lord.

707 David Hind

Great, O Lord is your holiness,
is your loveliness.
Great, O Lord is your holiness,
is your loveliness;
and I'll proclaim
Jesus is Lord,
Jesus is wonderful;
the Name above all names.
And I'll proclaim
Jesus is Lord,
Jesus is wonderful.
Great is the Lord;
great is the Lord.

708 William Williams

Guide me, O thou great Jehovah,
pilgrim through this barren land;
I am weak, but thou art mighty,
hold me with thy pow'rful hand:
Bread of heaven, Bread of heaven,
feed me now and evermore,
feed me now and evermore.

Open now the crystal fountain
whence the healing stream doth flow;
let the fiery, cloudy pillar
lead me all my journey through:
strong Deliverer, strong Deliverer,
be thou still my strength and shield,
be thou still my strength and shield.

When I tread the verge of Jordan
bid my anxious fears subside;
death of death, and hell's destruction,
land me safe on Canaan's side:
songs of praises, songs of praises,
I will ever give to thee,
I will ever give to thee.

709   <small>James Montgomery, based on Psalm 72</small>

Hail to the Lord's anointed,
great David's greater son!
Hail, in the time appointed,
his reign on earth begun!
He comes to break oppression,
to set the captive free;
to take away transgression,
and rule in equity.

He comes with succour speedy
to those who suffer wrong;
to help the poor and needy,
and bid the weak be strong;
to give them songs for sighing,
their darkness turn to light,
whose souls, condemned and dying,
were precious in his sight.

He shall come down like showers
upon the fruitful earth,
and love, joy, hope, like flowers,
spring in his path to birth:
before him on the mountains
shall peace the herald go;
and righteousness in fountains
from hill to valley flow.

Kings shall fall down before him,
and gold and incense bring;
all nations shall adore him,
his praise all people sing;
to him shall prayer unceasing
and daily vows ascend;
his kingdom still increasing,
a kingdom without end.

O'er ev'ry foe victorious,
he on his throne shall rest,
from age to age more glorious,
all-blessing and all-blest;
the tide of time shall never
his covenant remove;
his name shall stand for ever;
that name to us is love.

710   <small>V. Masongo and M. DuPlessis</small>

Hallelujah, hosanna!
Hallelujah, hosanna!
Hallelujah, hosanna!
Hallelujah, hosanna!
Hallelujah, hosanna!
(Repeat)

God has exalted Jesus to the highest place,
and given him the name that is above ev'ry
  name.
That at the name of Jesus ev'ry knee shall
  bow,
and ev'ry tongue confess that he is Lord.

Halala ngo Jesu,
halala ngo Jesu,
halala ngo Jesu,
halala, O halala.
Halala ngo Jesu,
halala ngo Jesu,
halala ngo Jesu Nkosi!

711   <small>Elisha A. Hoffman</small>

Have you been to Jesus for the cleansing
  pow'r?
Are you washed in the blood of the Lamb?
Are you fully trusting in his grace this hour?
Are you washed in the blood of the Lamb?

Are you washed in the blood,
in the soul-cleansing blood of the Lamb?
Are your garments spotless?
Are they white as snow?
Are you washed in the blood of the
  Lamb?

Are you walking daily by the Saviour's side?
Are you washed in the blood of the Lamb?
Do you rest each moment in the Crucified?
Are you washed in the blood of the Lamb?

Continued overleaf

When the Bridegroom cometh will your
  robes be white?
Are you washed in the blood of the Lamb?
Will your soul be ready for the mansions
  bright,
and be washed in the blood of the Lamb?

  Are you washed in the blood,
  in the soul-cleansing blood of the Lamb?
  Are your garments spotless?
  Are they white as snow?
  Are you washed in the blood of the
    Lamb?

Lay aside the garments that are stained with
  sin,
and be washed in the blood of the Lamb.
There's a fountain flowing for the soul
  unclean,
O be washed in the blood of the Lamb.

712 Claire Cloninger and Don Moen

Have your way, have your way,
Holy Spirit, fill our hearts
and have your way.
As we wait, as we pray,
speak your word into our hearts
and have your way.

713 Tanya Riches

Hear our pray'r,
Spirit, come.
How I long for
your sweet touch.

On my knees,
I cry out,
Jesus, Saviour,
behold your child.

  Like a deer longing for water,
  my soul yearns.
  Only you can fill my deep hunger.
  My heart burns, my heart burns.

Oceans deep,
mountains high,
O my God,
I cannot live without your love,
I cannot live without your love.

714 Don Moen

Hear our pray'r, we are your children,
and we've gathered here today;
we've gathered here to pray;
hear our cry, we need your mercy,
and we need your grace today,
hear us as we pray.

  Our Father, who art in heaven,
  hallowed be thy name;
  our Father, hear us from heaven;
  forgive our sins, we pray.

Hear our song as it rises to heaven;
may your glory fill the earth
as the waters cover the sea;
see our hearts and remove anything
that is standing in the way
of coming to you today.

Though we are few
we're surrounded by many
who have crossed that river before,
and this is the song we'll be singing for ever:
Holy is the Lord, holy is the Lord.

715 Russell Fragar

Hear these praises from a grateful heart.
Each time I think of you, the praises start.
Love you so much, Jesus, love you so much.

  How my soul longs for you,
  longs to worship you for ever,
  in your power and majesty.
  Lift my hands, lift my heart,
  lift my voice towards the heavens,
  for you are my sun and shield.

Lord I love you, my soul sings.
In your presence carried on your wings.
Love you so much, Jesus, love you so much.

716 Ian Mizen and Andy Pressdee

Heavenly Father, may your holy name
be lifted high in all the earth.
Heavenly Father, let your kingdom come,
and your will be done in all the earth.

I will follow you to the ends of the earth.
I will give to you ev'ryday of my life.
I will thirst for you from the depths of
*   my soul,*
I will worship you 'til the end of time.

Heavenly Father, wash away our sins
and make us holy in your eyes.
Heavenly Father, guide our hearts and minds
and keep us hidden in your love.

717 Darrell Evans and Eric Nuzum

He has come to bring light into the darkness;
he has come to bring freedom to the captives;
he has come to restore the broken-hearted,
it's time to proclaim the year of the Lord.

Prepare the way (prepare the way),
prepare the way for our Redeemer;
prepare the way (prepare the way),
prepare the way for our Restorer.
Make ready your heart,
make ready your home,
make ready the people of God,
prepare the way.

He has come to bring hope to the hopeless;
he has come to comfort all who mourn;
he has come the heal our ev'ry sickness,
it's time to proclaim the year of the Lord.

718 Rory Noland and Greg Ferguson

He is able, more than able
to accomplish what concerns me today.
He is able, more than able
to handle anything that comes my way.
He is able, more than able
to do much more than I could ever dream.
He is able, more than able
to make me what he wants me to be.

719 Michelle Hira

He is our God,
let all creation bow,
the sov'reign King: most holy One.
He sacrificed his life,
washed and cleansed within,
portioned by faith
we're destined to win.

Ev'rything that has breath,
praise the Lord,
ev'rything that's in me,
praise the Lord.
I can praise him
on the highest mountain,
praise him in the lowest valley;
ev'rything that's in me,
praise the Lord.

720 Kandela Groves

He is our peace,
who has broken down ev'ry wall.
He is our peace,
he is our peace.
(Repeat)

Cast all your cares on him,
for he cares for you.
He is our peace,
he is our peace.
(Repeat)

721 Paul Oakley

Here I am, and I have come
to thank you, Lord, for all you've done:
thank you, Lord;
you paid the price at Calvary,
you shed your blood, you set me free:
thank you, Lord;
no greater love was ever shown,
no better life ever was laid down.

And I will always love your name;
and I will always sing your praise;

You took my sin, you took my shame,
you drank my cup, you bore my pain:
thank you, Lord;
you broke the curse, you broke the chains,
in victory from death you rose again:
thank you, Lord;
and not by works, but by your grace
you clothe me now in your righteousness.

You bid me come, you make me whole,
you give me peace, you restore my soul:
thank you, Lord;
you fill me up, and when I'm full
you give me more till I overflow:
thank you, Lord;
you're making me to be like you,
to do the works of the Father, too.

722 Stuart Garrard and Martin Smith

Here I am, in that old place again,
down on my face again.
Crying out, I want you to hear my plea,
come down and rescue me.
How long will it take?
How long will I have to wait?

And all I want is all you have.
Come to me, rescue me,
fall on me with your love.
And all you want is all I have.
Come to me, rescue me,
fall on me with your love.

Sanctify, I want to be set apart
right to the very heart.
Prophesy to the four winds
and breathe life to this very place.
How long will it take?
How long will I have to wait?

Lifted up, I've climbed
with the strength I have,
right to this mountain top.
Looking out,
the cloud's getting bigger now,
it's time to get ready now.
How long will it take?
How long will I have to wait?

And all I want is all you have.
Come to me, rescue me,
fall on me with your love.
And all you want is all I have.
Come to me, rescue me,
fall on me with your love.

723 Craig Musseau

Here I am once again,
I pour out my heart
for I know that you hear ev'ry cry.
You are listening
no matter what state my heart is in.
You are faithful to answer
with words that are true
and a hope that is real.
As I feel your touch,
you bring a freedom to all that's within,
in the safety of this place.

I'm longing to pour out my heart,
say that I love you,
pour out my heart,
say that I need you;
pour out my heart,
say that I'm thankful,
pour out my heart,
say that you're wonderful.

724 Reuben Morgan

Here I am waiting,
abide in me I pray,
here I am longing for you.
Hide me in your love,
bring me to my knees,
may I know Jesus more and more.

Come, live in me all my life,
take over.
Come, breathe in me and I will rise
on eagles' wings.

725 A. Smith, J. Markin and C. Bowater

Here, in the dawning of hope,
in the wake of a rising wave,
clear, from the throne of our God
comes a strength for approaching days.
We have a house God has called us to build,
we have a challenge before us.
Raise up your standard in days such as these,
for the year of his favour has come.

Proclaim the favour of God.
Make known the justice of God.
Comfort the mourning,
provide for the grieving,
bestowing a crown of beauty.
Proclaim the favour of God.
Display the splendour of God.
Healing the hurting
as hope is returning,
declaring the day of our God.

Rise, for the light which has come
is the glory that shines on you.
See, though the darkness is strong,
yet the nations will come to your light.
We have a house God has called us to build,
we have a challenge before us.
Raise up your standard in days such as these,
for the year of his favour has come.

Proclaim the favour of God.
Make known the justice of God.
Comfort the mourning,
provide for the grieving,
bestowing a crown of beauty.
Proclaim the favour of God.
Display the splendour of God.
Healing the hurting
as hope is returning,
declaring the day of our God.

726 Ned Davies

Here in this house of the great King,
we've come together now to worship him.
This house is built on Christ our Rock,
cannot be shaken, cannot be shaken.

God is awesome in this place,
we sense his presence
as we sing his praise.
There is power here for miracles,
to set the captives free,
and make the broken whole.
God is awesome,
he's so awesome,
God is awesome in this place.

I've found where I belong,
I'm a living stone.
And in this house I will grow.
We've found where we belong,
we are living stones.
And in this house we will grow.

727 Colin Battersby

Here in your presence, Lord,
is where I wanna be.
Closer to you, my Jesus, I belong.
Here in your presence, Lord,
is where I wanna live,
I was made for this;
I was made to lift your name.

Continued overleaf

'Cause, you're my God,
on the throne,
and my delight is to worship you alone.
All my praise I will give,
you are the reason why I live.

728 Billie Mallett

Here I stand before you,
before your throne of grace,
to find help in time of need,
to seek your lovely face.
(Repeat)

> *God of glory,*
> *God of power,*
> *God of majesty.*
> (Repeat)

Father, I come to you
through the blood of Christ.
I bring to you an off'ring of
a consecrated life.
(Repeat)

729 Michael Sandeman

Here is the risen Son
riding out in glory,
radiating light all around.
Here is the Holy Spirit,
poured out for the nations,
glorifying Jesus the Lamb.
We will stand as a people
who are upright and holy,
we will worship the Lord of hosts.
We will watch, we will wait
on the walls of the city,
we will look and see what he will say to us.
Ev'ry knee shall bow before him,
ev'ry tongue confess
that he is King of kings,
Lord of lords, and ruler of the earth.

730 Richard Lewis

He rides on the wings of the wind,
his chariot the clouds of heaven;
holy is he, holy is he.
He's clothed in a garment of light,
his messengers are flames of fire;
holy is he, holy is he.

It's an awesome thing, to be in his presence,
oh, how I need his Spirit's work in me.
Consuming fire, my heart's desire,
come, Spirit fire, burn afresh in me.
Consuming fire, my heart's desire,
come, Spirit fire, burn afresh in me.

His hair is as white as the snow,
his eyes are a flame of fire;
holy is he, holy is he.
His feet are like glowing bronze,
his voice like the many waters;
holy is he, holy is he.

731 Mike Anderson
based on Isaiah 9,11

> *He shall be called 'Mighty!'*
> *He shall be called 'Wonder-Counsellor!'*
> *He shall be called 'Eternal Father,*
> *Prince of Peace!'*
> *And he will bring justice.*
> *Yes, he will bring peace eternally,*
> *for he is our eternal Father,*
> *Prince of Peace.*

The people who wandered in darkness
have seen a great light.
On people who lived in the shadowlands,
majestic light has shone!

The goat shall lie down with the panther,
the wolf with the lamb!
The infant will play by the viper's lair,
but never come to harm!

A child has been born to the people,
a son given us!
And he shall reign with integrity,
and justice shall be ours!

732 Kathryn Kuhlman

He's the Saviour of my soul.
My Jesus, my Jesus.
He's the Saviour of my soul.
He's the Saviour of my soul.
His name is Jesus, Jesus, Jesus, Jesus.
He's the Saviour of my soul.
He's the Saviour of my soul.

733 Jon Mohr

He who began a good work in you,
he who began a good work in you
will be faithful to complete it;
he'll be faithful to complete it;
he who started the work
will be faithful to complete it in you.

734 Dennis Jernigan

Hide me in the cleft of the rock,
clothe me in the love of the Son,
Lord, surround me, surround me.
I release the joy of my heart,
flowing from the river of life,
Lord, surround me
with your love.

For you are my refuge,
a present help in my trouble,
a river of gladness,
my help as the morning comes.
You are my refuge,
though the world falls around me,
no, I will not fear, Lord,
for I have your love.

Hide me in the cleft of your heart,
surround me with the pow'r
of your love,
Lord, surround me, surround me.
You are like a tower of strength,
your faithfulness a shelter for me,
so Lord, surround me
with your love.

735 Graham Kendrick

High above the dark horizon,
we have seen the morning star,
promise of a cloudless morning
lights up our hearts,
bright eternal day is breaking,
chasing shadows of the night,
open faces upward gazing,
we await the day of Christ.

Take the news to earth's far corners,
soon the promised King will come,
time's decay and death's dominion
will soon be gone,
there will be a new creation
in the twinkling of an eye,
hear his voice of invitation
calling 'Don't be left behind.'

Coming soon on clouds descending
east to west the skies will blaze,
earth made bright with angel splendour,
all the world amazed,
ev'ry eye shall see his glory,
King of kings and Lord of lords,
saints from ev'ry age will greet him,
caught up with him in the clouds.

So until that perfect morning
we will run to win the race,
till we're changed into his likeness,
see him face to face,
now unto the One who loves us,
and redeemed us by his blood,
be all honour, power and glory,
so shall his kingdom come.

Continued overleaf

Now unto the One who loves us,
and redeemed us by his blood,
be all honour, power and glory,
so shall his kingdom come.
Yes! Amen! Lord Jesus come!

736 Richard Lewis

High praises, high praises,
high praises, high praises,
high praises, high praises:
these are the praises of heaven.
(Repeat)

Legions of angels in bright array
worship the great 'I Am'.
Singing with joy of that glorious day
when he will come to reign.
Singing . . .

Glory and honour and pow'r to him
who's seated upon the throne.
This is the everlasting song
that they sing to him alone.
Singing . . .

737 Unknown

His name, his name
shall be called wonderful
his name, his name
shall be called Counsellor.

The Mighty God
the everlasting Father
the Prince of Peace
through all eternity. *(x2)*

738 Johnny Markin

Holy breath of God,
find me in this place.
Fall, sweet mercy, fall on me,
healing by your grace.

Tender hand of God,
hold me in your care.
All my fears and broken dreams,
ev'ry burden bear.

Come, O breath of God,
breathe your life again.
Stir the embers of this heart,
set my soul aflame.
Come, O breath of God,
draw me once again.
Ever closer to your heart,
to your burning flame.

Light of Life Divine,
search my selfish ways.
Tear from me my foolish will;
lead me all my days.
Ageless God of Hope,
stay for ever near
to the wounded broken heart;
scatter ev'ry fear.

739 Steve Mitchinson and Brian Doerkson

Holy fire from heaven,
descend to us, we pray,
let us burn again.
Holy fire from heaven,
consume our hearts today,
let us burn again,
let us burn again.

Waiting in expectancy,
surrendered to your sov'reignty,
we're hungry for true intimacy,
Lord, for the things of your heart.

Holy breath from heaven,
descend to us, we pray,
let us breathe again.
Holy breath from heaven,
revive our hearts today,
let us breathe again,
let us breathe again.

Holy stream from heaven,
descend to us, we pray,
let us drink again.
Holy stream from heaven,
bring new life today,
let us drink again,
let us drink again.

740 Gary Oliver

Holy, holy, holy,
holy, holy, holy,
holy is the Lord God Almighty!
Worthy to receive glory,
worthy to receive honour,
worthy to receive all our praise today.

Praise him,
praise him and lift him up;
praise him,
exalt his name for ever.
Praise him,
praise him and life him up;
praise him,
exalt his name for ever.

741 Nolene S. Prince

Holy, holy, holy is the Lord of hosts.
Holy, holy, holy is the Lord of hosts.
The whole earth is full of his glory,
the whole earth is full of his glory,
the whole earth is full of his glory,
holy is the Lord.

742 Richard Lewis

Holy, holy, so holy
is the Lord God Almighty.
Heaven and earth
are filled with your glory,
holy, holy is the Lord.
(Repeat)

I lift my hands
up to your throne of grace
and I bow before
your beauty and your majesty.
By the blood I enter in,
join with angels as they sing:

743 Kelly Green

Holy is the Lord.
(Holy is the Lord.)
Holy is the Lord.
(Holy is the Lord.)
(Repeat)

Righteousness and mercy,
(Righteousness and mercy,)
judgement and grace,
(judgement and grace,)
faithfulness and sov'reignty;
(faithfulness and sov'reignty;)
holy is the Lord, (holy is the Lord,)
holy is the Lord, (holy is the Lord.)

744 Ian Mizen and Andy Pressdee

Holy Jesus, burn your fire in me,
holy Jesus, sanctify.
Holy Jesus, full of grace and mercy,
holy Jesus, we lift you high.
Son of God, Word of God,
fill me up with your love.
Son of God, Word of God,
fill me up with your love,
with your love, with your love,
with your love, with your love.

745 Russell Fragar

Holy Spirit, rain down, rain down.
oh Comforter and Friend,
how we need your touch again.
Holy Spirit, rain down, rain down.
Let your power fall,
let your voice be heard.
Come and change our hearts,
as we stand on your word.
Holy Spirit, rain down.
(Repeat)

No eye has seen, no ear has heard,
no mind can know what God has in store.
So open up heaven, open it wide,
over your church, and over our lives.
(Repeat)

746 Dottie Rambo and David Huntsinger

Holy Spirit, thou art welcome in this place.
Holy Spirit, thou art welcome in this place.
Omnipotent Father of mercy and grace,
thou art welcome in this place.

747 Joel Houston

Hope has found its home within me
now that I've been found in you.
Let all I am be all you want me to be,
'cause all I want is more of you,
all I want is more of you.

Let your presence fall upon us,
I want to see you face to face.
Let me live for ever lost in your love,
'cause all I want is more of you,
all I want is more of you.

I'm living for this cause,
I lay down my life into your hands.
I'm living for the truth,
the hope of the world, in you I'll stand.
All I want is you.

All I want is you,
all I want is you . . . Jesus.

748 Mark Altrogge

How do I know you love me?
I look around and see
the sunshine, the rain and the wind in
    the trees.
But should these gracious tokens
all fade from my sight,
I won't doubt your love
for I fix my eyes.

I look to the cross where I most clearly
    see
your awesome love displayed for me.
For even when I was dead in sin,
you died for me.
Oh, I look to the cross.

How do I know you love me?
At times I'm so aware.
I sense your Holy Spirit,
I see you ev'rywhere.
But when I leave the mountain
and your face is hid from sight,
I won't doubt your love
for I fix my eyes.

I look to the cross where I most clearly
    see
your awesome love displayed for me.
For even when I was dead in sin,
you died for me.
Oh, I look to the cross.

749 Lynn DeShazo

How great are you, Lord,
how great is your mercy.
How great are the things
that you have done for me.
How great are you, Lord,
your loving kindness
is filling my heart as I sing,
how great are you, Lord.
How great is your love,
it reaches to the heavens,
how great is the heart
that sought and rescued me.

750 Joel Engle

How lovely is your dwelling-place,
O Jesus, my Saviour.
I long to see your holy face,
O Jesus, my Saviour.

Sing to my heart, sing to my soul;
whisper your words of healing to me.
Take hold of me and never let me go:
I long to hear you sing, sing to my heart.

751 Wes Sutton

How sweet your presence is,
how sweet your presence is, O Lord.
How sweet your presence is,
how sweet your presence is, O Lord.
I want to be where you are,
I want to rest in your love.
If I should stray from your heart
run after me, bring me home in your arms.

752 Dave Bilbrough

Humble yourselves
under God's mighty hand,
so that he will lift you up.
(Repeat)

Cast all anxiety on him,
because he cares for you.

Open your hearts
to the Lord your God,
and know his love for you.
(Repeat)

I bow down before you, my Lord.
I bow down before you, my Lord.

753 Kathryn Scott

Hungry, I come to you,
for I know you satisfy.
I am empty, but I know
your love does not run dry.
So I wait for you;
so I wait for you.

I'm falling on my knees,
offering all of me.
Jesus, you're all this heart is living for.

Broken, I run to you,
for your arms are open wide.
I am weary, but I know
your touch restores my life.
So I wait for you;
so I wait for you.

754 David Gate

I am yours,
and you are mine,
friend to me
for all of time.

And all I have now I give to you;
and all I want now is to be pure,
pure like you.

I'm not afraid
of earthly things,
for I am safe
with you, my King.

755 Stuart Bell, Johnny Markin & Paul Cruickshank

I believe in angels,
God's messengers of fire,
and I believe in prophets
who with God's word inspire,
and I believe in miracles
and that the strongholds fall,
and I believe in Jesus,
the highest name of all.

I believe in worship
that touches heaven's throne.
I believe his Spirit
renews the faithful one.
I believe the word of God,
his truth revealed to all,
yes, I believe in Jesus,
the highest name of all.

It's the highest name,
the name that's over all;
it's the highest name,
the name on which we call.
(Repeat)

I believe that suff'ring
and martyrs' cries will cease,
I believe that healing
will find its full release.
I believe the Son of God,
word of heaven come.
Trust in his salvation
born of faith alone.

I believe revival
will touch the earth again,
I believe his Kingdom
will rule without an end,
and I believe that unity
will see his blessing fall,
for I believe in Jesus,
the highest name of all.

It's the highest name,
the name that's over all;
it's the highest name,
the name on which we call.
(Repeat)

It's the name at which we fall,
it's the highest name of all!

756 David Hind

I believe in the gospel,
it's the hope for our world,
I believe in the cross,
it's the place where we find life.
So I pray, Father, come now,
release your fire,
your Spirit in our land.
I believe in Jesus Christ,
the Son of God, he is alive.

Lift up your heads, you ancient doors,
that the King may come in.
Open your eyes, body of Christ,
see the King, now come in.

We believe there is mercy;
we believe there is hope.
We believe in forgiveness,
that God's grace still shines forth.
So we pray, Father, come now,
release your fire,
your Spirit in our land.
We believe in Jesus Christ,
the Son of God, he is alive.

We believe in the Church,
it's the body of Christ on the earth.
We believe there is one way,
there's one faith, one baptism, one Lord.
So we pray, Father, come now,
release your fire,
your Spirit in our land.
We believe in Jesus Christ,
the Son of God, he is alive.

So here he comes; this is his city
let the King now come in.
Open your eyes, he is alive;
see the King now come in.

757 Ascribed to St Patrick
trans. Cecil Frances Alexander, alt.

I bind unto myself today
the strong name of the Trinity,
by invocation of the same,
the Three in One and One in Three.

I bind this day to me for ever,
by pow'r of faith, Christ's incarnation,
his baptism in the Jordan river,
his death on cross for my salvation;
his bursting from the spicèd tomb,
his riding up the heav'nly way,
his coming at the day of doom,
I bind unto myself today.

I bind unto myself the pow'r
of the great love of cherubim;
the sweet 'Well done!' in judgement hour;
the service of the seraphim,
confessors' faith, apostles' word,
the patriarchs' prayers, the prophets' scrolls,
all good deeds done unto the Lord,
and purity of faithful souls.

PART TWO

Christ be with me, Christ within me,
Christ behind me, Christ before me,
Christ beside me, Christ to win me,
Christ to comfort and restore me.
Christ beneath me, Christ above me,
Christ in quiet, Christ in danger,
Christ in hearts of all that love me,
Christ in mouth of friend and stranger.

DOXOLOGY

I bind unto myself the name,
the strong name of the Trinity,
by invocation of the same,
the Three in One and One in Three,
of whom all nature hath creation,
eternal Father, Spirit, Word.
Praise to the Lord of my salvation:
salvation is of Christ the Lord.
Amen.

758 Wendy O'Connell

I call out to you, my Lord.
Hear the cry of my heart.
Change me, to be like you, I pray.
Come, Lord Jesus, have your way.

I surrender all to you.
I give up my life
to live for you.

759 Michael Battersby

I can feel the Spirit of God is moving,
I can feel his power in this place.
I believe that God is more than able
to perform all that's in his word.

Pour on your power, Lord,
display your mighty strength.
This is the hour, Lord,
when your people rise in faith.
I take up the challenge, Lord,
as I stand and take my place.
Let the heavens roar as your people soar
to a higher place with you,
selah, selah.

760 Andrew Bromley

I come to you,
laying my life before you;
come to you,
in brokenness again.
I come to you,
needing your grace and mercy,
come to you
to know your love again.

Let your grace flow like a river,
let your mercy fall like rain,
let your love become a fountain,
to my heart again.

761 Jeff Nelson

I delight in you, I delight in you,
O Lord my God.
You're the only one I long for,
I delight in you, I delight in you,
O Lord my God, I delight in you.

How I love you, how I love you,
O Lord my God.
You're the only one I long for,
how I love you, how I love you,
O Lord my God, how I love you.

I will worship you, I will worship you,
O Lord my God.
You're the only one I long for,
I will worship you, I will worship you,
O Lord my God, I will worship you.

762 Lamont Hiebert

If we call to him, he will answer us;
if we run to him, he will run to us;
if we lift our hands, he will lift us up;
come now, praise his name, all you saints of
    God.

O sing for joy to God, our strength;
O sing for joy to God, our strength,
our strength.

Draw near to him, he is here with us;
give him your love, he's in love with us;
he will heal our hearts, he will cleanse our
    hands;
if we rend our hearts, he will heal our land.

763 Scott Wesley Brown

If you need Jesus, come;
if you need Jesus, run;
if you can see how great your need,
fall on your knees and come.
If you need Jesus, if you need Jesus, come.

If you are hungry, come now and taste
the goodness of God, his mercy and grace;
if you are weary and you are lost,
come and find life through his death on
    the cross.
If you need Jesus, If your need Jesus, come.

If you are thirsty, come;
if you are thirsty, run;
if your heart cries and your soul is dry,
fall on your knees and come.
If you need Jesus, if you need Jesus, come.

764 J. B. Arthur

I have absolute trust
in the Infinite One
who gave his life to me.
In my arrogant, proud, selfish state
he reached down,
he opened my eyes to see
the vast expanse of his wondrous grace,
forgiveness and love.
My mind's been renewed by the Spirit's pow'r
to prove his good and perfect will for me.

And I'll praise you, Infinite One;
I will serve you, glorious Son;
and I love you, Jesus my Lord,
your truth has set me free.

765 David Wellington

I have been lifted up,
lifted up to the heavenly places.
I have been lifted up,
seated now with Christ.

Once, once I was dead,
dead in my sin,
dead to your way of living.
You, you were a dream
ever so far away.
There, there came a day,
day of your will,
day of my destination.
You, you stole my heart
making me so alive.

Now, now I have peace,
peace in my heart,
peace with Almighty living God,
and you have sent,
sent your own Spirit.
We, we have been joined,
joined two as one,
joined as a holy temple;
now no longer alone
but part of your family.

766 Unknown

I have decided to follow Jesus,
I have decided to follow Jesus,
I have decided to follow Jesus,
no turning back, no turning back.

The world behind me, the cross before me;
the world behind me, the cross before me;
the world behind me, the cross before me,
no turning back, no turning back.
No turning back, I have decided to follow.
No turning back, no turning, no turning,
no turning back.

Though none go with me, I still will follow,
though none go with me, I still will follow,
though none go with me, I still will follow.
No turning back, no turning back.

767 Michael Frye and Helen Frye

I have sung my songs of praise,
thanksgiving on my lips,
bowed low and worshipped you;
but now I'm coming close, closer than before,
for the veil is torn in two.

Now that I am here with you,
there's no place I'd rather be.
Now that I have felt your touch,
make your home in me.

I feel so safe with you,
acceptance in your voice;
you whisper tenderly:
'You are my belov'd, chosen one, my friend;
you're so precious to me.'

768 Reuben Morgan

I know he rescued my soul,
his blood has covered my sin,
I believe, I believe.
My shame he's taken away,
my pain is healed in his name,
I believe, I believe.
I'll raise a banner;
my Lord has conquered the grave.

My Redeemer lives, my Redeemer lives;
my Redeemer lives, my Redeemer lives.
(Repeat)

You lift my burden, I'll rise with you:
I'm dancing on this mountain-top
to see your kingdom come.

769 D.W. Whittle alt. Stuart Townend

I know not why God's wondrous grace
to me hath been made known;
nor why, unworthy as I am,
he claimed me for his own.

But I know whom I've believèd;
he's able now to save
what I've committed unto him
until that final day.

I know not how this saving faith
to me he did impart;
or how believing in his word
wrought peace within my heart.

Continued overleaf

I know not how the Spirit moves,
convincing men of sin;
revealing Jesus through the word,
creating faith in him.

But I know whom I've believèd;
he's able now to save
what I've committed unto him
until that final day.

I know not what of good or ill
may be reserved for me,
of weary ways or golden days
before his face I see.

I know not when my Lord may come;
I know not how or where,
if I shall pass the vale of death,
or meet him in the air.

770   Darrell Evans and Chris Springer

I know you had me on your mind
when you climbed up on that hill,
for you saw me with eternal eyes,
while I was yet in sin,
Redeemer, Saviour, Friend.

Ev'ry stripe upon your battered back,
ev'ry thorn that pierced your brow,
ev'ry nail drove deep through guiltless hands
said that your love knows no end,
Redeemer, Saviour, Friend.

Oh, Redeemer, redeem my heart again.
Saviour, come and shelter me from sin.
You're familiar with my weakness,
devoted to the end,
Redeemer, Saviour, Friend.

So the grace you pour upon my life
will return to you in praise,
and I'll gladly lay down all my crowns
for the name of which I'm saved,
Redeemer, Saviour, Friend.

771   Andrew Bromley

I lay my life down at your feet,
surrender all you've given me,
my fondest thoughts, my wildest dreams,
all I am and hope to be.
I give my heart, I give my soul,
to the one who gave his all,
to my Saviour,
all to you.
All for you,
all my dreams and plans,
surrendered to you;
guide me by your hand.
All for you,
laying down my life,
I trust in you.
To my Saviour,
all for you.

772   Martin Smith

I lift my eyes to you,
eyes that have seen a thing or two,
who is this stranger in my life?
I lift my hands to you,
hands that have carried what is true,
intimate stranger, be my life.

And Jesus, I love you,
Jesus, I adore you.
Jesus, you still have my affection,
and my song will be 'I love you'.

I lift my voice to you,
lips that have cried a pray'r or two,
beautiful stranger, fill my life,
I lift my heart in praise to the Saviour
whose death made all things new,
intimate stranger, only you.

773 Darlene Zschech & Reuben Morgan

I lift up my eyes to your throne,
Lord, as I lose myself in you.
The song in my heart will be
yours alone.

My treasure is in the cross,
Jesus, I love to meet you there.
I hunger and thirst for you,
now flood my soul.
River of love,
river of healing,
Holy Spirit, flow,
river of grace,
river of mercy, flow.
River of peace,
river of promise,
Holy Spirit, flow,
river of joy,
river of blessing, flow.

Jesus, come again. *(x2)*

774 Marc James

I'm giving you my heart,
and all that is within,
I lay it all down
for the sake of you my King.
I'm giving you my dreams,
I'm laying down my rights,
I'm giving up my pride
for the promise of new life.

And I surrender all to you,
all to you.
And I surrender all to you,
all to you.

I'm singing you this song;
I'm waiting at the cross.
And all the world holds dear,
I count it all as loss.

For the sake of knowing you,
the glory of your name,
to know the lasting joy,
even sharing in your pain.

775 Steve Earl

I'm gonna trust in God, I'm gonna trust in
    Jesus
without shame and without fear,
I'm gonna fix my eyes on the hope of glory
for his day is drawing near.

How great is the love of God.
How steady is his hand to
guide me through this world,
and though I am weak, in him I stand,
and you will hear me say today,
in faith, I'm gonna trust in God.

Now when the cares of life seem
    overwhelming
and my heart is sinking down,
I'm gonna lift my hands to the one who'll
    help me,
to the one who holds my crown.

776 Reuben Morgan

I'm reaching for the prize,
I'm giving ev'rything,
I give my life for this,
it's what I live for.
Nothing will keep me from
all that you have for me;
you hold my head up high,
I live for you.
Greater is he that's living in me
than he that is in the world.

Faith! I can move the mountain,
I can do all things through Christ, I know.
Faith! Standing and believing
I can do all things through Christ,
    who strengthens me.

777 Kylie Adcock

I'm running the race, I'm moving in faith,
I'm walking the walk, and I'm talking the talk;
I'm shouting it out, and jumping about,
I'm soaring up high like the eagle above.

I've been put to the test, I'm giving my best,
I'm giving my all, and I'm standing tall;
I'm a soldier of God, a child of the King,
who sits on the throne, reigns over ev'rything.

*'Cause Jesus brought me
to a place where I should be;
'cause Jesus takes me to a place of
victory;
'cause Jesus gives me hope and destiny.
I'm gonna tell it, I'm gonna shout it,
'cause Jesus sets me free!*

© Rhema Publishing/worldwide worship ltd.

778 Camp Kirkland

I'm so glad, Jesus lifted me!
I'm so glad, Jesus lifted me!
I'm so glad, Jesus lifted me!
Singing glory, hallelujah! Jesus lifted me!

I'm so glad, Jesus set me free,
I'm so glad, Jesus set me free!
I'm so glad, Jesus set me free,
singing glory, hallelujah! Jesus set me free.

Satan had me bound, but Jesus set me free.
Satan had me bound, but Jesus set me free.
Satan had me bound, but Jesus set me free.
Singing glory, hallelujah! Jesus set me free!

Out of sin and shame Jesus set me free.
Out of sin and shame Jesus set me free.
Out of sin and shame Jesus set me free.
Singing glory, hallelujah! Jesus set me free!

I'm so glad Christ the Lord came down,
I'm so glad Christ the Lord came down.
Left his Father's glory, left his heav'nly crown.
Oh, glory, hallelujah! I'm so glad.

I'm so glad he's my Lord and King,
I'm so glad he's my Lord and King.
That is why I praise him, that is why I sing.
Oh, glory, hallelujah! I'm so glad.

I'm so glad he's living in my soul,
I'm so glad he's living in my soul.
Walking right beside me ev'rywhere I go.
Oh, glory, hallelujah! I'm so glad.

On my way to heaven, I'll shout the victory.
On my way to heaven, I'll shout the victory.
On my way to heaven, I'll shout the victory.
Singing glory, hallelujah, I shout the victory.

I'll tell the world Jesus lifted me.
I'll tell the world Jesus lifted me.
I'll tell the world Jesus lifted me;
singing glory, hallelujah! Jesus lifted me.

I was bound, Jesus set me free.
I was bound, Jesus set me free.
I was bound, Jesus set me free;
singing glory, hallelujah! Jesus lifted me.

© 1997 Integrity's Hosanna! Music

779 Darrell Evans

I'm trading my sorrows,
I'm trading my shame,
I'm laying them down
for the joy of the Lord.
I'm trading my sickness,
I'm trading my pain,
I'm laying them down
for the joy of the Lord.

Yes, Lord, yes, Lord,
yes, yes, Lord; yes Lord,
yes, Lord, yes, yes, Lord;
yes, Lord, yes, Lord,
yes, yes, Lord, Amen.

I'm pressed but not crushed,
persecuted, not abandoned,
struck down, but not destroyed;
I'm blessed beyond the curse,
for his promise will endure,
that his joy's gonna be my strength.
Though the sorrow may last for a night,
his joy comes with the morning.

La, la, la . . . Amen.

780 Reuben Morgan

In awe of you we worship
and stand amazed at your great love.
We're changed from glory to glory;
we set our hearts on you, our God.

Now your presence fills this place.
Be exalted in our praise!
As we worship, I believe
you are near.
(Repeat)

Blessing and honour and glory and power
for ever, for ever.
(Repeat)

In awe of you we worship.

781 Wes Sutton

I never want anything
in my life to take your place.
I never want to live
by any other grace.
My longing and my heart's desire
is to see your face, O Lord,
and become a friend of God.

I love you, day and night,
I love you, all my life,
I love you, Lord, heart and soul,
I long to be a friend of God.

782 Anna Laetitia Waring

In heav'nly love abiding,
no change my heart shall fear;
and safe is such confiding,
for nothing changes here.
The storm may roar without me,
my heart may low be laid,
but God is round about me,
and can I be dismayed?

Wherever he may guide me,
no want shall turn me back;
my Shepherd is beside me,
and nothing shall I lack.
His wisdom ever waketh,
his sight is never dim,
he knows the way he taketh,
and I will walk with him.

Green pastures are before me,
which yet I have not seen;
bright skies will soon be o'er me,
where the dark clouds have been.
My hope I cannot measure,
my path to life is free,
my Saviour has my treasure,
and he will walk with me.

783 Dick and Melodie Tunney

In his presence there is comfort,
in his presence, there is peace.
When we seek the Father's heart
we will find such bless'd assurance,
in the presence of the Lord.

In your presence there is comfort,
in your presence, there is peace.
When we seek to know your heart
we will find such bless'd assurance,
in your holy presence, Lord.

784 Geron Davis

In his presence there is joy beyond measure,
and at his feet peace of mind can still be
    found;
and if you have a need, I know he has
    ev'ry answer,
but you've got to reach out and claim it,
for you are standing on holy ground.

We are standing on holy ground,
and I know that there are angels all
    around;
let us praise Jesus now,
we are standing in his presence on
    holy ground.

785 Eric Grover

In my heart there is a stirring,
one that did not start with me;
a love to worship my Creator,
to show his love for all to see.

I will worship, I will honour,
I will exalt the Lord above;
all my days I'll sing the praises
of his great redeeming love.

In my heart there is a treason,
one that poisons all my love.
Take my heart and consecrate it,
wash it in your cleansing flood.

Tie me to the Rock unchanging,
tie me to his wondrous cross.
I'll fix my eyes upon the Saviour,
all other things I count as loss.

786 Kate Spence

In my life you've heard me say I love you;
how do I show you it's true?
Hear my heart, it longs for more of you;
I've fallen deeply in love with you.

You have stolen my heart,
I'm captivated by you.
Never will you and I part,
I've fallen deeply in love with you.
(Repeat)

You and I together for ever,
nothing can stand in the way.
My love for you grows stronger each new day,
I've fallen deeply in love with you.

787 Geoff Bullock

In my life proclaim your glory,
in my heart reveal your majesty;
then my soul shall speak the wonders of
    your grace,
and this heart of mine shall sing your praise.
In my words proclaim your mercy,
in my life reveal your power;
then my soul shall be a mirror of your love,
and this heart of mine shall sing your praise.

Lord of all mercy, God of all grace,
Lord of all righteousness;
Lord of the heavens, Lord of the earth,
enthroned in majesty.
Worthy of honour, worthy of praise,
all glory and majesty:
I give you the honour,
I give you the praise,
and proclaim your glorious pow'r.

In my soul unveil your love, Lord,
deep within my heart, renewing me.
Day by day, your life transforming all I am,
as this heart of mine reflects your praise.
Lord of all, enthroned in glory,
grace and mercy, truth and righteousness,
ev'ry knee shall bow before this Christ, our Lord,
as all creation sings your praise.

Lord of all mercy, God of all grace,
Lord of all righteousness;
Lord of the heavens, Lord of the earth,
enthroned in majesty.

Worthy of honour, worthy of praise,
all glory and majesty:
I give you the honour,
I give you the praise,
and proclaim your glorious pow'r.

788 Shonelle Barnes

In so many ways you love me
just as I am, not as I should be,
and as your child you take hold of me.
I see just why I've fallen in love with you.

The purest love I've ever known
was that you chose to give and die,
and the blood that poured from your open
      hands:
all, so I could fall in love with you.

I've got to worship you my God,
I can't contain the way I feel;
I dance free before you, Lord,
for it's you that I adore.

789 Christina Georgina Rossetti

In the bleak midwinter
frosty wind made moan,
earth stood hard as iron,
water like a stone;
snow had fallen, snow on snow,
snow on snow,
in the bleak midwinter, long ago.

Our God, heav'n cannot hold him
nor earth sustain;
heav'n and earth shall flee away
when he comes to reign.
In the bleak midwinter
a stable-place sufficed
the Lord God almighty, Jesus Christ.

Enough for him, whom cherubim
worship night and day,
a breastful of milk
and a mangerful of hay:
enough for him, whom angels
fall down before,
the ox and ass and camel which adore.

Angels and archangels
may have gathered there,
cherubim and seraphim
thronged the air;
but only his mother
in her maiden bliss
worshipped the belovèd with a kiss.

What can I give him,
poor as I am?
If I were a shepherd
I would bring a lamb;
if I were a wise man
I would do my part,
yet what I can I give him:
give my heart.

790 Steve Richardson, Mark Carouthers and
Jeff Harpole

In the darkness where ev'rything is unknown
I face the power of sin on my own.
I did not know of a place I could go
where I could find a way to heal my
      wounded soul.
He said that I could come into his presence
without fear,
into the holy place where his mercy hovers
      near.

I'm runnin', I'm runnin', I'm runnin' to the
   mercy-seat
where Jesus is callin', he said his grace
would cover me.
His blood will flow freely, it will provide the
   healing,
I'm runnin' to the mercy-seat. I'm runnin'
to the mercy-seat.

Continued overleaf

Are you livin' where hope has not been,
lost in the curse of a lifetime of sin.
Lovely illusions, they never come true,
I know where there's a place of mercy for you.
He said that you could come into his
    presence without fear,
into the holy place where his mercy
    hovers near.

Come runnin', come runnin', come runnin'
    to the mercy-seat
where Jesus is callin', his grace will be a
    covering.
His blood will flow freely, it will provide the
    healing,
come runnin' to the mercy-seat.
    Come runnin' to the mercy-seat.

791 Janine Price

In the mornin' hour, in the evenin' late,
I'm gonna praise your name.
In the mornin' hour, in the evenin' late,
I'm gonna praise your name.
(Repeat)

For when I praise your name
my strength is renewed,
you strengthen me, you strengthen me,
you strengthen me, Lord.
For when I praise your name
the demons flee,
tremble at the sound of your name,
tremble at the sound of your name.

792 Martin Smith and Stuart Garrard

Investigate my life and make me clean,
shine upon the darkest place in me,
to you my life's an open book,
so turn the page and take a look,
upon the life you've made,
always, my days, I'll praise.
Fly away where heaven calls my name,
fly away, I'll never be the same.
Investigate, I can't wait, excavate, recreate.

Investigate my life and take me through,
shine upon the road that leads to you,
I know you'd heard the words I'd say,
before I'd even lived one day,
you knew the life you'd made,
always, my days, I'll praise.
Fly away where heaven calls my name,
fly away, I'll never be the same.
Fly away, fly away, fly away,
fly away, fly away.

Investigate my life and make me clean,
shine upon the darkest place in me,
when I go, when I return,
you've seen your holy fire burn,
upon the life you've made, always.

793 Wayne and Libby Huirua

In your presence there is joy,
in your presence there is freedom,
but the greatest joy of all
is to know we've made you smile.
In your presence there is life,
in your presence there is healing,
but the greatest joy of all
is to know we've reached your heart.
God of glory, we give you praise,
lift you up in this holy place,
our hearts are ready, our lives made new,
it's all we long to do.
God of glory, we give you praise,
lift you up in this holy place,
our hearts are ready, our lives made new,
God of glory, we worship you.

794 Tanya Riches

I open my life to you, Lord,
I want to be pure.
Jesus, you're breath to my soul;
you know what I think, what I feel.

Jesus, I adore you;
to you, my Saviour,
I will sing,
you know me through and through;
you're the closest to my heart
that one could be.

And, Jesus, I adore you,
I love you with the deepest of my soul,
I rest inside your arms and I trust you to lead
me on.

795   Paul Baloche

I see the Lord and he is seated on the
throne;
the train of his robe is filling the heavens.
I see the Lord and he is shining like the sun;
his eyes full of fire, his voice like the waters.
Surrounding his throne are thousands
singing:
'Holy, holy, holy is the Lord God Almighty.
Holy, holy, holy is the Lord.
Holy, holy, holy is the Lord God Almighty.
Holy, holy, holy is the Lord.'

796   Matthew Lockwood

I see you now,
I see you high and lifted up,
I see your glory fill the whole earth,
I see your throne,
I see your majesty and splendour,
and I join with angels cheering:

Glory, glory, glory to the Lamb enthroned
on high.
Glory, glory to the Lamb upon the throne.
He is high above the nations.
Glory, glory, glory to the Lamb enthroned
on high.
Glory, glory to the Lamb upon the throne.
He is high above the nations.

I hear your voice,
I hear you call in softest whispers,
I hear the shout of triumph,
I hear the sound
as the nations call upon your name
and I hear all heaven cry:

797   Janine Price

Isn't it good to know the Lord?
Isn't it good to praise his name?
Isn't it good to know that he's always
there for us?
Isn't it good to know the Lord?
(Repeat)

Well I know him to be my help in time of
need
and I know him to be the one that leadeth
me.
And I know him to be my true liberty,
the one that I can trust; and I will never,
never, walk alone, for he is always there.

798   Edmund Hamilton Sears, alt.

It came upon the midnight clear,
that glorious song of old,
from angels bending near the earth
to touch their harps of gold:
'Peace on the earth, goodwill to all,
from heav'n's all-gracious King!'
The world in solemn stillness lay
to hear the angels sing.

Still through the cloven skies they come,
with peaceful wings unfurled;
and still their heav'nly music floats
o'er all the weary world:
above its sad and lowly plains
they bend on hov'ring wing;
and ever o'er its Babel-sounds
the blessèd angels sing.

Continued overleaf

Yet with the woes of sin and strife
the world has suffered long;
beneath the angel-strain have rolled
two thousand years of wrong;
and warring humankind hears not
the love-song which they bring;
O hush the noise of mortal strife,
and hear the angels sing!

And ye, beneath life's crushing load,
whose forms are bending low,
who toil along the climbing way
with painful steps and slow:
look now! for glad and golden hours
come swiftly on the wing;
O rest beside the weary road,
and hear the angels sing.

For lo, the days are hast'ning on,
by prophets seen of old,
when with the ever-circling years
comes round the age of gold;
when peace shall over all the earth
its ancient splendours fling,
and all the world give back the song
which now the angels sing.

799 Lincoln Brewster

I thank the Lord for what,
for what he's done in us;
I thank the Lord for his love;
and I thank the Lord for what
he's gonna do in us
from the heavens above.

And I thank the Lord
for the smile that he's put on my face;
I thank the Lord for his grace;
and I thank the Lord for the joy
that he has given to me,
'cause now I know that I am really set free.

> Ev'rybody, ev'rybody,
> ev'rybody praise the Lord.
> Ev'rybody, ev'rybody,
> ev'rybody praise the Lord.

800 Colin Dye and Richard Lewis
(revised and adapted Richard Lewis)

I thank you for the precious blood of Jesus
as of a Lamb without blemish or stain.
I thank you that the blood pleads for me
all the mercy and provisions of your grace.
And I thank you that the blood
has made a way for me
into the presence of a holy God;
salvation is purchased for me;
I'm forgiven, the blood has set me free.

> I say 'Thank you for the blood,
> thank you for the blood;
> the blood that gives me freedom,
> the blood that gives me life.'
> I say 'Thank you for the blood,
> thank you for the blood,
> thank you for the blood you shed for me.'

I thank you that the blood is ever cleansing
me
from ev'ry sin, whether thought, word or
deed.
Now evil has no hold on me,
I'm redeemed by the Lamb of victory.
And I thank you that the blood's my full
assurance
of peace with God and a destiny changed.
You've called me from death into life;
out of darkness into your marv'llous light.

801 William Walsham How

It is a thing most wonderful,
almost too wonderful to be,
that God's own Son should come from
heav'n,
and die to save a child like me.

And yet I know that it is true:
he chose a poor and humble lot,
and wept and toiled, and mourned and died,
for love of those who loved him not.

I sometimes think about the cross,
and shut my eyes, and try to see
the cruel nails and crown of thorns,
and Jesus crucified for me.

But even could I see him die,
I could but see a little part
of that great love which, like a fire,
is always burning in his heart.

I cannot tell how he could love
a child so weak and full of sin;
his love must be most wonderful,
if he could die my love to win.

It is most wonderful to know
his love for me so free and sure;
but 'tis more wonderful to see
my love for him so faint and poor.

And yet I want to love thee, Lord;
O light the flame within my heart,
and I will love thee more and more,
until I see thee as thou art.

For though we struggle
and trials and troubles still come our way,
you won't forsake us;
your word has told us
your promises will never end,
Sing it again . . .

(Leader – All)
Why give him praise?
Because he is worthy.
Why should we sing?
He loves you and me.
Why give him thanks?
Because he forgave us.
Why celebrate?
Because we are free.
And when should we thank him?
In morning and evening.
In what circumstance?
The good and the bad.
Is it always easy?
No, it's not so easy.
But is it good?
*Yes, it's good, it is good,
it is good.*

802   Dan Adler

*It is good, it is good,
it is good to give thanks to the Lord on
    high,
to sing of your faithfulness
and loving kindness both day and night;
to play on our instruments
sweet songs of praise for the things you
    do.
It is good, it is good,
it is good to give thanks to you.*

For though the wicked
spring up like the grass and are ev'rywhere,
soon they will perish;
but all those planted in your house
will grow without end.
Sing it again . . .

803   Mary Shekleton

It passeth knowledge, that dear love of
    thine,
my Saviour, Jesus! yet this soul of mine
would of thy love, in all its breadth and
    length,
its height and depth, and everlasting
    strength,
know more and more.

It passeth telling, that dear love of thine,
my Saviour, Jesus! yet these lips of mine
would fain proclaim, to sinners, far and near,
a love which can remove all guilty fear,
and love beget.

Continued overleaf

It passeth praises, that dear love of thine,
my Saviour, Jesus! yet this heart of mine
would sing that love, so full, so rich, so free,
which brings a rebel sinner, such as me,
nigh unto God.

O fill me, Saviour Jesus, with thy love;
lead, lead me to the living fount above;
thither may I, in simple faith, draw nigh,
and never to another fountain fly,
but unto thee.

And then, when Jesus face to face I see,
when at his lofty throne I bow the knee,
then of his love, in all its breadth and length,
its height and depth, its everlasting strength,
my soul shall sing.

804   Darlene Zschech

I trust in you, my faithful Lord,
how perfect is your love.
You answer me before I call,
my hope, my strength, my song.
And I shout for joy, I thank you, Lord,
your plan stands firm for ever.
And your praise will be continually
pouring from my heart.

I will bless you, Lord,
I will bless you, Lord,
how my soul cries out for you, my God.
I will bless you, Lord.

© 1997 Darlene Zschech/Hillsong Publishing/Kingsway's Thankyou Music

805   Mark Altrogge

It's all for you, creation, Lord,
the universe, it's all for you.
The starry sky, the em'rald earth,
it's all for you, all to bring you glory.
It's all for you, the one who came to
    seek and serve,
it's all for you, who died the death that
    we deserve,
it's all for you, all to bring you glory.

It's all for you and the worship of
    your name.
It's all for you, for your honour and
    your fame.
From the heights to the depths let all that
has breath
proclaim that it's all for you.

It's all for you, our joy, our adoration,
Lord, it's all for you.
Our songs, our celebration, Lord, it's all for
you,
all to bring you glory, it's all for you.
Our trials and temptations, Lord, they're
    all for you.
Our suffering, our patience,
Lord, it's all for you, all to bring you glory.

© 1997 PDI Praise/CopyCare

806   Michael Battersby

I've come to this house
to celebrate the goodness
of God in my life,
and for all that you've done.
And after ev'rything you give to me
the best is still to come.
So I dedicate my life
to seeking your face,
'cause no one compares to you,
I'm still amazed at your grace.

God is so good,
there ain't no doubt about it,
and his mercy endures for ever and ever.
God is so good
and Lord, I'm gonna shout it
'till the nations hear
and I've made it clear
what you've done,
what you've done in my life,
'cause God is so good.

© Michael Battersby/1998 Smart Productions

807 Wes Sutton

I wait in your sanctuary
to behold your glory,
the glory of my God and King.
I bow down before you
to worship and adore you,
my God, the Holy One, the King.

Leaving all my many burdens,
those well known and those uncertain,
I approach you in the holy place.
Gazing here upon your glory,
touched by you I am made holy,
not through my own effort but by your grace.

I worship you (I worship you),
I worship you (I worship you),
I worship you (I worship you),
I worship you.

808 Paul Oakley and Alan Rose

I want to be holy, I want to be righteous,
I want to live my life the way you want me to.
I want to be blameless, not walking in darkness,
I want to be a living sacrifice to you.
I'm gonna run the race, I'm gonna run to win,
throw off ev'rything that hinders me, yeah,
    yeah.
I'm gonna fix my eyes upon the King,
and leave my sin behind.
(Repeat)

I want to be so much better,
I want to be more like you.
Keep taking me further and deeper,
I want to right the wrong,
I want to live this song,
now I'm pressing on,
I'm gonna leave my sin behind.

Singing, 'Goodbye rage, goodbye hate,
goodbye anger, goodbye malice,
goodbye bitterness and slander,
goodbye fear of man!'

809 Joel Engle

I want to seek your face,
I want to know your ways,
I want to give you praise,
O Lord, most high.
You are the holy One,
you are the anointed One,
you are the only One.

And your love is better than life,
it's sweeter than anything
under the sun and the moon
and the stars in the sky.
Oh, your love is better than life,
is better than life.

810 Mick Dalton

I was on your mind
long before you formed the earth.
By your grace you gave me life;
I was on your mind.

Take me by the hand,
lead me down your paths of truth.
Mark my ways with peace and love;
I am on your mind.

You know all my thoughts and ways,
show me all of yours.
All I am is all I have,
in this gift of life.

811 Richard Lewis

I will awaken the dawn,
I will sing praises till the heavens come
    down,
I won't give up till you come,
I won't give up until the fire is falling.
(Repeat)

Continued overleaf

You are the lily of the valley,
you are the hope when hope has gone,
you are the light that shines for ever:
Jehovah is your name
and I've never been the same
since I put my trust in you.

Jehovah, your love will never end,
Jehovah, your love will never end.
(Repeat)

812   Mark Naea & Vernon Katipa

I will bless the Lord at all times,
no matter what may come my way;
always looking unto Jesus,
the author of my faith.
As my heart is filled with praises
I will glorify your name.

Lord, I give you ev'rything
and worship you, my one and only King;
you are worthy of all praises.
Lord, I give my heart and soul,
in ev'rything I do in you I know
you will be glorified.

I will bless the Lord at all times
and give honour to your name.
All I have I will surrender;
Holy Spirit have your way.
Take this vessel, Lord, and use me
to bring glory to your name.

813   Rita Baloche

I will celebrate, sing unto the Lord,
sing to the Lord a new song.
I will celebrate, sing unto the Lord,
sing to the Lord a new song.
With my heart rejoicing within,
with my mind focused on him,
with my hands raised to the heavens,
all I am worshipping him.

814   Martin Nystrom

I will come and bow down at your feet, Lord
    Jesus.
In your presence is fullness of joy.
There is nothing, there is no one who
    compares with you.
I take pleasure in worshipping you, Lord.

815   Billy Funk

I will come into your presence, Lord,
with a sacrifice of praise;
with a song I will exalt you, Lord,
blessèd be your holy name.

I will give you all the glory,
you delivered me from shame;
I'm created in your righteousness,
blessèd be your holy name.

> *Lift him up, his name be lifted higher,*
> *lift him up, exalt his holy name;*
> *lift him up, his name be lifted higher,*
> *exalt his holy name.*

816   Reuben Morgan

I will come to you with an open heart,
bring a sacrifice of praise.
I have seen your pow'r in the holy place,
I have known your mighty ways.
I will remember your mercy,
and, Lord, your faithfulness.

> *Lord, your goodness and your love*
> *will follow me all the days of my life,*
> *I'm surrounded with the favour of the*
>   *Lord*
> *always and for ever.*

817 Brent Chambers

I will give thanks to thee,
O Lord, among the peoples,
I will sing praises to thee among the nations.
For thy steadfast love is great,
is great to the heavens,
and thy faithfulness, thy faithfulness, to
   the clouds.
Be exalted, O God, above the heavens,
let thy glory be over all the earth!

© 1977 Scripture in Song/Integrity Music/Kingsway's Thankyou
Music

818 Joel Engle

I will live to declare your glory
and my heart is filled with praise.
I will shout and I will sing
for all of my days.
I want to walk in your holiness, Lord,
I want to stand for all your ways.
When you call I will say 'yes',
for all of my days.

I want to die so you can live,
resurrect my heart again.
I will tell the world that
you are the Holy One.
(Repeat)

   You are the Holy One,
   and I worship your name.
   You are the Holy One,
   and I stand amazed.
   You are the Holy One,
   you are the Holy One.

© 1999 Spin Three-Sixty Music/Music Services/CopyCare

819 Wes Sutton

I will not live by power or might
but by your Spirit,
by your Spirit.
(Repeat)

So fill me again,
glorify your name,
fill me again,
by your Spirit,
by your Spirit.

© 1995 Sovereign Lifestyle Music

820 Matt Poole

I will sing of your faithfulness,
of your mercy and your love.
I will say this is the day
that the Lord has made.
I hold on to your promise
and the resurrection pow'r,
restore to me your joy;
I will praise you now.

   Be glad and rejoice
   for the Lord our Saviour reigns
   and the joy of the Lord
   shall be our strength.
   I was born to be
   your dwelling place.
   This is the day
   that the Lord has made.

© 1998 Matt Poole/Sounds of Paradise

821 Francis Harold Rawley

I will sing the wondrous story
of the Christ who died for me;
how he left his home in glory,
for the cross on Calvary.
I was lost: but Jesus found me –
found his sheep that went astray;
threw his loving arms around me,
drew me back into his way.

I was bruised; but Jesus healed me –
faint was I from many a fall;
sight was gone, and fears possessed me:
but he freed me from them all.
Days of darkness still come o'er me;
sorrow's paths I often tread:
but the Saviour still is with me,
by his hand I'm safely led.

Continued overleaf

He will keep me till the river
rolls its waters at my feet;
then he'll bear me safely over,
where the loved ones I shall meet.
Yes, I'll sing the wondrous story
of the Christ who died for me;
sing it with the saints in glory,
gathered by the crystal sea.

822 Richard Lewis

I will testify of the Saviour whom I love,
who laid down his life for all my guilt
    and shame.
He was crucified to take away my sin;
he has paid the price with his never
    ending love.

Deep as the ocean, high as the highest
    heav'n above,
wide as the east is from the west is your
    great love.
Deep as the ocean, high as the highest
    heav'n above,
wide as the east is from the west is your
    great love.

823 Reuben Morgan

I will wait,
reach out my hands before you,
my keeper.
I will come running
into your arms.
It's you I long for
with all my heart.

I want to know you,
you are all I want.
I want to know you more.

824 Geoff Bullock

I will worship you,
my Lord and Saviour.
I am overwhelmed
by your love,
for I am so amazed
by your gift of grace:

I will worship,
I will worship,
I will worship you.

I am loved by you,
oh Lord of mercy.
I am held secure
by your grace,
and I am lifted up
through your faithfulness:

Held by love and healed by grace,
mercy's crown in Jesus' face,
peace eternal, hope secured,
love revealed, and life renewed.

825 Jennifer Atkinson and Robin Mark

Jesus, all for Jesus;
all I am and have and ever hope to be.
(Repeat)

All of my ambitions, hopes and plans,
I surrender these into your hands.
(Repeat)

For it's only in your will that I am free.
For it's only in your will that I am free.

826 Michael Frye

Jesus, be the centre,
be my source, be my light,
Jesus.

Jesus, be the centre,
be my hope, be my song,
Jesus.

Be the fire in my heart,
be the wind in these sails,
be the reason that I live,
Jesus, Jesus.

Jesus, be my vision,
be my path, be my guide,
Jesus.

© 1999 Vineyard Songs (UK/Eire)/CopyCare

827 Andy Pressdee and Ian Mizen

Jesus Christ, you are the Son of God,
Holy One, you gave ev'rything
to become like one of us.
Heaven's Son came to earth,
showed a selfless way to live and how to
    love.

On my knees I will fall
in surrender to your love.
On my knees I will fall
in surrender to your love.
(Repeat)

You obeyed God's plan to the very end,
Holy One, became the sacrifice
that would show us the Father's love.
You came to die to give us life,
and now I give myself to you the humble
    King.

One day all the world will see you,
one day all the world will see
all creation kneel before you,
all creation sing.

© 2000 Brown Bear Music

828 Mike Norman and Mike Little

Jesus, how I love your name,
I will sing your praise
for ever and ever.
Jesus, how you've set me free,
I will magnify your name
in honour and glory today.
(Repeat)

Lord, without you I am nothing at all
but with you I can do anything.
Dreams that reach for the sky;
hopes created on high;
Lord, I trust you with the rest of my life.

© 1997 Kingsong/Alliance Media Ltd./CopyCare

829 Steve and Vikki Cook

Jesus, how we love you,
how we long to sing your praise,
to join the mighty chorus
that is worshipping your name,
for you are surrounded
by an endless sea of joy.
Multitudes rejoicing
and declaring with one voice.

You're the glory of the ages,
you're eternity's delight,
you're the hope of all creation,
and the fountain of all life.
You're the glory of the ages
and the Lord of history;
your great throne will stand for ever,
Jesus, you will always be the glory of the
    ages.

Jesus, how we love you,
for you proved your love for us
when you became the Lamb of God
by dying on the cross.
Now you are exalted
as our great Redeemer, King,
throughout time our praise
will be for ever echoing.

© 1998 PDI Worship/CopyCare

830 Wes Sutton

Jesus, I see in you all that is holy.
And, Jesus, I see in you the Father's glory.
And so I'll worship none but you,
I'll worship none but you.

Jesus, I have found in you complete
    forgiveness.
And, Jesus, I have found in you love
    without limit.
And so I'll love no one but you,
I'll love no one but you.

831 Jayne and Luke Weller

Jesus, Jesus, Jesus, Jesus.
Open up the heavens,
let your glory, let your glory fall.
Open up the heavens,
let your fire, let your fire fall.

832 Suzette Thorndycraft

Jesus, Jesus, Jesus, Jesus,
Holy One, Mighty One,
Son of God,
I worship you, Lord.
Jesus, Jesus, Jesus, Jesus,
Holy One, Mighty One,
Son of God,
I give my life to you.

Take me as I am
and I will call you Lord,
come, take me here and now,
and be my Saviour.
(Repeat)

Jesus, Jesus,
Jesus, Jesus.

833 William J. Gaither and Gloria Gaither

Jesus, Jesus, Jesus;
there's just something about that name.
Master, Saviour, Jesus,
like the fragrance after the rain.
Jesus, Jesus, Jesus,
let all heaven and earth proclaim;
kings and kingdoms will all pass away,
but there's something about that name.

834 Frances Jane van Alstyne (Fanny J. Crosby)

Jesus, keep me near the Cross;
there a precious fountain,
free to all, a healing stream,
flows from Calv'ry's mountain.

> *In the Cross, in the Cross,*
> *be my glory ever;*
> *till my raptured soul shall find*
> *rest beyond the river.*

Near the Cross, a trembling soul,
love and mercy found me;
there the bright and morning star
shed its beams around me.

Near the Cross: O Lamb of God,
bring its scenes before me;
help me walk from day to day,
with its shadow o'er me.

Near the Cross I'll watch and wait,
hoping, trusting ever,
till I reach the golden strand,
just beyond the river.

835 Chris Rolinson

Jesus, King of kings,
we worship and adore you.
Jesus, Lord of heav'n and earth,
we bow down at your feet.
Father, we bring to you our worship,
your sov'reign will be done,
on earth your kingdom come,
through Jesus Christ, your only Son.

Jesus, sov'reign Lord,
we worship and adore you.
Jesus, name above all names,
we bow down at your feet.
Father, we offer you our worship,
your sov'reign will be done,
on earth your kingdom come,
through Jesus Christ, your only Son.

Jesus, light of the world,
we worship and adore you.
Jesus, Lord Emmanuel,
we bow down at your feet.
Father, for your delight we worship,
your sov'reign will be done,
on earth your kingdom come,
through Jesus Christ, your only Son.

836 Geoff Baker

Jesus, Light of the world,
shine your light on me.
Jesus, Light of the world,
cause these blinded eyes to see.
See your glory, see your face,
know the joy of your wonderful grace.
Jesus, Light of the world,
shine your light on me.

Jesus, Hope of the world,
set your hope in me.
Jesus, Hope of the world,
cause these blinded eyes to see.
See your sov'reign will be done,
know by faith that your Kingdom is come.
Jesus, Hope of the world,
set your hope in me.

Jesus, Joy of the world
put your joy in me.
Jesus, Joy of the world,
cause these blinded eyes to see.
See the vict'ry of the cross,
know the place you're preparing for us.
Jesus, Joy of the world
put your joy in me.

837 Paul Oakley

Jesus, lover of my soul,
all consuming fire is in your gaze.
Jesus, I want you to know
I will follow you all my days.
For no one else in history is like you,
and history itself belongs to you.
Alpha and Omega, you have loved me,
and I will share eternity with you.

It's all about you, Jesus,
and all this is for you,
for your glory and your fame.
It's not about me,
as if you should do things my way;
you alone are God,
and I surrender to your ways.

838 Charles Wesley

Jesus, lover of my soul,
let me to thy bosom fly,
while the nearer waters roll,
while the tempest still is high;
hide me, O my Saviour, hide,
till the storm of life is past;
safe into the haven guide,
O receive my soul at last.

Other refuge have I none,
hangs my helpless soul on thee;
leave, ah, leave me not alone,
still support and comfort me.
All my trust on thee is stayed,
all my help from thee I bring;
cover my defenceless head
with the shadow of thy wing.

Thou, O Christ, art all I want;
more than all in thee I find;
raise the fallen, cheer the faint,
heal the sick, and lead the blind.
Just and holy is thy name,
I am all unrighteousness;
false and full of sin I am,
thou art full of truth and grace.

Continued overleaf

Plenteous grace with thee is found,
grace to cover all my sin;
let the healing streams abound,
make and keep me pure within.
Thou of life the fountain art;
freely let me take of thee;
spring thou up within my heart,
rise to all eternity.

839 Bernard of Clairvaux
(revised and adapted Graham Kendrick)

Jesus, the joy of loving hearts,
fountain of life, true light of man,
from the best bliss that earth imparts } x2
we turn unfilled to you again.

Your truth unchanged has ever stood,
you rescue those who on you call.
To those who seek, you're always good, } x2
to those who find you, all in all.

We taste of you, O living bread,
and long to feast upon you still.
We drink of you, the fountain head, } x2
here may our thirsty souls be filled.

Our restless spirits yearn for you
through changing scenes, uncertain paths;
glad when your smile of grace we see, } x2
happy when faith can hold you fast.

O Jesus, ever with us stay,
your presence here so calm and bright.
Chase the dark night of sin away, } x3
bathe all the world in holy light.

© 2001 Make Way Music

840 Wes Sutton

Jesus, there's no one like you.
Jesus, no one loves like you do.
Jesus, the glory of God,
no one compares with you.
Jesus, the Father's delight,
Jesus, the world's brightest light.
Jesus, I want you to know
that all that I want is you.
All that I want is you.

© 1997 Sovereign Lifestyle Music

841 Nicolaus Ludwig von Zinzendorf
Trans. John Wesley

Jesus, thy blood and righteousness
my beauty are, my glorious dress;
midst flaming worlds, in these arrayed,
with joy shall I lift up my head.

Bold shall I stand in thy great day;
for to my charge who aught shall lay?
Fully absolved through these I am,
from sin and fear, from guilt and shame.

That holy, meek, unspotted Lamb,
who from the Father's bosom came,
who suffered for me, to atone,
now for my Lord and God I own.

Lord, I believe thy precious blood,
which at the mercy-seat of God
for ever doth for sinners plead,
for me, e'en for my soul, was shed.

When from the dust of death I rise
to claim my mansion in the skies,
e'en then this shall be all my plea –
Jesus hath lived, hath died for me!

842 Martin E. Leckebusch

Jesus, we have heard your Spirit
saying we belong to you,
showing us our need for mercy,
focusing our hopes anew;
you have won our hearts' devotion,
now we feel your guiding hand:
where you lead us, we will follow
on the paths your love has planned.

As a chosen, pilgrim people
we are learning day by day
what it means to be disciples,
to believe and to obey.
Word and table show your purpose;
hearts and lives we gladly bring -
where you lead us, we will follow,
suffering Saviour, risen King.

How we yearn that ev'ry people
should exalt your matchless name,
yet so often this world's systems
countermand your regal claim.
If we stand for truth and justice
we, like you, may suffer loss;
where you lead us, we will follow -
give us grace to bear our cross.

So we journey on together,
keen to make our calling sure;
through our joys, our fears, our crises,
may our faith be made mature.
Jesus, hope of hearts and nations,
Sov'reign Lord of time and space,
where you lead us, we will follow
till we see you face to face.

© 1999 Kevin Mayhew Ltd.

843   Richard Lewis

Jesus, what a wonder you are;
Jesus, your word is a lamp to my feet,
a light to my path:
O what a friend and guide.
Jesus, what a wonder you are;
you know my thoughts from afar
and you care for my ev'ry need:
O what a friend and guide!

O, how long to see your face,
beautiful Saviour, King of grace.
There is such peace in your embrace:
Jesus, what a wonder you are.

Jesus, what a wonder you are;
no greater love can be found
than you gave your life for me:
O what a friend and guide!
Jesus, what a wonder you are;
you carried all of my sorrows and shame
there on the cross:
O what a friend and guide!

© 2001 Kevin Mayhew Ltd.

844   William Cowper

Jesus, where'er thy people meet,
there they behold thy mercy-seat;
where'er they seek thee thou art found,
and ev'ry place is hallowed ground.

For thou, within no walls confined,
inhabitest the humble mind;
such ever bring thee when they come,
and, going, take thee to their home.

Dear Shepherd of thy chosen few,
thy former mercies here renew;
here to our waiting hearts proclaim
the sweetness of thy saving name.

Here may we prove the pow'r of prayer
to strengthen faith and sweeten care,
to teach our faint desires to rise,
and bring all heav'n before our eyes.

Lord, we are few, but thou art near;
nor short thine arm, nor deaf thine ear;
O rend the heav'ns, come quickly down,
and make a thousand hearts thine own.

845   Paul Banderet

Jesus, you are Lord of heaven
yet to earth you gladly came.
Because you gave your life up for me
I will never be the same.

You are so good,
you are so wonderful.
How I love to know you love me,
your saving grace I see.
You are so good,
you are Emmanuel.
Just to know you as my Saviour
means ev'rything to me.

Jesus, I have come to wonder
at the beauty of your name.
And as I live each moment for you
I will never be the same.

© 2001 Kevin Mayhew Ltd.

846 Darlene Zschech

Jesus, you're all I need, you're all I need.
Now I give my life to you alone,
you are all I need,
Jesus, you're all I need,
you're all I need.
Lord, you gave yourself so I could live,
you are all I need.

Oh, you purchased my salvation
and wiped away my tears,
now I drink your living waters
and I'll never thirst again.
For you alone are holy,
I'll worship at your throne,
and you will reign for ever,
holy is the Lord.

847 Tommy Coomes

Jesus, you're the sweetest name of all;
Jesus, you always hear me when I call.
O Jesus, you pick me up each time I fall;
you're the sweetest, the sweetest name of all.

Jesus, how I love to praise your name;
Jesus, you're still the first, the last, the same.
O Jesus, you died and took away my shame;
you're the sweetest, the sweetest name of all.

Jesus, you're the soon and coming King;
Jesus, we need the love that you can bring.
O Jesus, we lift our voices up and sing;
you're the sweetest, the sweetest name of all.

848 Isaac Watts and Bob Kauflin

Join all the glorious names
of wisdom, love and pow'r
that mortals ever knew,
that angels ever bore;
all are too poor to speak
your vast and priceless worth,
too poor to set my Saviour forth.

Jesus, your name is glorious,
our Prophet, Priest and King.
Jesus, you're reigning over us
and for evermore,
your praises we will sing.

Great Prophet of my God,
my tongue would bless your name,
through you the joyful news of our salvation
    came.
The long-awaited news
of ev'ry sin forgiv'n,
of hell subdued and peace with heav'n.

Jesus, my great high Priest,
you shed your blood and died,
my guilty conscience seeks no sacrifice
    beside.
Your pure and precious blood
for all my sin atoned,
and now it pleads before the throne.

849 Henry van Dyke

Joyful, joyful, we adore thee,
God of glory, Lord of love;
hearts unfold like flow'rs before thee,
op'ning to the sun above.
Melt the clouds of sin and sadness;
drive the dark of doubt away.
Giver of immortal gladness,
fill us with the light of day!

All thy works with joy surround thee,
earth and heav'n reflect thy rays.
Stars and angels sing around thee,
centre of unbroken praise.
Field and forest, vale and mountain,
flow'ry meadow, flashing sea,
chanting bird and flowing fountain
call us to rejoice in thee!

Thou art giving and forgiving,
ever blessing, ever blest,
wellspring of the joy of living,
ocean depth of happy rest!

Thou our Father, Christ our brother,
all who live in love are thine.
Teach us how to love each other;
life us to the joy divine!

Mortals, join the mighty chorus
which the morning stars began;
love divine is reigning o'er us,
leading us with mercy's hand.
Ever singing, march we onward,
victors in the midst of strife.
Joyful music leads us sunward
in the triumph-song of life!

© Control

850 Geoff Bullock

Just let me say how much I love you,
let me speak of your mercy and grace,
just let me live in the shadow of your
    beauty,
let me see you face to face.
And the earth will shake
as your word goes forth
and the heavens can tremble and fall.
Just let me say how much I love you,
O my Saviour, my Lord and friend.

Just let me hear your finest whispers
as you gently call my name.
And let me see your power and your glory,
let me feel your Spirit's flame.
Let me find you in the desert
'til this sand is holy ground
and I am found completely surrendered
to you, my Lord and friend.

So let me say how much I love you,
with all my heart I long for you.
For I am caught in this passion of knowing
this endless love I've found in you.
And the depth of grace,
the forgiveness found
to be called a child of God
just makes me say how much I love you,
O my Saviour, my Lord and friend.

© 1994 Word Music/Maranatha! Music/CopyCare

851 Darlene Zschech

Lamp unto my feet,
light unto my path.
It is you,
Jesus, it is you.

This treasure that I hold,
more than finest gold.
It is you,
Jesus, it is you.

With all my heart,
with all my soul,
I live to worship you and
praise for evermore,
praise for evermore.
Lord ev'ry day I need you more,
on wings of heaven I will soar
with you.

You take my brokenness,
call me to yourself,
there you stand,
healing in your hands.

© 1999 Darlene Zschech/Hillsong Publishing/Kingsway's Thankyou
Music

852 James Lewis

Lead me, Lord,
lead me in your ways;
not in my strength
but by your Spirit.
(Repeat)

As I rise,
to when I sleep,
I will praise you.
When I'm strong
or when I fall,
Lord, let me praise you.
Lord, let me praise you
and as I worship you,
lead me, Lord.

© 1999 Kevin Mayhew Ltd.

853 Mark Naea, Vernon Katipa and Frank Kereopa

Lead me on, Holy Spirit,
fill my heart, come flood my soul;
lead me on, into your presence,
touch me, Lord Jesus, I need you.
I can't live without you,
I can't walk this road alone;
in my heart I need you,
Holy One, come and take my hand.

854 Matt Redman

Let ev'rything that, ev'rything that,
ev'rything that has breath,
praise the Lord.
Let ev'rything that, ev'rything that,
ev'rything that has breath,
praise the Lord.

Praise you in the morning,
praise you in the evening,
praise you when I'm young and when I'm old.
Praise you when I'm laughing,
praise you when I'm grieving,
praise you ev'ry season of the soul.
If we could see how much you're worth,
your pow'r, your might, your endless love,
then surely we would never cease to praise.

Praise you in the heavens,
joining with the angels,
praising you for ever and a day.
Praise you on the earth now,
joining with creation,
calling all the nations to your praise.
If they could see how much you're worth,
your pow'r, your might, your endless love,
then surely we would never cease to praise.

Let ev'rything that, ev'rything that,
ev'rything that has breath,
praise the Lord.
Let ev'rything that, ev'rything that,
ev'rything that has breath,
praise the Lord.

855 Jamie Burgess

Let ev'rything that isn't
pure in your sight, Lord Jesus,
be swept away by your power, Lord.
I want to stand before you
dressed in the finest linen:
holy, in purity, my Lord.

Pure and holy, giving glory
to the King of kings.
Here, before you, I adore you,
praises I will bring.

I set my eyes upon you,
I focus my mind on you,
I want to give you, oh, so much.
Touch me and move my spirit,
love me without a limit.
Oh Lord, I cry out for your touch.

856 Jim Cernero

Let my heart be the temple of your Spirit.
Let my spirit feel the warmth of your
    embrace.
Let me be a holy habitation
where your Spirit is pleased to dwell.
Oh Lord, I long to know your glory.
I want to offer the sacrifice of praise.
Fill this temple, Lord,
with your Spirit once again.
Fill this temple, Lord,
with your Spirit once again.

857 Dave Bilbrough

Let the chimes of freedom ring
all across the earth;
lift your voice in praise to him
and sing of all his worth,
and sing of all his worth.

Open wide your prison doors
to greet the Lord of life;
songs of triumph fill the air,
Christ Jesus is alive,
Christ Jesus is alive.

Let all the people hear the news
of the One who comes to save:
he's the Lord of all the universe,
and for ever he shall reign.

In ev'ry corner of the earth
to ev'ry tribe and tongue,
make known that God so loved this world
that he gave his only Son,
he gave his only Son.

Spread the news and make it plain:
he breaks the pow'r of sin.
Jesus died and rose again,
his love will never end,
his love will never end.

Let all the people hear the news
of the One who comes to save:
he's the Lord of all the universe,
and for ever he shall reign.
And for evermore, and for evermore,
and for evermore he shall reign.
And for evermore, and for evermore,
and for evermore he shall reign.

He will return in majesty
to take his rightful place
as King of all eternity,
the Name above all names,
the Name above all names.

© 1997 Kingsway's Thankyou Music

858 Paul Baloche and Gary Sadler

Let the heavens rejoice,
let the earth be glad;
let the people of God sing his praise
all over the land.
Ev'ryone in the valley,
come, and lift your voice;
all those on the mountain top
be glad and shout for joy.

Rise up and praise him,
he deserves our love;
rise up and praise him,
worship the Holy One.
With all your heart,
with all your soul,
with all your might,
rise up and praise him.

© 1996 Integrity's Hosanna! Music/Kingsway's Thankyou Music

859 Darrell Evans

Let the poor man say, 'I am rich in him,'
let the lost man say, 'I am found in him,'
and let the river flow;
let the blind man say, 'I can see again,'
let the dead man say, 'I am born again,'
and let the river flow, let the river flow.

Let the river flow, let the river flow;
Holy Spirit, come, move in power.
Let the river flow, let the river flow;
Holy Spirit come, move in power.
Let the river flow, let the river flow,
let the river flow.

© 1995 Mercy/Vineyard Publishing/CopyCare

860 Dick and Melodie Tunney

Let there be praise,
let there be joy in our hearts.
Sing to the Lord, give him the glory (glory).

Let there be praise,
let there be joy in our hearts.
For evermore let his love fill the air
and let there be praise.

© BMG Songs Inc./Pamela Kay Music/Charlie Monk Music/EMI
Christian Publishing/CopyCare

861 Graham Kendrick

Let the same mind that was in Jesus
be found among you, his attitude.
Who, though he was in nature God
did not consider it something to grasp,
but emptied himself,
and took the form of a servant,
and in the likeness of man he was born.

Continued overleaf

Then being found in human form,
humbled himself, was obedient to death,
death on a cross.

Therefore God has exalted him
(God has exalted him),
highly exalted him
(highly exalted him),
given to him the Name above all names,
that at the name of Jesus,
ev'ry knee should bow
(ev'ry knee should bow),
ev'ry tongue confess
(ev'ry tongue confess),
Jesus is Lord of heaven and earth
to God the Father's glory, glory.
God has exalted him
(God has exalted him),
highly exalted him
(highly exalted him),
Jesus is Lord of heaven and earth
to God the Father's glory,
to God the Father's glory.

862 Reuben Morgan

Let the weak say 'I am strong',
let the poor say 'I am rich',
let the blind say 'I can see,
it's what the Lord has done in me'.

Hosanna, hosanna
to the Lamb that was slain!
Hosanna, hosanna!
Jesus died and rose again!

Into the river I will wade;
there my sins are washed away.
From the heavens mercy streams
of the Saviour's love for me.

I will rise from waters deep
into the saving arms of God.
I will sing salvation songs;
Jesus Christ has set me free.

863 Don Moen

Let your glory fall,
we are thirsty, Lord;
hear us as we call,
fill us now.
Let your glory fall,
let your glory fall,
let your glory fall.

Ev'ry tongue and tribe
gathered 'round your throne;
with one voice we cry,
'Holy Lord.'
Ev'ry tongue and tribe,
ev'ry tongue and tribe,
ev'ry tongue and tribe.

Glory to the Lamb,
Lamb upon the throne;
all the saints proclaim,
'Jesus reigns.'
Glory to the Lamb,
glory to the Lamb,
glory to the Lamb.

864 Tommy Walker

Lift up your heads (lift up your heads),
O you gates (O you gates);
swing open wide (swing open wide),
you ancient doors (you ancient doors);
let the King of kings (let the King of kings)
take his rightful place (take his rightful place);
make room, make way (make room, make way)
for our King of grace (for our King of grace).

Lift up your hands (lift up your hands),
open up your hearts (open up your hearts);
his vict'ry over sin (his vict'ry over sin)
and death is ours (and death is ours);
let the King of kings (let the King of kings)
take his rightful place (take his rightful place);
make room, make way (make room, make way)
for our King of grace (for our King of grace).

Who is this King of glory, Lord of pow'r?
His name is Jesus, our risen King.
Who is this King, so mighty,
  Lord of strength?
His name is Jesus, our risen King.

865 Richard Lewis

Lift up your heads, O you gates,
be lifted up, O ancient doors,
that the King of glory may come in,
that the King of glory may come in.
(Repeat)

Who is this King of glory?
The Lord strong and mighty.
Who is this King of glory?
The Lord strong and mighty in battle.
Worthy is he to receive all honour,
worthy is he to receive all praise,
worthy is he to receive the glory.
Glory to God, glory to God, glory to God.
(Repeat)

866 Frances Ridley Havergal

Like a river glorious is God's perfect peace,
over all victorious, in its bright increase:
perfect, yet it floweth fuller ev'ry day;
perfect, yet it groweth deeper all the way.

> *Stayed upon Jehovah, hearts are fully blest,*
> *finding, as he promised, perfect peace and*
> *rest.*

Hidden in the hollow of his blessèd hand,
never foe can follow, never traitor stand;
not a surge of worry, not a shade of care,
not a blast of hurry touched the Spirit there.

Ev'ry joy or trial falleth from above,
traced upon our dial by the sun of love.
We may trust him fully, all for us to do;
they who trust him wholly find him wholly
true.

867 Fred Pratt Green

Long ago, prophets knew
Christ would come, born a Jew,
come to make all things new,
bear his people's burden,
freely love and pardon.

> *Ring, bells, ring, ring, ring!*
> *Sing, choirs, sing, sing, sing!*
> *When he comes, when he comes,*
> *who will make him welcome?*

God in time, God in man,
this is God's timeless plan:
he will come, as a man,
born himself of woman,
God divinely human.

Mary, hail! Though afraid,
she believed, she obeyed.
In her womb, God is laid:
till the time expected,
nurtured and protected.

Journey ends! Where afar
Bethlem shines, like a star,
stable door stands ajar.
Unborn Son of Mary,
Saviour, do not tarry!

868 Eoghan Heaslip and M. Goss

Look what you've done in my life,
see what you've done in this heart,
you've brought hope, healing and freedom,
look what you've done in my life.
(Repeat)

And though I'm not deserving of your love,
you give it all to me,
with open arms you welcome me.

Continued overleaf

Your love is higher than the mountains,
your love is deeper than the sea,
Jesus, you came to pay my ransom,
it's your love, Jesus, that sets me free.

869 Thomas Kelly

Look, ye saints, the sight is glorious:
see the Man of Sorrows now;
from the fight returned victorious,
ev'ry knee to him shall bow:
Crown him, crown him! *(x2)*
Crowns become the Victor's brow.

Crown the Saviour! Angels, crown him!
Rich the trophies Jesus brings;
in the seat of pow'r enthrone him,
while the vault of heaven rings:
Crown him, crown him! *(x2)*
Crown the Saviour King of kings!

Sinners in derision crowned him,
mocking thus the Saviour's claim;
saints and angels crowd around him,
own his title, praise his name:
Crown him, crown him! *(x2)*
spread abroad the Victor's fame.

Hark, those bursts of acclamation!
Hark those loud triumphant chords!
Jesus takes the highest station:
O what joy the sight affords!
Crown him, crown him! *(x2)*
King of kings and Lord of lords!

870 George Hugh Bourne

Lord, enthroned in heav'nly splendour,
first begotten from the dead,
thou alone, our strong defender,
liftest up thy people's head.
Alleluia, alleluia,
Jesu, true and living bread.

Here our humblest homage pay we,
here in loving rev'rence bow;
here for faith's discernment pray we,
lest we fail to know thee now.
Alleluia, alleluia,
thou art here, we ask not how.

Though the lowliest form doth veil thee
as of old in Bethlehem,
here as there thine angels hail thee,
Branch and Flow'r of Jesse's Stem.
Alleluia, alleluia,
we in worship join with them.

Paschal Lamb, thine off'ring, finished
once for all when thou wast slain,
in its fullness undiminished
shall for evermore remain.
Alleluia, alleluia,
cleansing souls from ev'ry stain.

Life-imparting heav'nly manna,
stricken rock with streaming side,
heav'n and earth with loud hosanna
worship thee, the Lamb who died.
Alleluia, alleluia,
ris'n, ascended, glorified!

871 Clive Goodwill

Lord, how you came and rescued me,
saved me from such misery;
O how I want to thank you.
You, how you've loved me from the start,
entered in and won my heart,
O, is there any wonder

I love you, I love you.
I love you, I love you.

Lord how you gave yourself for me,
hung upon that cursèd tree;
I'm ever thankful to you.
You, how you've shown me your great love,
even now you're praying above
that I would always love you.

Lord, help me do your will today,
hear you, trust you, then obey,
so I may always please you.
Lord, how your love will draw me on
'til all trace of self is gone
and I'll be yours completely.

872 Craig Gower

Lord, I lift my voice in praise to you
for the love you placed inside of me.
Lord, I give my life, my heart and soul
to you alone.

And with ev'ry breath that comes from me
will flow your mercy and your grace,
proclaiming love and liberty,
for all who have an ear to hear.

And your love stirs faith and hope in me,
and your grace brings pow'r
to set this sinner free,
and your blood pours joy into my life;
Jesus, you gave it all for me.

873 Steve McPherson

Lord, I long to see you glorified
    in ev'rything I do;
all my heartfelt dreams I put aside,
to see your Spirit move with power in my life.

Jesus, Lord of all eternity,
your children rise in faith;
all the earth displays your glory,
and each word you speak brings life to
    all who hear.

Lord of all,
all of creation sings your praise
in heaven and earth.
Lord, we stand,
hearts open wide, be exalted.

874 Lowell Mason

Lord Jesus Christ, we seek thy face
within the veil we bow the knee.
Oh, let thy glory fill the place,
and bless us while we wait on thee.

We thank thee for the precious blood
that purged our sins and brought us nigh.
All cleansed and sanctified to God,
thy holy name to magnify.

The brow that once with thorns was bound,
thy hands, thy side we fain would see;
draw near, Lord Jesus, glory crowned,
and bless us while we wait on thee.

875 Trish Morgan

Lord, my heart before you
is open and bare.
I stand in need of your mercy,
in need of your care.
Wash my sins away in this falling rain.
In this day of grace, fill me once again.
With an honest heart,
Lord, I worship you,
with an honest heart, I worship you.

876 R. Holden

Lord of glory, we adore you,
Christ of God, ascended high.
Heart and soul we bow before you,
glorious now beyond the sky.
You we worship, you we praise;
excellent in all your ways.

Mighty King in heav'n exalted,
rightful heir and Lord of all,
once despised, disowned, rejected
by the ones you came to call;
you we honour, you adore,
glorious now and evermore.

Continued overleaf

Lord of life, to death made subject,
blesser, yet a curse once-made,
of your Father's heart the object,
yet in depths of anguish laid;
you we gaze on, you recall,
bearing here our sorrows all.

877 Janine Price

Lord of hosts, Alpha and Omega,
you are Lord of hosts,
the beginning and the end,
you reign on high.
King of kings, majesty enthroned on high,
you're Lord of lords.
Victorious over sin and death.
And I worship you, O Lord God on high,
for you sent your Son who was crucified
and I worship you, O Lord God on high,
I worship you, worship you,
I worship you, Lord on high.

878 Shaun and Mel Griffiths

Lord of the heavens,
I bow my knee and worship you,
I stand before you and I am amazed,
I see your beauty
displayed in ev'rything you do.
For you are my Saviour,
Lord and King;
you are the only one for me,
you are the only one that I adore.
In your Son atonement, sacrifice;
through his death
redemption gives new life
and I reach out,
receive your endless love.

879 Scott Wesley Brown

Lord, we come before your throne
humbled and amazed,
your greatness overshadows
ev'ry idol of this age;
for all the treasures of this world,
Lord, cannot replace
the greatest joy of knowing you,
and walking in your grace.

We will worship you,
there is none beside you,
we will worship you,
there is none beside you,
we will worship you,
there is none beside you, Lord.

Lord, we come with thankful hearts
into your courts with praise,
rejoicing in your favour,
delighting in your ways;
for all we've lost cannot compare,
Lord, to what we've gained,
for there is none like you, O God,
Name above all names!

880 Eoghan Heaslip, M. Goss and B. Heaslip

Lord, we turn to you and pray,
we come to seek your face,
to call upon your name.
So, Lord, open up the doors,
the flood-gates of your love,
Lord, we pray that you'd reveal your glory.

For, O, that the heavens would rend and be
  opened,
and you, you would come down.
The mountains would tremble,
our hearts would be humbled before you.

Won't you open up the heavens, Lord,
and shower down with your love,
pour out your presence on us, we pray,
that you would come and heal our land,
let your love flood our barrenness,
pour out your presence on us,
we pray, Lord, we pray.

881 Tommy Coomes and Don Moen

Lord, we've come to worship,
and we have come to pray;
Lord, we've come to listen,
and hear what you would say;
O Lord, our hearts are longing
to meet with you today;
for we have come to seek you,
and we have come to say.

Worthy, you are worthy,
King of kings, Lord of lords,
you are worthy.
All blessing and power,
all riches and wisdom,
all glory and honour and praise
to the Lamb.

Lord, we need forgiveness,
we've wandered far away;
look down in tender mercy,
forgive our sins, we pray;
O Lord, we need revival,
all across this land;
come move among your people,
with your mighty hand.

Worthy, you are worthy,
King of kings, Lord of lords,
you are worthy.
All blessing and power,
all riches and wisdom,
all glory and honour and praise to the Lamb.
To the Lamb that was slain
to redeem us back to God again;
to the Lamb who will reign
for ever and ever, amen.

882 Graham Kendrick

Lord, you've been good to me
all my life, all my life;
your loving kindness never fails.
I will remember all you have done,
bring from my heart thanksgiving songs.

New ev'ry morning is your love
filled with compassion from above.
Grace and forgiveness full and free,
Lord, you've been good to me.

So may each breath I take be for you, Lord,
only you, giving you back the life I owe.
Love so amazing, mercy so free,
Lord, you've been good, so good to me.

883 George Wade Robinson

Loved with everlasting love,
led by grace that love to know;
Spirit breathing from above,
thou hast taught me it is so.
O this full and perfect peace!
O this transport all divine!
In a love which cannot cease,
I am his and he is mine.

Heaven above is softer blue,
earth around is sweeter green;
something lives in every hue
Christless eyes have never seen;
birds with gladder songs o'erflow,
flowers with deeper beauties shine,
since I know, as now I know,
I am his, and he is mine.

Things that once were wild alarms
cannot now disturb my rest;
closed in everlasting arms,
pillowed on the loving breast.
O to lie for ever here,
doubt and care and self resign,
while he whispers in my ear,
I am his and he is mine.

Continued overleaf

His for ever, only his;
who the Lord and me shall part?
Ah, with what a rest of bliss
Christ can fill the loving heart!
Heaven and earth may fade and flee;
firstborn light in gloom decline;
but, while God and I shall be,
I am his, and he is mine.

884 Noel and Tricia Richards

Love songs from heaven are filling the earth,
bringing great hope to all nations;
evil has prospered, but truth is alive,
in this dark world the light still shines.

Nothing has silenced this gospel of Christ,
it echoes down through the ages.
Blood of the martyrs has made your
    Church strong,
in this dark world the light still shines.

For you we live, and for you we may die,
through us may Jesus be seen;
for you alone we will offer our lives,
in this dark world our light will shine.

Let ev'ry nation be filled with your song;
this is the cry of your people,
'We will not settle for anything less,
in this dark world our light must shine.'

For you we live, and for you we may die,
through us may Jesus be seen;
for you alone we will offer our lives,
in this dark world our light will shine.

© 1996 Kingsway's Thankyou Music

885 Andy Park

Many waters cannot quench your love,
rivers cannot overwhelm it.
Oceans of fear cannot conceal your love for me.
Many waters cannot quench your love,
rivers cannot overwhelm it.

Oceans of fear cannot conceal your love for me,
your love for me.
Holy love, flow in me,
fill me up like the deepest sea.
Like a crashing wave pouring over me,
holy love flow in me.

Many sorrows cannot quench your love,
darkness cannot overwhelm it.
I will not fear, your love is here to comfort me.
Many sorrows cannot quench your love,
darkness cannot overwhelm it.
I will not fear, your love is here to comfort me,
you comfort me.

When I find you I find healing,
when I find you I find peace,
and I know that there's no river so wide,
no mountain so high, no ocean so deep
that you can't part the sea.

© 1995 Mercy/Vineyard Publishing/CopyCare

886 Reuben Morgan

May our homes be filled with dancing,
may our streets be filled with joy;
may injustice bow to Jesus
as the people turn to pray.

From the mountain to the valley,
hear our praises rise to you.
From the heavens to the nations,
hear our singing fill the air.

May a light shine in the darkness,
as we walk before the cross;
may your glory fill the whole earth
as the water o'er the seas.

Hallelujah!

© 1998 Reuben Morgan/Hillsong Publishing/Kingsway's Thankyou
Music

887 Katie Barclay Wilkinson

May the mind of Christ my Saviour
live in me from day to day,
by his love and pow'r controlling
all I do and say.

May the word of God dwell richly
in my heart from hour to hour,
so that all may see I triumph
only through his pow'r.

May the peace of God my Father
rule my life in ev'rything,
that I may be calm to comfort
sick and sorrowing.

May the love of Jesus fill me,
as the waters fill the sea;
him exalting, self abasing,
this is victory.

May I run the race before me,
strong and brave to face the foe,
looking only unto Jesus
as I onward go.

May his beauty rest upon me
as I seek the lost to win,
and may they forget the channel,
seeing only him.

888 Lynne Deshazo and Gary Sadler

Mercy, mercy, Lord,
your mercy is how we are restored.
Mercy, O mercy, Lord,
help us to show your mercy, Lord.

You have been patient with our offences,
you have forgiven all of our sins;
we were deserving only your judgement,
but your great mercy triumphed again.

Mercy, mercy, Lord,
your mercy is how we are restored.
Mercy, O mercy, Lord,
help us to show your mercy, Lord.
(Repeat)

Lord, you have taught us
'Love one another'.
As You have loved us
so we must love,
always forbearing,
always forgiving,
showing to others
the mercy we've known.

889 Chris Orange

Mercy and love, a pure offering,
you gave your life, freed me from sin.
Let now the oil of this thankful heart
flow out to you, my Lord.

Faithful and true, your word never ends.
Strength for the weak, life for the dead.
My great Redeemer, my closest friend,
empow'r me to live for you.

> *With my hands raised up to your throne,*
> *I will love, Jesus, you alone.*
> *You're my all, my ev'rything, my grace,*
> *and I'll live to ever sing your praise.*

890 Scott Wesley Brown

> *More like you, Jesus, more like you,*
> *fill my heart with your desire*
> *to make me more like you.*
> *More like you, Jesus, more like you,*
> *touch my lips with holy fire*
> *and make me more like you.*

Lord, you are my mercy,
Lord, you are my grace,
all my deepest sins have forever been
erased.
Draw me in your presence,
lead me in your ways,
I long to bring you glory
in righteousness and praise.

Continued overleaf

Lord, you are compassion,
and never-ending love,
for you have redeemed me
by your precious blood.
Create in me a clean heart,
a spirit that is new,
the joy of my salvation
is only found in you.

891 Bryn Haworth

More, Lord, I must have more, Lord,
more of your presence, more of your love.
More, Lord, I must have more, Lord,
more of your Spirit flowing through me.

For you, Lord, you are the fountain
of living water that never runs dry.
So come, now, come to the waters,
all who are thirsty will be satisfied.

More Lord, I must have more Lord,
more of your kingdom, more of your will.

892 Richard Lewis

More, Lord, give us more of your Spirit,
give us more, we open our hearts.
More, Lord.
Give us more of your Spirit in our lives;
we yield them to you, give us more of
    your Spirit,
give us more of the Son, give us more of
    the Father,
come and fill ev'ry one.
I receive your Spirit, I receive your love,
I receive the power of the Lord God above.

Glorify your name, glorify your name,
glorify your name in all the earth.
(Repeat)

893 Reuben Morgan

More than I could
hope or dream of,
you have poured
your favour on me.
One day in the house of God is
better than a thousand
days in the world.

> So blessed, I can't contain it,
> so much I've got to give it away.
> Your love
> has taught me to live now.
> You are more than enough for me.

Lord, you're more than enough for me.
Lord, you're more than enough for me.

894 Nick and Anita Haigh

My eyes be open to your presence,
my ears to hear your call.
My heart be open to your love
and in your arms to fall.
My mind be open to your word,
my soul to heaven's cure,
that I be open to you, Lord,
this day and evermore.

My life be open to your leading,
my hands to do your will.
My lips be open in your praise
and for your truth to tell.
My home be open in your name
for weary ones and poor,
that I be open to you, Lord,
this day and evermore.

My door be open to the other
wherever we may meet.
My arms be open to the one
in whom I am complete.
My self be open to your world
and in it see your face,
that I be open to you, Lord,
held fast in your embrace.

895 Don Harris and Gary Sadler

My eyes can see your hand
at ev'ry passing glance;
your glory covers all the earth and sky.
Your goodness fills my life
in ev'ry circumstance;
my heart is open wide,
my hands are lifted high.

You are my God and I am your servant,
I am in awe of your love for me.
Your mercy flows though I don't
*   deserve it,*
I want to shout it out:
I'm in awe of your love for me.

I found a deeper faith
within your love's embrace;
where all I want is what you have for me.
I'm drinking from the cup
of pure and endless grace;
my heart is open wide,
my hands are lifted high.

© 2000 Integrity's Hosanna! Music/Kingsway's Thankyou Music

896 Frederick William Faber

My God, how wonderful thou art,
thy majesty how bright,
how beautiful thy mercy-seat,
in depths of burning light!

How dread are thine eternal years,
O everlasting Lord,
by prostrate spirits day and night
incessantly adored!

How wonderful, how beautiful,
the sight of thee must be,
thine endless wisdom, boundless pow'r,
and aweful purity!

Yet I may love thee too, O Lord,
almighty as thou art,
for thou has stooped to ask of me
the love of my poor heart.

No earthly father loves like thee,
no mother e'er so mild,
bears and forbears as thou hast done
with me thy sinful child.

Father of Jesus, love's reward,
what rapture will it be,
prostrate before thy throne to lie,
and gaze and gaze on thee!

897 Samuel Crossman and John Ireland

My song is love unknown,
my Saviour's love to me;
love to the loveless shown,
that they might lovely be.
O who am I,
that for my sake
my Lord should take
frail flesh and die?

He came from his blest throne
salvation to bestow;
but men made strange, and none
the longed-for Christ would know:
but O, my friend,
my friend indeed,
who at my need
his life did spend.

Sometimes they strew his way,
and his sweet praises sing;
resounding all the day
hosannas to their King:
then 'Crucify!'
is all their breath,
and for his death
they thirst and cry.

They rise and needs will have,
my dear Lord made away;
a murderer they save,
the Prince of Life they slay;
yet cheerful he
to suff'ring goes,
that he his foes
from thence might free.

Continued overleaf

Here might I stay and sing,
no story so divine;
never was love, dear King!
Never was grief like thine.
This is my friend,
in whose sweet praise
I all my days
could gladly spend.

898 Neil Bennetts

Name above all names,
the Saviour for sinners slain.
You suffered for my sake,
to bring me back home again.
When I was lost,
you poured your life out for me.
Name above all names,
Jesus, I love you.

Giver of mercy,
the fountain of life for me.
My spirit is lifted
to soar on the eagle's wings.
What love is this
that fills my heart with treasure?
Name above all names,
Jesus, I love you.

High King eternal,
the one true and faithful God.
The beautiful Saviour,
still reigning in pow'r and love.
With all my heart
I'll worship you for ever:
Name above all names,
Jesus, I love you.

© 2000 Daybreak Music Ltd.

899 Mark Altrogge

No eye has seen and no ear has heard
and no mind has ever conceived
the glorious things that you have prepared
for ev'ryone who has believed.
You brought us near and you called us your
    own,
and made us joint heirs with your Son.

*How high and how wide,
how deep and how long,
how sweet and how strong is your love.
How lavish your grace,
how faithful your ways,
how great is your love, O Lord.*

Objects of mercy who should have known
    wrath,
we're filled with unspeakable joy,
riches of wisdom, unsearchable wealth
and the wonder of knowing your voice.
You are our treasure and our great reward,
our hope and our glorious King.

© 1990 Integrity's Hosanna! Music/PDI Praise/Kingsway's Thankyou
Music

900 Graham Kendrick

No one like you, no one like you,
no one like you, no one like you.
No one like you, no one like you,
no one like you, no one like you.

Beautiful, wonderful, merciful, holy,
faithful, forgiving, God with us.
Beautiful, wonderful, merciful, holy,
faithful, forgiving, God with us.

All wisdom, all kindness,
all justice, all love,
all glorious, magnificent,
majestic, Jesus.

No one like you, no one like you,
no one like you, no one like you.

Son of God, Son of Man, Word of God, holy,
full of grace, full of truth, God with us.
Sufferer, sacrifice, crucified, buried,
risen, ascended, God with us.

Victorious, exalted,
Redeemer, Judge of all,
our High Priest in heaven
we worship you, Jesus.

All wisdom, all kindness,
all justice, all love,
all glorious, magnificent,
majestic, Jesus, Jesus, Jesus,
God with us.

901   Martin E. Leckebusch

No other prophet ever spoke
so clearly to our race;
no bright and shining angel matched
the glory on his face;
through him the universe was made,
by him our debt for sin was paid:
in Christ, at last, we see in full
God's splendour and God's grace.

Majestic angels swiftly fly
on wings of wind and flame;
his servants' servants, low they bend
in honour of his name.
The Father's precious Son is he,
the Lord from all eternity:
yet taking human flesh and blood
a baby he became.

His throne is built on righteousness,
established firm and sure;
the oil of joy anoints the one
who values what is pure!
The wonder of the Maker's skill
is seen throughout creation still:
but when this age has run its course
his kingdom will endure.

God's matchless pow'r confirms that Christ
is all our life and light;
his word proclaims the solemn truth
dividing wrong from right,
and those who cast that word aside
are lost like driftwood on the tide:
but Jesus reigns eternally
in majesty and might!

902   Rachel Judd

O come and praise him, come on, let's
*   praise him!*
O come and praise the living God!
O come and praise him, come on, let's
*   praise him!*
O come and praise the living God!

Your love, O Lord, is higher than the
   mountains,
your love, O Lord, is deeper than the oceans.
Your love, O Lord, it reaches to the heavens,
I will praise you for your love!

* O, I will praise you, yes, I will praise you!*
* O, I will praise you for your love.*
* O, I will praise you, yes, I will praise you!*
* O, I will praise you for your love.*

Your faithfulness is higher than the
   mountains,
your faithfulness is deeper than the oceans.
Your faithfulness, it reaches to the heavens,
I will praise you, faithful God!

* O, I will praise you, yes, I will praise you!*
* O, I will praise you, faithful God!*
* O, I will praise you, yes, I will praise you!*
* O, I will praise you, faithful God!*

903   William Cowper

O for a closer walk with God,
a calm and heav'nly frame;
a light to shine upon the road
that leads me to the Lamb!

Where is the blessedness I knew
when first I saw the Lord?
Where is that soul-refreshing view
of Jesus and his word?

Continued overleaf

What peaceful hours I once enjoyed!
How sweet their mem'ry still!
But they have left an aching void
the world can never fill.

Return, O holy Dove! Return,
sweet messenger of rest!
I hate the sins that made thee mourn,
and drove thee from my breast.

The dearest idol I have known,
whate'er that idol be,
help me to tear it from thy throne.
And worship only thee.

So shall my walk be close with God,
calm and serene my frame;
so purer light shall mark the road
that leads me to the Lamb.

904 Charles Wesley

O for a heart to praise my God,
a heart from sin set free;
a heart that's sprinkled with the blood
so freely shed for me.

A heart resigned, submissive, meek,
my great Redeemer's throne;
where only Christ is heard to speak,
where Jesus reigns alone.

A humble, lowly, contrite heart,
believing, true and clean,
which neither life nor death can part
from him who dwells within.

A heart in ev'ry thought renewed,
and full of love divine;
perfect and right and pure and good –
a copy, Lord, of thine.

Thy nature, gracious Lord, impart,
come quickly from above;
write thy new name upon my heart,
thy new best name of love.

905 Isaac Watts, alt.

O God, our help in ages past,
our hope for years to come,
our shelter from the stormy blast,
and our eternal home.

Beneath the shadow of thy throne,
thy saints have dwelt secure;
sufficient is thine arm alone,
and our defence is sure.

Before the hills in order stood,
or earth received her frame,
from everlasting thou art God,
to endless years the same.

A thousand ages in thy sight
are like an evening gone;
short as the watch that ends the night
before the rising sun.

Time, like an ever-rolling stream,
will bear us all away;
we fade and vanish, as a dream
dies at the op'ning day.

O God, our help in ages past,
our hope for years to come,
be thou our guard while troubles last,
and our eternal home.

906 Beaker

O God, you are my God,
and I will ever praise you;
O God, you are my God,
and I will ever praise you.

I will seek you in the morning,
I will learn to walk in your ways;
and step by step you lead me,
and I will follow you all of my days.

© Control

907 Darrell Evans and Matt Jones

O God, you've been so good to me,
you came and found this orphan
and you brought me right into your family;

O God, you've been so good to me,
you threw away my past
and you never count my sins against me.
Oh, thank you, Lord.

You got me dancing
and now I'm shouting,
you got me leaping
and now I'm spinning, hallelujah,
you're so good to me,

you're so good to me,
you're so good to me.

O God, you've been so good to me,
and ev'ry day I wake up
I breathe another breath of your mercy;
O God, you've been so good to me,
and my delight is in you
'cause I know that your hand is upon me.
Oh, thank you, Lord.

You got me dancing
and now I'm shouting,
you got me leaping
and now I'm spinning, hallelujah,
you're so good to me,

you're so good to me,
you're so good to me.
Jesus, you're the one
who saved myself from me,
so I will be the one
to praise you in the streets.
You're so good to me.

© 1998 Integrity's Hosanna! Music/Kingsway's Thankyou Music

908 Unknown

O happy day! (O happy day!)
O happy day! (O happy day!)
when Jesus washed (when Jesus washed),
when Jesus washed (when Jesus washed),
when Jesus washed (when Jesus washed),
he washed my sins away. (O happy day!)
(O happy day!).
(Repeat)

He taught me how to watch,
watch and pray, watch and pray;
and live rejoicing ev'ry,
ev'ry day, ev'ry day.

909 Matthew Ling

Oh how great is the Father's love,
that we should be called children of God.
How extravagant is his grace,
that we stand before him unashamed.

Like the sun upon my face,
is the warming of your grace,
and you've become my resting place, O God.
And so I come to offer my life,
what a joyful sacrifice,
to worship you for evermore.

Though we cannot comprehend
your love, O Lord, that never ends,
yet we know it in our lives today.
From bursting hearts our songs arise,
until your praises fill the skies,
we worship you for evermore.

© 1995 Restoration Music/Sovereign Music UK

910 Wes Sutton

Oh how my spirit rejoices.
My soul will glorify,
the Lord, my God, my Saviour,
sending his mercy from on high.
His presence shadows o'er me
I stand beneath his grace.
His eyes are ever on me
shows me the favour of his face.

Oh how my spirit rejoices.
My soul will glorify,
the Lord, my God, my Saviour,
sending his mercy from on high.
He lifts the broken and humble.
Proud men, he makes to fall,
fills hungry hearts with treasures,
hears the cry of those who call.

Continued overleaf

Oh how my spirit rejoices.
My soul will glorify,
the Lord, my God, my Saviour,
sending his mercy from on high.
My life will give him glory,
for all his faithfulness.
This now the ageless story
all who call on him are blessed.

911 Brenton Brown

Oh, kneel me down again, here at your feet;
show me how much you love humility.
Oh, Spirit, be the star that leads me to
the humble heart of love I see in you.
You are the God of the broken,
the friend of the weak;
you wash the feet of the weary,
embrace the ones in need.
I want to be like you, Jesus,
to have this heart in me.
You are the God of the humble,
you are the humble King.

912 Michael Battersby

Oh Lord, you're amazing,
how your love for me will never end.
Your grace, it surrounds me,
you're my Saviour,
you're my closest friend.

Your love's deeper
than the deepest sea,
I feel it shining like
the midday sun on me
and I'm here to worship you.

Ev'ry day that I live
I will live it for you
and I'm here to worship you.
With everything that's within me
I will bless your holy name,
my Emmanuel.

913 Kevin Simpson

Oh taste and see that the Lord is good
and his mercies endureth for ever.
Oh taste and see that the Lord is good
and his mercies endureth for ever.
(Repeat)

They are new ev'ry morning,
they are new ev'ry morning,
they are new ev'ry morning,
the mercies of the Lord.

914 Geoff Bullock

Oh, the mercy of God, the glory of grace,
that you chose to redeem us, to forgive and
    restore,
and you call us your children chosen in him
    to be holy
and blameless to the glory of God.

To the praise of his glorious grace,
to the praise of his glory and power,
to him be all glory, honour and praise,
for ever and ever and ever, amen.

Oh, the richness of grace, the depths of his
    love,
in him is redemption, the forgiveness of sin.
You called us as righteous, predestined in him
for the praise of his glory, included in Christ.

Oh, the glory of God expressed in his Son,
his image and likeness revealed to us all;
the plea of the ages completed in Christ,
that we be presented perfected in him.

915 Marjorie Tancock and Helen Frye

O Jesus mine, O Jesus mine,
you've filled us with a love divine.
Our hearts have found no resting-place but
    thee,
O Jesus, Jesus, Jesus mine.

916 Michael W. Smith

O Lord, our Lord, how majestic
is your name in all the earth.
O Lord, our Lord, how majestic
is your name in all the earth.
O Lord, we praise your name,
O Lord, we magnify your name;
Prince of Peace, Mighty God,
O Lord God Almighty.

917 George Matheson

O Love that wilt not let me go,
I rest my weary soul in thee;
I give thee back the life I owe,
that in thine ocean depths its flow
may richer, fuller be.

O Light that follow'st all my way,
I yield my flick'ring torch to thee;
my heart restores its borrowed ray,
that in thy sunshine's blaze its day
may brighter, fairer be.

O Joy that seekest me through pain,
I cannot close my heart to thee;
I trace the rainbow through the rain,
and feel the promise is not vain
that morn shall tearless be.

O Cross that liftest up my head,
I dare not ask to fly from thee:
I lay in dust life's glory dead,
and from the ground there blossoms red
life that shall endless be.

918 Unknown
revised and adapted Graham Kendrick

O mystery of love divine!
where righteousness and peace combine
and truth and mercy meet;
God manifest in flesh behold,
in Jesus see that love unfold,
the work of grace complete.
Love, only love, your heart inclined
and brought you, Saviour of mankind,
down from the throne above;
love made you here a Man of Grief,
distressed you sore for our relief –
O mystery of love.

Love's glorious triumph now appears
for you will have your children near
where grief can never come;
where ev'ry heart is filled with joy
and praise shall ev'ry tongue employ
in love's eternal home.
Love there will crown what love began,
its wondrous ways of grace to man
in its fair home above.
All, all, O Lord, will there proclaim
through endless years your blessèd name
supreme, almighty love.

919 Steve & Velvita Thompson /Andy Mitchell

One Lord, one faith, we stand together,
one Lord and Father of us all.
In unity and by God's Spirit,
we walk as one to reach our goal.

Increase in me the flame that's burning.
Ignite in us your passion for the lost.
Enlarge our hearts, the harvest is here.
O Lord, increase in me.

To reach the lost is our commission;
to stretch our hands to those in need.
Reflect God's heart, fulfil his calling,
and then his kingdom will increase.

Continued overleaf

Enlarge your hearts, rise up in faith,
do not hold back, do not delay.
Enlarge your hearts, rise up in faith,
from east to west prepare the way.

920 Johnny Markin

One name scatters my fear,
one name brings me to tears
when I think of the scars borne for me.
One name brings me such peace,
one name never will cease
to be held in my heart tenderly.

I will speak the name of Jesus,
I will worship at his feet;
like the purest gold his name shall be:
more than treasure to me.

One name to which I'll bow,
one name to which I vow
to be faithful in all that I do.
One name, hope for the lost;
one name shines from the cross
where salvation is found;
life made new.

I will speak the name of Jesus,
I will worship at his feet;
like the purest gold his name shall be:
more than treasure to me.

I will speak the name of Jesus,
I will worship at his feet;
in my heart his name will always be
more than treasure to me.

921 Scott Wesley Brown

Only your mercy, only your grace,
only your Spirit brings us to faith;
O what a wonder that you chose us first,
not by our merit, but your perfect work.

Jesus, we long to worship you,
and give you all glory and praise;
all that you are, all that you have,
we have received by faith.

Only your goodness, only your love,
only your pardon poured out in blood;
your righteousness exchanged for our sin,
O what a Saviour, O what a friend!

922 Graham Kendrick

On the blood-stained ground, where the
    shadow falls,
of a cross and a crown of thorns,
I kneel down, I kneel down.
I lift my eyes to a tear-stained face,
who is this dying in my place?
I kneel down, I kneel down.

I come just as I am,
this is my only plea;
one hope in which I trust,
this blood was shed for me.

As you wash the stains of my guilty heart
'til I'm clean in ev'ry part,
I kneel down, I kneel down.
Wash away my shame, my pain, my pride,
ev'ry sin that I once denied,
I kneel down, I kneel down.

This is where I'll always come,
this is where I'll always run,
to worship you.
This is where I'll always come,
this is where I'll always run,
to worship you, Jesus.

923 Geoff Baker

On the cross, on the cross,
where the King of Glory died,
here is grace, here is love,
flowing from that wounded side.
Amazing mystery,
that he should die for me,
as a perfect sacrifice.
On the cross, on the cross,
love incarnate on the cross.

At the cross, at the cross,
all my sin on Jesus laid.
Mine the debt, his the cost,
by his blood the price is paid.
And through his suffering,
that fragrant offering,
arms of love are opened wide.
At the cross, at the cross,
there is healing at the cross.

To the cross, to the cross,
Spirit lead me to the cross.
Bowed in awe at his feet,
richest gain I count as loss.
Nothing compares with this,
to share his righteousness
and be called a child of God.
To the cross, to the cross,
Spirit lead me to the cross.

© 1998 Daybreak Music Ltd.

924 James Montgomery

On this assembled host,
in this accepted hour,
O Spirit, as at Pentecost,
descend in all your pow'r!
We meet with one accord
in our appointed place,
and wait the promise of our Lord,
the Spirit of all grace.

Like mighty rushing wind
upon the waves beneath,
move with one impulse ev'ry mind;
one soul, one feeling, breathe.
Both young and old inspire
with wisdom from above;
and give us hearts and tongues of fire,
to pray and praise and love.

Spirit of light, explore
and chase our gloom away,
with brightness shining more and more
until the perfect day.
Spirit of truth, we pray,
for ever be our guide;
O Spirit of adoption, may
we all be sanctified.

925 Alan Rose

O our Lord and King,
our praise to you we bring,
there is no other Rock but you.
Seated high above, you are the one we
*   love,*
this is our song of praise to you.

King for ever!
You are the first and you're the last,
you are sov'reign,
all your commands will always
come to pass,
to give you glory!

Who else is like you?
Who else is worthy of your praise?
We exalt you;
you reign in majesty and
awesome splendour,
king for ever!

Abba Father,
your steadfast love will never fail.
You are faithful,
you are God and I will
worship in your
courts for ever.

© 1997 Kingsway's Thankyou Music

926 Paul Baloche

Open the eyes of my heart, Lord,
open the eyes of my heart;
I want to see you, I want to see you.
Open the eyes of my heart, Lord,
open the eyes of my heart;
I want to see you, I want to see you.
(Repeat)

To see you high and lifted up,
shining in the light of your glory.
Pour out your pow'r and love;
as we sing holy, holy, holy.

Holy, holy, holy,
holy, holy, holy,
holy, holy, holy,
I want to see you.

927 David Bird, Richard Lacy and Sarah Lacy

O praise the holy Lord above,
you people in his temple.
Praise him, for the Lord is good
and you are his possessions.
The Lord above is Lord of all,
the earth is here to please him,
from deepest sea to cloudy sky
and wind and rain in season.
Praising the name of the Lord,
praising the name of the Lord,
praising the name of the Lord,
praising the name of the Lord.

Your name, O Lord, and your renown
endure through generations.
You will free your people,
have compassion on your servants.
All the nations of the earth
come to him and praise him.
All of you who fear the Lord,
come to him and praise him.
Praise him, the name of the Lord;
praise him, the name of the Lord;
praise him, the name of the Lord;
praise him, the name of the Lord.

928 Paulus Gerhardt

O sacred head, once wounded,
with grief and pain weighed down,
how scornfully surrounded with thorns,
thine only crown!
How pale art thou with anguish,
with sore abuse and scorn!
How does that visage languish,
which once was bright as morn!

O Lord of life and glory,
what bliss till now was thine!
I read the wondrous story,
I joy to call thee mine.
Thy grief and thy compassion
were all for sinners' gain;
mine, mine was the transgression,
but thine the deadly pain.

What language shall I borrow
to praise thee, heav'nly friend,
for this, thy dying sorrow,
thy pity without end?
Lord, make me thine for ever,
nor let me faithless prove;
O let me never, never
abuse such dying love!

Be near me, Lord, when dying;
O show thyself to me;
and for my succour flying:
come, Lord, to set me free:
these eyes, new faith receiving,
from Jesus shall not move;
for he who dies believing,
dies safely through thy love.

929 D. R. Edwards (revised and adapted Graham Kendrick)

O, the love of God is boundless,
perfect, causeless, full and free!
Doubts have vanished, fears are groundless,
now I know that love to me.

Love, the source of all my blessing,
love, that set itself on me.
Love, that gave the sinless victim,
love, told out at Calvary.

O, the cross of Christ is wondrous!
There I learn God's heart to me
'midst the silent, deep'ning darkness
'God is light' I also see.
Holy claims of justice finding
full expression in that scene;
light and love alike are telling
what his woe and suff'ring means.

O, the sight of heav'n is glorious!
Man in righteousness is there.
Once the victim, now victorious,
Jesus lives in glory fair!
Him, who met the claims of glory
and the need of ruined man
on the cross, O wondrous story!
God has set at his right hand.

O, what rest of soul in seeing
Jesus on his Father's throne!
Yes, what peace for everflowing
from God's rest in his own Son!
Gazing upward into heaven,
reading glory in his face,
knowing that 'tis he, once given
on the cross to take my place.

930 Gary Sadler

O the passion, O the wonder
of the fiery love of Christ;
king of glory on the altar,
perfect Lamb of sacrifice.

Who are we that he would love us?
Who, but he would give his life?
O the passion, O the wonder
of the fiery love of Christ.

O the wisdom, O the wonder
of the power of the cross;
love so rare no words could tell it,
life himself has died for us.

Who are we that he would save us?
Crucified to give us life;
O the wisdom, O the wonder
of the power of the cross.

O the passion, O the wonder
of the fiery love of Christ;
death defeated by his rising,
darkness conquered by his light.

We will sing his praise for ever,
worthy is the Lamb of Life;
O the passion, O the wonder
of the fiery love of Christ.

Who are we that he would love us?
Who, but he would give his life?
O the passion, O the wonder
of the fiery love of Christ.

931 Brian Doerksen and Michael Hansen

Our Father in heaven holy is your name.
Forgive us our sins, Lord, as we forgive.
Our Father in heaven give us our bread.
Lead us not into temptation,
but deliver us from the evil one.
Your kingdom come, your will be done.
Your kingdom come, your will be done.

Our Father in heaven holy is your name.
Forgive us our sins, Lord, as we forgive.
Our Father in heaven give us our bread.
Lead us not into temptation,
but deliver us from the evil one.
Your kingdom come, your will be done.
Your kingdom come, your will be done
on the earth as it is in heaven.
Let it be done on the earth.
Amen. *(x2)*

932 Paul Field and Stephen Deal

Our Father, who art in heaven,
hallowed be thy name.
Thy kingdom come,
thy will be done
on earth as in heav'n.
Give us today our daily bread
and forgive our sins,
as we forgive each one of those
who sins against us;
and lead us not to the time of trial
but deliver us from evil,
for thine is the kingdom,
the power and the glory.
(Repeat)

Let all the people say 'Amen'
in ev'ry tribe and tongue;
let ev'ry heart's desire be joined
to see the kingdom come.
Let ev'ry hope and ev'ry dream be born
    in love again;
let all the world sing with one voice,
let the people say 'Amen'.

933 Dave Bilbrough

Our God is great. Our God is great.
Our God is great. Our God is great.

He gave us the wind, the sun and the snow,
the sand on the seashore, the flowers
    that grow.
Morning and evening, winter and spring;
come join all creation and sing!

The gifts that he brings are new ev'ry day,
from glorious sunset to soft falling rain.
The mist on the hills, the light and the shade;
come join all creation in praise!

For music and dancing, the sounds that
    we hear;
for colours and words, the life that we
    share, we say:

934 Tim Smith

Our God is lifted up midst the shouts of joy,
our God is lifted up in the sounding of the
    trumpets;
our God is lifted up midst the shouts of joy –
shout joyfully unto our God, shout joyfully
    unto our God.
Let the trumpets make a joyful noise,
let us clap our hands and praise our God;
for our God is lifted up, our God is lifted up,
our God is lifted up on high.

935 John Chisum and George Searcy

Our heart, our desire,
is to see the nations worship;
our cry, our prayer,
is to sing your praise to the ends of the
    earth,
that with one mighty voice
ev'ry tribe and tongue rejoices;
our heart, our desire,
is to see the nations worship you.
Heavenly Father,
your mercy showers down upon your
    people,
ev'ry race upon this earth;
may your Spirit pierce the darkness,
may it break the chains of death upon us;
let us rise in honest worship,
to declare your matchless worth.

936 Brenton Brown

Over all the earth, you reign on high,
ev'ry mountain stream, ev'ry sunset sky.
But my one request, Lord, my only aim
is that you'd reign in me again.

Lord, reign in me, reign in your pow'r
over all my dreams, in my darkest hour.
You are the Lord of all I am,
so won't you reign in me again.

Over ev'ry thought, over ev'ry word,
may my life reflect the beauty of my Lord;
'cause you mean more to me than any
    earthly thing,
so won't you reign in me again.

937   Martin Smith

O, your hands of kindness
are here for me,
and I've heard they are silken
and can carry me.

> *How I love you,*
> *all I am is you,*
> *King of love, I bow.*

O, your hands of mercy
were scarred for me,
and your body was broken
so that I can go free.

O, your love that burns me,
deeper than the sea,
and the treasure I find here:
the Saviour's love for me.

938   Rita Baloche

Pour your Holy Spirit upon me,
let your presence fill me up;
make my life a flowing river
of your everlasting love.
Like a living stream
flowing from your mighty ocean;
purify in me my desire
and my devotion;
make my life a flowing river
of your everlasting love.

939   Richard Lewis

Power and riches belong to you,
my Saviour, Redeemer and friend.
And all the nations belong to you;
your kingdom, it shall never end.
Soon all the peoples
will bow before your throne,
lifting praises to your name.
Ev'ry knee will bow
and ev'ry tongue confess
and proclaim that you reign.

> *Yes, you reign,*
> *for ever in the heavens you reign.*
> *Jesus, you will always be the same,*
> *for ever you reign.*
> *Yes, you reign,*
> *your faithfulness and love will never end,*
> *Jesus, my deliverer and friend.*
> *For ever you reign.*
> *Yes, you reign,*
> *for ever in the heavens you reign.*
> *Jesus, you will always be the same,*
> *for ever you reign.*
> *Yes, you reign,*
> *your faithfulness and love will never end,*
> *Jesus, my deliverer and friend.*
> *For ever, O Lord, you reign.*
> *In wisdom and strength,*
> *blessing, honour and praise,*
> *for ever, O Lord, you reign.*
> *In wisdom and strength,*
> *blessing, honour and praise,*
> *for ever, O Lord, you reign.*

940   Clive A. Goodwill

> *Praise him, come on, let's praise him,*
> *   come on and praise him.*
> *Shout, ev'rybody, let's praise him,*
> *show him your love now, let's praise the*
> *   Lord.*
> *Praise him, ev'ryone praise him,*
> *joyfully praise him, lovingly singing a song*
> *   to him.*
> *Praise him, give him your love now,*
> *praise the Lord!*

Continued overleaf

He's full of glory, powerful and mighty,
Alpha and Omega, worthy of all honour,
the Lily of the Valley, bright and morning
  star,
shepherd, physician, Lord, that's who you
  are.
Prince of Peace and Saviour,
Lamb of God, Redeemer,
Emmanuel, God with us,
Lord, we've come to worship and to sing.
You are amazing, yes Lord, you are our King.

941 Frances Jane van Alstyne (Fanny J. Crosby)

Praise him, praise him!
Jesus, our blessèd Redeemer!
Sing, O earth,
his wonderful love proclaim!
Hail him, hail him!
Highest archangels in glory;
strength and honour
give to his holy name!
Like a shepherd,
Jesus will guard his children,
in his arms he carries
them all day long.
Praise him, praise him!
tell of his excellent greatness;
praise him, praise him
ever in joyful song!

Praise him, praise him!
Jesus, our blessèd Redeemer!
For our sins
he suffered, and bled, and died!
He – our rock,
our hope of eternal salvation,
hail him, hail him!
Jesus the crucified!
Sound his praises
– Jesus who bore our sorrows,
love unbounded, wonderful,
deep and strong.

Praise him, praise him!
Jesus, our blessèd Redeemer!
Heav'nly portals,
loud with hosannas ring!
Jesus, Saviour,
reigneth for ever and ever:
crown him, crown him!
Prophet, and Priest, and King!
Christ is coming,
over the world victorious,
pow'r and glory
unto the Lord belong.

942 Russell Fragar

Praise him, you heavens
and all that's above.
Praise him, you angels
and heavenly hosts.
Let the whole earth praise him.

Praise him, the sun, moon
and bright shining stars.
Praise him, you heavens
and waters and skies.
Let the whole earth praise him.

Great in power,
great in glory.
Great in mercy,
King of heaven.
Great in battle,
great in wonder.
Great in Zion,
King over all the earth.

943 Bryn Haworth

Praise the Lord, praise the Lord,
praise the Lord with all of your mind,
and all of your strength praise the Lord.
let all that has breath call on his name
for he is worthy to be praised;
merciful, strong to save, praise the Lord.

O what a gracious Father,
so faithful through the years.
I called and then he answered,
delivered me from all my fears;
pour out your hearts before him,
our times are in his hands.
My heart will always trust him,
he's the Rock on which I stand.

O what a friend is Jesus,
his love will never end.
Cast all your cares upon him,
he's our refuge and our strength.
He heals the broken-hearted
and sets the captives free;
place no one else above him,
all the earth will one day sing.

944 Tim Lomax

Praise the Lord,
praise the Lord!
Praise the Lord, you heavens,
praise him in the heights above.
Praise him, all you angels,
all his heav'nly hosts.

Let ev'rything he made praise the Lord,
for he alone is worthy and true.
Hallelujah!
Praise the Lord. Hallelujah!
Praise the Lord!

Praise him, sun,
praise him, moon.
Praise him all you bright stars,
praise him, all you highest heav'ns.
All you deepest oceans,
come and praise the Lord.

(Repeat refrain)

945 Joachim Neander
trans. Catherine Winkworth

Praise to the Lord,
the Almighty, the King of creation!
O my soul, praise him,
for he is thy health and salvation.
All ye who hear,
now to his temple draw near;
joining in glad adoration.

Praise to the Lord,
who o'er all things so wondrously reigneth,
shieldeth thee gently from harm,
or when fainting sustaineth:
hast thou not seen
how thy heart's wishes have been
granted in what he ordaineth?

Praise to the Lord,
who doth prosper thy work and defend thee,
surely his goodness and mercy
shall daily attend thee:
ponder anew
what the Almighty can do,
if to the end he befriend thee.

Praise to the Lord,
O let all that is in us adore him!
All that hath life and breath,
come now with praises before him.
Let the 'Amen'
sound from his people again,
gladly for ay we adore him.

946 Jamie Harvill

Put on the garments of praise
for the spirit of heaviness,
let the oil of gladness flow down from your
    throne.
Put on the garments of praise
for the spirit of heaviness,
your joy is my strength alone,
my strength alone.

Continued overleaf

Make these broken, weary bones
rise to dance again.
Wet this dry and thirsty land with a river.
Lord, our eyes are fixed on you
and we are waiting
for your garland of grace
as we praise your name.

Hallelujah, sing hallelujah,
we'll give all honour
and praise to your name.
Hallelujah, sing hallelujah,
we trade our sorrows
for garments of praise.

947 Richard Lewis

Rain down, Holy Spirit,
rain down on this thirsty land.
We need your love,
we need your pow'r,
we need a touch from your hand this hour.
We cry for more of you,
Holy Spirit, rain down. *(x2)*

Pour down sweet rain,
come and fill this vessel again.
Father of love, come and
pour out your riches from above.
We need your presence like the desert needs
rain.
Father, send the rain,
Father, send the rain. *(x2)*

For your glory and your honour,
for your glory, Holy Spirit, rain down.

948 Charles Wesley

Rejoice, the Lord is King!
Your Lord and King adore;
mortals, give thanks and sing,
and triumph evermore.

> *Lift up your heart, lift up your voice;*
> *rejoice, again I say, rejoice.*

Jesus the Saviour reigns,
the God of truth and love;
when he had purged our stains,
he took his seat above.

His kingdom cannot fail;
he rules o'er earth and heav'n;
the keys of death and hell
are to our Jesus giv'n.

He sits at God's right hand
till all his foes submit,
and bow to his command,
and fall beneath his feet.

949 Nick Coetzee

Right now the presence of the Lord is in this
place,
right now the presence of the Lord is in this
place.
He will heal the broken-hearted,
he will bind up their wounds.
The healing, cleansing fire of the Lord
is in this place, is in this place.

950 Augustus Montague Toplady, alt.

Rock of ages, cleft for me,
let me hide myself in thee;
let the water and the blood,
from thy riven side which flowed,
be of sin the double cure:
cleanse me from its guilt and pow'r.

Not the labours of my hands
can fulfil thy law's demands;
could my zeal no respite know,
could my tears for ever flow,
all for sin could not atone:
thou must save, and thou alone.

Nothing in my hands I bring,
simply to thy cross I cling;
naked, come to thee for dress;
helpless, look to thee for grace;
tainted, to the fountain fly;
wash me, Saviour, or I die.

While I draw this fleeting breath,
when mine eyelids close in death,
when I soar through tracts unknown,
see thee on thy judgement throne;
Rock of ages, cleft for me,
let me hide myself in thee.

951 Augustus Montague Toplady
(revised and adapted by Graham Kendrick)

Rock of ages, cleft for me,
let me hide myself in thee.
Let the water and the blood
from your wounded side which flowed
be of sin the double cure,
cleanse me from its guilt and pow'r.

My Rock (my Rock),
my Jesus, my Rock.
My Rock (my Rock),
my Jesus, my Rock.

Not the labours of my hands
can fulfil your law's demands.
Could my zeal no respite know,
could my tears for ever flow,
all for sin could not atone,
you must save and you alone.

Nothing in my hand I bring,
simply to your cross I cling.
Naked, come to you for dress,
helpless, look to you for grace.
Foul, I to the fountain fly,
wash me, Saviour, or I die.

While I draw this fleeting breath,
when my eyelids close in death,
when I soar to worlds unknown,
see you on your judgement throne,
Rock of ages, cleft for me,
let me hide myself in thee.

© 2001 Make Way Music

952 *Hymns for the young (1836)* attributed to
Dorothy A. Thrupp

Saviour, like a shepherd lead us,
much we need thy tender care;
in thy pleasant pastures feed us,
for our use thy folds prepare:
blessèd Jesus, blessèd Jesus,
thou hast bought us, thine we are;
blessèd Jesus, blessèd Jesus,
thou hast bought us, thine we are.

We are thine, do thou befriend us,
be the guardian of our way;
keep thy flock, from sin defend us,
seek us when we go astray:
blessèd Jesus, blessèd Jesus,
hear, O hear us when we pray;
blessèd Jesus, blessèd Jesus,
hear, O hear us when we pray.

Thou hast promised to receive us,
poor and sinful though we be;
thou hast mercy to relieve us,
grace to cleanse and pow'r to free:
blessèd Jesus, blessèd Jesus,
early let us turn to thee;
blessèd Jesus, blessèd Jesus,
early let us turn to thee.

Early let us seek thy favour;
early let us do thy will;
blessèd Lord and only Saviour,
with thy love our beings fill:
blessèd Jesus, blessèd Jesus,
thou hast loved us, love us still;
blessèd Jesus, blessèd Jesus,
thou hast loved us, love us still.

953 Graham Kendrick

Say the name of love: Jesus, Jesus.
Say the name of peace: Jesus, Jesus.
Say the name of mercy: Jesus, Jesus.
Say the name of goodness: Jesus, Jesus.

Continued overleaf

May that name be lifted high,
may that name be glorified
as we gather here.
All that's beautiful and true,
all that's good is found in you,
the Name above all names.

Say the name of wisdom: Jesus, Jesus.
Name of revelation: Jesus, Jesus.
Say the name of justice: Jesus, Jesus.
Pardon and forgiveness: Jesus, Jesus.

      May the name . . .

Jesus, worship Jesus.
Jesus, worship Jesus.

Say the name of healing: Jesus, Jesus.
Miracles and wonders: Jesus, Jesus.
Say the name of power: Jesus, Jesus.
Here among us now: Jesus, Jesus.

Jesus, worship Jesus.
Jesus, worship Jesus.

© 2000 Make Way Music

954   Russell Fragar

Say the word,
and I will sing for you.
Over oceans deep
I will follow.
If each star was a song,
and ev'ry breath of wind, praise,
it would still fail by far
to say all my heart could say.
I simply live,
I simply live for you.
(Repeat)

    As the glory of your presence
    now fills this place,
    in worship we will meet you face to face.
    There is nothing in this world
    to which you can be compared,
    glory to glory, praise upon praise.

You bind the broken-hearted
and save all my tears,
and by your word,
you set the captives free.
There is nothing in this world
that you cannot do.
I simply live,
I simply live for you.

© 1999 Russell Fragar/Hillsong Publishing/Kingsway's Thankyou Music

955   Ian Mizen and Andy Pressdee

Search me, O God, and know my heart,
lead me in your ways for ever.
Search me, O God, and know my heart,
lead me in your ways for ever.

I want to be holy, giving ev'rything to you.
I want to be pure in heart and pure in mind.
I want to be holy, always pleasing you,
I want to live for you.

© 1994 Brown Bear Music

956   Edward Caswall

See, amid the winter's snow,
born for us on earth below,
see, the Lamb of God appears,
promised from eternal years.

    Hail, thou ever-blessèd morn!
    Hail, redemption's happy dawn!
    Sing through all Jerusalem:
    Christ is born in Bethlehem!

Lo, within a manger lies
he who built the starry skies,
he who, throned in height sublime,
sits amid the cherubim.

Say, ye holy shepherds, say,
what your joyful news today;
wherefore have ye left your sheep
on the lonely mountain steep?

'As we watched at dead of night,
lo, we saw a wondrous light;
angels, singing peace on earth,
told us of the Saviour's birth.'

Sacred infant, all divine,
what a tender love was thine,
thus to come from highest bliss,
down to such a world as this!

Teach, O teach us, holy child,
by thy face so meek and mild,
teach us to resemble thee
in thy sweet humility.

957 Dave Wellington

Send us the rain, Lord,
rain of your Spirit,
rain on this dry barren land.
Send us the rain, Lord,
rain to revive us;
cleanse us and fill us again.
Here we are of one accord,
calling to you, singing:
send your Spirit,
send your Spirit,
send the rain on us again.

Pour out your wine, Lord,
wine of your Spirit,
wine that would teach us to love.
Pour out your wine, Lord,
oh, how we need you
to quench the thirst of our hearts.
Here we are of one accord,
calling to you, singing:
send your Spirit,
send your Spirit,
pour your wine on us again.

Breathe now upon us,
breath of your Spirit,
breath to bring life to these bones.
Breathe now upon us
life of abundance,
holiness, wisdom, love, truth.
Here we are of one accord,
calling to you, singing:
send your Spirit,
send your Spirit,
breathe your life on us again.

Send down the fire,
fire of your Spirit,
Refiner's fire to fulfil.
Send down the fire,
fire to consume us,
reveal your power once more.
Here we are of one accord,
calling to you, singing:
send your Spirit,
send your Spirit,
send the fire on us again.

958 Paul Banderet

Send your word, O God,
that cuts to the heart of me.
Plant your word, O God,
that becomes a part of me.
Reveal your vision
of what you want of me,
O make me ready for your coming, Lord.

Plough my heart, O God,
cut deep a furrow with your Word.
Break the hardest ground,
make it a place where you can sow seeds of
    revival.
Plough my heart, O God,
cut deep a furrow with your Word.
Break the hardest ground,
make it a place where you can sow seeds of
    revival
for this land.

959 William J. Gaither

Shackled by a heavy burden,
'neath a load of guilt and shame;
then the hand of Jesus touched me,
and now I am no longer the same.

*He touched me, O, he touched me,
and O, the joy that floods my soul!
Something happened, and now I know,
he touched me and made me whole.*

Continued overleaf

Since I met this blessèd Saviour,
since he cleansed and made me whole;
I will never cease to praise him,
I'll shout it while eternity rolls.

960   Mark Altrogge

Should he who made the stars
be hung upon a tree?
And should the hands that healed
be driven through for me?
Should he who gave us bread
be made to swallow gall?
Should he who gave us breath and life
be slaughtered for us all?

We sing your mercies,
we sing your endless praises,
we sing your everlasting love.
We sing your mercies,
we sing your endless praises,
Sov'reign One who died,
Sov'reign One who died for us.

Should he who is the light
be cast into the dark?
And should the Lord of love
be pierced through his own heart?
Should he who called us friends
be deserted by us all?
Should he who lived a sinless life
be punished for our fall?

We sing your mercies,
we sing your endless praises,
we sing your everlasting love.
We sing your mercies,
we sing your endless praises,
Sov'reign One who died,
Sov'reign One who died for us.

961   Andy Smith

Sing a song for the nations,
sing a song for the earth;
God's chosen people
to shine out his worth.
Brothers and sisters with harmonies rare.
Beautiful music is filling the air.

Let our songs ring out all over the earth.
Jesus is Lord over every nation,
only in Christ can we find salvation and
    hope.
Let our songs ring out all over the earth.
Joining the praise of all creation,
saints with one voice in celebration,
lifting up high the name of Jesus our King.

Sing a song from your heart now,
sing a song with your life.
You are a vessel
for the glory of Christ.
Sing to the broken:
'Your healer has come.
You can find rest in the arms of the Son'.

962   Stuart Garrard

Sing to the Lord with all of your heart;
sing of the glory that's due to his name.
Sing to the Lord with all of your soul,
join all of heaven and earth to proclaim:

You are the Lord, the Saviour of all,
God of creation, we praise you.
We sing the songs that awaken the dawn,
God of creation, we praise you.

Sing to the Lord with all of your mind,
with understanding give thanks to the King.
Sing to the Lord with all of your strength,
living our lives as a praise offering.

963 Leon Patillo

Sing unto the Lord a new song,
let his praises fill the temple.
He is the King of kings and the Lord of lords.
Bow down before him.

Sing unto the Lord a new song,
for he loves to hear our praises.
Let all of creation sing,
'Glory to our God!'
Bow down before him.
Hallelujah! Glory to God.
Hallelujah! Glory to God.

© World Music Inc./CopyCare

964 David Bird, Richard Lacy and Sarah Lacy

Son of Man, led to die on a cross,
nailed and bleeding,
and the heavens darkened in your name.
There was dust, there was heat,
there was pain and there was glory
and fulfilment of the prophet's words.
Son of Man, you shed your blood,
I could know no greater love.
As your life ebbed away,
though my sins were red as scarlet,
your blood has washed them white as snow,
and a death bringing life,
though beyond my understanding,
is made real in me if I believe.
Son of Man, you shed your blood,
I could know no greater love.
Open hearts will receive
all the joy they could imagine,
and the gift of life from you, Son of Man.

© 1997 Whole World Publishing/CN Publishing/CopyCare

965 Steve and Vikki Cook

Spirit, how we hunger for your presence,
with nothing else will we be satisfied.
How we long to taste your lavish goodness,
and fill our souls with heaven's bread of life.
And so we come to you with great
    anticipation,
knowing how you love, our celebration
    overflows.

We've come to feast at your table,
feast at your table
and drink from your fountain of delights.
We've come to feast at your table,
feast at your table,
in our joy you are glorified.
We've come to feast.

Father you've prepared for us a banquet,
in honour of the vict'ry of your Son.
For he secured the way for our communion,
that we could know the fullness of your love.
And so we come to you with great
    anticipation,
knowing how you love, our celebration
    overflows.

We've come to feast at your table,
feast at your table
and drink from your fountain of delights.
We've come to feast at your table,
feast at your table,
in our joy you are glorified.
We've come to feast.

© 1997 PDI Worship/CopyCare

966 Billy Funk

Spirit of the living God,
you bring new life to me;
Spirit of the living God,
flow like a river through me.

Flow like a river with streams of life,
flow like a river, flow free,
flow like a river with streams of life,
setting your people free.

© 1997 Integrity's Hosanna! Music/Kingsway's Thankyou Music

967 Darlene Zschech

Standing in your presence,
Lord, my heart and life are changed;
just to love you and to live to see
your beauty and your grace.

Continued overleaf

Heaven and earth cry out your name,
nations rise up and see your face;
and your kingdom is established
as I live to know you more.
Now I will never be the same;
Spirit of God, my life you've changed,
and I'll for ever sing your praise.
I live to know you, Lord.
I live to know you, Lord.

You've called me, I will follow
your will for me I'm sure.
Let your heart beat be my heart's cry,
let me live to serve your call.

968 Andy Smith and Johnny Markin

Sunrise awakening joy to our lips;
dawn is bringing revival.
Heaven is sounding a glorious beat;
saints come alive to its rhythm.
Rising, turning hearts to the call of theSaviour.
Breaking, burning chains that have kept
    us from faith.

Call forth the songs that will ring
    celebration,
come and rejoice in the Day of the Dance.
Shout out your praise to the Lord of
    the nations.
Herald the dawn of the Day of the Dance;
herald the dawn of the Day of the Dance.

See, now, the lame as they rise to their feet;
hear, now, the mute tongue is singing.
Hearts that were barren in winter's decay
spring forth in joyous abandon.

Call forth the songs that will ring
    celebration,
come and rejoice in the Day of the Dance.
Shout out your praise to the Lord of
    the nations.
Herald the dawn of the Day of the Dance,
herald the dawn of the Day of the Dance.

969 B. Mansell Ramsey

Teach me thy way, O Lord,
teach me thy way!
Thy gracious aid afford,
teach me thy way!
Help me to walk aright,
more by faith, less by sight;
lead me with heav'nly light:
teach me thy way.

When doubts and fears arise,
teach me thy way!
When storms o'erspread the skies,
teach me thy way!
Shine through the cloud and rain,
through sorrow, toil, and pain;
make thou my pathway plain:
teach me thy way!

Long as my life shall last,
teach me thy way!
Where'er my lot be cast,
teach me thy way!
Until the race is run,
until the journey's done,
until the crown is won,
teach me thy way!

970 C. Mundy, L. Petersen and J. Price

Thank you for your mighty power
that you showed on Calvary.
Lord, I'm here today, praising your name
'cause you set me free.

Free from sin, free from shame,
free from all that hurt within.
Now I'm free to dance and praise your name.
Lord, you've been so good to me.

Thank you for life in the Spirit,
that gives me liberty,
all my days are filled with victory
'cause you set me free.

Free to dance, free to sing,
free to give my ev'rything.
Jesus, you're the joy that is within,
Lord, you've been so good to me.

Lord, you've been so good,
Lord, you've been so good,
Lord, you've been so good to me.

971 Richard Lewis

The angels around your throne, they cry
   'Holy is the Lamb.'
The angels around your throne, they cry
   'Holy is the Lamb.'
So we sing 'Holy, holy, holy, holy is the Lamb.'
So we sing 'Holy, holy, holy, holy is the Lamb.'

The angels around your throne, they cry
   'Worthy is the Lamb.'
The angels around your throne, they cry
   'Worthy is the Lamb.'
So we sing 'Worthy, worthy, worthy,
   worthy is the Lamb.'
So we sing 'Worthy, worthy, worthy,
   worthy is the Lamb.'

972 Andraé Crouch

The blood that Jesus shed for me
way back on Calvary,
the blood that gives me strength from day to
   day,
it will never lose its pow'r.

It reaches to the highest mountain;
it flows to the lowest valley.
The blood that gives me strength
from day to day, it will never lose its pow'r!

It soothes my doubt and calms my fears,
and it dries all my tears;
the blood that gives me strength from day to
   day,
it will never lose its pow'r.

973 G. R. Cowell

The darkest hour, Lord Jesus,
that rolled o'er your blest head
called forth the sweetest fragrance
that e'er on earth was shed.
That cup so full, so bitter –
the wormwood and the gall –
directly from your Father
you did accept it all.

What perfect, meek submission!
Your will, not mine be done.
Obedience full, unquestioned;
perfection of a Son!
Thus prostrate there before him,
your sweat as drops of blood
and so to be the victim,
the spotless Lamb of God!

Yet, you, O holy suff'rer,
could 'Abba, Father!' cry
through all your woe abiding
in sonship's perfect tie.
Through suffering made perfect
in heav'n our leader now;
captain of our salvation!
With rev'rent hearts we bow.

By this you have, Lord Jesus,
our hearts' affection gained.
How can we give you comfort
for what you have sustained?
Entire and full devotion
alone can worthy be
till, love to love responsive,
your glorious face we see.

974 From William Sandys' 'Christmas Carols, Ancient and Modern', alt.

The first Nowell the angel did say
was to certain poor shepherds in fields as
   they lay:
in fields where they lay keeping their sheep,
on a cold winter's night that was so deep.

Continued overleaf

Nowell, Nowell, Nowell, Nowell,
born is the King of Israel!

They lookèd up and saw a star,
shining in the east, beyond them far,
and to the earth it gave great light,
and so it continued both day and night.

And by the light of that same star,
three wise men came from country far;
to seek for a king was their intent,
and to follow the star wherever it went.

This star drew nigh to the north-west,
o'er Bethlehem it took its rest,
and there it did both stop and stay
right over the place where Jesus lay.

Then entered in those wise men three,
full rev'rently upon their knee,
and offered there in his presence,
their gold and myrrh and frankincense.

Then let us all with one accord
sing praises to our heav'nly Lord,
who with the Father we adore
and Spirit blest for evermore.

He by himself has sworn –
we on his oath depend –
we shall, on eagles' wings upborne,
to heav'n ascend:
we shall behold his face,
we shall his pow'r adore,
and sing the wonders of his grace
for evermore.

There dwells the Lord our King,
the Lord our righteousness,
triumphant o'er the world and sin,
the Prince of Peace,
on Zion's sacred height
his Kingdom still maintains,
and glorious with his saints in light
for ever reigns.

The whole triumphant host
give thanks to God on high:
'Hail, Father, Son and Holy Ghost!'
they ever cry:
Hail, Abraham's God and ours!
We join the heav'nly throng,
and celebrate with all our pow'rs
in endless song.

975 Thomas Olivers
based on the Hebrew 'Yigdal', alt.

The God of Abraham praise,
who reigns enthroned above,
Ancient of everlasting Days,
and God of love:
Jehovah, great 'I Am,'
by earth and heav'n confessed;
we bow and bless the sacred name,
for ever blest.

The God of Abraham praise,
at whose supreme command
from earth we rise, and seek the joys
at his right hand:
we all on earth forsake,
its wisdom, fame and pow'r,
and him our only portion make,
our shield and tow'r.

976 Tim Lomax

The grace of our Lord, Jesus Christ,
and the love of God,
and the fellowship of the Holy Spirit,
be with us for evermore.

© 1999 Kevin Mayhew Ltd.

977 Mark Pendergrass

The greatest thing in all my life is knowing
    you;
the greatest thing in all my life is knowing
    you.
I want to know you more, I want to know
    you more.
The greatest thing in all my life is knowing
    you.

The greatest thing in all my life is loving you;
the greatest thing in all my life is loving you.
I want to love you more, I want to love you
more.
The greatest thing in all my life is loving you.

The greatest thing in all my life is serving you;
the greatest thing in all my life is serving you.
I want to serve you more, I want to serve
you more.
The greatest thing in all my life is serving you.

978 H. R. Bramley

The great God of heaven is come down to
earth,
his mother a virgin, and sinless his birth;
the Father eternal his Father alone:
he sleeps in the manger; he reigns on the
throne:

> *Then let us adore him, and praise his
> great love:*
> *to save us poor sinners he came from
> above.*

A babe on the breast of a maiden he lies,
yet sits with the Father on high in the skies;
before him their faces the seraphim hide,
while Joseph stands waiting, unscared, by
his side:

Lo! here is Emmanuel, here is the Child,
the Son that was promised to Mary so mild;
whose pow'r and dominion shall ever
increase,
the Prince that shall rule o'er a kingdom of
peace:

The Wonderful Counsellor, boundless in
might,
the Father's own image, the beam of his
light;
behold him now wearing the likeness of man,
weak, helpless, and speechless, in measure a
span:

O wonder of wonders, which none can
unfold:
the Ancient of Days is an hour or two old;
the maker of all things is made of the earth,
man is worshipped by angels, and God
comes to birth:

> *Then let us adore him, and praise his
> great love:*
> *to save us poor sinners he came from
> above.*

The word in bliss of the Godhead remains,
yet in flesh comes to suffer the keenest of
pains;
he is that he was, and for ever shall be,
but becomes that he was not, for you and
for me.

979 Thomas Kelly

The head that once was crowned with thorns
is crowned with glory now:
a royal diadem adorns
the mighty victor's brow.

The highest place that heav'n affords
is his, is his by right.
The King of kings and Lord of lords,
and heav'n's eternal light.

The joy of all who dwell above,
the joy of all below,
to whom he manifests his love,
and grants his name to know.

To them the cross, with all its shame,
with all its grace is giv'n;
their name an everlasting name,
their joy the joy of heav'n.

They suffer with their Lord below,
they reign with him above,
their profit and their joy to know
the myst'ry of his love.

The cross he bore is life and health,
though shame and death to him;
his people's hope, his people's wealth,
their everlasting theme.

980 Jo Puleston

The heavens are open now; *(x3)*
The presence of God is here. } *x2*

The blind shall see,
the lame shall walk,
the captive shall see their freedom.
The deaf shall hear,
the dead man rise,
salvation come for my brother.

O, the tears, the pray'rs,
the years of our care,
O dear King, sov'reign Lord,
could this be time for rain?
(Repeat)

We're praying, we're praying,
we're praying for the rain.

981 Lex Loizides

The heavens, they preach, they preach,
they preach the glorious splendour of God.
The stars in the sky seem so out of reach,
yet they whisper his wonderful love.
Day after day in a sermon of nature
the works of his hands lift their voice:
'Wake up, you nations, and serve your
    creator,
there's mercy in him, so rejoice!'

And I'll lift my heart and my hands to him,
and I'll let my life shine with love to
*   God's wonderful Son.*
He wears the crown, he's the King.
Come and behold him now,
come and delight in his excellent virtues;
seek him while he can be found,
for he is the help and the hope for all
*   the world.*

The prophets, they preached, they preached,
they preached that one day a Saviour
    would come;
and suddenly men heard a heavenly speech,
the voice of God's only Son.
Day after day in the streets and the temple
he taught them and met their needs,
and now through his death and his great
    resurrection
his glorious purpose succeeds.

And I'll lift my heart and my hands to him,
and I'll let my life shine with love to
*   God's wonderful Son.*
He wears the crown, he's the King.
Come and behold him now,
come and delight in his excellent virtues;
seek him while he can be found,
for he is the help and the hope for all
*   the world.*

Your people will preach, we'll preach,
we'll preach the unfailing riches of Christ,
there's no one who's fallen too far from
    his reach,
who can't come from death into life.
Day after day at the dawn of revival
the multitudes seek his face,
as we work to speed on his final arrival
and crown him with glory and praise!

And I'll lift my heart and my hands to him,
and I'll let my life shine with love to
*   God's wonderful Son.*
He wears the crown, he's the King.
Come and behold him now,
come and delight in his excellent virtues;
seek him while he can be found,
for he is the help and the hope for all
*   the world.*

982 Russell Fragar

The Holy Spirit is here,
and his power is real.
Anything can happen,
and it probably will.
Something very good,
something good is going on around here.

Well there's a light that shines
to make the darkness disappear,
there's a power at work,
but there's nothing to fear.
Something very good,
something good is going on around here.

This is a church on fire,
this is the Holy Spirit flame.
We have a burning desire,
to lift up Jesus' name.
Let the fire burn in ev'ry heart,
to light the way, defeat the dark.
Let the flame of love burn higher.
This is a church, this is a church on fire.

983 Stuart Townend and Kevin Jamieson

The King of love is my delight,
his eyes are fire, his face is light,
the First and Last, the Living One,
his name is Jesus.
And from his mouth there comes a sound
that shakes the earth and splits the ground,
and yet this voice is life to me,
the voice of Jesus.

And I will sing my songs of love,
calling out across the earth;
the King has come,
the King of love has come.
And troubled minds can know his peace,
captive hearts can be released;
the King has come,
the King of love has come.

My Lover's breath is sweetest wine,
I am his prize, and he is mine;
how can a sinner know such joy:
because of Jesus.
The wounds of love are in his hands,
the price is paid for sinful man;
accepted child, forgiven son:
because of Jesus.

And I will sing my songs of love,
calling out across the earth;
the King has come,
the King of love has come.
And troubled minds can know his peace,
captive hearts can be released;
the King has come,
the King of love has come.

And my desire is to have you near,
Lord, you know that you are welcome here.
Before such love, before such grace
I will let the walls come down

And I will sing my songs of love,
calling out across the earth;
the King has come,
the King of love has come.
And troubled minds can know his peace,
captive hearts can be released;
the King has come,
the King of love has come.

984 Henry Williams Baker, based on Psalm 23

The King of love my shepherd is,
whose goodness faileth never;
I nothing lack if I am his
and he is mine for ever.

Where streams of living water flow
my ransomed soul he leadeth,
and where the verdant pastures grow
with food celestial feedeth.

Continued overleaf

Perverse and foolish oft I strayed,
but yet in love he sought me,
and on his shoulder gently laid,
and home, rejoicing, brought me.

In death's dark vale I fear no ill
with thee, dear Lord, beside me;
thy rod and staff my comfort still,
thy cross before to guide me.

Thou spread'st a table in my sight,
thy unction grace bestoweth:
and O what transport of delight
from thy pure chalice floweth!

And so through all the length of days
thy goodness faileth never;
good Shepherd, may I sing thy praise
within thy house for ever.

985 Graham Ord

The Lord is gracious and compassionate,
slow to anger and rich in love.
The Lord is gracious and compassionate,
slow to anger and rich in love.
The Lord is good to all,
he has compassion on all that he has made.
As far as the east is from the west,
that's how far he has removed our
    transgressions from us.
As far as the east is from the west,
that's how far he has removed our
    transgressions from us.

Praise the Lord, oh my soul,
    praise the Lord.
Praise the Lord, oh my soul,
    praise the Lord.
(Repeat)

986 Richard Lewis

The Lord is marching out like a mighty
    man of war,
stirring up his zeal with a shout and a roar.

The Lord is marching out like a mighty
    man of war,
stirring up his zeal with a shout and a roar.
And he'll triumph . . . . triumph,
triumph over his foes.

Jesus (Jesus),
Jesus (Jesus).

987 Graham Kendrick

The Lord is present here,
the Lord is present here,
the Lord is present here, come worship.
The Lord is present here,
the Lord is present here,
the Lord is present here, come worship.

Brought near by Jesus' blood,
brought near by Jesus' blood,
brought near by Jesus' blood we worship.
With angels round your throne,
with angels round your throne,
with angels round your throne we worship.

We offer up our lives a living sacrifice,
pouring out our gifts of thanks and praise.
This is your holy hill, you call us higher
    still,
joining with all heaven to acclaim:
Holy, holy, holy Lord, God of pow'r and
    might,
heav'n and earth are full of your glory.
Holy, holy, holy Lord, God of pow'r and
    might,
heav'n and earth are full of your glory.

Let all the nations come,
let all the nations come,
let all the nations come and worship.
Let all creation come,
let all creation come,
let all creation come, and worship.

988 Stuart Townend, based on Psalm 23

The Lord's my shepherd, I'll not want;
he makes me lie in pastures green,
he leads me by the still, still waters,
his goodness restores my soul.

    And I will trust in you alone,
    and I will trust in you alone,
    for your endless mercy follows me,
    your goodness will lead me home.

He guides my ways in righteousness,
and he anoints my head with oil;
and my cup - it overflows with joy,
I feast on his pure delights.

And though I walk the darkest path -
I will not fear the evil one,
for you are with me, and your rod and staff
are the comfort I need to know.

989 William Cowper

There is a fountain filled with blood,
drawn from Immanuel's veins,
and sinners plunged beneath that flood
lose all their guilty stains.

    Lose all their guilty stains,
    lose all their guilty stains;
    and sinners plunged beneath that flood
    lose all their guilty stains.
    Wash all my sins away,
    wash all my sins away;
    and there may I, though vile as he,
    wash all my sins away.

The dying thief rejoiced to see
that fountain in his day;
and there may I, though vile as he,
wash all my sins away.

I do believe, I will believe,
that Jesus died for me!
That on the cross he shed his blood,
from sin to set me free.

Dear dying Lamb! Thy precious blood
shall never lose its pow'r,
till all the ransomed church of God
be saved to sin no more.

    Lose all their guilty stains,
    lose all their guilty stains;
    and sinners plunged beneath that flood
    lose all their guilty stains.
    Wash all my sins away,
    wash all my sins away;
    and there may I, though vile as he,
    wash all my sins away.

E'er since by faith I saw the stream
thy flowing wounds supply,
redeeming love has been my theme,
and shall be till I die.

990 Cecil Frances Alexander

There is a green hill far away,
outside a city wall,
where the dear Lord was crucified,
who died to save us all.

We may not know, we cannot tell,
what pains he had to bear,
but we believe it was for us
he hung and suffered there.

He died that we might be forgiv'n,
he died to make us good;
that we might go at last to heav'n,
saved by his precious blood.

There was no other good enough
to pay the price of sin;
he only could unlock the gate
of heav'n, and let us in.

O dearly, dearly has he loved,
and we must love him too,
and trust in his redeeming blood,
and try his works to do.

991 F. Whitfield

There is a name I love to hear,
I love to speak its worth;
it sounds like music in my ear,
the sweetest name on earth.

O how I love the Saviour's name,
O how I love the Saviour's name,
O how I love the Saviour's name,
the sweetest name on earth.

It tells me of a Saviour's love,
who died to set me free;
it tells me of his precious blood,
the sinner's perfect plea.

It tells of one whose loving heart
can feel my deepest woe;
who in my sorrow bears a part
that none can bear below.

It bids my trembling heart rejoice,
it dries each rising tear;
it tells me in a still, small voice,
to trust and never fear.

992 Michael Battersby

There is a sound of great
rejoicing before the Lord
and there is an awesome
expectation here today,
'cause ev'ry hill and ev'ry mountain
will be moved in Jesus' name;
'cause we serve a God
who's more than able
to make a way.

Make a way through the desert,
make a way through the storm,
make a way when there is no way:
my God will make a way.
(Repeat)

So I'm giving you
the best I've got today.
And I'm living in
the brightness of your mighty, mighty ways.

993 David Jones

There is freedom at the cross,
endless hope for all of us,
the price was paid
now we can all go free.
No greater love was ever shown,
you were broken, I am whole.
I can't believe what you have done for me.
King of heaven died for me.
Amazing love that sets me free.

You bought me freedom,
took my chains and cut me loose.
You bought me freedom
my soul sings with thanks to you.
All you gave was all I needed,
beaten, broken, torn and wounded.
You were crushed but not defeated,
the Son has set me free, set me free.

There is mercy at the cross,
we were broken, dead and lost
but you've rescued me,
I've been redeemed.
I did not deserve this grace,
out of love you freely gave
life to ransom me, now I'm saved.
King of heaven died for me.
Amazing love that sets me free.

994 Andy Smith

There is no higher call,
than to live ev'ry day for the glory of God.
There is no greater joy,
than surrendering all for a kingdom that
won't pass away.

You are the reason, there's no other reason
to live
all of my strength and my passion I willingly
give.
You are my hope, my celebration.
Who could want more than your sweet
salvation?

Throwing off all that would hinder I run for
    the prize.
Living my life all for Jesus without
    compromise.
Your grace, your love will keep me from
    falling;
I won't be swayed from your higher calling.

995 Colin Battersby

There is no other name
by which we can be saved,
there is no other name like Jesus.
You give me joy, you give me peace,
you set my spirit free,
you lift me up to higher ground,
you're all I need.

I'm gonna praise you all my days,
I'm gonna follow you,
there's no other way.
I'm gonna lift the name of Jesus higher now:
you're the one.
(Repeat)

Singin' Jesus, Jesus, Jesus . . .
you're all I need.

996 Robin Mark

There is no other name
by which man can be saved,
there is no other name under heaven.
There is rest for my soul,
and the wounded made whole,
and the captives set free and forgiven.
Such love as I had never known,
I've found in the grace that flowed
to me
in my unrighteousness;
this is why my heart and soul
and tongue confess:

997 David Bird, Richard Lacy and Sarah Lacy

There's a distant voice,
an awak'ning cry
for a land in darkest night,
and it calls you now to shed the past
and move into the light.

Let your heart be clean
as you search for him
and seek for what is right,
for where darkness reigned,
now the dawn will break
as you move into the light.

> *Rise! Rise! O sleeper.*
> *Rise! Rise ! O sleeper.*

Bring your heartfelt thanks
to the Lord of all,
in the name of Jesus Christ,
make righteousness
and truth your goal
as children of the light.

998 David Jones

There's an army raising up a shout of praise,
the sound of freedom, hope and liberty.
Mighty people with a passion in their hearts
all for Jesus, King above all kings.
Let the earth sing out your name,
hear our vict'ry shout of praise.

> *We will lift our voice,*
> *we will raise a shout,*
> *in the song of vict'ry: hallelujah.*
> *Lift our voice,*
> *shout it out,*
> *Jesus, Jesus, Jesus,*
> *you are Lord.*

There's an army marching out in vict'ry,
overcomers through the cross of Calvary.
Darkness trembles at the sound of their
    voice,
one in praises they magnify the King.
Let the earth sing out your name,
hear the vict'ry shout of praise.

999 Darrell Evans

*There's a new song arising in the
 hearts of his children,
a new song arising in the hearts of his
 own.*
(Repeat)

A song of hope, a song of peace,
the sound of liberation,
the shout of victory,
the hymn of praise,
the new song of God,
many will see and fear
and put their trust in our Lord.

*With the oil of joy he's anointing his
 children,
the music he gives sets the nations free.
With the oil of joy he's anointing his
 children
and the dance of our Father's
 bringing liberty.*

©1997 Integrity's Hosanna! Music/Kingsway's Thankyou Music

1000 David Klassen

There's a song, all the time
stirring in this heart of mine
unto you, Lord Divine,
songs of exultation.
Let the cymbals ring out loud,
let the trumpets shout it out
and from a joyful crowd,
sounds of adoration.
The only One who's worthy,
receiving all the glory,
your presence right in this place.

*To you, Lord, who reigns for ever,
be my praises now and ever.
Songs of exultation rise to gather at your
 throne.
May the praise in me be pleasing,
may your joy be never ceasing,
as I bring my sacrifice of praise to you
 alone.*

Be glorified, be glorified.
Be glorified, be glorified.
Be glorified, be glorified.
Be glorified, be glorified.

© 2000 Rhema Publishing/world wide worship ltd.

1001 Vicky Beeching and Steve Mitchinson

*There's no one like our God, no one at all.
He gave his Son for us, Jesus the Lord.
And who can love us like he does? No one
 at all.
Oh how we love you, Lord.*

You are high above all nations,
your glory shines above the heavens;
humbled yourself to love and save us:
be praised through endless generations.

You lift the needy from the ashes
and seat them high up with the princes.
You give the barren woman healing;
she'll dance for joy like the mother of children.

© 1999 Vineyard Songs (UK/Eire)/CopyCare

1002 Graham Kendrick

The Spirit of the Lord is on me now,
poured out like oil over me.
For the Lord has called and anointed me
to preach good news to the poor,
to bind the broken heart, to free the
 captive soul,
open blind eyes, make broken people whole.
And I know this is the hour
of his favour and his pow'r,
and his Spirit is upon me now.

© 1997 Make Way Music

1003 Dave Bilbrough

The waves are breaking, the tide is turning,
God's Spirit is coming to this earth;
the harvest is waiting, and we have been
 called
to go to the nations of this world.

To the ends of the earth,
to the ends of the earth,
to the ends of the earth we will go;
bearing the message that our God can
be known,
to the ends of the earth we will go.

The fire is falling, the wind is blowing,
the flame is spreading across our land;
revival is coming, let the world hear,
tell ev'ry woman, child and man.

The drums are beating, the trumpet is
sounding,
a warrior spirit he's put in our hearts;
in the name of the Father, Spirit and Son,
we'll take this word to ev'ryone.

1004 Don Wallace

The wonder of your mercy, Lord,
the beauty of your grace,
that you would even pardon me
and bring me to this place.
I stand before your holiness,
I can only stand amazed:
the sinless Saviour died to make
a covenant of grace.

I only want to serve you,
bring honour to your name,
and though I've often failed you,
your faithfulness remains.
I'll glory in my weakness,
that I might know your strength.
I will live my life at the cross of Christ,
and raise a banner to proclaim.

You welcome us before you,
into this holy place;
the brilliance of your glory
demands our endless praise.
The one, the only Saviour
has opened heaven's doors;
we can enter in, free from all our sin,
by your cleansing sacrifice.

1005 Russell Fragar

The word of God is planted and living in my
heart.
I'm an overcomer, I live his promise out.
This was not a new thing until it happened
to me.
Now I walk in power, I walk in victory.
Jesus gave the power to be all you were
meant to be,
people get free!

You lose your fears when you stand in faith.
You lose your tears when you trust his grace.
You lose your pain when you know his
touch.
Only Christ can turn your bitter into sweet,
people get free!

Jesus gave the power to be all you were
meant to be,
and people get free!
People get free! *(x4)*

1006 Martin Smith and Stuart Garrard

The world's shaking with the love of God,
great and glorious, let the whole earth sing,
and all you ever do is change the old for
new,
people we believe that:

God is bigger than the air we breathe,
the world we'll leave, God will save the day
and all will say: my glorious!

Clouds are breaking, heaven's come to earth,
hearts awak'ning, let the church bells ring,
and all you ever do is change the old for the
new,
people we believe that:

1007 Marie Barnett

This is the air I breathe,
this is the air I breathe;
your holy presence living in me.

This is my daily bread,
this is my daily bread;
your very word spoken to me.

And I, I'm desp'rate for you.
And I, I'm lost without you.

1008 Dave Bilbrough

This is the place
where dreams are found;
where vision comes,
called holy ground.

Holy ground,
I'm standing on holy ground
for the Lord my God is here with me.

Your fire burns
but never dies;
I realise
this is holy ground

The great 'I Am'
revealed to man;
take off your shoes,
this is holy ground.

1009 Graham Kendrick

This is the year when hearts go free
and broken lives are mended,
I hear the sound of jubilee,
the song of sorrow ended,
love is the greatest story the world has known,
the beacon in the darkness,
the way back home.

This is the year of joy for tears
and beauty out of ashes.
When skies will clear if we will share,
forgive and learn what love is.
Let's crown the year with kindness
and live in peace;
fill all the world with songs
that never cease.

These are the days of heaven's grace
and favour smiling on us.
Two thousand years of hopes and prayers
are met in one great chorus.
A light has dawned upon us
and will increase,
and countless captive souls
shall be released.

1010 Graham Kendrick

This is your house,
and we your people,
the object of your love,
purchased by your blood.
We are living stones built together
to reveal the glories of your grace.

And by your grace,
and by the pow'r that works within us,
and by your word,
as we daily seek your face,
we'll choose to live for you
and die to our way
so we can be your holy dwelling place.

Fill your house with glory,
fill your house with praise, Father.
Fill your house with prayer
for all the nations,
to your house of blessing
let the nations run,
to worship Jesus,
O let the people come.

1011 Darlene Zschech

This song in my heart,
this song in my soul,
this song I was born to sing.
It's your song of freedom,
now I'm free to dance again.

I'll sing in the darkness,
I'll laugh in the rain,
rejoice in your love again.
It's your song of freedom,
now I'm free to dance again.
Your Spirit brings me liberty,
your breath of life has set me free.

Jesus, your love, it lifts me high,
gives me reason to run this race with joy.
This song within me, Lord,
will bless your holy name.
Jesus, I'll dance before your throne,
bring this heavenly sound to you alone.
This song within me, Lord,
will bless your holy name.

1012 Darlene Zschech

This yearning deep within me
reaches out to you.
Your oil of joy for mourning
soaks me, makes me new.

And I will go to your secret place,
bow my knee to your glorious throne,
have your way in my heart, O Lord,
have your way.

I need you, Holy Spirit,
fire to my soul.
Consume my total being,
Jesus, take control.

1013 David Klassen

Those who wait on the Lord
shall mount up with wings as eagles,
shall walk and they shall not faint.
In the strength of our God
we'll run and we'll not grow weary
if we wait on the Lord.
(Repeat)

How great are your thoughts towards me,
they number more than the sand of the sea.
I'll follow wherever you lead me,
I will wait on you.
No valley deep, no mountain too high,
I spread my wings I know I can fly.
I set my sights up, way in the sky,
I will wait on you.

Those who wait on the Lord
shall mount up with wings as eagles,
shall walk and they shall not faint.
In the strength of our God
we'll run and we'll not grow weary
if we wait on the Lord.

We'll fly so much higher, higher and higher.
Our strength will be more than before
'cause we'll fly with the Father,
he'll give the power to overcome.
(Repeat)

Those who wait on the Lord
shall mount up with wings as eagles,
shall walk and they shall not faint.
In the strength of our God
we'll run and we'll not grow weary
if we wait on the Lord.

1014 Karen Eagen

Thou art worthy, great Jehovah.
Thou art worthy, mighty God.
Thou art worthy, Abba Father.
Thou art worthy, Lamb of God.

1015
Emily Elizabeth Steele Elliott
adapted by Michael Forster

Thou didst leave thy throne
and thy kingly crown
when thou camest to earth for me,
but in Bethlehem's home
was there found no room
for thy holy nativity.

O come to my heart, Lord Jesus,
there is room in my heart for thee.

Heaven's arches rang
when the angels sang
and proclaimed thee of royal degree,
but in lowliest birth
didst thou come to earth
and in deepest humility.

Though the fox found rest,
and the bird its nest
in the shade of the cedar tree,
yet the world found no bed
for the Saviour's head
in the desert of Galilee.

Though thou camest, Lord,
with the living word
that should set all thy people free,
yet with treachery,
scorn and a crown of thorn
did they bear thee to Calvary.

When the heav'ns shall ring
and the angels sing
at thy coming to victory,
let thy voice call me home,
saying, 'Heav'n has room,
there is room at my side for thee.'

1016
Graham Kendrick

Though trials will come, don't fear, don't run.
Lift up your eyes, hold fast, be strong.
Have faith, keep on believing.
Lift up your eyes for God is at work in us,
moulding and shaping us out of his love for
us,
making us more like Jesus.

Consider it joy, pure joy when troubles
come.
Many trials will make you strong.
Consider it joy, pure joy and stand your
ground,
then at last you'll wear a crown.

Though trials will come, won't fear, won't
run.
We'll lift up our eyes, hold fast, be strong.
Have faith, keep on believing.
We'll lift up our eyes for God is at work in us,
moulding and shaping us out of his love for
us,
making us more like Jesus.
Patiently trusting him, ready for anything,
'til we're complete in him,
in ev'rything more like Jesus.

1017
Donn Thomas and Charles Williams

Thou, O Lord, art a shield about me;
you're my glory, you're the lifter of my head.

Hallelujah! Hallelujah! Hallelujah!
You're the lifter of my head.

1018
Bishop Frank Houghton

Thou who wast rich beyond all splendour,
all for love's sake becamest poor;
thrones for a manger didst surrender,
sapphire-paved courts for stable floor.
Thou who wast rich beyond all splendour
all for love's sake becamest poor.

Thou who art God beyond all praising,
all for love's sake becamest Man;
stooping so low, but sinners raising
heav'nwards by thine eternal plan.
Thou who art God beyond all praising,
all for love's sake becamest Man.

Thou who art love beyond all telling,
Saviour and King, we worship thee.
Emmanuel, within us dwelling,
make us what thou wouldst have us be.
Thou who art love beyond all telling,
Saviour and King, we worship thee.

© Control

1019   Graham Kendrick

Through days of rage and wonder
we pursue the end of time,
to seize the day eternal,
the reign of love divine.

Fixing our eyes on Jesus,
we will press on day by day;
this world's vain passing pleasures
are not our destiny.
Our ancient rites of passage
still are the bread and wine:
our hope a cross that towers
over the wrecks of time.

Through days of rage and wonder,
by the awesome pow'r of prayer
God will shake ev'ry nation,
secrets will be laid bare.
And if his light increasing
casts deeper shadows here,
safe in his holy presence,
love will cast out our fear.

Through days of rage and wonder
you will give us grace to stand
and seek a heav'nly city
not built by human hands.
Now is the only moment
within our pow'r to change:
to give back in obedience
while life and breath remain.

© 1998 Make Way Music

1020   Mike Burn

Through the cross, Jesus you triumphed,
by your blood you bought our peace.
Where there once was death and separation
your healing river flows.

Let it flow, let it flow,
let the healing river flow.
Gracious God we cry to you:
let the healing river flow.

Bind up wounds within our homes, Lord,
reconcile husbands and wives.
Turn the fathers' hearts towards their
    children,
O, let the river flow.
Break down walls of isolation,
rescue those who live in fear.
May the lonely find love in your fam'ly,
O, let the river flow.

May your church rise up as one now,
join the streams in one accord.
Young and old will stand and sing with
    one voice
to praise our risen Lord.

Let it flow, let it flow,
let the healing river flow.
Gracious God we cry to you:
let the healing river flow.

© 1996 Daybreak Music Ltd.

1021   Andraé Crouch

To God be the glory,
to God be the glory,
to God be the glory
for the things he has done.
With his blood he has saved me;
with his pow'r he has raised me.
To God be the glory
for the things he has done.

© 1971 Bud John Songs Inc/EMI Christian Music Publishing/
CopyCare

1022 Debbye Graafsma

To him who sits on the throne and unto the
    Lamb,
to him who sits on the throne and unto the
    Lamb
be blessing and glory and honour and
    power for ever;
be blessing and glory and honour and
    power for ever.

1023 Graham Kendrick

To the King eternal, immortal,
invisible, the only God.
To the King eternal, immortal,
invisible, the only God.
Honour and glory for ever and ever.
Honour and glory for ever and ever.
(Repeat)

To the King of creation,
of the saints and of angels, sov'reign of all,
who calls the nations to feast at his table,
almighty Lord.
To him who was and is and is to come.
The first, the last and everliving One.

To the King eternal, immortal,
invisible, the only God.
To the King eternal, immortal,
invisible, the only God.
Honour and glory for ever and ever.
Honour and glory for ever and ever.

Let all the world in ev'ry corner sing:
all that has life and breath your praises
    bring.
Honour and glory for ever and ever.
Honour and glory for ever and ever.
Honour and glory for ever and ever.
Amen! Amen! Amen! Amen!

1024 Liz Fitzgibbon

Turn the hearts of the fathers
to the hearts of the children,
O Lord, come and heal, heal our land.
Take the pain, take the shame
of the past generation,
O Lord, come and heal, heal our land.

Lord, heal our land; O Lord, heal our land,
heal our land, O Lord, heal our land,
heal our land.

Come repair what is broken,
in the heart, in the spirit,
O Lord, come and heal, heal our land.
Restoring the fathers
in the heart of the nation,
O Lord, come and heal, heal our land.

We are fathered by you,
you are faithful and true,
restore and renew what is lost.
Change the face of this land,
touch with your tender hand,
O Lord, come and heal, heal our land.

Son of righteousness,
come arise over us,
O Lord, come and heal, heal our land.
With healing in your wings,
your love changes all things,
O Lord, come and heal our land.

1025 Carol Mundy

Under the shadow of your wings
I find shelter from the storm.
You are my refuge, you are my fortress
and in your love I will abide.

Woke up this morning with you on my mind;
I'm so grateful, that you live inside.
You are my stronghold, you are my Father;
and in your arms I will abide.

Because you're my refuge and my hiding
 place,
I walk in vict'ry every day.
I'll love you for ever, your praises I'll sing;
thank you, God, for being my King.

1026 Lynn DeShazo and Gary Sadler

We are a moment, you are for ever,
Lord of the ages, God before time.
We are a vapour, you are eternal,
love everlasting, reigning on high.

Holy, holy, Lord God Almighty.
Worthy is the Lamb who was slain.
Highest praises, honour and glory
be unto your name, be unto your name.

1027 Richard Lewis

We ask you, O Lord, for the rain of your
 Spirit,
we ask you, O Lord, for the rain of your
 Spirit.
For now is the time, for now is the time
of the latter rain, of the latter rain.
(Repeat)

Send your rain, cleanse us by your word,
let us be your pure and radiant Bride.
Make us strong, prepare us for revival,
let us see the nations turn their hearts,
let us see the nations turn their hearts,
let us see the nations turn their hearts to
you, to you.

Send your rain, mercy from heaven,
send your rain, the grace of your Son.
Send your rain, Word of your power,
send your rain, come fill ev'ryone.
(Repeat)

1028 Viola Grafstrom

We bow down and confess
you are Lord in this place.
We bow down and confess
you are Lord in this place.
You are all I need;
it's your face I seek.
In the presence of your light
we bow down, we bow down.

1029 Russell Fragar and Darlene Zschech

We come into your presence with singing,
come into your presence with praise,
and enter your gates with thankful hearts;
we are going to celebrate.
All of heaven's waiting, pow'r is on its way,
so we shout 'hallelujah',
lifting to you a mighty roar of praise.

You deserve the highest praise
that we can give, and more.
Lord, we give you our praise,
that's what we came here for.
You deserve the highest praise
that we can give and more.
Lord, we give you our praise,
that's what we came here for.

Ev'rything within me reaches out to you;
your power and majesty,
grace and mercy too.
There'll be singing, and dancing,
hearts and voices raised.
You have set your people free,
now the house is filled with praise.
(Repeat)

You deserve the highest praise
that we can give, and more.
Lord, we give you our praise,
that's what we came here for.
You deserve the highest praise
that we can give and more.
Lord, we give you our praise,
that's what we came here for.

Continued overleaf

You deserve the highest praise.
You deserve the highest praise.
You deserve the highest praise.
You deserve the highest praise.

1030 Brian Doerksen and Steve Mitchinson

We come to you with a heart of thanks,
for your love.
To be a living sacrifice, brought with love.
We come to you with a heart of thanks,
for your love;
an offering of all we are, brought with love.

All creation looks to you.
All provision comes from you.
In ev'ry sunrise, hope shines through.
For your mercy, we thank you.

We come to you with a song of praise,
for your love.
The music of our soul's delight,
brought with love.
We come to you with a song of praise,
for your love.
Sounds of joy and gratefulness,
brought with love.

All creation looks to you.
All provision comes from you.
In every rhythm we thank you, for your love.
All creation looks to you.
All provision comes from you.
In every season we thank you, for your love.

1031 Chris Falson

We have a vision for this nation,
we share a dream for this land,
we join with angels in celebration,
by faith we speak revival to this land.

Where ev'ry knee shall bow and worship
   you,
and ev'ry tongue confess that you are Lord;
give us an open heaven, anoint our prayers
   this day,
and move your sov'reign hand across this
   nation.

1032 Janine Price

We have come just to praise
our awesome Father in this place.
It's his love that makes us sing,
he's become our ev'rything.
So let us dance before him,
and make a joyful noise,
so let us shout aloud
for he is our delight,
he's the giver of new life.

Awesome Father, it's you we praise;
precious Jesus, in this place.
Holy Spirit, holy fire,
help us lift his name up higher,
praise Almighty God!

So praise him, praise him,
so praise him, praise him!

1033 Bruce Ballinger

We have come into his house
and gathered in his name
to worship him.
We have come into his house
and gathered in his name
to worship him.
We have come into his house
and gathered in his name
to worship Christ the Lord.
Worship him, Christ the Lord.

Let's forget about ourselves
and magnify his name
and worship him.
Let's forget about ourselves
and magnify his name
and worship him.
Let's forget about ourselves
and magnify his name
and worship Christ the Lord.
Worship him, Christ the Lord.

© 1976 Universal/MCA/Music Sales Ltd.

1034 Russ Hughes

We have come to a holy mountain,
joining angels in celebration,
a thousand thousand lift their voices
as the firstborn Church sings her praises
to the Holy One, to the Holy One.

We've come to God the judge of all men,
to those made perfect by his own Son;
a thousand thousand lift their voices
as God's redeemed sing their praises
to the Holy Lamb, to the Holy Lamb.

O Holy God, we have come to you,
consuming fire to be refined in you,
O Holy One, how we long for you,
our one desire is found in you.

We have come to a holy mountain,
not in fear but with rejoicing;
a thousand thousand lift their voices
as cleansing flows through the blood of
    Jesus,
the Holy Lamb, the Holy Lamb.

© 2000 Joshua Music/Alliance Media Ltd./CopyCare

1035 Mark Altrogge

We have come to a throne of grace,
where our mighty Saviour
perfects our praise;
where wrath and judgement
have been put away,
where not a trace
of all our sin remains.

You're the King of grace unending,
to your open arms we run.
You're the King of grace unending;
and we rest in your unfailing love,
and we rest in your unfailing love.

We have come to your throne of grace,
where our Prince of Peace
    ever lives,
to pray for those his sacrifice
has bought and saved,
where saints and angels
sing eternal praise.

© 2000 PDI Praise/CopyCare

1036 David Horton

We have come to worship the Lord,
we have come to worship the Lord,
bow down before him,
love and adore him,
we have come to worship the Lord.

Enter in, in the Holy Place;
enter in, and look upon his face;
he is worthy, he is holy, he is wonderful,
enter in.

© 1997 David Horton/Harp and Bowl Music/1999 Spiritsound Music Group

1037 Stuart Townend

We have sung our songs of vict'ry,
we have prayed to you for rain;
we have cried for your compassion
to renew the land again.
Now we're standing in your presence,
more hungry than before;
now we're on your steps of mercy,
and we're knocking at your door.

How long
before you drench the barren land?
How long
before we see your righteous hand?
How long
before your name is lifted high?
How long
before the weeping turns to songs of joy?

Continued overleaf

Lord, we know your heart is broken
by the evil that you see,
and you've stayed your hand of judgement
for you plan to set men free.
But the land is still in darkness,
and we've fled from what is right;
we have failed the silent children
who will never see the light.

But I know a day is coming
when the deaf will hear his voice,
when the blind will see their Saviour,
and the lame will leap for joy;
when the widow finds a husband
who will always love his bride,
and the orphan finds a father
who will never leave her side.

How long
before your glory lights the skies?
How long
before your radiance lifts our eyes?
How long
before your fragrance fills the air?
How long
before the earth resounds with songs of
joy?

1038 Steve and Velveta Thompson

We lift our hands to worship you,
we raise our voice in praise.
For you alone are worthy:
in majesty you reign.

We love you, adore you,
we bow down before you.

We stand in awe before you,
we worship at your feet.
Your holiness surrounds us,
your beauty, Lord, we see.

1039 Isi de Gersigny

We lift up our eyes
above the troubles in our land,
and together we stand
to declare you as king.
In times like these
we choose to praise you,
for it's you, it's you who really matter.

You are worthy of all praise,
and we will say that you are good,
and all the miracles you've done
have brought us joy,
for we are changed,
and all the hope we have
we place in you right now.

Father, we declare that we love you.
We declare our everlasting love for you.
Father, we declare that we love you.
We declare our everlasting love for you.

1040 Capt. Alan Price

We're a bright light together,
with the light of Jesus we shine;
we're a grand band together,
with our friend Jesus it's fine.
We're a swell smell together,
it's the fragrance of Jesus we share!
Whenever we are together,
Jesus is specially there.
Even before time began,
we were part of God's great plan;
'cos of Jesus we would be part of his great
family!

1041 Matt Redman

We're looking to your promise of old,
that if we pray and humble ourselves,
you will come and heal our land,
you will come, you will come.

We're looking to the promise you made,
that if we turn and look to your face,
you will come and heal our land,
you will come, you will come to us.

Lord, send revival, start with me.
For I am one of unclean lips,
and my eyes have seen the King,
your glory I have glimpsed,
send revival, start with me.

1042   Chris Cartwright & Richard Lewis

We're so thankful to you,
we're so grateful for the things you've done,
that you died for us on the cross
such a painful death,
that you paid the price for us,
you paid the price for us.

And we say thank you, Lord.
We say thank you, Lord.
We say thank you for what you have done.
And we say thank you, Lord.
We say thank you, Lord.
We say thank you for the things you
    have done.

It's so wonderful that you rose,
victorious over death and hell.
All authority is now yours,
and the Comforter
you have sent in fullness to us,
you have come to us.

1043   Edith Gilling Cherry

We rest on thee, our shield and our
    defender!
We go not forth alone against the foe;
strong in thy strength, safe in thy keeping
    tender,
we rest on thee, and in thy name we go.
Strong in thy strength, safe in thy keeping
    tender,
we rest on thee, and in thy name we go.

Yes, in thy name, O captain of salvation!
In thy dear name, all other names above;
Jesus our righteousness, our sure foundation,
our prince of glory and our king of love.
Jesus our righteousness, our sure foundation,
our prince of glory and our king of love.

We go in faith, our own great weakness
    feeling,
and needing more each day thy grace to know:
yet from our hearts a song of triumph pealing,
'We rest on thee, and in thy name we go.'
Yet from our hearts a song of triumph pealing,
'We rest on thee, and in thy name we go.'

We rest on thee, our shield and our defender!
Thine is the battle, thine shall be the praise;
when passing through the gates of pearly
    splendour,
victors, we rest with thee, through
    endless days.
When passing through the gates of pearly
    splendour,
victors, we rest with thee, through
    endless days.

1044   Matt Redman and Steve Cantellow

We will give ourselves no rest
'til your kingdom comes on earth;
you've positioned watchmen on the walls.
Now our prayers will flow like tears,
for you've shared your heart with us;
God of heaven, on our knees we fall.
Come down in power, reveal your heart again;
come hear our cries, the tears that plead for
    rain.

We're knocking, knocking on the door of heaven;
we're crying, crying for this generation;
we're praying for your name to be known
in all of the earth.
We're watching, watching on the walls to see
    you;
we're looking, looking for a time of break-
    through;
we're praying for your word to bear fruit
in all of the earth.

1045 Michael Battersby

We will never be the same,
we've been touched by your love,
never going back again,
we've been washed by your blood.
Deep calls, deep calls to deep,
and you're closer than a brother,
you've put your life inside of me,
now I'm free for ever.

You are the Lord of my life,
my reason for living.
You are my day and my night.
That's why I'm giving all to you,
'cause when all is said and done
we will never be the same
because of you.

© 1996 Michael Battersby/Smart Productions

1046 Reuben Morgan

We will seek your face, almighty God,
turn and pray for you to heal our land.
Father, let revival start in us,
then ev'ry heart will know your kingdom
    come.

Lifting up the name of the Lord,
in power and in unity.
We will see the nations turn.
Touching heaven, changing earth.
Lifting up the name of the Lord,
in power and in unity.
We will see the nations turn.
Touching heaven, changing earth.
Touching heaven, changing earth.

Never looking back we'll run the race,
giving you our lives we'll gain the prize.
We will take the harvest given us,
though we sow in tears, we'll reap in joy.

Lifting up the name of the Lord,
in power and in unity.
We will see the nations turn.
Touching heaven, changing earth.
Lifting up the name of the Lord,
in power and in unity.
We will see the nations turn.
Touching heaven, changing earth.
Touching heaven, changing earth.

Send revival, send revival,
send revival to us.
(Repeat)

© 1997 Reuben Morgan/Hillsong Publishing/Kingsway's Thankyou
Music

1047 Elisha A. Hoffman

What a fellowship, what a joy divine,
leaning on the everlasting arms.
What a blessedness, what a peace is mine,
leaning on the everlasting arms.

Leaning, leaning, safe and secure from all
*   alarms;*
leaning, leaning, leaning on the
*   everlasting arms.*

O how sweet to walk in this pilgrim way,
leaning on the everlasting arms.
O how bright the path grows from day to day,
leaning on the everlasting arms.

What have I to dread, what have I to fear,
leaning on the everlasting arms?
I have blessèd peace with my Lord so near,
leaning on the everlasting arms.

1048 Mary Brown

What a healing, Jesus,
I've found in you.
What a healing, Jesus,
you restore, refresh, and renew.
You're my healing, Jesus,
for such a time as this.
Arise on healing wings,
Son of Righteousness.

© 1989 Rooted and Grounded

1049 Mark Altrogge

What a hope you've treasured up for us,
wealth and riches hidden in Jesus.
What a wondrous gift to be invited
to your throne,
to find mercy and grace in our need.

*Such great and precious promises you've
  given,
all we need for holiness and life.
Great and precious promises you've given,
purchased by the blood of Jesus Christ.
All of them are 'Yes',
ev'ry promise 'Yes',
all of them are 'Yes' in Christ.*

The faithfulness you've shown us in the past,
assures us of your goodness in the future.
You who did not spare your Son,
but gave him for us all,
you will surely give us all other things.

(Repeat refrain)

1050 Unknown

What a mighty God we serve,
what a mighty God we serve;
angels bow before him,
heaven and earth adore him,
what a mighty God we serve.

1051 Robert Lowry

What can wash away my sin?
Nothing but the blood of Jesus.
What can make me whole again?
Nothing but the blood of Jesus.

*O, precious is the flow
that makes me white as snow;
no other fount I know,
nothing but the blood of Jesus.*

For my pardon this I see,
nothing but the blood of Jesus;
for my cleansing, this my plea:
nothing but the blood of Jesus.

Nothing can for sin atone,
nothing but the blood of Jesus;
naught of good that I have done,
nothing but the blood of Jesus.

This is all my hope and peace,
nothing but the blood of Jesus;
this is all my righteousness,
nothing but the blood of Jesus.

1052 Joel Houston

What to say, Lord?
It's you who gave me life and I
can't explain just how
much you mean to me now
that you have saved me, Lord.
I give all that I am to you,
that ev'ry day I can
be a light that shines your name.

Ev'ry day, Lord, I'll
learn to stand upon your word.
And I pray that I,
that I may come to know you more,
that you would guide me
in ev'ry single step I take,
that ev'ry day I can
be your light unto the world.

*Ev'ry day it's you I live for,
ev'ry day I'll follow after you.
Ev'ry day I'll walk with you, my Lord.*

It's you I live for ev'ry day. *(x3)*

1053   Richard Lewis

When I pray, the Devil trembles;
when I sing, the strongholds fall;
for I know my God is for me,
and the Devil cannot stand,
and the Devil cannot stand,
and the Devil cannot stand
when I pray.

Fire fall! Fire fall!
And release the kingdom of the living God.
(Repeat)

For my praise, it burns like incense,
and my prayers rise to your throne;
they release fire from the altar,
and the Devil cannot stand,
and the Devil cannot stand,
and the Devil cannot stand
when I pray.

1054   German (19th century)
trans. Edward Caswall

When morning gilds the skies,
my heart awaking cries,
may Jesus Christ be praised.
Alike at work and prayer
to Jesus I repair;
may Jesus Christ be praised.

The night becomes as day,
when from the heart we say:
may Jesus Christ be praised.
The pow'rs of darkness fear,
when this sweet chant they hear:
may Jesus Christ be praised.

In heav'n's eternal bliss
the loveliest strain is this:
may Jesus Christ be praised.
Let air, and sea, and sky
from depth to height reply:
may Jesus Christ be praised.

Be this, while life is mine,
my canticle divine:
may Jesus Christ be praised.
Be this th'eternal song
through all the ages on:
may Jesus Christ be praised.

1055   Steve and Vikki Cook

When the cares of life
come and darken my eyes;
there's only you for me.
When my heart grows cold
you bring fire to my soul;
there's only you for me.
You're all I desire,
Lord, you're all I need.

I want only you for me.
No other god will I ever seek,
I want only you for me.
Through all of eternity
there'll be only you for me.

When the way is hard
and the valley dark;
there's only you for me.
In my deepest loss
I will cling to the cross;
there's only you for me.
In love's sov'reign hand
is all I could need.

As I run the race
I will hope in your grace;
there's only you for me.
When my flesh has failed
and I step through the veil;
there's only you for me.
And I'll fully know
that you're all I need.

1056 Reuben Morgan

When the darkness
fills my senses,
when my blindness
keeps me from your touch,
Jesus, come.

When my burden
keeps me doubting,
when my mem'ries
take the place of you,
Jesus, come.

And I'll follow you there
to the place where we meet,
and I'll lay down my pride
as you search me again.
(Repeat)

Your unfailing love,
your unfailing love,
your unfailing love
over me again.

1057 Johnson Oatman Jr.

When upon life's billows you are tempest-
    tossed,
when you are discouraged, thinking all is lost,
count your many blessings, name them one
    by one,
and it will surprise you what the Lord has done.

Count your blessings, name them one by one;
count your blessings, see what God has done.
Count your blessings, name them one by one;
count your many blessings, see what God
    has done.

Are you ever burdened with a load of care?
Does the cross seem heavy you are called to
    bear?
Count your many blessings; ev'ry doubt will fly,
and you will be singing as the days go by.

When you look at others with their lands
    and gold,
think that Christ has promised you his
    wealth untold;
count your many blessings; money cannot buy
your reward in heaven nor your home on high.

So amid the conflict, whether great or small,
do not be discouraged; God is over all.
Count your many blessings; angels will attend,
help and comfort give you to your journey's
    end.

1058 Reuben Morgan

Where the Spirit is
there is liberty,
fullness of joy.
With a heart of praise
I will lift my voice
in the holy place.

Your love
has lifted me up again,
now I'm free to live.
Your grace
has lifted me high again.

You are awesome
in this place, O Lord,
we exalt your name.
For the hope you set
inside of me,
I will ever sing.

There's no higher
love that I could find.
For this joy
I will thank you,
I will thank you.

1059 Nahum Tate

While shepherds watched their flocks
   by night,
all seated on the ground,
the angel of the Lord came down,
and glory shone around.

'Fear not,' said he, (for mighty dread
had seized their troubled mind);
'glad tidings of great joy I bring
to you and all mankind.

'To you in David's town this day
is born of David's line
a Saviour, who is Christ the Lord;
and this shall be the sign:

'The heav'nly babe you there shall find
to human view displayed,
all meanly wrapped in swathing bands,
and in a manger laid.'

Thus spake the seraph, and forthwith
appeared a shining throng
of angels praising God, who thus
addressed their joyful song:

'All glory be to God on high,
and on the earth be peace,
goodwill henceforth from heav'n to earth
begin and never cease.'

1060 Mike Burn

Whiter than the snow,
purer than the clearest stream;
wash me and I'll be bathed in purity,
I long to feel clean.
A robe of righteousness,
a robe that I could not afford;
my Lord, you paid the price,
your perfect sacrifice
has covered up my shame.
And so I thank you, Jesus,
for the sweet forgiveness of the cross.
It's a mystery, to amaze even angels,
that when Father looks into my heart,
he sees me now as whiter than the snow.

© 1998 Daybreak Music Ltd.

1061 Gary Sadler

Who compares to your matchless beauty?
What can equal your warm embrace,
O Lord, my Lord?
Who could challenge your strength and
   glory?
Who can rise up to take your place?
For you are God,
so I throw down my earthly idols,
I remove them from my heart.

Jesus, Jesus,
you're the only God I come to;
Jesus, Jesus,
you're the only rock I run to.
When I think about the cross,
how you died for us,
rose again to set us free;
I say, Jesus, Jesus,
you're the only God,
the only God for me;
the only God for me.

Who could show me a heart so faithful?
What could give me a joy so deep,
O Lord, my Lord?
Who could open the gates of heaven?
Only you have such love for me,
for you are God.
So I throw down my earthly idols,
I remove them from my heart.

© 1999 Integrity's Hosanna! Music/Kingsway's Thankyou Music

1062 Art Bain

Who'd be found worthy
in the heavens or the earth,
to pay the debt of sin for ev'ryone?
Who could win the vict'ry
over death, hell and the grave?
He's the Lion of the tribe of Judah,
Jesus Christ, the Son.

He alone is worthy to worship and adore,
the Lamb of God, victorious, our risen
*   Lord;*
he purchased our redemption,
our righteousness is he;
exalt the name of Jesus, he is worthy.

Praise Adonai,
from the rising of the sun
'til the end of ev'ry day;
praise Adonai,
all the nations of the earth,
all the angels and the saints
*   sing praise.*

1063 Lynn DeShazo

Who holds the heavens in his hands?
Who made the stars by the word of his
power?
Who put the spirit in man
and causes all the earth to cry out glory?

Glory to the Lord,
worship him,
the God of our salvation.
Glory to the Lord,
honour him, he reigns,
he rules the nations;
he is righteous and worthy
to be worshipped and adored;
lift your voices
and give glory to the Lord.

Who holds the righteous by the hand?
Who is the way in this marvellous hour?
Who stirs the heart of a man
and causes all his saints to cry out glory?

1064 Paul Baloche

Who is like him,
the Lion and the Lamb,
seated on the throne?
Mountains bow down,
ev'ry ocean roars
to the Lord of hosts.

1065 Brian Duane, Brian Doerksen and Brian Thiessen

Who is like our God?
Who is like our God?
Holy and intimate, tender and strong,
patient and powerful.
Who is like our God?

Who is like our God?
Who is like our God?
Mighty and innocent, jealous and kind,
sov'reign and merciful.
Who is like our God?

All of man's glory fades away
like a spring flower in the rain.
No fallen angel is worthy to be worshipped,
nor anything created.

1066 Frances Ridley Havergal

Who is on the Lord's side?
Who will serve the King?
Who will be his helpers,
other lives to bring?
Who will leave the world's side?
Who will face the foe?
Who is on the Lord's side?
Who for him will go?
By thy call of mercy,
by thy grace divine,
we are on the Lord's side,
Saviour, we are thine.

Continued overleaf

Jesus, thou hast bought us
not with gold or gem,
but with thine own life-blood,
for thy diadem.
With thy blessing filling
each who comes to thee,
thou hast made us willing,
thou hast made us free.
By thy grand redemption,
by thy grace divine,
we are on the Lord's side,
Saviour, we are thine.

Fierce may be the conflict,
strong may be the foe,
but the King's own army
none can overthrow:
round his standard ranging,
vict'ry is secure;
for his truth unchanging
makes the triumph sure.
Joyfully enlisting,
by thy grace divine,
we are on the Lord's side,
Saviour, we are thine.

Chosen to be soldiers
in an alien land,
chosen, called, and faithful,
for our Captain's band;
in the service royal
let us not grow cold,
let us be right loyal,
noble, true, and bold.
Master, thou wilt keep us,
by thy grace divine,
always on the Lord's side,
Saviour, we are thine.

1067

D. Klassen, T. Klassen, J. Price, L. Petersen, T. Sampson and S. A. Sampson

Who is there like Almighty God?
Jehovah! Jehovah!
He is the one who sustains all the earth.
Jehovah! Jehovah!
Giver of breath to all that's alive.
Jehovah! Jehovah!
All of creation gives praise to our God.
Jehovah! Almighty! Almighty! Almighty!

You bring salvation upon the earth.
Jehovah! Jehovah!
At your rebuke all chains will be broken.
Jehovah! Jehovah!
River of hope in a barren land.
Jehovah! Jehovah!
You are the peace that will tear down the
    walls.
Jehovah! Almighty!

Jehovah, strong and mighty.
Mighty God, Jehovah.
Ruler, awesome in power.
Mighty God, Jehovah.

Unamandla N'kulu, N'kulu
Namandla, Jehovah.
Unamandla, Ubaba soamandla
'Namandla, Jehovah.

1068   Michael and Helen Frye

Who is this that appears like the dawn?
Fairer than the moon, brighter than the sun;
you're the lover of my soul.
Draw me into you, draw me into you.

Who is this that beckons me to come close?
Beauty beyond words surrounds me when
    you're near;
you're the lover of my soul.
Draw me into you, draw me into you.

We will run, we will fly,
we will be together.
We will laugh, we will cry,
we will be together.

Who is this that wipes the tears from my eyes?
Just one glimpse of you steals my heart
    away;
you're the lover of my soul.
Draw me into you, draw me into you.

Draw me into you, draw me into you.
Draw me into you, draw me into you.

1069   Matt Spencer

Who then is this,
that even the wind and the waves obey him?
Who then is this, says 'Peace, be still'
and the storm is over?
Master, Teacher, Lord and Saviour;
Son of God and Son of Man.
Lover, Healer, King for ever,
friend of mine, Emmanuel.

Who then is this, who shatters the chains
and heals the spirit?
Who then is this, says 'Peace be still'
and the storm is over?
Master, Teacher, Lord and Saviour;
Son of God and Son of Man.
Lover, Healer, King for ever;
friend of mine, Emmanuel.

1070   John Pantry

Wonderful grace,
that gives what I don't deserve,
pays me what Christ has earned,
then let's me go free.
Wonderful grace,
that gives me the time to change,
washes away the stains
that once covered me.

And all that I have
I lay at the feet
of the wonderful Saviour
who loves me.

Wonderful grace,
that held in the face of death,
breathed in its latest breath
forgiveness for me.
Wonderful love,
whose pow'r can break ev'ry chain,
giving us life again,
setting us free.

1071   Don Moen

Worthy, you are worthy,
King of kings, Lord of lords,
you are worthy;
worthy, you are worthy,
King of kings, Lord of lords,
I worship you.

Holy, you are holy,
King of kings, Lord of lords,
you are holy;
holy, you are holy,
King of kings, Lord of lords,
I worship you.

Jesus, you are Jesus,
King of kings, Lord of lords,
you are Jesus;
Jesus, you are Jesus,
King of kings, Lord of lords,
I worship you.

1072   Lewis E. Jones

Would you be free from your burden of sin?
There's pow'r in the blood, pow'r in the
    blood;
would you, o'er evil, a victory win?
There's wonderful pow'r in the blood.

Continued overleaf

There is pow'r, pow'r,
wonder-working pow'r
in the blood of the Lamb.
There is pow'r, pow'r,
wonder-working pow'r
in the precious blood of the Lamb.

Would you be free from your passion and
    pride?
There's pow'r in the blood, pow'r in the
    blood;
come for a cleansing to Calvary's tide.
There's wonderful pow'r in the blood.

Would you be whiter, much whiter than
    snow?
There's pow'r in the blood, pow'r in the
    blood;
sin stains are lost in its life-giving flow.
There's wonderful pow'r in the blood.

Would you do service for Jesus, your King?
There's pow'r in the blood, pow'r in the
    blood;
would you live daily his praises to sing?
There's wonderful pow'r in the blood.

© New Music Enterprises

1073 William R. Newell

Years I spent in vanity and pride,
caring not my Lord was crucified,
knowing not it was for me he died
on Calvary.

   Mercy there was great and grace was
       free;
   pardon there was multiplied to me;
   there my burdened soul found liberty, at
       Calvary.

By God's Word at last my sin I learned;
then I trembled at the law I'd spurned,
till my guilty soul imploring turned
to Calvary.

Now I've giv'n to Jesus ev'rything;
now I gladly own him as my King;
now my raptured soul can only sing
of Calvary.

O the love that drew salvation's plan!
O the grace that bro't it down to man!
O the mighty gulf that God did span
at Calvary!

© Control

1074 Charles Wesley

Ye servants of God,
your Master proclaim,
and publish abroad
his wonderful name;
the name all-victorious
of Jesus extol;
his kingdom is glorious,
and rules over all.

God ruleth on high,
almighty to save;
and still he is nigh,
his presence we have;
the great congregation
his triumph shall sing,
ascribing salvation
to Jesus our King.

'Salvation to God
who sits on the throne',
let all cry aloud,
and honour the Son:
the praises of Jesus
the angels proclaim,
fall down on their faces,
and worship the Lamb.

Then let us adore,
and give him his right -
all glory and pow'r,
all wisdom and might:
all honour and blessing,
with angels above;
and thanks never-ceasing,
and infinite love.

1075 John Hampden Gurney

Yes, God is good – in earth and sky,
from ocean-depths and spreading wood,
ten thousand voices seem to cry:
'God made us all, and God is good.'

The sun that keeps his trackless way
and downward pours his golden flood,
night's sparkling hosts, all seem to say
in accents clear that God is good.

The merry birds prolong the strain,
their song with ev'ry spring renewed;
and balmy air and falling rain,
each softly whispers: 'God is good.'

We hear it in the rushing breeze;
the hills that have for ages stood,
the echoing sky and roaring seas,
all swell the chorus: 'God is good.'

For all thy gifts we bless thee, Lord,
but chiefly for our heav'nly food,
thy pard'ning grace, thy quick'ning word,
these prompt our song, that God is good.

1076 Brian Duane & Kathryn Scott

You are a holy God,
an all-consuming fire.
You're robed in majesty,
bright, shining as the sun.

Your ways are not our ways.
Your thoughts are high above.
You are the fountain, Lord,
of mercy, truth and love.

> *And we cry: 'Holy, holy, is the Lord God*
> *   most high.'*
> *And we cry: 'Holy, holy, is the Lord most*
> *   high.'*

© 1999 Vineyard Songs (UK/Eire)/CopyCare

1077 Reuben Morgan

You are holy, holy,
Lord, there is none like you.
You are holy, holy,
glory to you alone.
(Repeat)

> *I'll sing your praises for ever,*
> *deeper in love with you.*
> *Here in your courts*
> *where I'm close to your throne,*
> *I've found where I belong.*
> (Repeat)

© 1997 Reuben Morgan/Hillsong Publishing/Kingsway's Thankyou
Music

1078 Scott Wesley Brown

You are holy, O Lord, so holy;
you are holy, O Lord, so holy.
What a priv'lege and an honour
to worship at your throne;
to be called into your presence as your own.

You are worthy, O Lord, so worthy ....

You are faithful, O Lord, so faithful ....

© 1995 Integrity's Hosanna! Music/Kingsway's Thankyou Music

1079 Ray Chee

You are Lord,
maker of the heavens,
you are Lord,
ruler of all nations.
I lift my voice
to worship you, Lord.

You are Lord,
healer and Messiah,
you are Lord,
wonderful Redeemer.
I crown you King of kings
and Lord of lords.

Continued overleaf

You are Lord,
I worship and adore you,
you are Lord,
creation bows before you,
you are Lord,
I lay my life before you.
Jesus, you are Lord.

1080 Michael Ledner

You are my hiding-place,
you always fill my heart
with songs of deliverance.
Whenever I am afraid
I will trust in you,
I will trust in you.
Let the weak say I am strong
in the strength of the Lord.

You are my hiding place,
you always fill my heart
with songs of deliverance.
Whenever I am afraid
I will trust in you,
I will trust in you.
Let the weak say I am strong
in the strength of the Lord.
I will trust in you.

1081 Dennis Jernigan

You are my strength when I am weak,
you are the treasure that I seek,
you are my all in all.
Seeking you as a precious jewel,
Lord, to give up I'd be a fool,
you are my all in all.
Jesus, Lamb of God,
worthy is your name.
Jesus, Lamb of God,
worthy is your name.

1082 David Grant, Carrie Grant & Richard Lewis

Oh, oh, oh, oh.
Oh, oh, oh, oh.

You are the anchor and foundation,
you are the Rock that will not roll;
you are the one provider, the purifier
and the lover of my soul.

Jesus, Saviour, you let me know
you made a covenant of love with me
and you'll never let me go.

You are the anchor and foundation,
you are the Rock that will not roll;
you are the one provider, the purifier
and the lover of my soul.

Jesus, Saviour, you let me know
you made a covenant of love with me
and you'll never let me go.

Never let me go,
never let me go, never let me go,
never let me go.

You are the King in all your glory,
you are the Lamb of victory,
you are the mercy-giver and you deliver
all the grace I'll ever need.

1083 Janine Price

You are the breath of life
and you are a shining light.
You are the only living God.
You are a mighty warrior
and you have conquered all;
you are the only living God.

Kings and kingdoms, they shall fall
while you remain the same.
Tribes and tongues will turn and know
that you're the one who reigns.

So reign, O God,
take your rightful place,
you're enthroned, O God,
in these praises we now raise.
So, reign, O God,
in and through our lives.
Reign, O God, reign, O Lord,
reign for evermore.

1084   Alvin Slaughter

You are the one
that makes my feet start dancing;
you are the one
that drives the dark clouds away;
you are the one,
you're my reason for living;
you are the one I praise.

I praise you for the very breath I breathe,
I praise you for supplying all my needs,
I praise you for amazing love, sweet amazing
    love,
that I've never, never known.
I praise you for the joy you've given me,
I praise you, for in you I am complete,
I give my heart, my mind, my soul,
I'm yours: take control, take control.

1085   Shannon J. Wexelberg

You are the Rose of Sharon,
the brightest morning star;
the fairest of ten thousand,
that is who you are.
You have crowned me with compassion,
you give me wings to soar;
turn my sorrows into gladness,
and so much more.

You give me all the riches of you,
you give me all the riches of you.
Nothing else on earth could ever satisfy,
for your love, O Lord, is so much better
    than life;
you give me all the riches of you,
you give me all the riches of you.

My Saviour and my Healer,
my Comforter and Friend;
my strength and my Redeemer,
a love that knows no end.
You're preparing now in glory
a place that waits for me,
where I'll worship you for ever,
my Lord and King.

1086   Brian Doerksen

You are the sov'reign 'I Am',
your name is holy.
You are the pure spotless Lamb,
your name is holy.

You are the Almighty One,
your name is holy.
You are the Christ,
God's own Son,
your name is holy.

In your name,
there is mercy for sin,
safety within, in your holy name.
In your name strength to remain,
to stand in spite of pain,
in your holy name.

1087 Nigel Hemming

You are warm like the sunshine
on a bright summer day.
You are clear as the blue sky
when the clouds have rolled away.
You are gentle as the evening breeze
that blows against my face;
and I love to be with you, beautiful God,
and I love to be with you, beautiful God.

You protect me with your arms of love,
and you take away my fear.
I'm reaching out my hands to you,
'cos I know that you are near.
Lord, I'll whisper words of tenderness,
which only you can hear;
and I love to be with you, beautiful God,
and I love to be with you, beautiful God.

As my love for you grows strong,
close to you is where I long to be.
As I gaze into your eyes
such a look of pure delight I see,
Lord, you're smiling at me.

© 1998 Vineyard Songs (UK/Eire)/CopyCare

1088 Bob Kauflin

You have been given the Name above all
    names,
and we worship you, yes we worship you.
You have been given the Name above all
    names,
and we worship you, and we worship you.

We are your people, made for your glory,
and we worship you, yes we worship you.
We are your people, made for your glory,
and we worship you, and we worship you.

You have redeemed us from ev'ry nation,
and we worship you, yes we worship you.
You have redeemed us from ev'ry nation,
and we worship you, and we worship you.

© 1987 PDI/CopyCare

1089 Andy and Wendy Rayner

You have chosen us,
set our lives apart
to declare the wonder of your name.
Awesome mighty God,
Saviour, friend and Lord,
of your love and grace we will proclaim.
We will tell the world
of your great faithfulness,
we will lift your name for all to see.
For you alone are God,
you alone are worthy,
we will live our lives to honour you.

© 2000 Kevin Mayhew Ltd.

1090 Jennifer Thune

You're Messiah,
you're Messiah,
you're Messiah.

From all the nations we come,
we come to your throne to seek your face,
in truth, in pow'r, in love.
No longer bound up by sin,
we lay it all down in humbleness,
your light breaks through our shame.

Now we lift up holy hands
in glorious joy and admiration,
to dance as David danced!
Our hearts are open to you,
to hear your voice,
show us your righteousness,
your grace, your light, your fire.

*You're Messiah. You have come to the
    world.
You're Messiah. Down from heaven to
    earth;
you're Messiah. Hear the cry of our
    nations to you.
You're Messiah. You're the lover of souls.
You're Messiah. You're the bridge
between foes.
You're Messiah. There is none who
    compares to you.*

We'll spread this passion for you;
revival will flow through all of our lands,
to glorify your name.
And then your kingdom will come,
your reign to begin in righteousness,
your sov'reign plan fulfilled!

1091 Gary Sadler

You're my rock of refuge,
the shelter of my life,
my merciful companion,
my comfort in the night;
though my heart falls hard,
still your love stands guard,
O Lord, you are my rock of refuge.

And I run to you,
and you hold me close,
you hide me under your shadow.
Yes, I run to you, it's so good to know,
O Lord, you are my rock of refuge.

You're my rock of refuge,
the calm within my storm,
a secret place of safety,
my barrier from harm;
when my eyes are tears,
through my worst of fears,
O Lord, you are my rock of refuge.

1092 Mark Altrogge

You're the One who flung the stars
across the heavens and you are
the One who spoke and mountains rose
above the foaming seas.
You're the One who sends the rain
and golden sun to drench the plains,
and gracious God, you always pour
such favour out on me.

You are the One who does awesome things,
you are the One who works wonders.
You are the One who does awesome things,
you are the One who works wonders.
And you are, you are the One I love.

You're the One whose bleeding head
was crowned with thorns,
and in my stead you took God's wrath,
and died my death that I might live your life.
And as I fix my gaze on you,
I'm captivated by the view,
becoming ever like the One
whose glory fills my eyes.

1093 Darlene Zschech

Your eye is on the sparrow
and your hand it comforts me.
From the ends of the earth
to the depths of my heart,
let your mercy and strength be seen.

And I will run to you,
to your words of truth,
not by might, not by power
but by the Spirit of God.
Yes, I will run the race,
'til I see your face.
Oh, let me live in the glory of your grace.

You call me to your purpose,
as angels understand.
For your glory may you draw
all men, as your love and grace demands.

1094 Darlene Zschech and David Moyse

Your kingdom generation
declares your majesty.
Our lives are resounding with your praise.
We see your Spirit moving,
we burn with holy fire.
Your glory is seen through all the earth.

You set eternity in my heart,
so I'll live for you, for you.

Continued overleaf

Hallelujah, hallelujah,
honour and praise for ever.
We'll shout a victory-cry
from here to eternity.
Hallelujah, hallelujah,
we'll take our place in history.
We'll shout your awesome love
from here to eternity.

1095 Reuben Morgan

Your light broke through my night,
restored exceeding joy.
Your grace fell like the rain,
and made this desert live.

You have turned my mourning into
dancing.
You have turned my sorrow into joy.

Your hand lifted me up,
I stand on higher ground.
Your praise rose in my heart,
and made this valley sing.

This is how we overcome.

1096 Brian Doerksen and Brenton Brown

Your love is amazing, steady and
    unchanging,
your love is a mountain, firm beneath my
    feet.
Your love is a myst'ry, how you gently lift me,
when I am surrounded, your love carries me.

Hallelujah, hallelujah,
hallelujah, your love makes me sing.
Hallelujah, hallelujah,
hallelujah, your love makes me sing.

Your love is surprising, I can feel it rising,
all the joy that's growing deep inside of me.
Ev'ry time I see you, all your goodness
shines through,
I can feel this God-song, rising up in me.

1097 Twila Paris

Your only Son, no sin to hide,
but you have sent him from your side,
to walk upon this guilty sod,
and to become the Lamb of God.

O Lamb of God, sweet Lamb of God;
I love the holy Lamb of God.
O wash me in his precious blood.
My Jesus Christ, the Lamb of God.

Your gift of love they crucified,
they laughed and scorned him as he died;
the humble King they named a fraud,
and sacrificed the Lamb of God.

I was so lost I should have died,
but you have brought me to your side
to be led by your staff and rod,
and to be called a lamb of God.

1098 . Andy Bromley

Your words of life burn in my soul,
I feel this hunger more and more,
compelling me to follow you,
calling me to walk in truth.
To walk in ways of righteousness,
to long and crave for holiness,
to live my life in purity,
to give my life up willingly.

Let this flame of love burn in my heart again.
Let this flame become a fire once again.
That I would seek your face,
that I would know you more,
let the flame of love burn in my heart again.

Your Spirit like a fire in me,
I feel this passion stirring me,
compassion's fire, this flame of love,
could only be from God above.
Open my eyes, my pray'r, O Lord,
to see the hungry, thirsty soul.
Reach out my hand to meet the need
to give your love so selflessly.

1099 Reuben Morgan

You said 'Ask and you will receive
whatever you need.'
You said 'Pray, and I'll hear from heaven
and I'll heal your land.'

You said your glory will fill the earth
like water the sea.
You said 'Lift up your eyes,
the harvest is here, the kingdom is here.'

You said, 'Ask and I'll give the nations to you.'
O Lord, that's the cry of my heart.
Distant shores and the islands
will see your light as it rises on us.

Indexes

Key Word Index

The key word categories appear alphabetically and are cross-referenced to make it as easy as possible for worship leaders to find songs and hymns suitable for various themes and occasions.

ADORATION AND PRAISE – GODHEAD

All my hope on God is founded	620
All people that on earth do dwell	13
All the world can offer	626
All things bright and beautiful	14
Almighty God, we bring you praise	16
Almighty God, my Redeemer	17
Among the gods	19
And here we are	630
Ascribe greatness	25
As I come into your presence	26
As long as there is air to breathe	635
As the deer pants (Lewis)	28
As we seek your face	31
Be glorified	42
Be still, for the presence of the Lord	47
Blessing and honour	54
Bless the Lord, my soul	56
Clothed with splendour and majesty	657
Come, now is the time to worship	662
Come, thou fount of every blessing	663
Come to the power	665
Exalt the Lord	87
Faithful God	88
Father, I come to you	95
Father in heaven, how we love you	96
Fill thou my life, O Lord, my God	683
For the fruits of his creation	685
For thou, O Lord, art high	112
Freedom and liberty	686
From the ends of the earth	115
Gloria	119
Glorious things of thee are spoken	691
God is good	124
God is good all the time	125
God is great	126
God of glory, we exalt your name	130
God's not dead	133
God, you're my God	703
Great and mighty is he	135
Great is the Lord and most worthy of praise	137
Great is your name	139
Guide me, O thou great Jehovah	708
Hallelujah, hallelujah	141
He's given me a garment of praise	166
Holy, holy, Lord God Almighty	177
Holy, holy, Lord, you're worthy	178
How great are you, Lord	749

How lovely is your dwelling-place	188
I am standing beneath your wings	193
I delight in you	761
I give you all the honour	203
I have come to love you	204
I have made you too small	205
I have sung my songs of praise	767
I just want to be where you are	207
I just want to praise you	208
I love to be in your presence	213
I'm gonna click	218
Immortal, invisible, God only wise	220
In heavenly armour	228
In so many ways you love me	788
In the mornin' hour	791
In the presence of a holy God	232
In your presence there is joy	793
I sing praises	240
I stand before your throne	245
I thank the Lord	799
I will enter his gates	262
I will live to declare your glory	818
I will praise you all my life	266
I will wave my hands	269
I worship you, Almighty God	271
Let everything that has breath	854
Let the heavens rejoice	858
Let there be praise	860
Let the righteous sing	316
Look what God has done	325
Lord, for the years	327
Lord, my heart cries out	331
Lord of lords	332
Lord, we long to see your glory	338
Lord, you are more precious	339
Lord, you are so precious to me	340
Lord, you have my heart	341
Lord, you put a tongue in my mouth	342
Make a joyful noise, all ye people	347
May our worship be as fragrance	351
Mighty is our God	357
More love, more power	359
My heart will sing to you	364
Now unto the King	378
O come and praise him	902
O give thanks	384
O God, you are my God	906
O Lord, how majestic is your name	395
O Lord our God	398
On this day	409
O praise the holy Lord above	927
O the glory of your presence	415
Our God is an awesome God	418
O worship the King	425

O worship the Lord in the beauty of holiness	426
Our God is great	933
Our God is lifted up	934
Praise him, you heavens	942
Praise, my soul, the King of heaven	433
Praise the Lord	944
Praise the Lord, O my soul	434
Praise to the Lord, the Almighty	945
Salvation belongs to our God	443
See his glory	446
Sing to the Lord	962
Sing, praise and bless the Lord	458
Sing unto the Lord	963
Streams of worship	464
Surely our God	466
Teach me to dance	469
Tell out, my soul	471
Thank you for your mercy	474
The angels, Lord, they sing	476
The God of Abraham praise	975
The Lord is gracious and compassionate	985
The Lord is our strength	484
The Lord reigns	485
Therefore we lift our hearts in praise	489
There is none like you	493
The steadfast love of the Lord	505
They that wait on the Lord	509
This is my desire	515
This is the day that the Lord has made	516
This is the day	517
Thou art worthy, great Jehovah	1014
Though the earth should tremble	523
To every good thing God is doing	525
To God be the glory!	526
To keep your lovely face	527
Tonight	528
To the King eternal	1023
To you, O Lord, I bring my worship	529
We are a moment	1026
We bring the sacrifice of praise	542
We come into your presence	1029
We declare your majesty	544
We have come to a holy mountain	1034
We lift our hands to worship you	1038
We rejoice in the goodness of our God	554
What noise shall we make	569
When I feel the touch	570
When I look into your holiness	571
Who holds the heavens in his hands?	1063
Who is like him	1064

CALL TO WORSHIP

CELEBRATION

CHILDREN AND FAMILY WORSHIP

LOVE - OUR LOVE FOR OTHERS

MARCH FOR JESUS

MARRIAGE

MISSION

NATURE

See **God - Creation**

OFFERING

OPENING OF SERVICE

See **Call to Worship**

PALM SUNDAY

See **Jesus - Life**

PEACE

PENTECOST

SANCTIFICATION

SECOND COMING
See **Jesus – Second Coming**

SOCIAL CONCERN

TRINITY

See **Adoration and Praise**

TRUST

UNITY

See **Church**

VICTORY

VISION

WORD OF GOD

WORSHIP

See **Adoration and Praise**

Index of First Lines and Titles

This index gives the first line of each hymn. If a hymn is known by an alternative title, this is also given, but indented and in italics.

Acknowledgements

The publishers wish to express their gratitude to the following for permission to include copyright material in this publication. Details of copyright owners are given underneath each individual hymn.

Ascent Music, PO Box 263, Croydon, CR9 5AP. All rights reserved. International copyright secured.

Ateliers et Presses de Taizé, F-71250 Taizé-Communauté, France.

Executors of A.C. Barham Gould, 34 Pollards Drive, Horsham, West Sussex, RH13 5HH.

Beracah Music, PO Box 361, Halfway House, Midrand, 1685, South Africa.

Brettian Productions, PO Box 96395, Brixton 2019, Johannesburg, South Africa.

Brown Bear Music, 154 Deptford High Street, London, SE8 3PQ.

Bucks Music Group, Onward House, 11 Uxbridge Street, London, W8 7TQ.

Christian Life Publications, PO Box 157, Folkestone, Kent, CT20 2YS.

Church House Publishing, Church House, Great Smith Street, London, SW1P 3NZ.

Clive Goodwill 60's Music, PO Box 4776, Cresta 2118, South Africa.

Jarrod Cooper (Ministries), New Life Christian Centre, Bridlington Avenue, Hull, HU2 0DU, UK.

CopyCare, PO Box 77, Hailsham, East Sussex, BN27 3EF. (music@copycare.com). On behalf of Sploshsongs; Spin Three-Sixty Music/Music Services; For the Shepherd Music/EMI Christian Music Publishing; Worshiptogether.Com Songs/EMI Christian Music Publishing; Meadowgreen Music/EMICMP/EMI Christian Music Publishing; Sampsongs Publishing; Maranatha! Music; Isondo Music/Maranatha! Praise; Awsum Songs; Dick and Mel Music/BMG Music Publishing/Pamela Kay Music/EMI Christian Music Publishing; Pamela Kay Music/EMI Christian Music Publishing/Lorenz Creative Services/BMG Music Publishing/Charlie Monk Music; Bud John Songs; CA Music/Music Services; CMI-HP Publishing/High Praises Publishing/Word Music Inc; Juniper Landing Music/Word Music Inc; Kingsong/Alliance Media Ltd; Meadowgreen Music/ Songchannel Music Co/EMI Christian Music; Zionsong Music; Straightway Music; Shepherds Heart Music Inc; Run Deep Music; Resource Christian Music Pty; Meadowgreen Music/EMI Christian Music Publishing/Stephen Deal; Birdwing Music/Garden Valley/Sparrow Song/EMI Christian Publishing/ Careers BMG Music/BMG Songs Inc; Coomsietunes; HarperCollins Religious; Jacobs Ladder Publishing; Heartservice Music/Music Services; Mercy/Vineyard Publishing; Vineyard Songs; PDI Praise; PDI Worship; Copycare/PDI; People of Destiny Int; Whole World Publishing/C N Publishing; Threefold Amen Music; Word's Spirit of Praise Music; Word/Maranatha! Music; Word Music/Spoone Music; Songward Music/The Copyright Company/Threefold Music; Deep Fryed Music/Music Services; .; Glory Alleluia Music/Word Music; Springtide/Word Music; Dancing Heart Music/Word Music; The Rodeheaver Co./Word Music; Shade Tree Music/Maranatha! Music; Word of God Music/ The Copyright Company; John T. Benson Publishing Co./Universal Songs; Straightway/Mountain Spring/Universal Songs; Latter Rain Music/Universal Songs; Singspiration Music/Universal Songs; Stamps Baxter Music/Universal Songs; Body Songs; Hope Publishing; PDI Music; Sound III/Tempo Music Publications; Fairhill Music; Bob Kilpatrick Music; Ampelos Music; Lillenas Publishing Co.

Daybreak Music Ltd, Silverdale Road, Eastbourne, East Sussex, BN20 7AB. All rights reserved. International copyright secured.

Bishop Timothy Dudley-Smith, 9 Ashlands, Ford, Salisbury, Wiltshire, SP4 6DY.

Far Lane Music Publishing, PO Box 2164, Florence, AL 35630, USA.

First Klas Publishing, PO Box 410, Olivedale 2158, South Africa.

FLAMME, 5 Rue Erik Satie, Apt. 278, 31100 Toulouse, France.

Gabriel Music Inc., PO Box 840999, Houston, Texas 77284, USA, on behalf of Pete Sanchez Jr.

Pamela Hayes RSCJ, Marden Lodge, Marden Park, Woldingham, Surrey, CR3 7YA.

Ice Music, Bayley's Plantation, St Philip, Barbados, West Indies.

IMP, Griffin House, 161 Hammersmith Road, London, W6 8BS.

IQ Music, Commercial House, 52 Perrymount Road, Haywards Heath, West Sussex, RH16 3DT.

Jubilate Hymns, Southwick House, 4 Thorne Park Road, Chelston, Torquay, TQ2 6RX.

Kingdom Faith Ministries, Foundry Lane, Horsham, West Sussex, RU13 5PX.

Kingsway's Thankyou Music, Lottbridge Drove, Eastbourne, East Sussex, BN23 6NT. On behalf of Arun Puddle/Hillsong Publishing (UK/Europe); Lensongs Publishing; Kingsway's Thankyou Music; Curious? Music UK (Worldwide excluding USA); Parachute Music New Zealand (UK/Europe); Darlene Zschech/Hillsong Publishing (UK/Europe); Integrity's Hosanna Music (UK only); Watershed Productions (UK only); Integrity's Praise! Music/We Mobile Music; Gaither Music Company/WJG Inc (UK/Eire); Tanya Riches/Hillsong Publishing (UK/Europe); Russell Fragar/Hillsong Publishing (UK/Europe); Reuben Morgan/Hillsong Publishing (UK/Europe); Ned Davies/Hillsong Publishing (UK/Europe); Joel Houston/Hillsong Publishing (UK/Europe); Scripture in Song (UK only); Kate Spence/SHOUT! Publishing (UK/Europe); Coronation Music Publishing (UK/Australia/New Zealand only); Craig Gower/Hillsong Publishing (UK/Europe); Stephen McPherson/Hillsong Publishing (UK/Europe); Signalgrade/Kingsway's Thankyou Music (Worldwide); Manna Music/Kingsway's Thankyou Music (British Commonwealth excluding Canada); Chris Falson Music (UK only); Peter West/ Integrity's Hosanna! Music; Curious? Music UK; Celebration (for Europe and British Commonwealth, excl. Canada, Australasia and Africa); Debbie and Rob Eastwood/Hillsongs Australia; Acts Music (Worldwide, excl. South Africa); Kempen Music (for Europe and British Commonwealth, excl. Canada); 7th Time Music (for Europe, excl. Germany, Austria, Switzerland, Liechtenstein and Luxembourg); J. Ezzy, D. Grul, S. McPherson/Hillsongs Australia; Lucy Fisher/ Hillsongs Australia; Stuart K. Hine (Worldwide, excl. USA and Canada); Little Misty Music (Worldwide, excl. Australia and New Zealand) and Signalgrade. Used by permission.

K.K. Foundation, 4140 Brownsville Road, STE 249, Pittsburgh, PA 15227, USA.

Lakes Music, PO Box 1038, Wangara, WA 6947, Australia.

Leosong Copyright Services, Greenland Place, 115/123 Bayham Street, London, NW1 0AG, on behalf of Rocksmith Music.

Littleway Music, 5 Littleway, Moortown, Leeds, LS17 6JN.

Make Way Music, PO Box 263, Croydon, CR9 5AP. All rights reserved. International copyright secured.

Ministry Management Associates, PO Box 1248, Decatur, Alabama 35602-1248, USA, on behalf of Exaltation Music.

Music Sales Ltd, 8/9 Frith Street, London, W1V 5TZ.

New Music Enterprises, The Dell, Reach Lane, Heath & Reach, Bedfordshire, LU7 0AL.

New Life Music, 10 Haggers Mead, Forward Green, Stowmarket, Suffolk, IP14 5JA.

Nodel Music, 92a Parchmore Road, 1-6 The Mews, Praize Rooms, Thornton Health, Surrey, CR7 1LX.

Novello & Co, 8/9 Frith Street, London, W1V 5TZ.

OCP Publications, 5536 NE Hassalo, Portland, OR 97213, USA, on behalf of OCP Publications and New Dawn Music. All rights reserved. Used by permission.

Oxford University Press, Great Clarendon Street, Oxford, OX2 6DP.

David Palmer, City Church Sunderland, Crown House, Borough Road, Sunderland, SR1 1HW.

Joel Pott, 14 Bonny Street, Camden, London, NW1 9PG.

Rain Music, PO Box 11, Mary Ester, FL 32569, USA.

Remission Music UK, 50 Parkview Crescent, Bentley, Walsall, WS2 8TY. (Taken from the album Melody of the Heart.)

Restoration Music Ltd, PO Box 356, Leighton Buzzard, Beds, LU7 8WP.

Rooted & Grounded, PO Box 580, Cordova, TN 38018, USA.

Sea Dream Music, PO Box 13533, London, E7 0SG.

Sixstepsrecords, PO Box 5, Roswell, Georgia 30077, USA. (www.sixstepsrecords.com)

Smart Productions, PO Box 6829, East Perth, WA6892, Australia.

Sounds of Paradise, 2 Crowle Road, Paradise, SA 5075, Australia.

Sovereign Music UK, PO Box 356, Leighton Buzzard, Beds, LU7 8WP.

Sovereign Lifestyle Music, PO Box 356, Leighton Buzzard, Beds, LU7 8WP.

Spiritsound Music Group, PO Box 2430, Cleveland, TN 37320, USA.

Stainer & Bell Ltd, PO Box 110, Victoria House, 23 Gruneisen Road, London, N3 1DZ

Swansound Music Publishing, PO Box 1250, Asheville, NC 28802, USA.

Shannon J. Wexelberg, 240 Hemlock Street, Broomfield, CO80020, USA.

Tevita Music, PO Box 46, Beckenham, Kent, BR3 4YR, UK.
A. P. Watt Ltd, Literary Agents, 20 John Street, London, WC1N 2DR, on behalf of The Grail, England.

Wild Goose Resource Group, Iona Community, Pearce Institute, 840 Govan Road, Glasgow, G51 3UU, Scotland.

Windswept Pacific Music Ltd, 27 Queensdale Place, London, W11 4SQ.

world wide worship ltd, Buxhall, Stowmarket, Suffolk, IP14 3BW.